TOKYO GHOUL

SUI ISHIDA

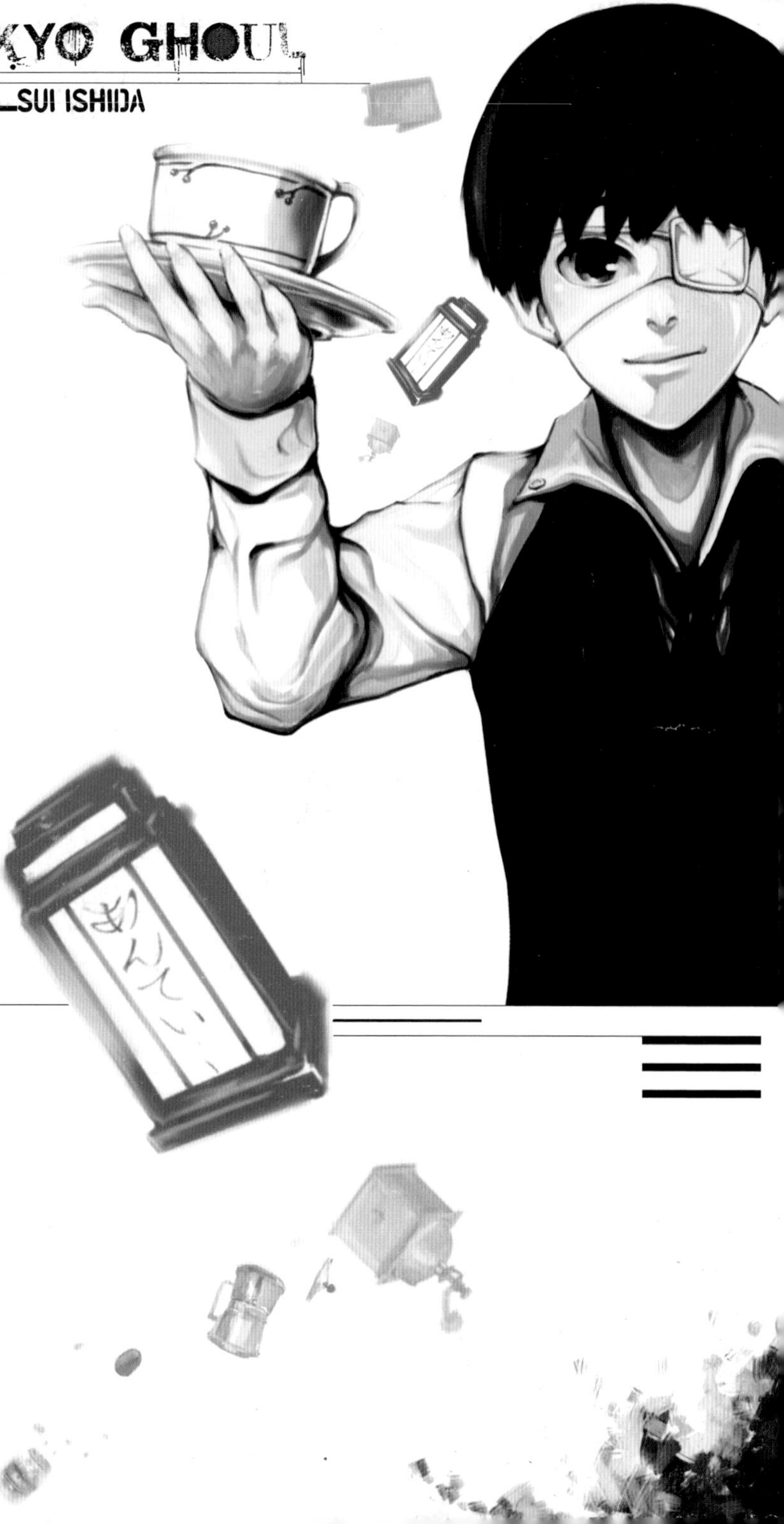

T O K Y O   G H O U L

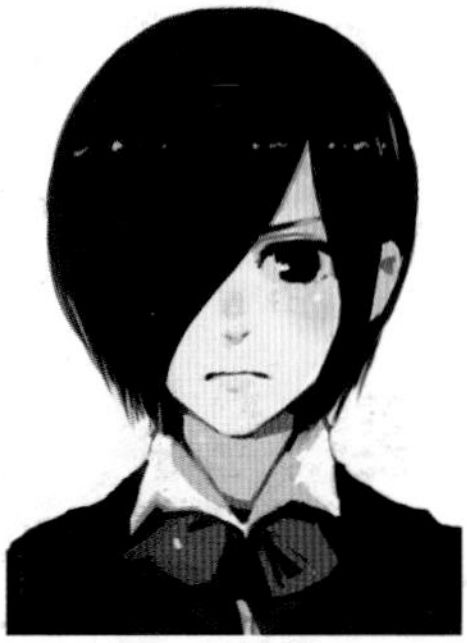

TOUKA KIRISHIMA

霧嶋董香（キリシマ トウカ）

BORN July 1st Cancer

Kiyomi High School, Sophomore
General Education Curriculum

BLOOD-TYPE: O

Size: 156 cm 45 kg F FEET 22.5 CM

Likes: School, rabbits

Hates: Ghoul investigators, dimwits, Classic Lit.

T O U K A   K I R I S H I M A

SUI ISHIDA was born in Fukuoka, Japan. He is the author of ***Tokyo Ghoul*** and several ***Tokyo Ghoul*** one-shots, including one that won him second place in the *Weekly Young Jump* 113th Grand Prix award in 2010. ***Tokyo Ghoul*** began serialization in *Weekly Young Jump* in 2011 and was adapted into an anime series in 2014.

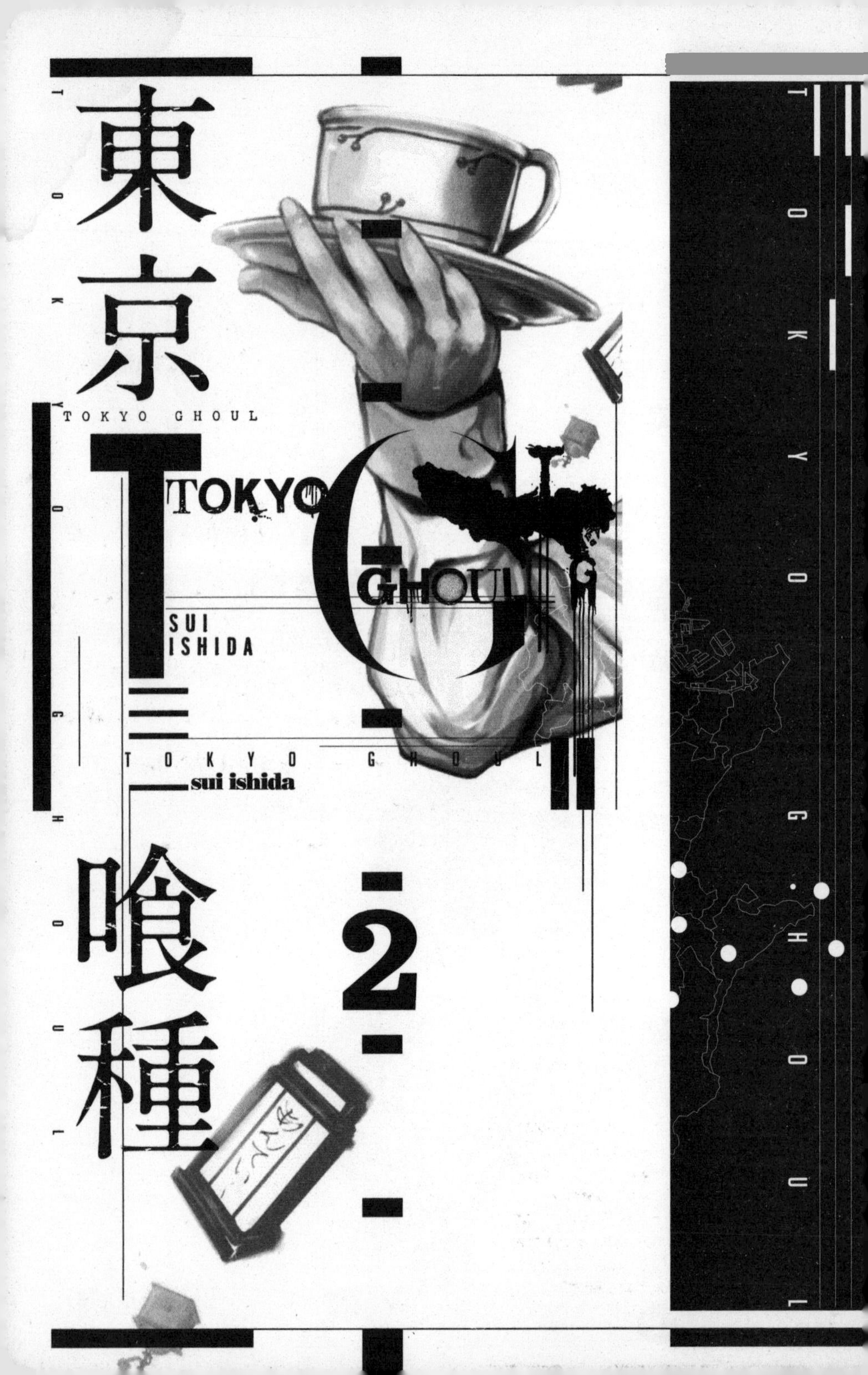
東京喰種
TOKYO GHOUL
TOKYO GHOUL
SUI ISHIDA
T O K Y O G H O U L
sui ishida
2
T O K Y O G H O U L

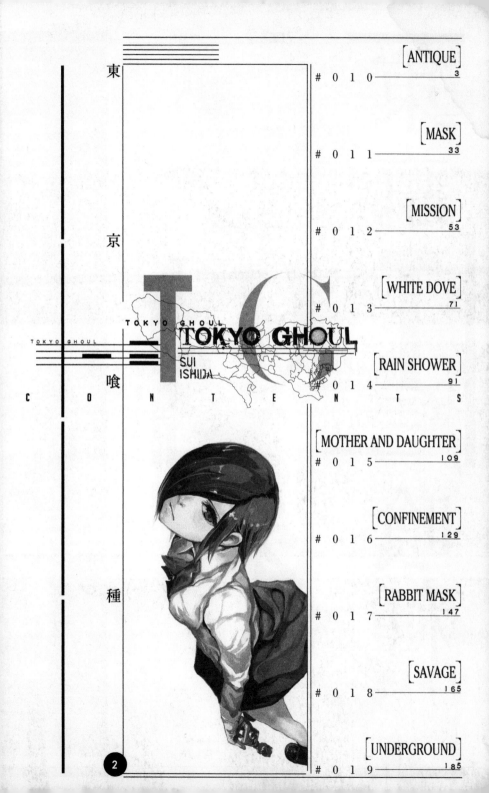

東 京 喰 種

TOKYO GHOUL

SUI ISHIDA

CONTENTS

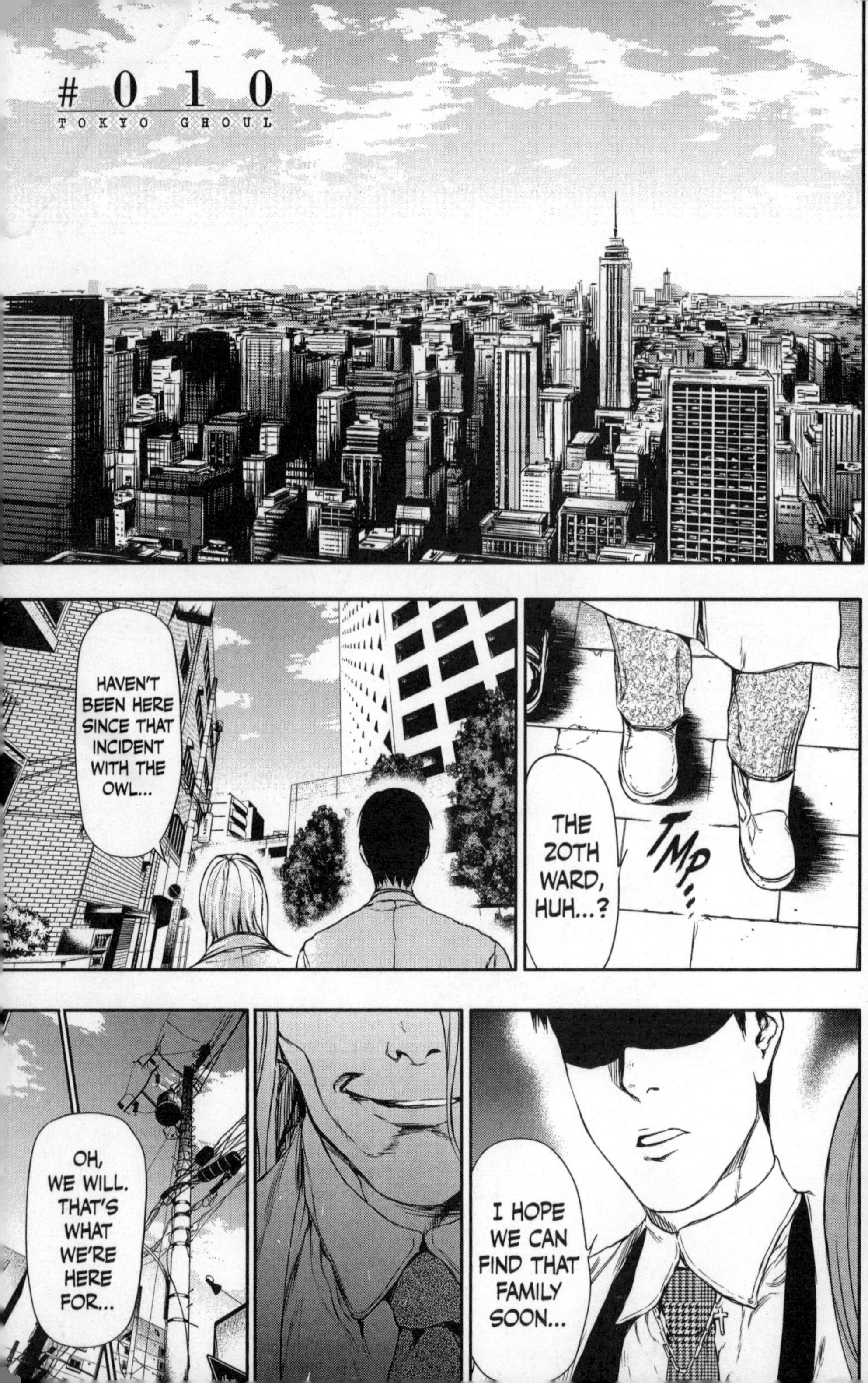
#010
TOKYO GHOUL
THE 20TH WARD, HUH...?
TMP...
HAVEN'T BEEN HERE SINCE THAT INCIDENT WITH THE OWL...
I HOPE WE CAN FIND THAT FAMILY SOON...
OH, WE WILL. THAT'S WHAT WE'RE HERE FOR...

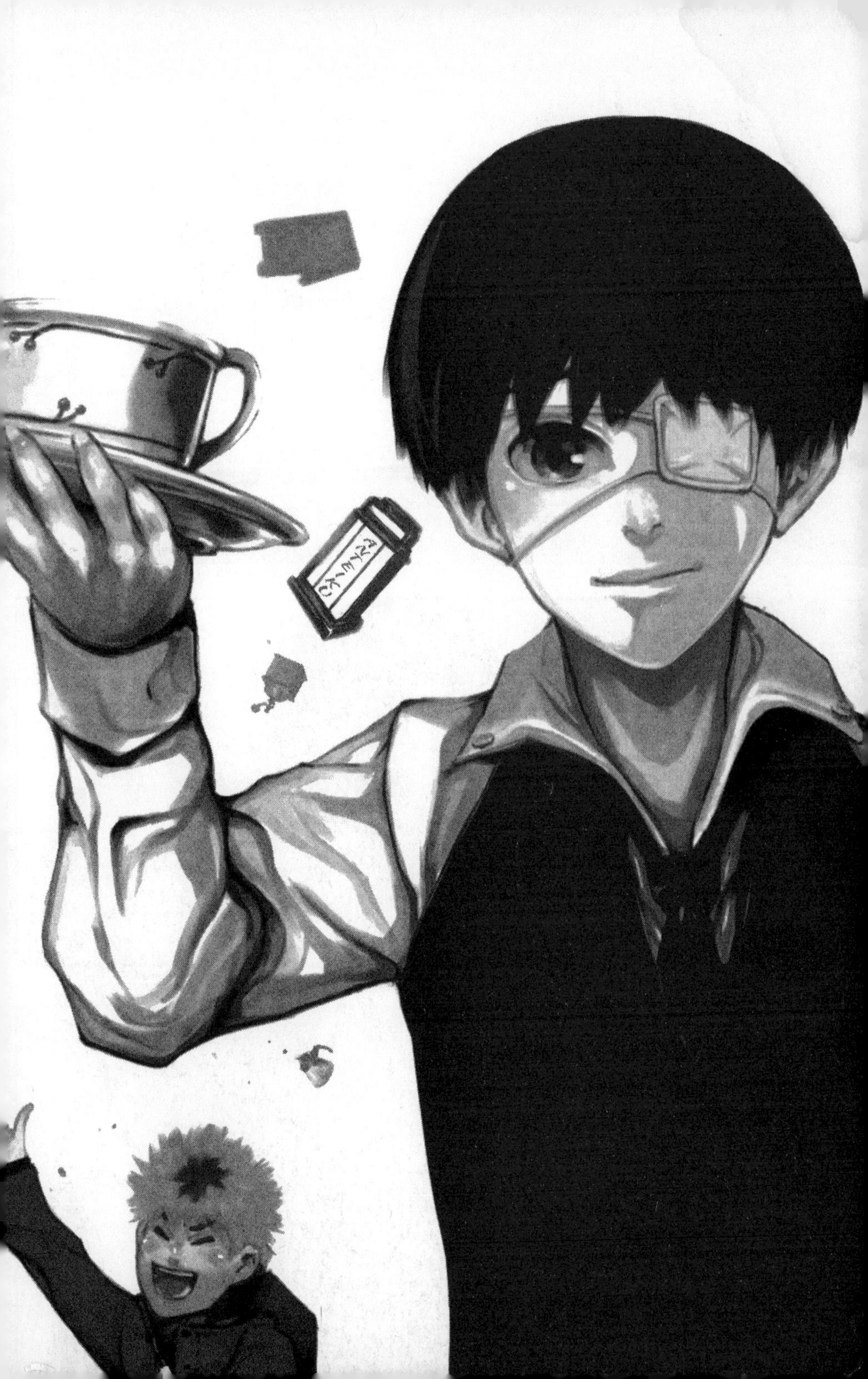
ANTEIKU

#010
TOKYO GHOUL
[ANTIQUE]

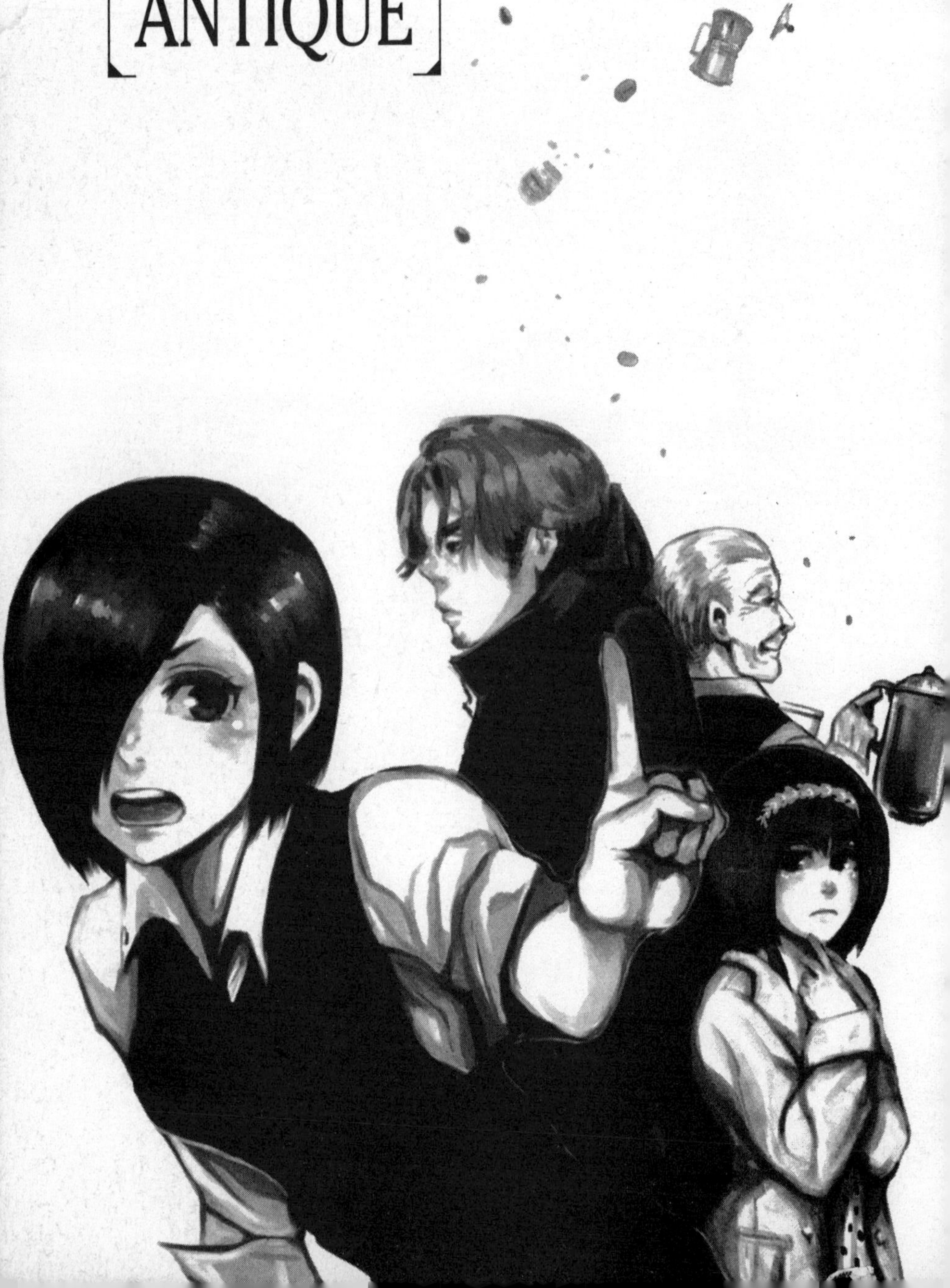

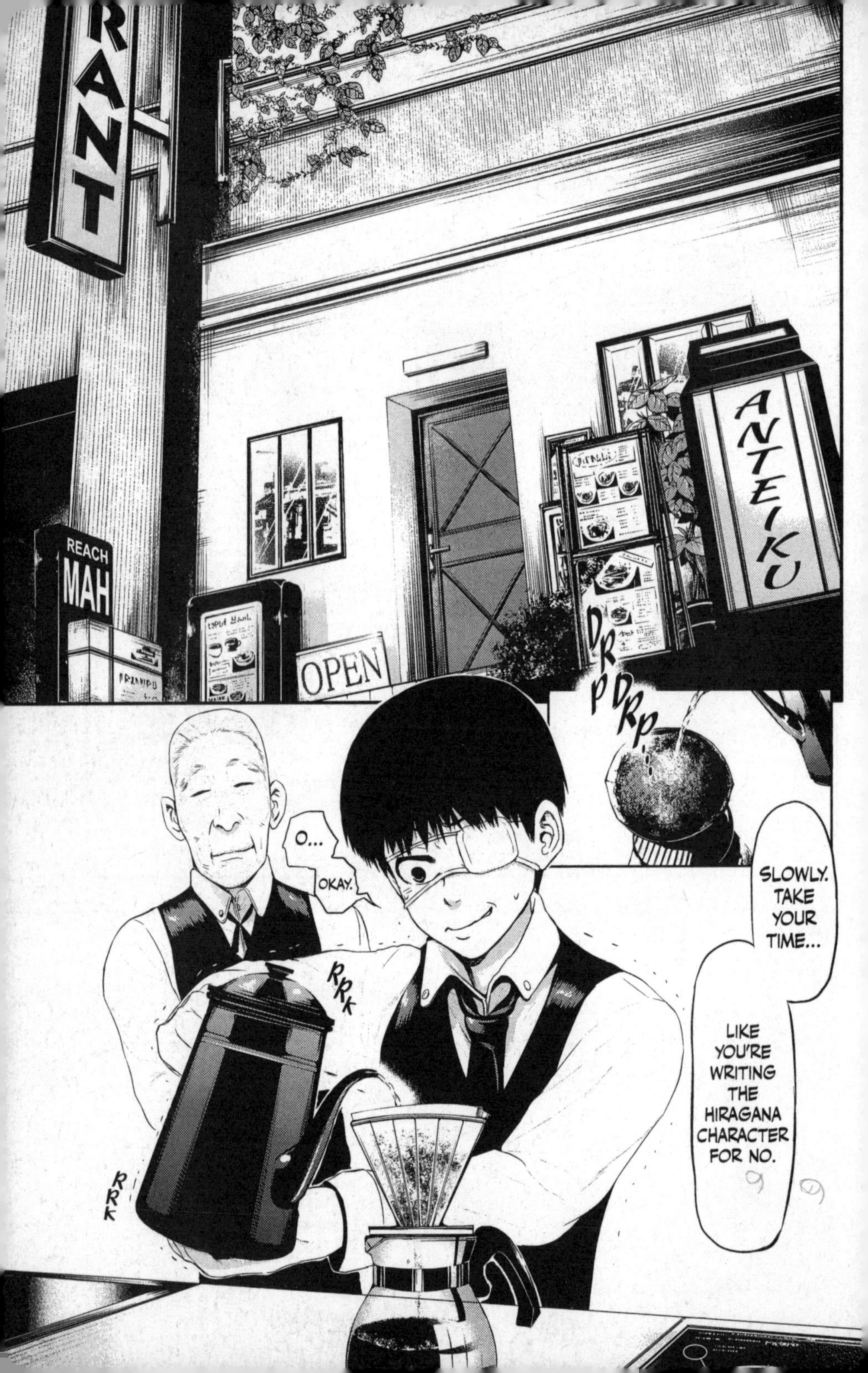
RANT
ANTEIKU
OPEN
REACH
MAH
DRP DRP DRP
SLOWLY. TAKE YOUR TIME...
LIKE YOU'RE WRITING THE HIRAGANA CHARACTER FOR NO.
O... OKAY.
RRK
RRK

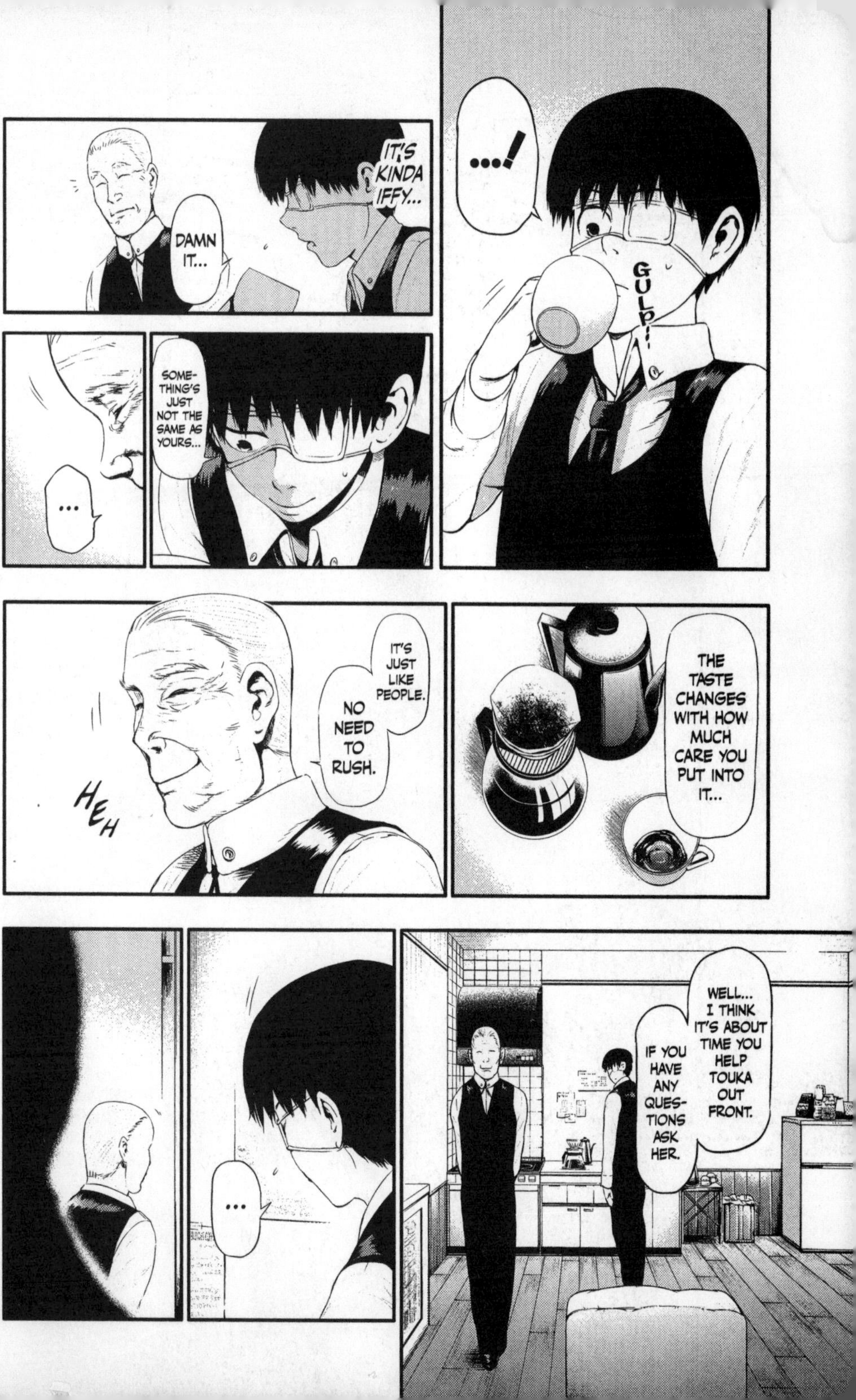
...!
GULP!!
IT'S KINDA IFFY...
DAMN IT...
SOME-THING'S JUST NOT THE SAME AS YOURS...
...
THE TASTE CHANGES WITH HOW MUCH CARE YOU PUT INTO IT...
IT'S JUST LIKE PEOPLE.
NO NEED TO RUSH.
HEH
WELL... I THINK IT'S ABOUT TIME YOU HELP TOUKA OUT FRONT.
IF YOU HAVE ANY QUES-TIONS ASK HER.
...

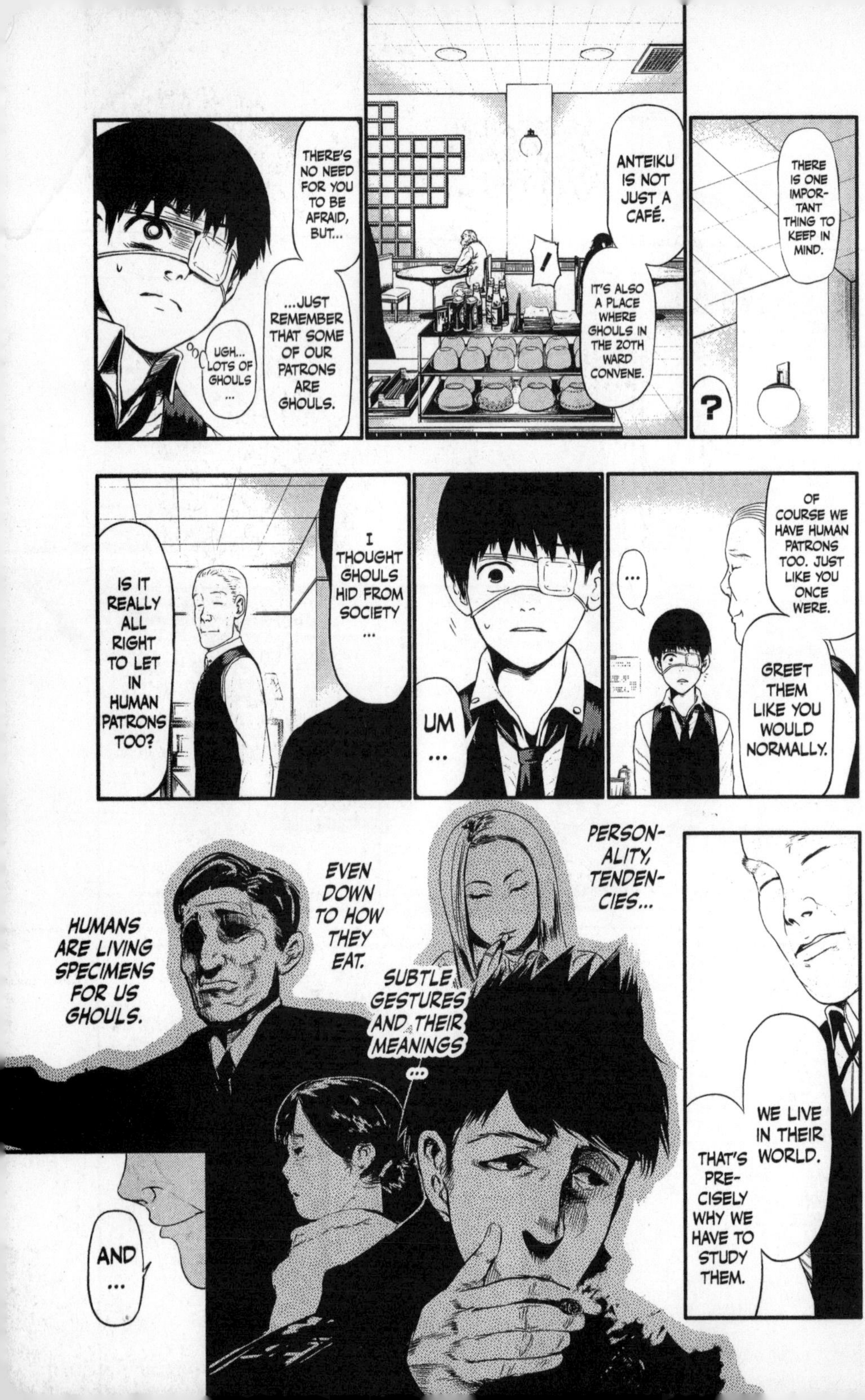
THERE IS ONE IMPORTANT THING TO KEEP IN MIND.
?
ANTEIKU IS NOT JUST A CAFÉ.
!
IT'S ALSO A PLACE WHERE GHOULS IN THE 20TH WARD CONVENE.
THERE'S NO NEED FOR YOU TO BE AFRAID, BUT...
...JUST REMEMBER THAT SOME OF OUR PATRONS ARE GHOULS.
UGH... LOTS OF GHOULS ...
OF COURSE WE HAVE HUMAN PATRONS TOO. JUST LIKE YOU ONCE WERE.
GREET THEM LIKE YOU WOULD NORMALLY.
...
UM ...
I THOUGHT GHOULS HID FROM SOCIETY ...
IS IT REALLY ALL RIGHT TO LET IN HUMAN PATRONS TOO?
WE LIVE IN THEIR WORLD.
THAT'S PRECISELY WHY WE HAVE TO STUDY THEM.
PERSONALITY, TENDENCIES...
EVEN DOWN TO HOW THEY EAT.
SUBTLE GESTURES AND THEIR MEANINGS ...
HUMANS ARE LIVING SPECIMENS FOR US GHOULS.
AND ...

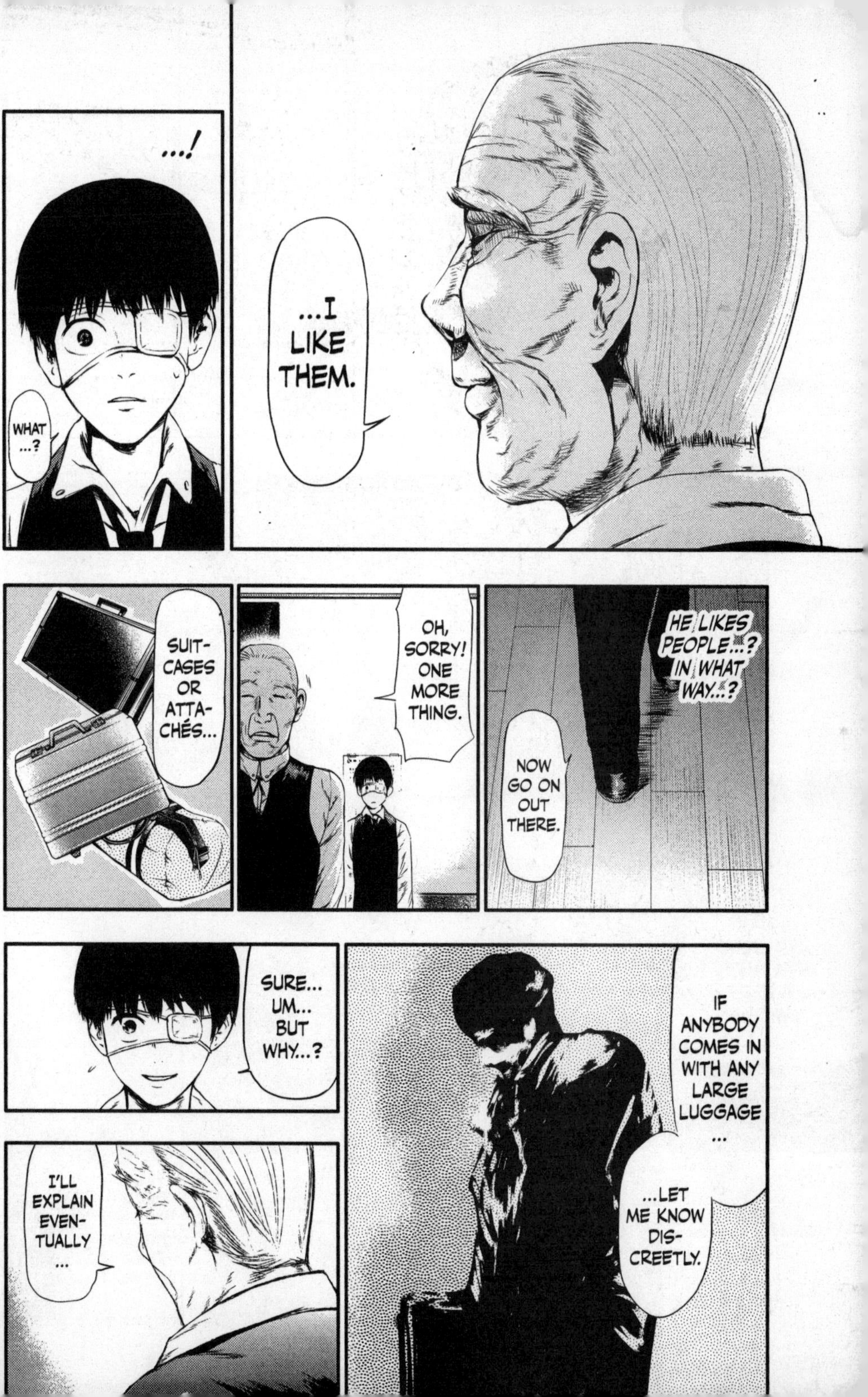
...I LIKE THEM.
...!
WHAT ...?
HE LIKES PEOPLE...? IN WHAT WAY...?
NOW GO ON OUT THERE.
OH, SORRY! ONE MORE THING.
SUIT-CASES OR ATTA-CHÉS...
IF ANYBODY COMES IN WITH ANY LARGE LUGGAGE ...
...LET ME KNOW DIS-CREETLY.
SURE... UM... BUT WHY...?
I'LL EXPLAIN EVEN-TUALLY ...

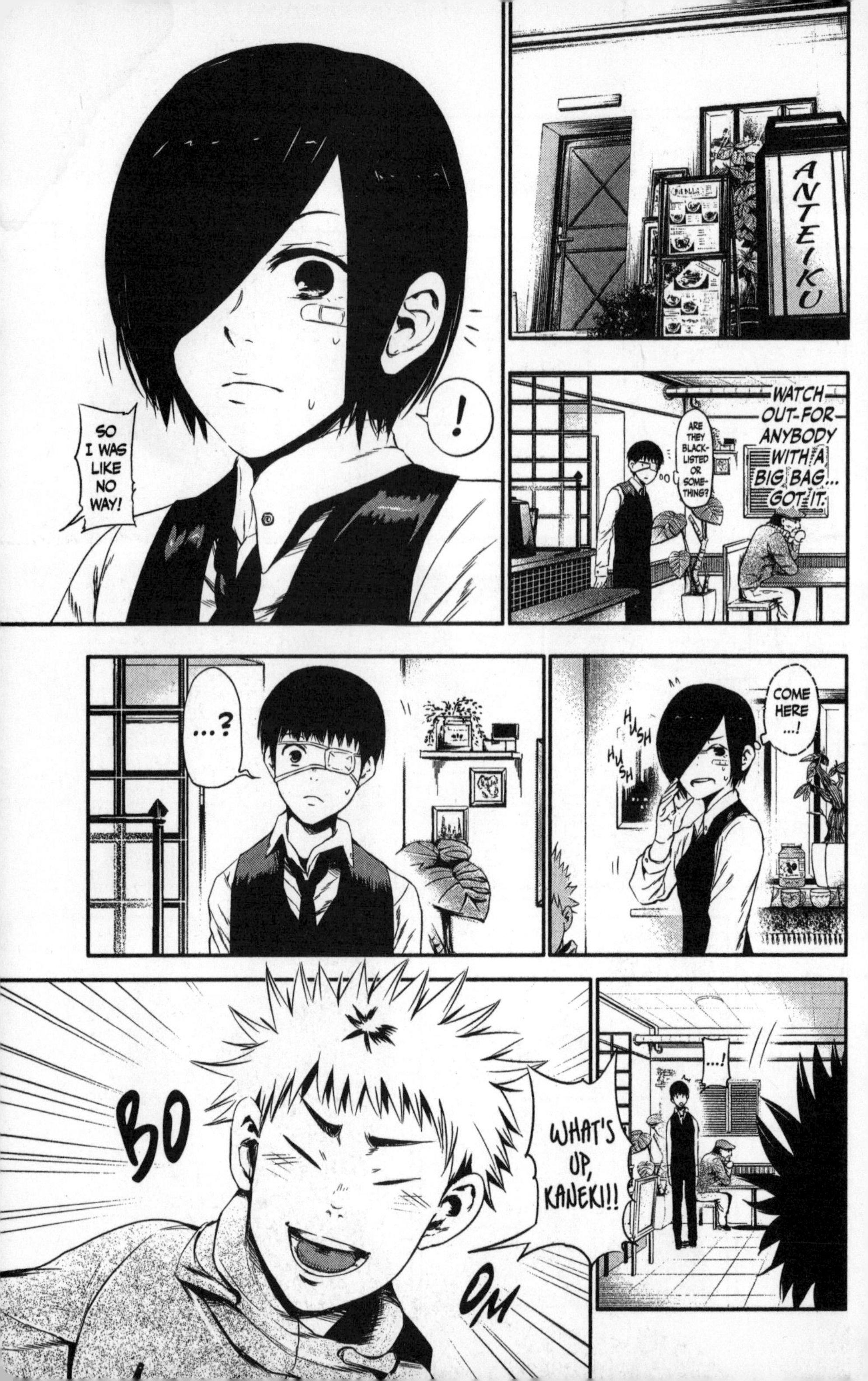
ANTEIKU
WATCH OUT FOR ANYBODY WITH A BIG BAG... GOT IT.
ARE THEY BLACK-LISTED OR SOME-THING?
!
SO I WAS LIKE NO WAY!
COME HERE ...!
HUSH HUSH
...?
...!
WHAT'S UP, KANEKI!!
BO
OM

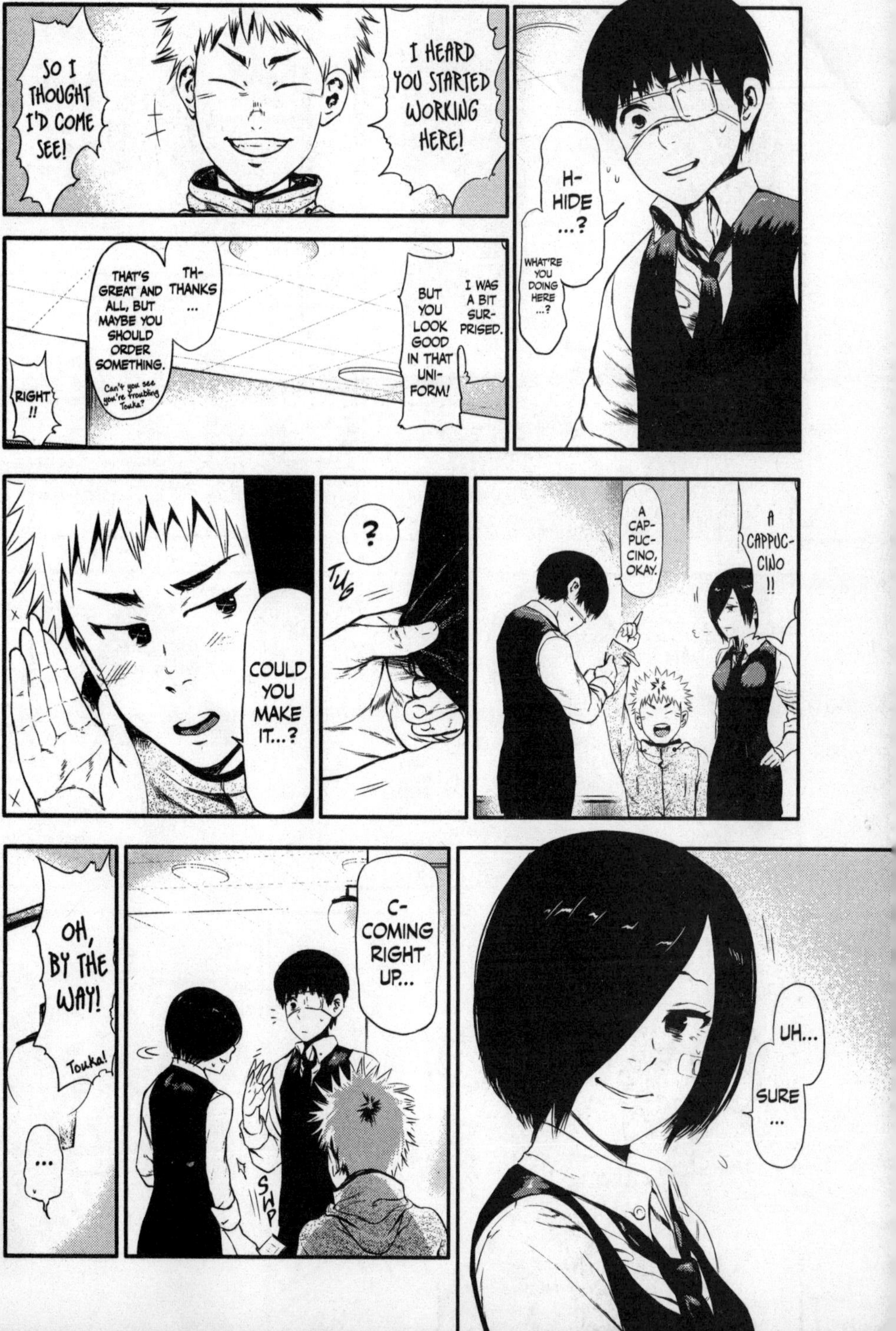
H-HIDE...?
WHAT'RE YOU DOING HERE...?
I HEARD YOU STARTED WORKING HERE!
SO I THOUGHT I'D COME SEE!
I WAS A BIT SURPRISED.
BUT YOU LOOK GOOD IN THAT UNIFORM!
TH-THANKS...
THAT'S GREAT AND ALL, BUT MAYBE YOU SHOULD ORDER SOMETHING.
Can't you see you're troubling Touka?
RIGHT!!
A CAPPUCCINO!!
A CAPPUCCINO, OKAY.
?
TUG
COULD YOU MAKE IT...?
UH...
SURE...
C-COMING RIGHT UP...
SWP
OH, BY THE WAY!
Touka!
...

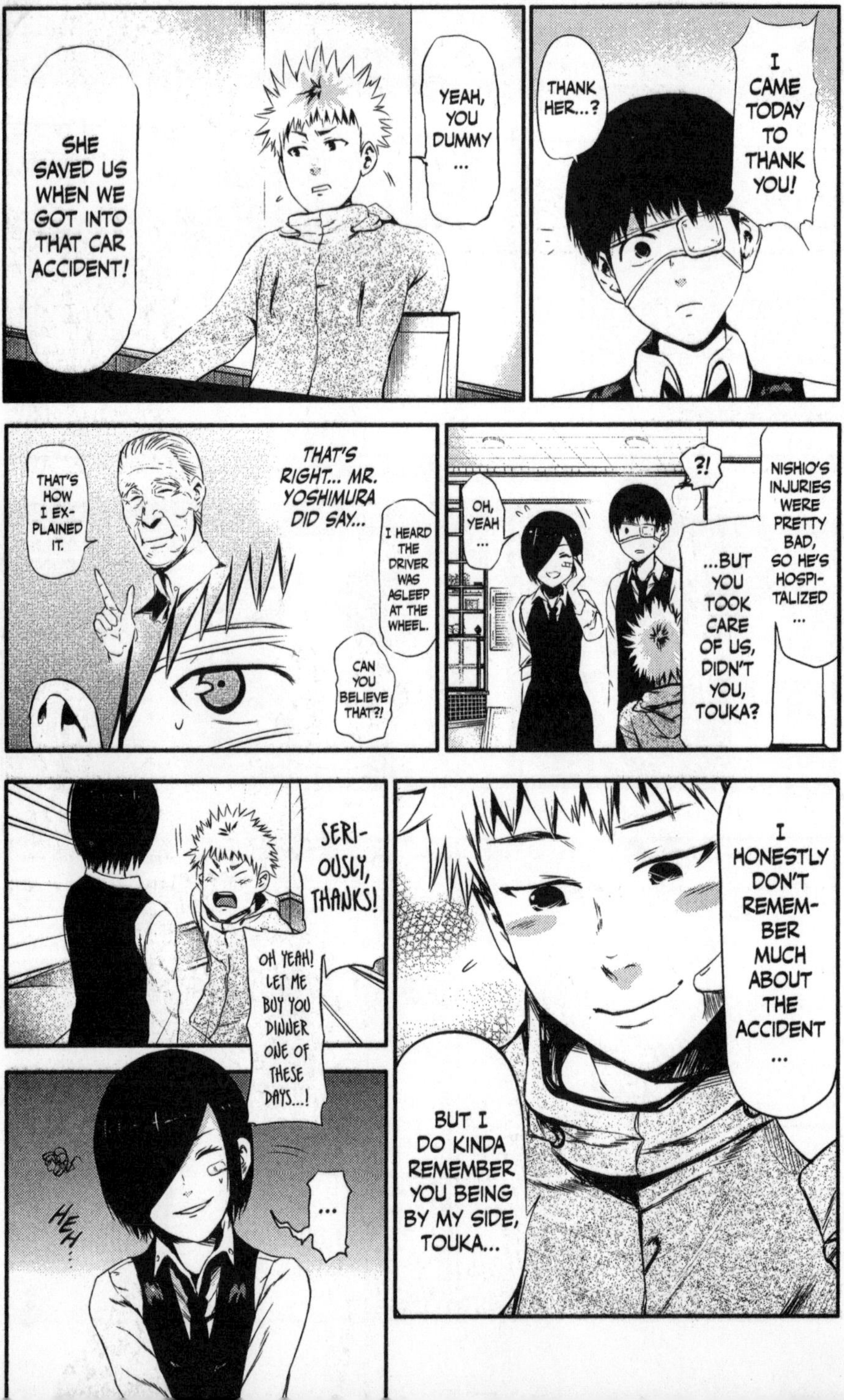
I CAME TODAY TO THANK YOU!
THANK HER...?
YEAH, YOU DUMMY ...
SHE SAVED US WHEN WE GOT INTO THAT CAR ACCIDENT!
NISHIO'S INJURIES WERE PRETTY BAD, SO HE'S HOSPITALIZED ...
?!
...BUT YOU TOOK CARE OF US, DIDN'T YOU, TOUKA?
OH, YEAH ...
THAT'S RIGHT... MR. YOSHIMURA DID SAY...
I HEARD THE DRIVER WAS ASLEEP AT THE WHEEL.
CAN YOU BELIEVE THAT?!
THAT'S HOW I EXPLAINED IT.
I HONESTLY DON'T REMEMBER MUCH ABOUT THE ACCIDENT ...
BUT I DO KINDA REMEMBER YOU BEING BY MY SIDE, TOUKA...
SERIOUSLY, THANKS!
OH YEAH! LET ME BUY YOU DINNER ONE OF THESE DAYS...!
...
HEH...

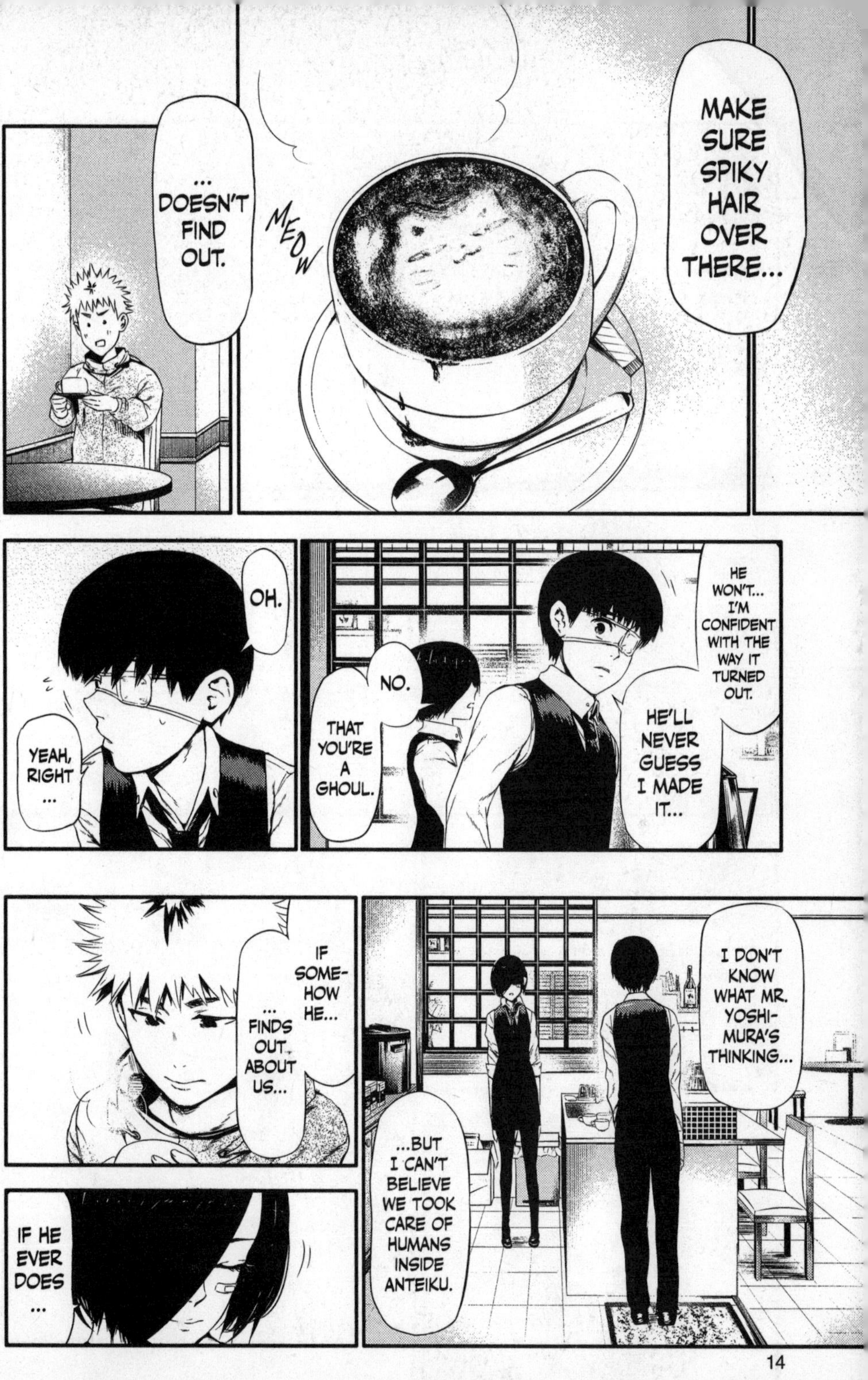
MAKE SURE SPIKY HAIR OVER THERE...
MEOW
... DOESN'T FIND OUT.
HE WON'T... I'M CONFIDENT WITH THE WAY IT TURNED OUT.
HE'LL NEVER GUESS I MADE IT...
NO.
THAT YOU'RE A GHOUL.
OH.
YEAH, RIGHT ...
I DON'T KNOW WHAT MR. YOSHI-MURA'S THINKING...
...BUT I CAN'T BELIEVE WE TOOK CARE OF HUMANS INSIDE ANTEIKU.
IF SOME-HOW HE...
... FINDS OUT ABOUT US...
IF HE EVER DOES ...

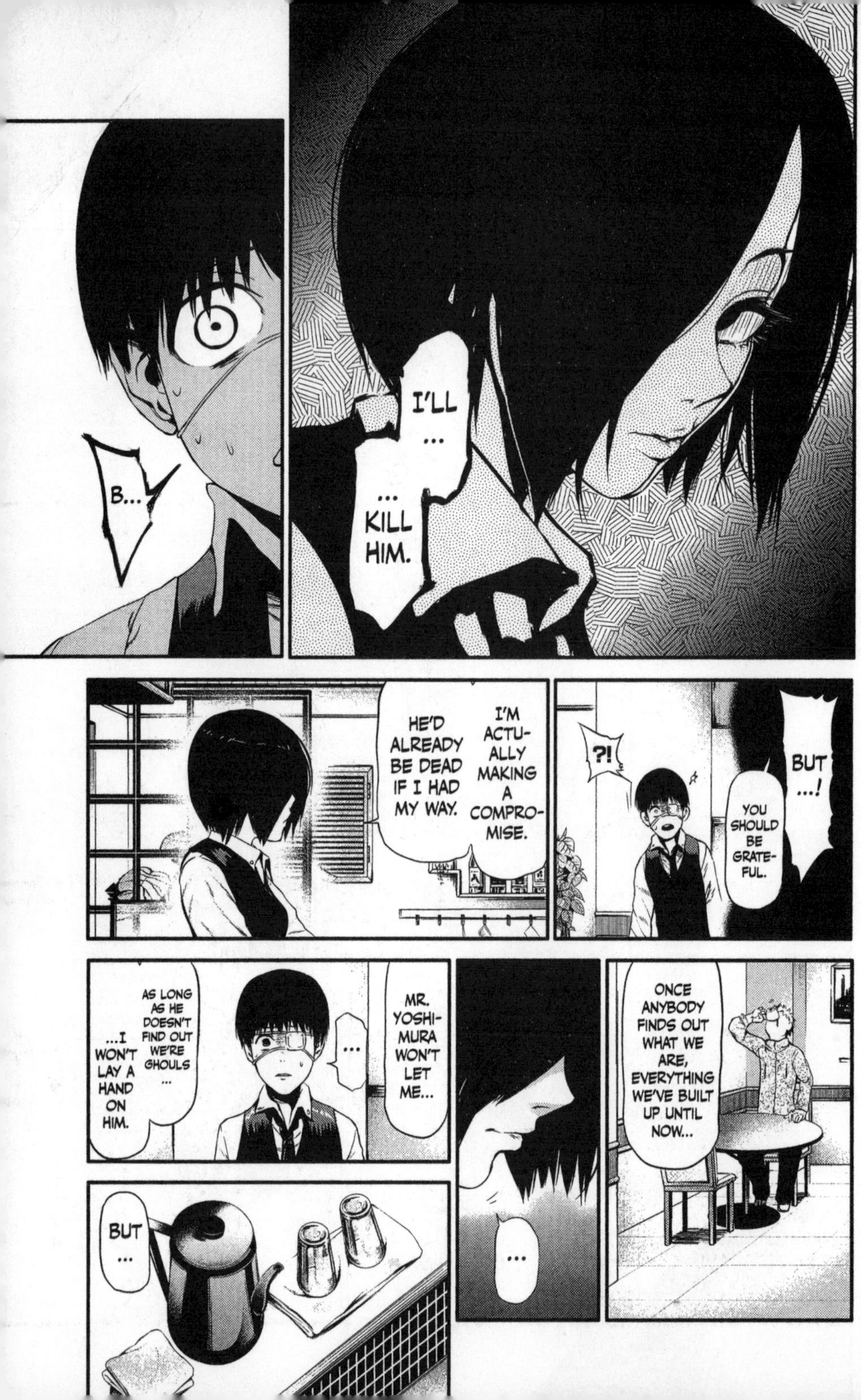
I'LL ...
... KILL HIM.
B...
BUT ...!
YOU SHOULD BE GRATE-FUL.
?!
I'M ACTU-ALLY MAKING A COMPRO-MISE.
HE'D ALREADY BE DEAD IF I HAD MY WAY.
ONCE ANYBODY FINDS OUT WHAT WE ARE, EVERYTHING WE'VE BUILT UP UNTIL NOW...
...
MR. YOSHI-MURA WON'T LET ME...
...
AS LONG AS HE DOESN'T FIND OUT WE'RE GHOULS ...
...I WON'T LAY A HAND ON HIM.
BUT ...

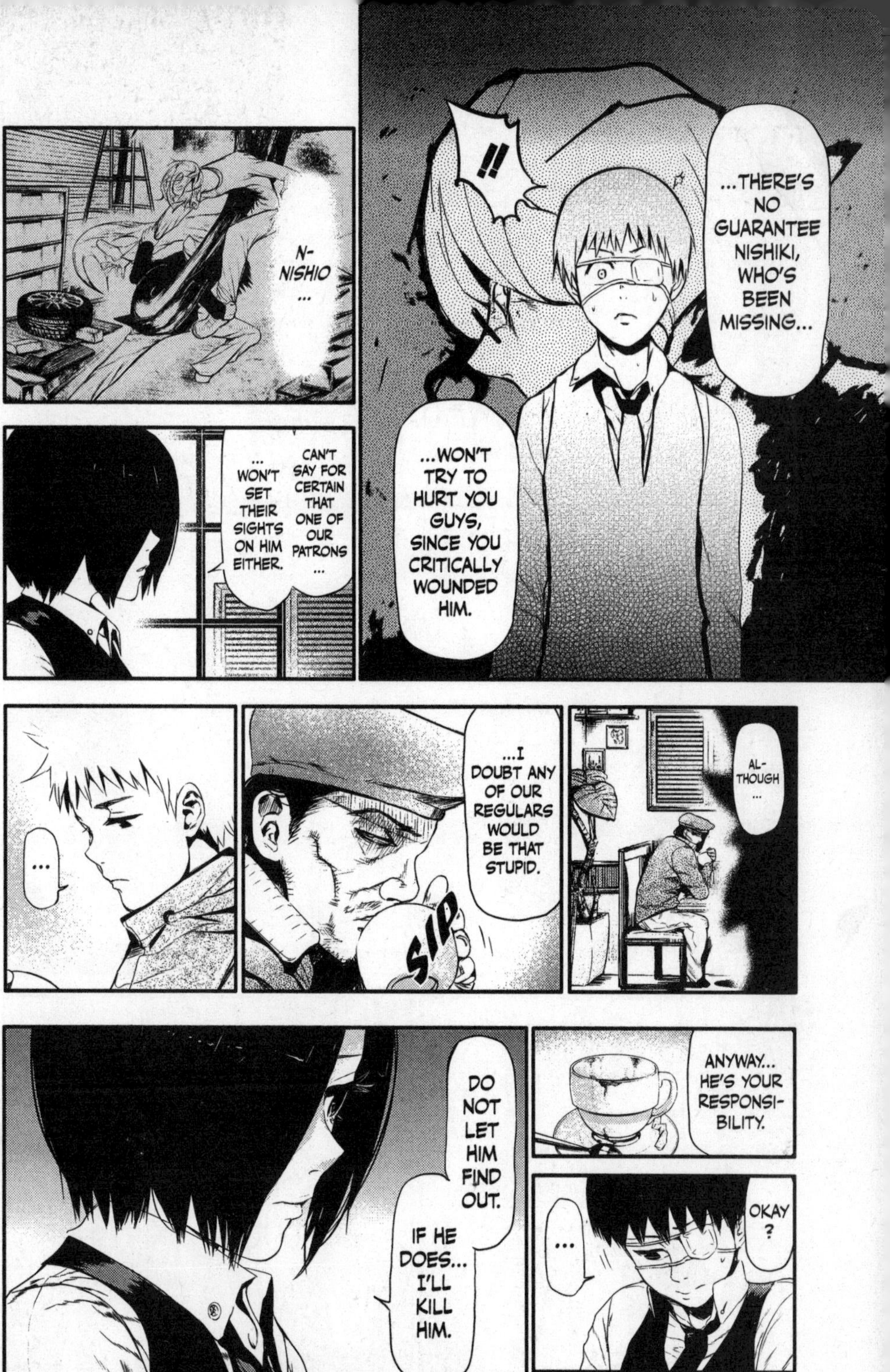
!!
...THERE'S NO GUARANTEE NISHIKI, WHO'S BEEN MISSING...
...WON'T TRY TO HURT YOU GUYS, SINCE YOU CRITICALLY WOUNDED HIM.
N-NISHIO ...
CAN'T SAY FOR CERTAIN THAT ONE OF OUR PATRONS ...
...WON'T SET THEIR SIGHTS ON HIM EITHER.
AL-THOUGH ...
...I DOUBT ANY OF OUR REGULARS WOULD BE THAT STUPID.
SIP
...
ANYWAY... HE'S YOUR RESPONSI-BILITY.
OKAY ?
...
DO NOT LET HIM FIND OUT.
IF HE DOES... I'LL KILL HIM.

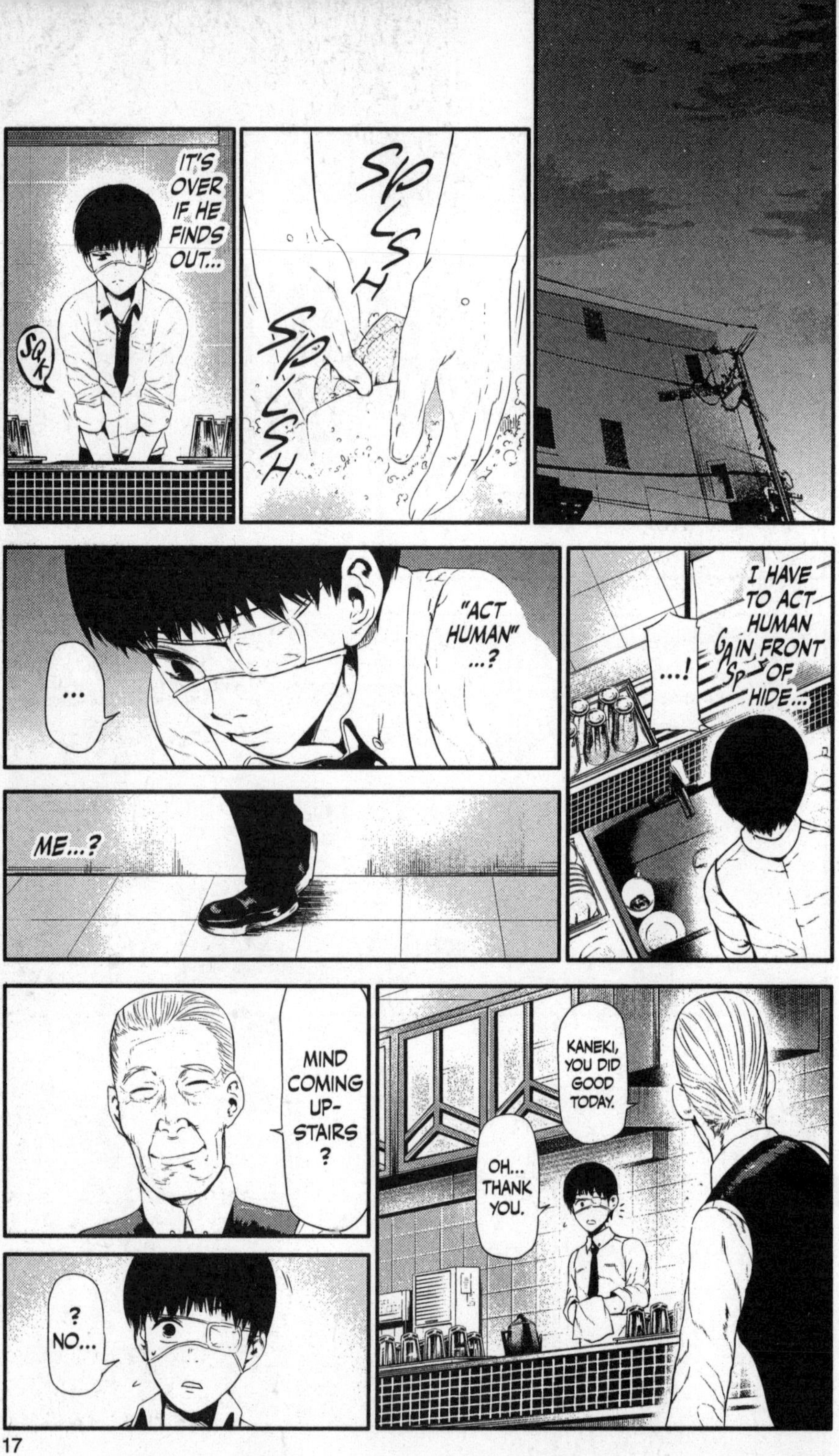
SPLSH
SPLSH
IT'S OVER IF HE FINDS OUT...
SQK
I HAVE TO ACT HUMAN IN FRONT OF HIDE...
GASP
...!
"ACT HUMAN" ...?
...
ME...?
KANEKI, YOU DID GOOD TODAY.
OH... THANK YOU.
MIND COMING UP-STAIRS ?
? NO...

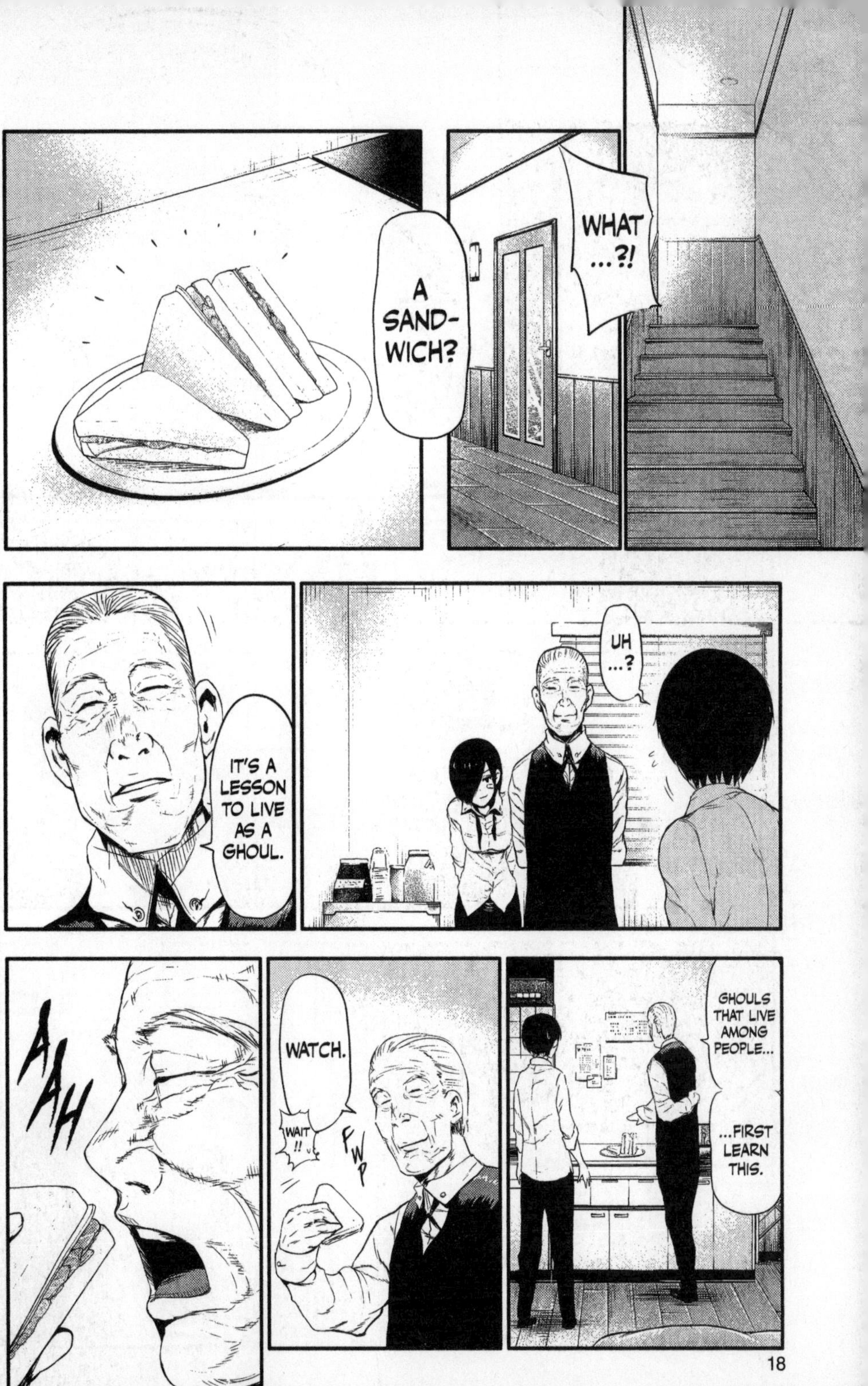
WHAT ...?!
A SAND-WICH?
UH ...?
IT'S A LESSON TO LIVE AS A GHOUL.
GHOULS THAT LIVE AMONG PEOPLE...
...FIRST LEARN THIS.
WATCH.
WAIT !!
FWP
AAH

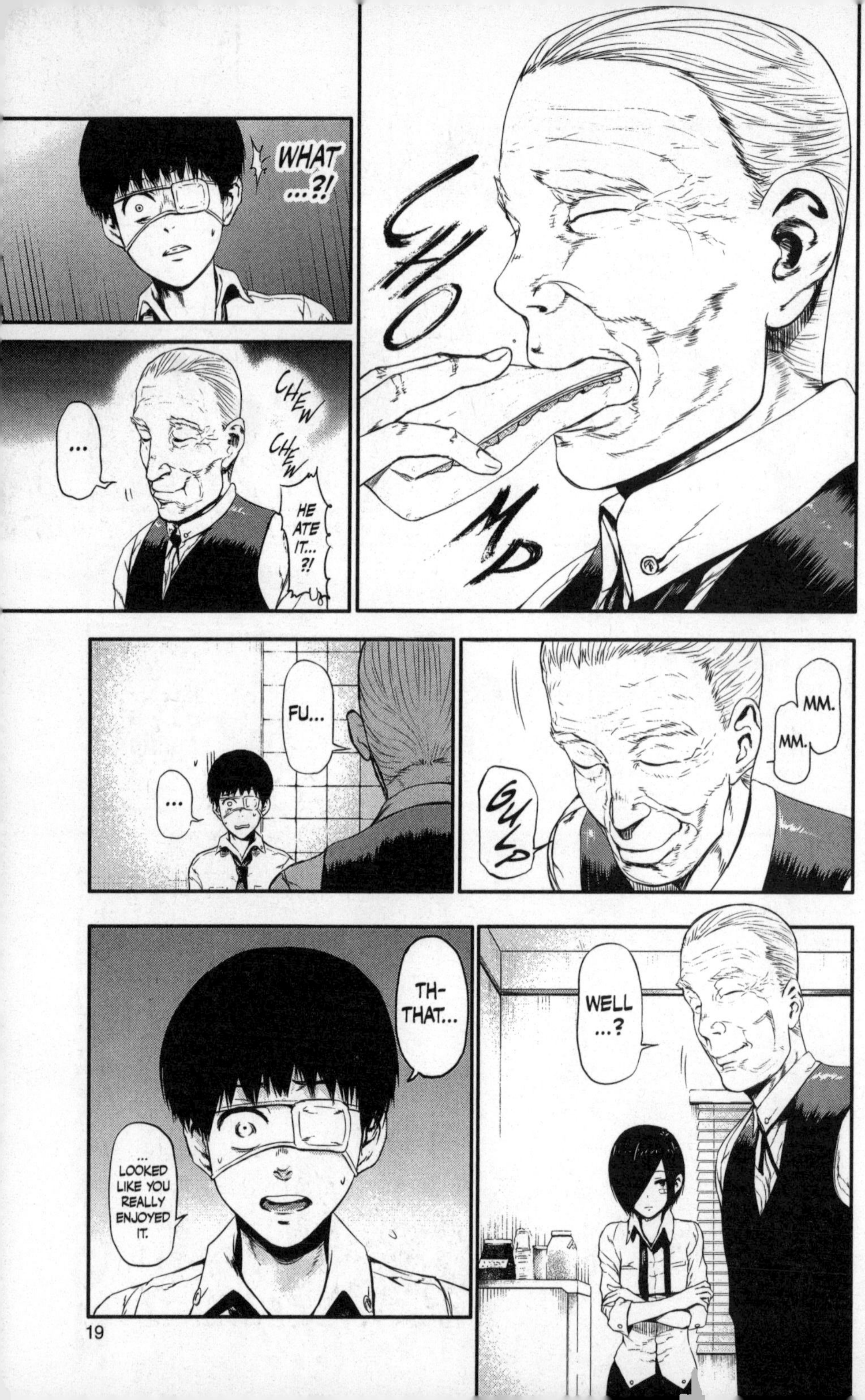
CHOMP
WHAT ...?!
CHEW CHEW
HE ATE IT... ?!
...
MM. MM.
GULP
FU...
...
WELL ...?
TH- THAT...
... LOOKED LIKE YOU REALLY ENJOYED IT.

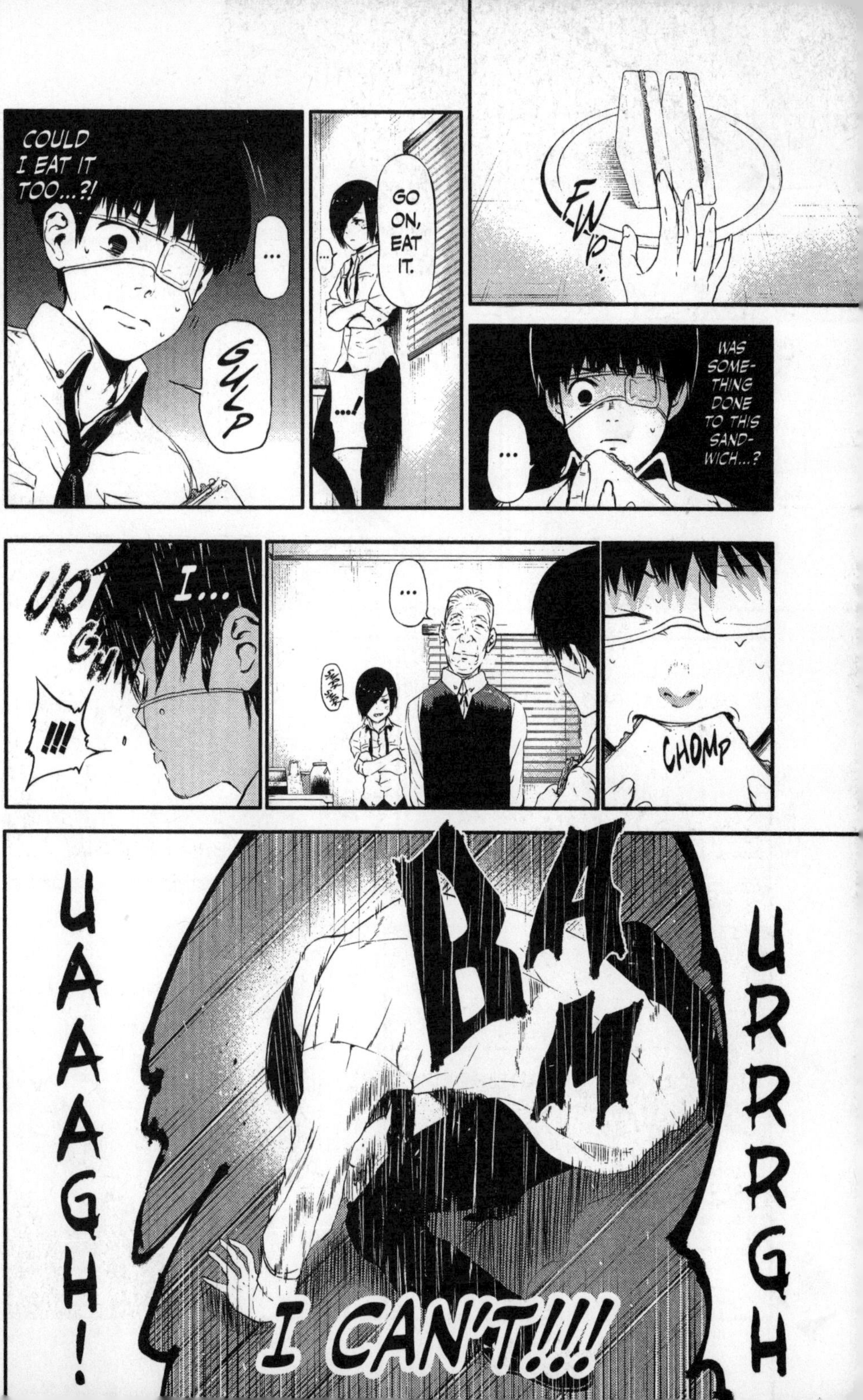
FWP...
...
WAS SOMETHING DONE TO THIS SANDWICH...?
GO ON, EAT IT.
...
...!
COULD I EAT IT TOO...?!
...
GULP
CHOMP
...
I...
URGH
!!!
URRRGH
I CAN'T!!!
UAAAGH!

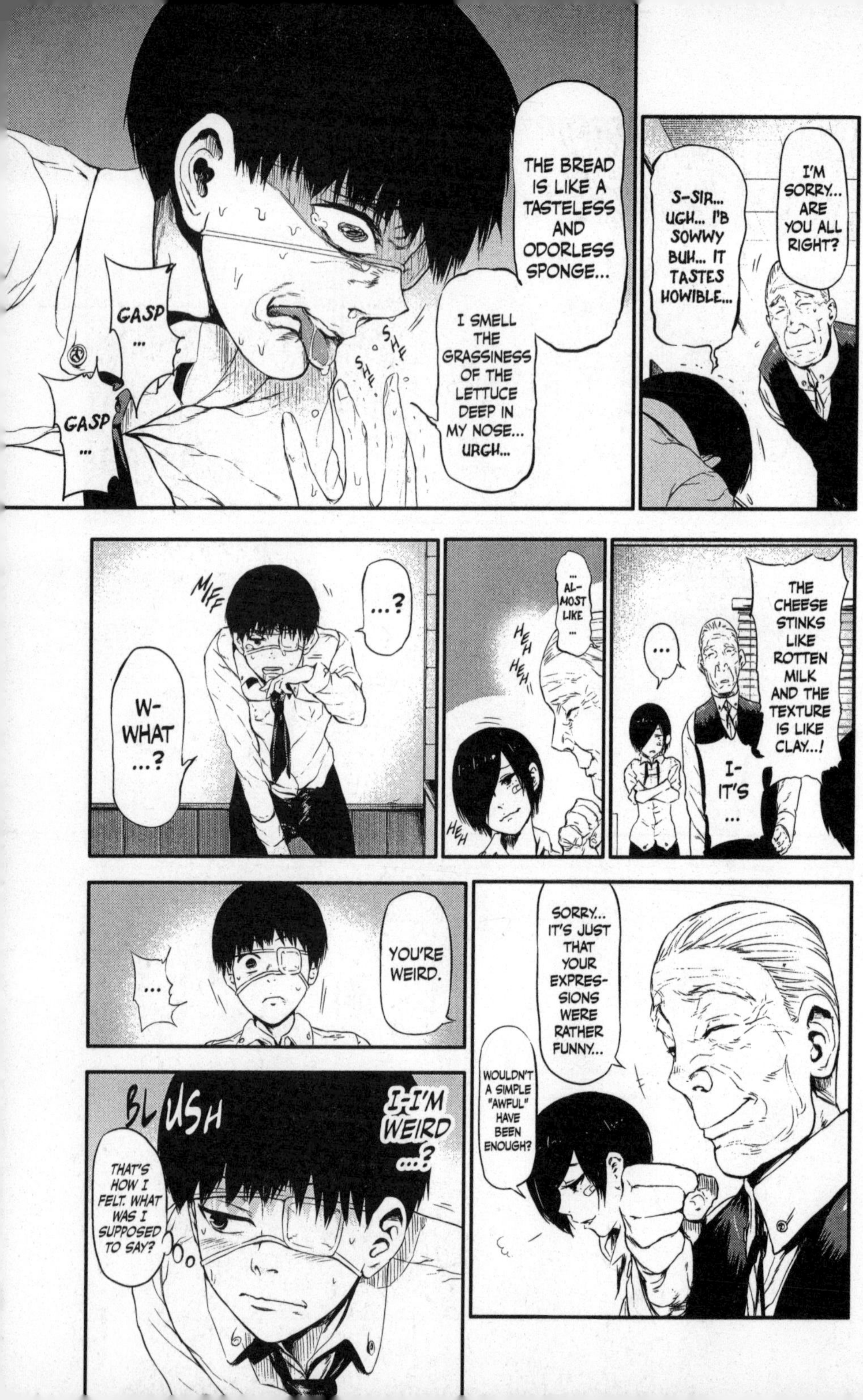
I'M SORRY... ARE YOU ALL RIGHT?
S-SIR... UGH... I'B SOWWY BUH... IT TASTES HOWIBLE...
THE BREAD IS LIKE A TASTELESS AND ODORLESS SPONGE...
I SMELL THE GRASSINESS OF THE LETTUCE DEEP IN MY NOSE... URGH...
GASP...
GASP...
THE CHEESE STINKS LIKE ROTTEN MILK AND THE TEXTURE IS LIKE CLAY...!
...
I- IT'S ...
...ALMOST LIKE ...
HEH HEH HEH
...?
W- WHAT ...?
SORRY... IT'S JUST THAT YOUR EXPRESSIONS WERE RATHER FUNNY...
WOULDN'T A SIMPLE "AWFUL" HAVE BEEN ENOUGH?
YOU'RE WEIRD.
...
BLUSH
I-I'M WEIRD ...?
THAT'S HOW I FELT. WHAT WAS I SUPPOSED TO SAY?

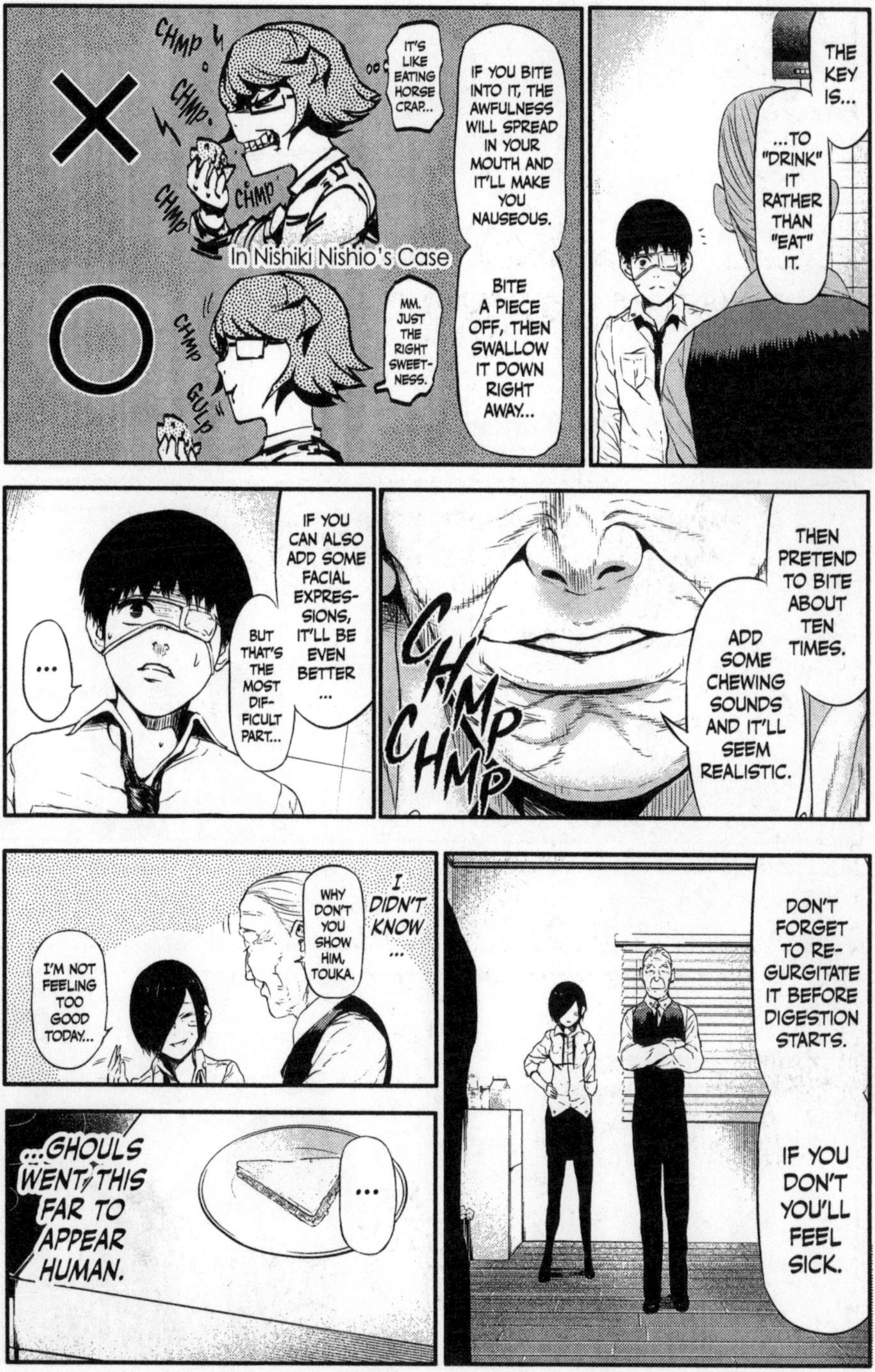
THE KEY IS...
...TO "DRINK" IT RATHER THAN "EAT" IT.
IF YOU BITE INTO IT, THE AWFULNESS WILL SPREAD IN YOUR MOUTH AND IT'LL MAKE YOU NAUSEOUS.
IT'S LIKE EATING HORSE CRAP...
CHMP
CHMP
CHMP
CHMP
In Nishiki Nishio's Case
BITE A PIECE OFF, THEN SWALLOW IT DOWN RIGHT AWAY...
MM. JUST THE RIGHT SWEETNESS.
CHMP
GULP
THEN PRETEND TO BITE ABOUT TEN TIMES.
ADD SOME CHEWING SOUNDS AND IT'LL SEEM REALISTIC.
CHMP CHMP
IF YOU CAN ALSO ADD SOME FACIAL EXPRESSIONS, IT'LL BE EVEN BETTER...
BUT THAT'S THE MOST DIFFICULT PART...
...
DON'T FORGET TO REGURGITATE IT BEFORE DIGESTION STARTS.
IF YOU DON'T YOU'LL FEEL SICK.
I DIDN'T KNOW...
WHY DON'T YOU SHOW HIM, TOUKA.
I'M NOT FEELING TOO GOOD TODAY...
...
...GHOULS WENT THIS FAR TO APPEAR HUMAN.

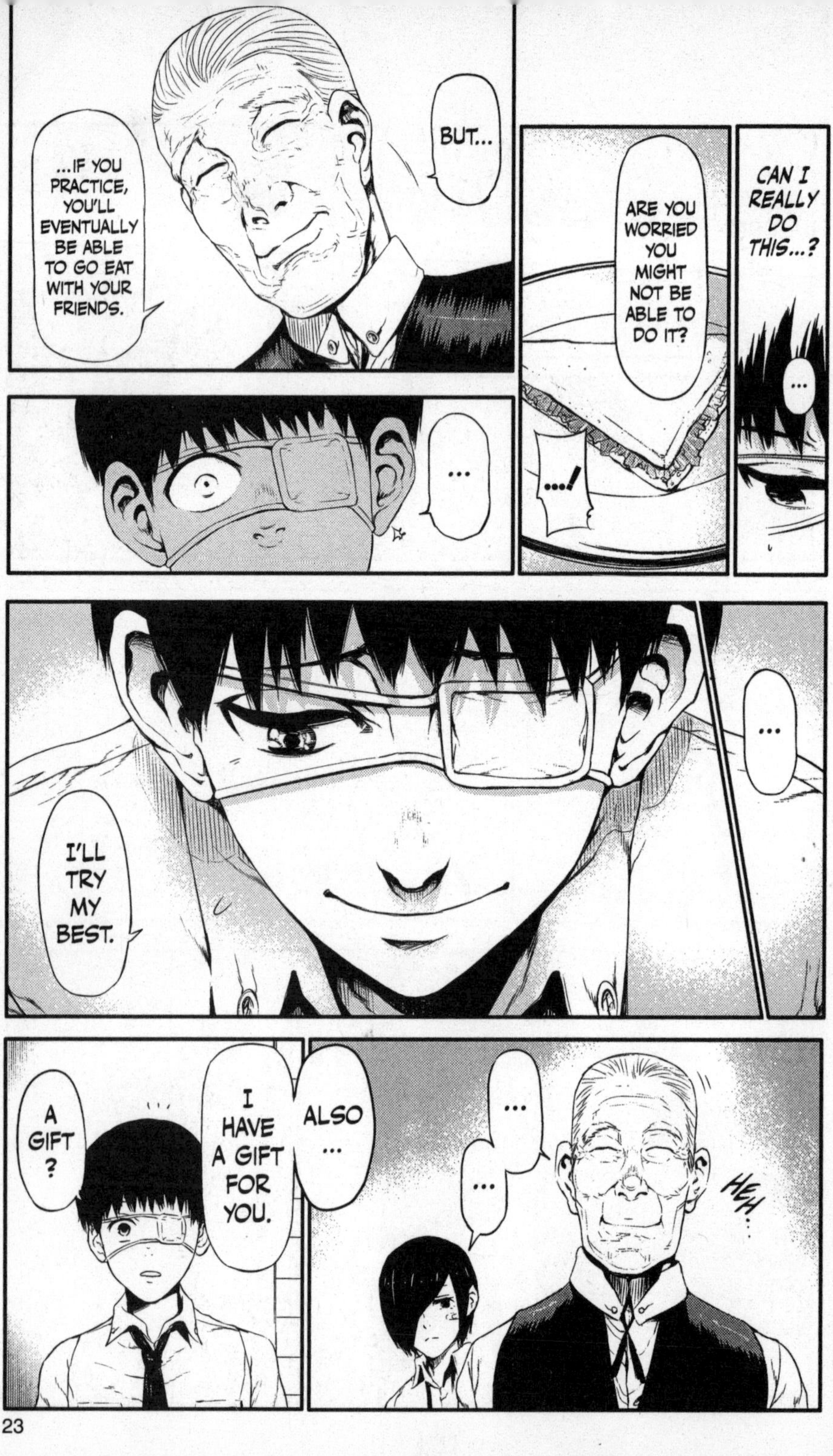
CAN I REALLY DO THIS...?
...
ARE YOU WORRIED YOU MIGHT NOT BE ABLE TO DO IT?
...!
BUT...
...IF YOU PRACTICE, YOU'LL EVENTUALLY BE ABLE TO GO EAT WITH YOUR FRIENDS.
...
...
I'LL TRY MY BEST.
...
...
HEH...
ALSO ...
I HAVE A GIFT FOR YOU.
A GIFT?

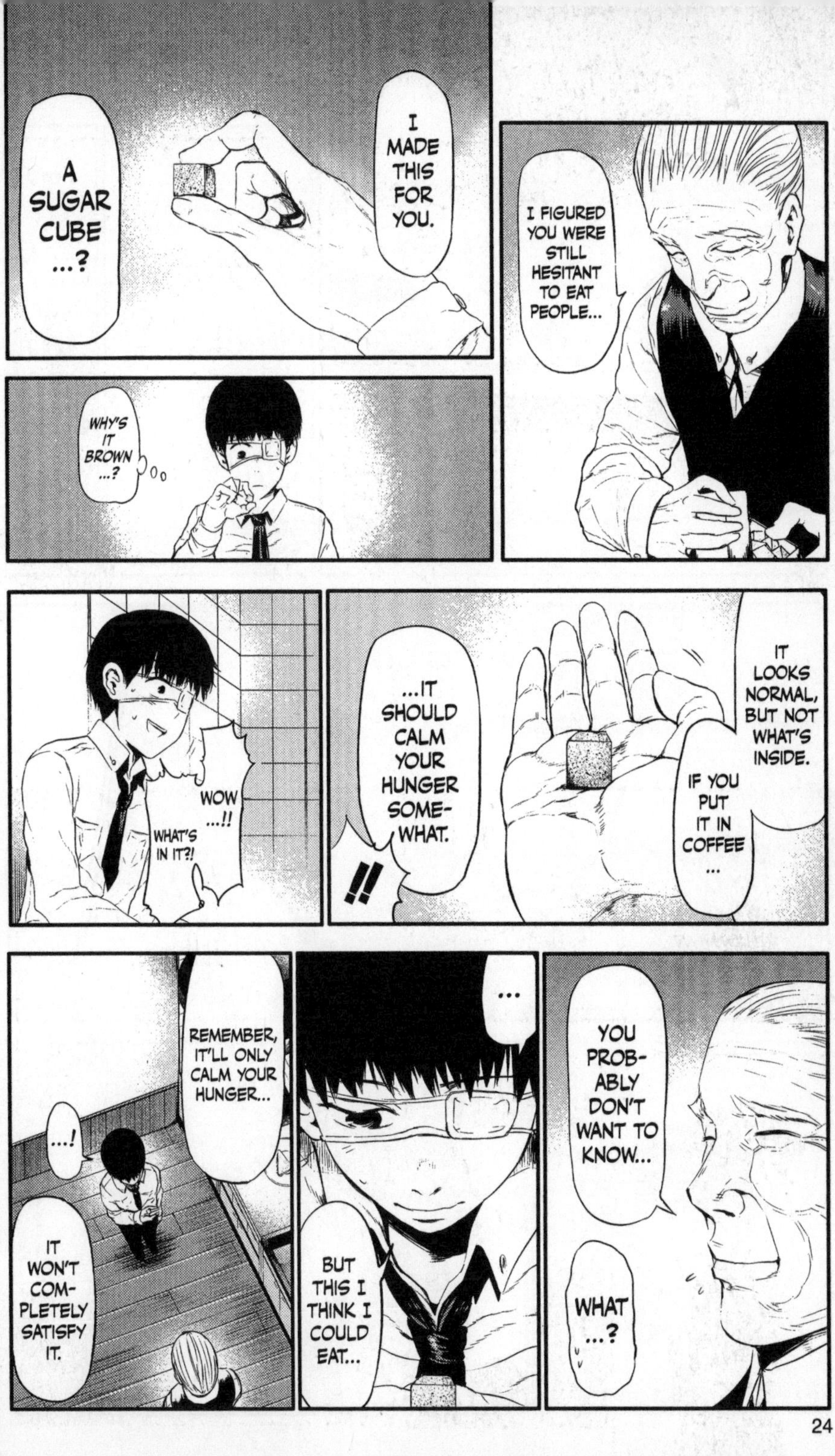
I FIGURED YOU WERE STILL HESITANT TO EAT PEOPLE...
I MADE THIS FOR YOU.
A SUGAR CUBE ...?
WHY'S IT BROWN ...?
IT LOOKS NORMAL, BUT NOT WHAT'S INSIDE.
IF YOU PUT IT IN COFFEE ...
...IT SHOULD CALM YOUR HUNGER SOME-WHAT.
!!
WOW ...!!
WHAT'S IN IT?!
YOU PROB-ABLY DON'T WANT TO KNOW...
WHAT ...?
...
BUT THIS I THINK I COULD EAT...
REMEMBER, IT'LL ONLY CALM YOUR HUNGER...
...!
IT WON'T COM-PLETELY SATISFY IT.

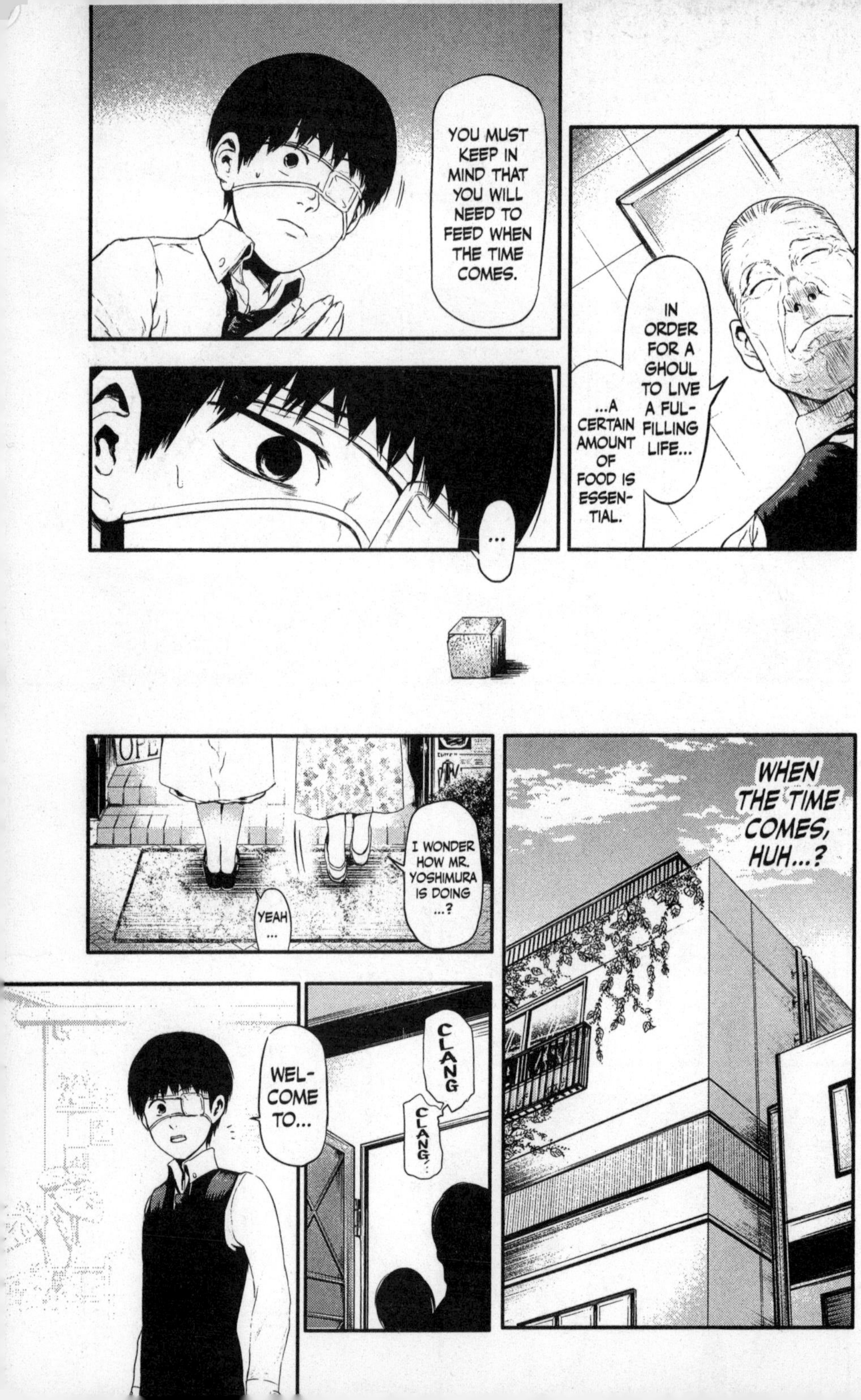

IN ORDER FOR A GHOUL TO LIVE A FUL-FILLING LIFE...
...A CERTAIN AMOUNT OF FOOD IS ESSEN-TIAL.
YOU MUST KEEP IN MIND THAT YOU WILL NEED TO FEED WHEN THE TIME COMES.
...
WHEN THE TIME COMES, HUH...?
I WONDER HOW MR. YOSHIMURA IS DOING ...?
YEAH ...
CLANG
CLANG
WEL-COME TO...

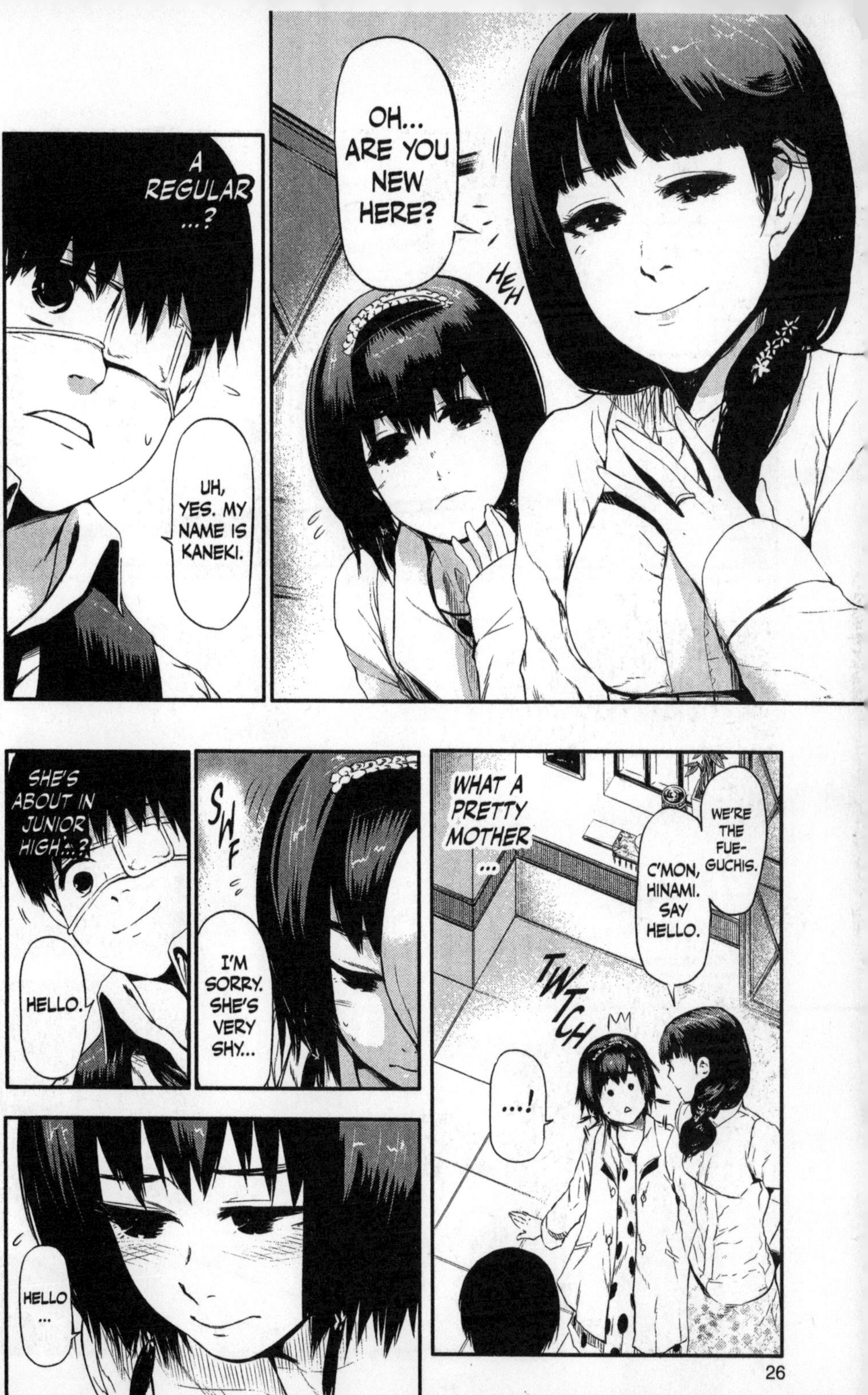

OH... ARE YOU NEW HERE?
HEH
A REGULAR ...?
UH, YES. MY NAME IS KANEKI.
WE'RE THE FUE-GUCHIS.
WHAT A PRETTY MOTHER ...
C'MON, HINAMI. SAY HELLO.
TWTCH
...!
SWF
I'M SORRY. SHE'S VERY SHY...
SHE'S ABOUT IN JUNIOR HIGH...?
HELLO.
HELLO ...

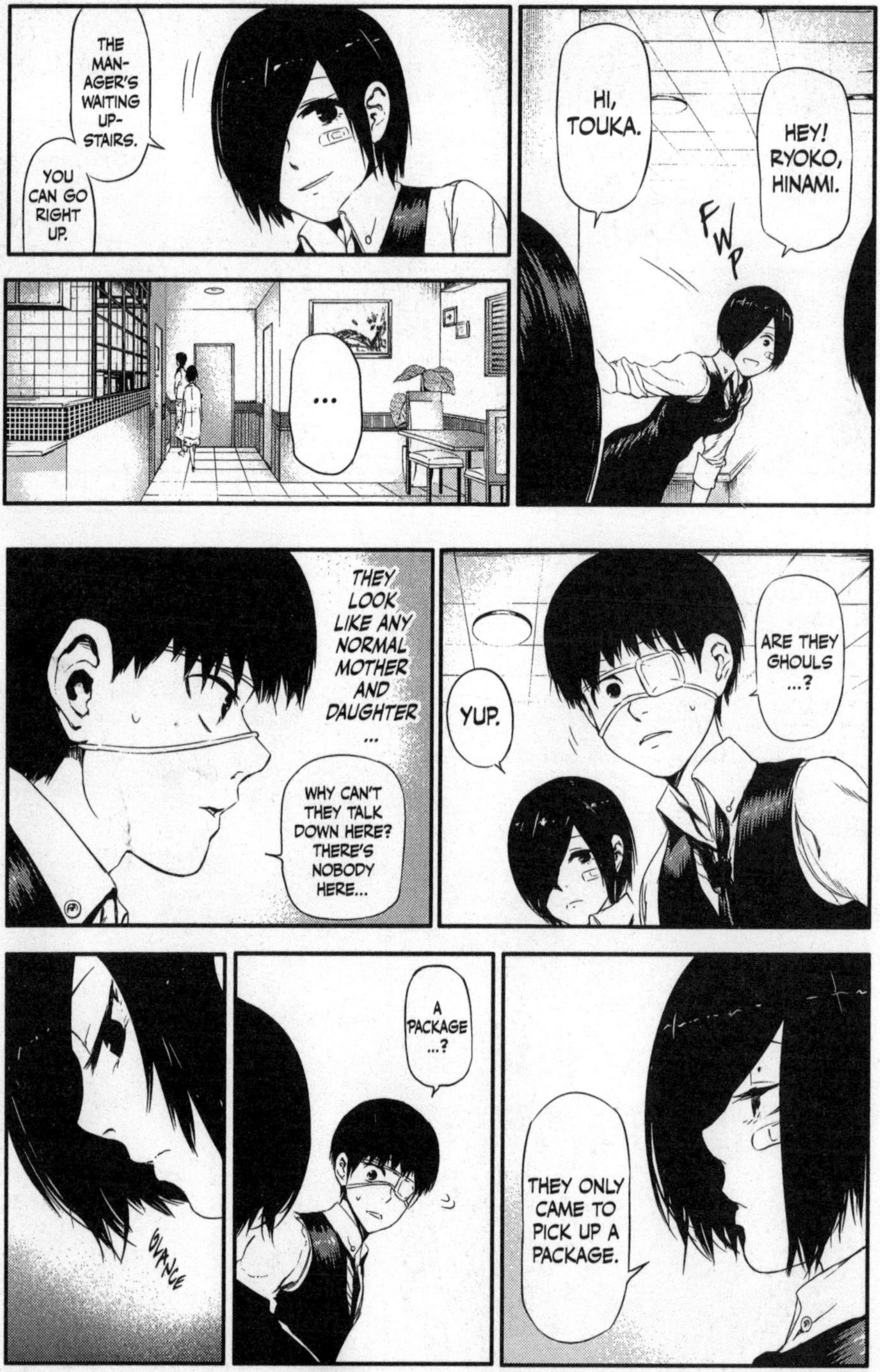
HEY! RYOKO, HINAMI.
HI, TOUKA.
FWP
THE MANAGER'S WAITING UPSTAIRS.
YOU CAN GO RIGHT UP.
...
ARE THEY GHOULS ...?
YUP.
THEY LOOK LIKE ANY NORMAL MOTHER AND DAUGHTER ...
WHY CAN'T THEY TALK DOWN HERE? THERE'S NOBODY HERE...
THEY ONLY CAME TO PICK UP A PACKAGE.
A PACKAGE ...?
GLANCE

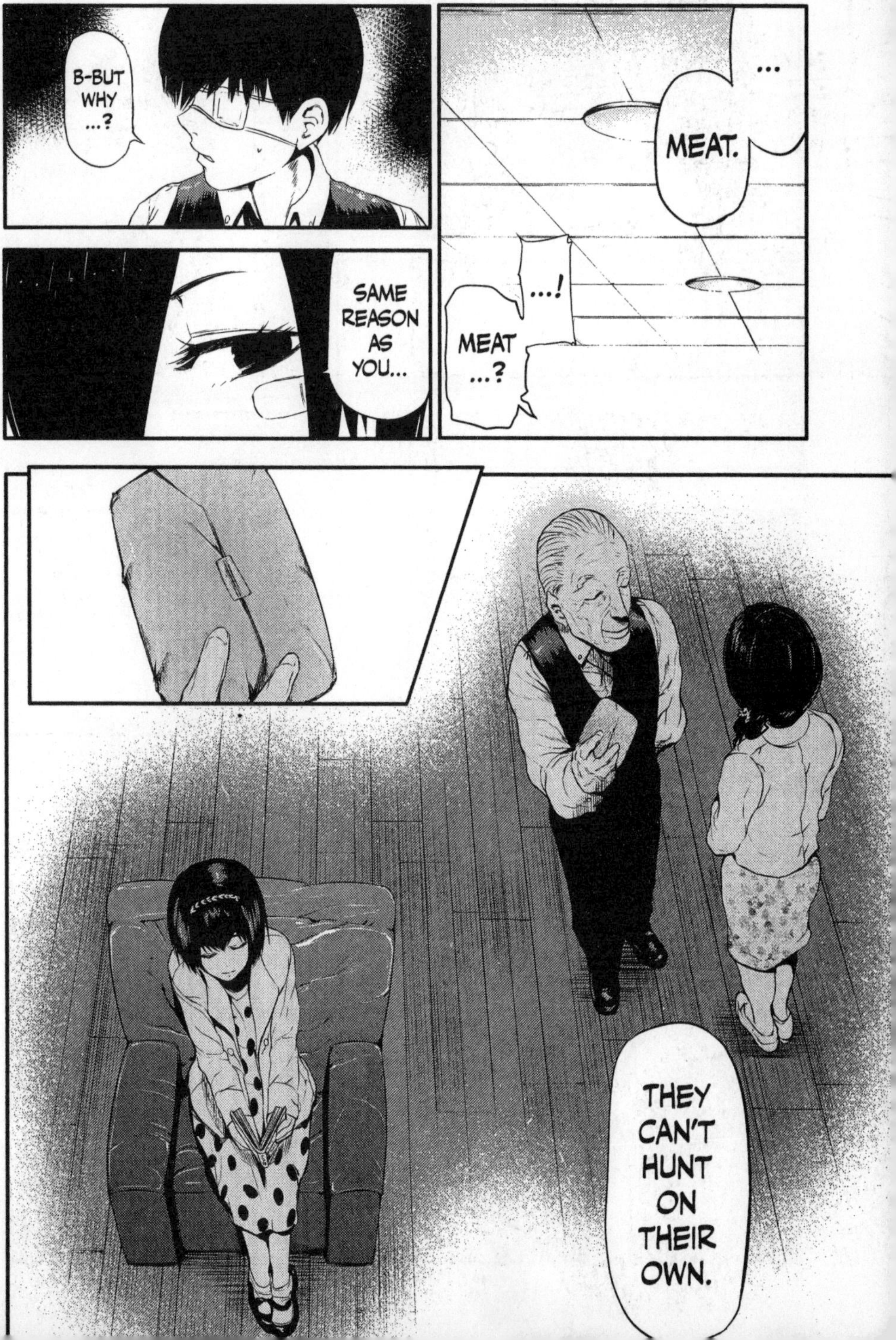
...
MEAT.
...!
MEAT ...?
B-BUT WHY ...?
SAME REASON AS YOU...
THEY CAN'T HUNT ON THEIR OWN.

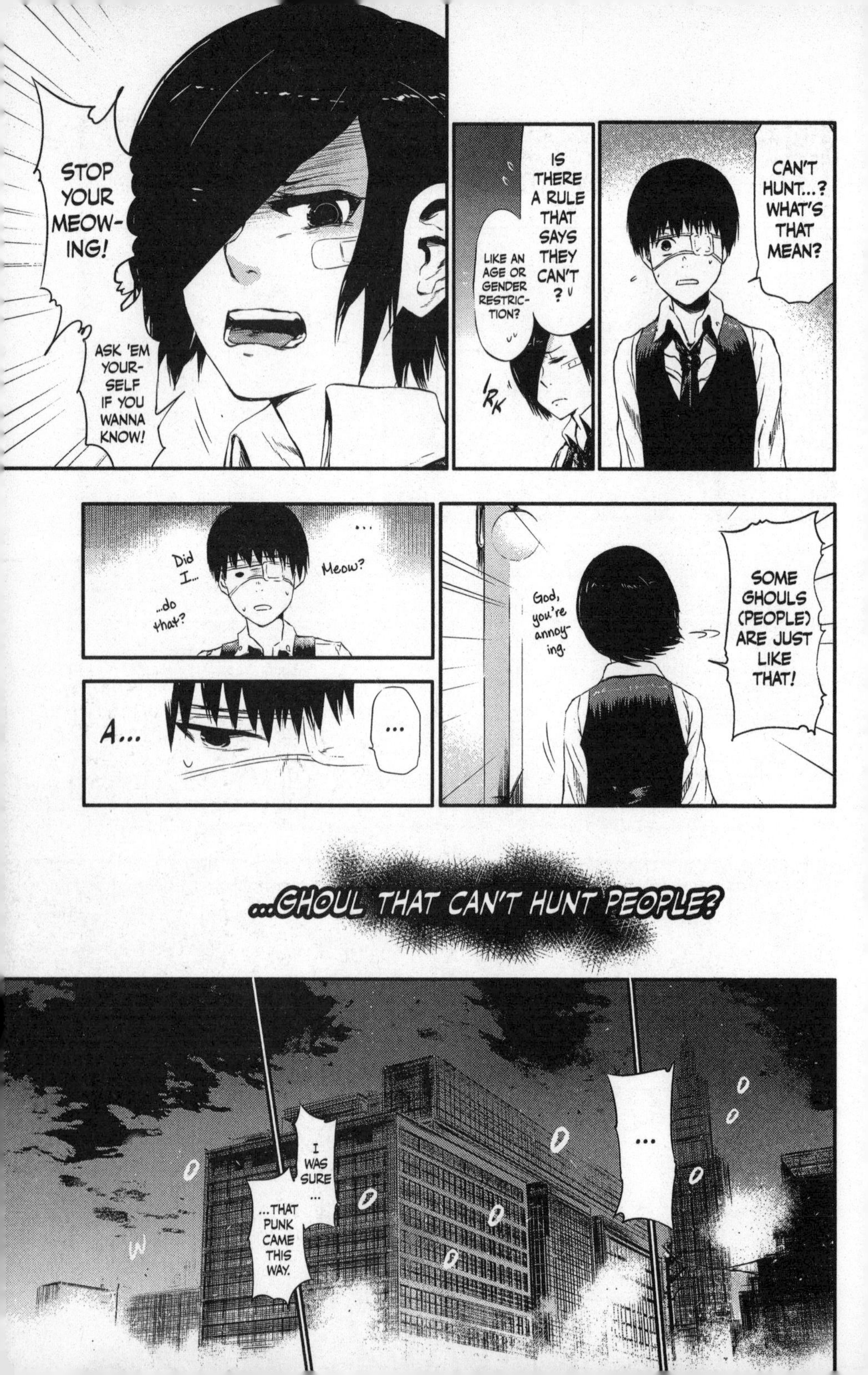
CAN'T HUNT...? WHAT'S THAT MEAN?
IS THERE A RULE THAT SAYS THEY CAN'T?
LIKE AN AGE OR GENDER RESTRICTION?
IRK
STOP YOUR MEOW-ING!
ASK 'EM YOUR-SELF IF YOU WANNA KNOW!
SOME GHOULS (PEOPLE) ARE JUST LIKE THAT!
God, you're annoy-ing.
...
Meow?
Did I...
...do that?
...
A...
...GHOUL THAT CAN'T HUNT PEOPLE?
...
I WAS SURE...
...THAT PUNK CAME THIS WAY.

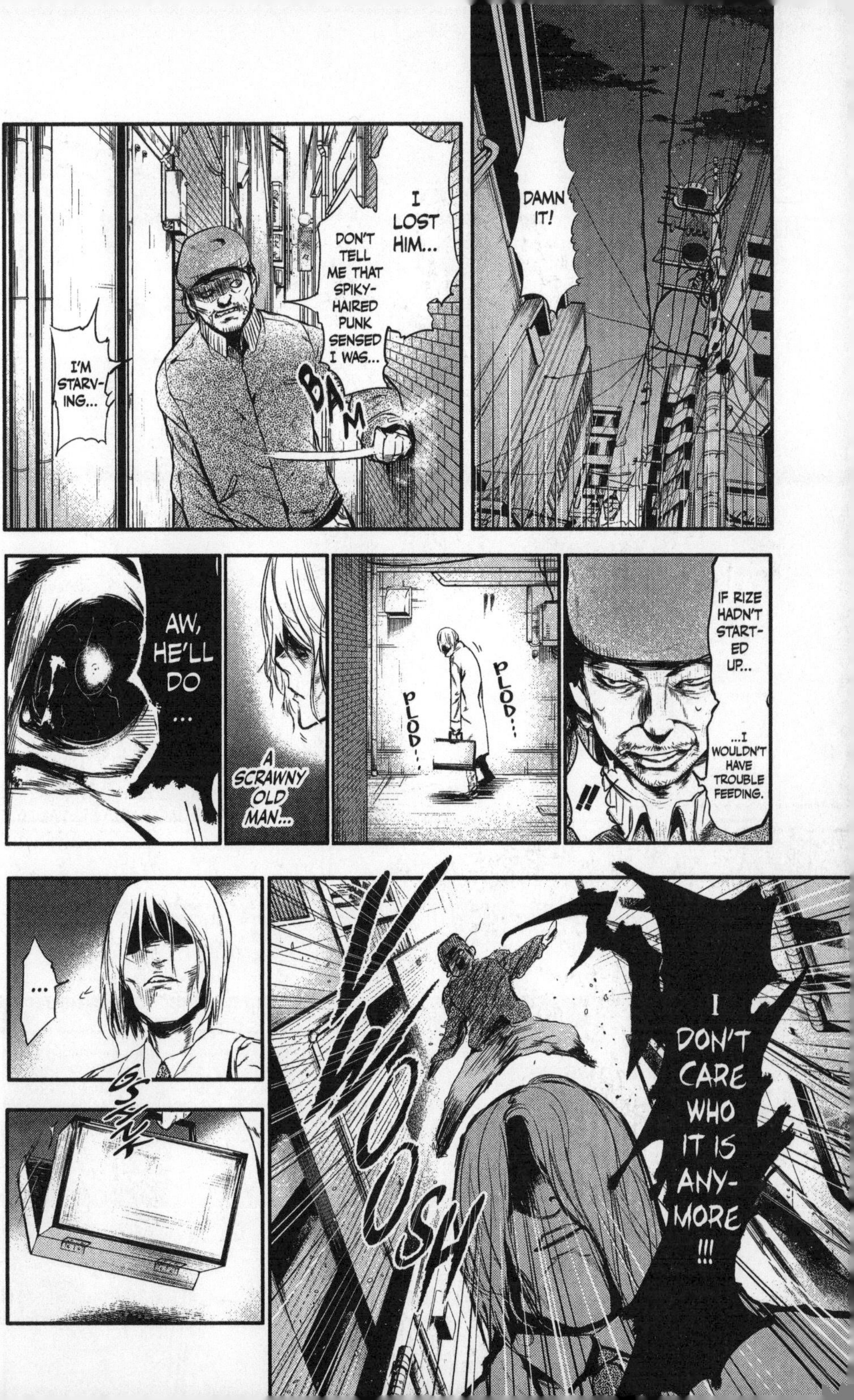
DAMN IT!
I LOST HIM...
DON'T TELL ME THAT SPIKY-HAIRED PUNK SENSED I WAS...
BAM
I'M STARV-ING...
IF RIZE HADN'T START-ED UP...
...I WOULDN'T HAVE TROUBLE FEEDING.
!!
PLOD...
PLOD...
A SCRAWNY OLD MAN...
AW, HE'LL DO ...
WHOOSH
I DON'T CARE WHO IT IS ANY-MORE !!!
...
GSHUNK

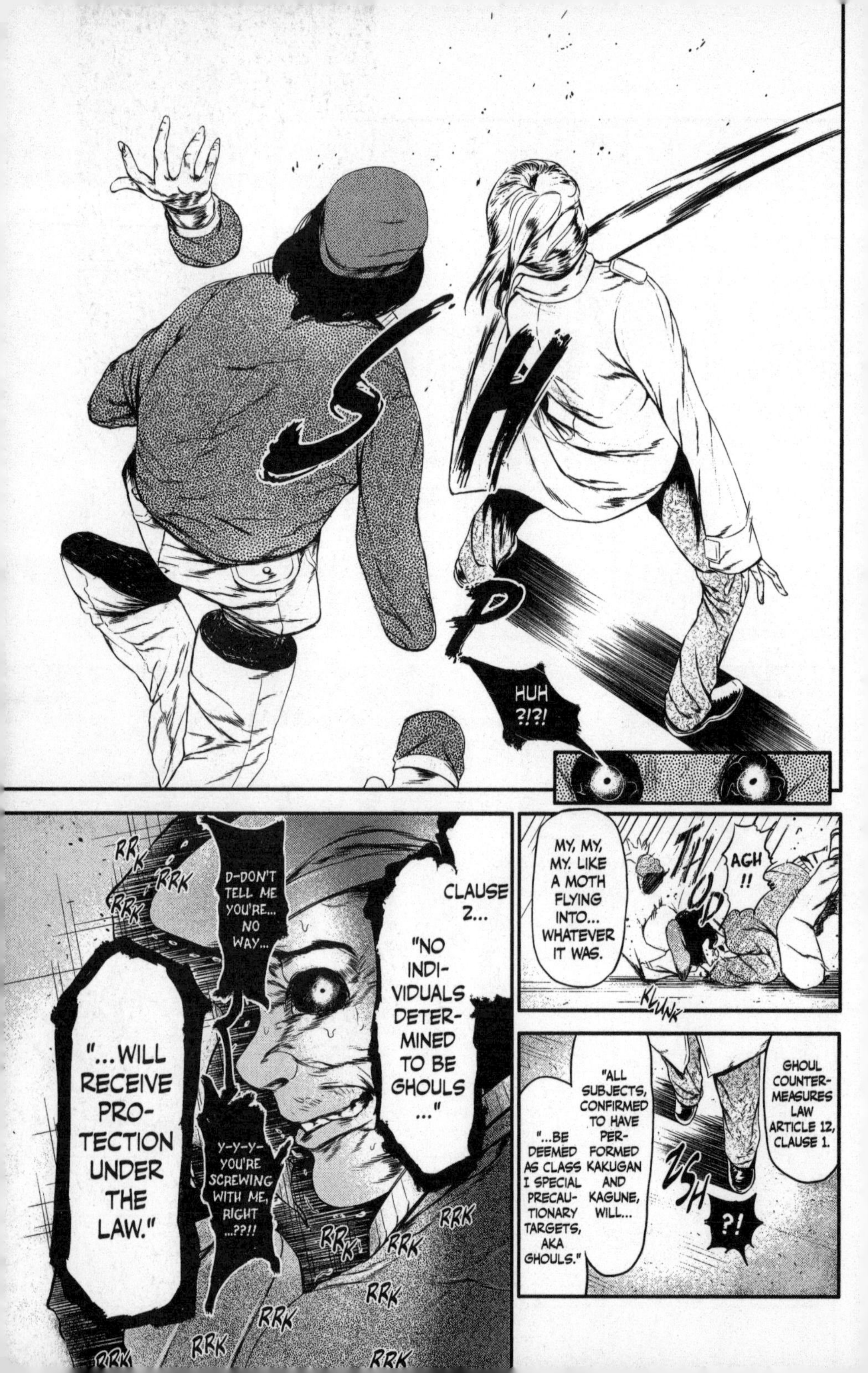
SHP
HUH ?!?!
AGH !!
THOD
MY, MY, MY. LIKE A MOTH FLYING INTO... WHATEVER IT WAS.
KLUNK
GHOUL COUNTERMEASURES LAW ARTICLE 12, CLAUSE 1.
ZSH
?!
"ALL SUBJECTS, CONFIRMED TO HAVE PERFORMED KAKUGAN AND KAGUNE, WILL...
"...BE DEEMED AS CLASS I SPECIAL PRECAUTIONARY TARGETS, AKA GHOULS."
CLAUSE 2...
"NO INDIVIDUALS DETERMINED TO BE GHOULS..."
D-DON'T TELL ME YOU'RE... NO WAY...
RRK RRK RRK
"...WILL RECEIVE PROTECTION UNDER THE LAW."
Y-Y-Y-YOU'RE SCREWING WITH ME, RIGHT ...??!!
RRK RRK RRK RRK RRK RRK RRK RRK

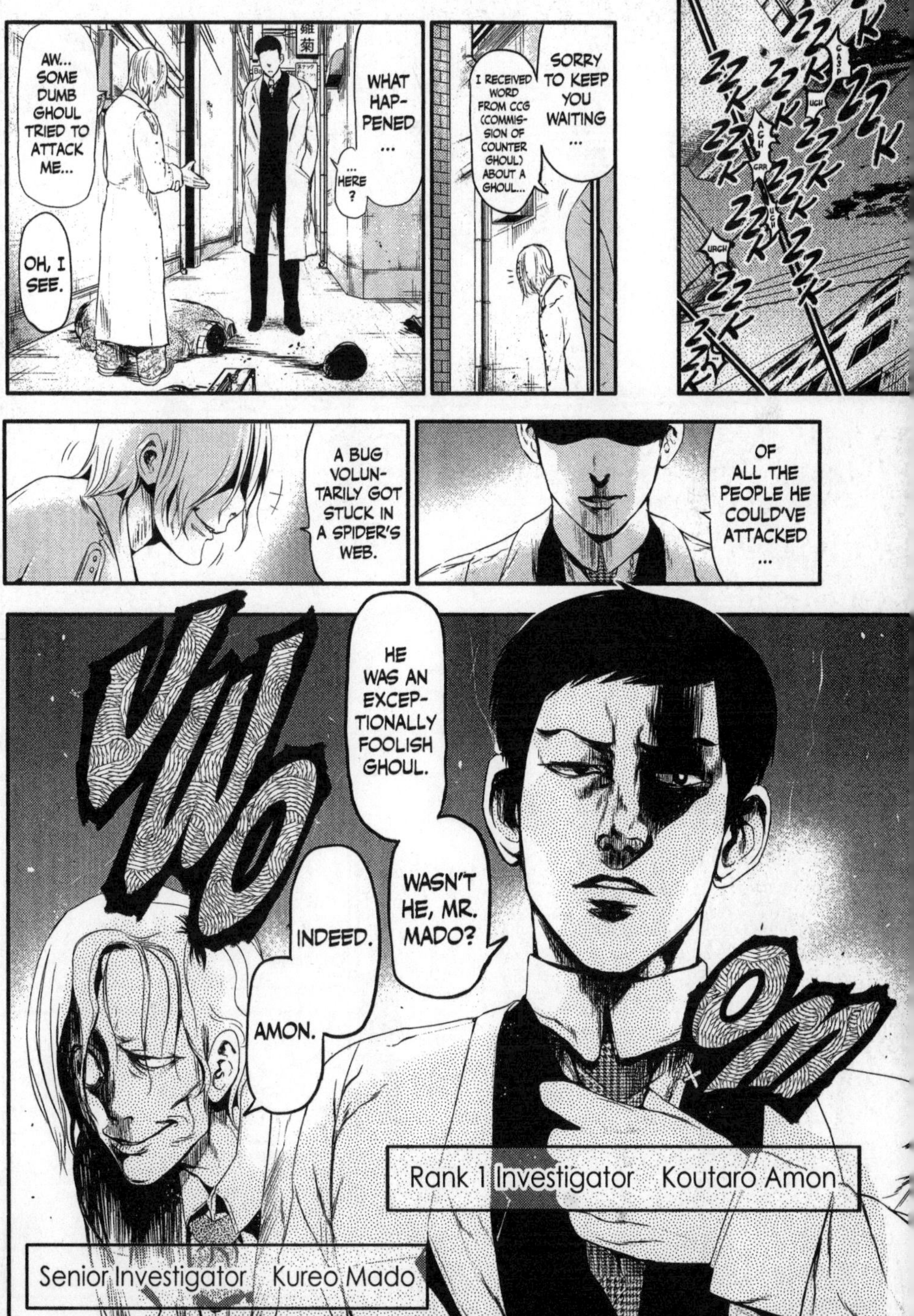
ZZK
GASP
UGH
ACGH
GRR
UGH
URGH
SORRY TO KEEP YOU WAITING ...
I RECEIVED WORD FROM CCG (COMMISSION OF COUNTER GHOUL) ABOUT A GHOUL...
WHAT HAPPENED ...
... HERE ?
AW... SOME DUMB GHOUL TRIED TO ATTACK ME...
OH, I SEE.
OF ALL THE PEOPLE HE COULD'VE ATTACKED ...
A BUG VOLUNTARILY GOT STUCK IN A SPIDER'S WEB.
HE WAS AN EXCEPTIONALLY FOOLISH GHOUL.
WASN'T HE, MR. MADO?
INDEED.
AMON.
Rank 1 Investigator Koutaro Amon
Senior Investigator Kureo Mado

#011
TOKYO GHOUL

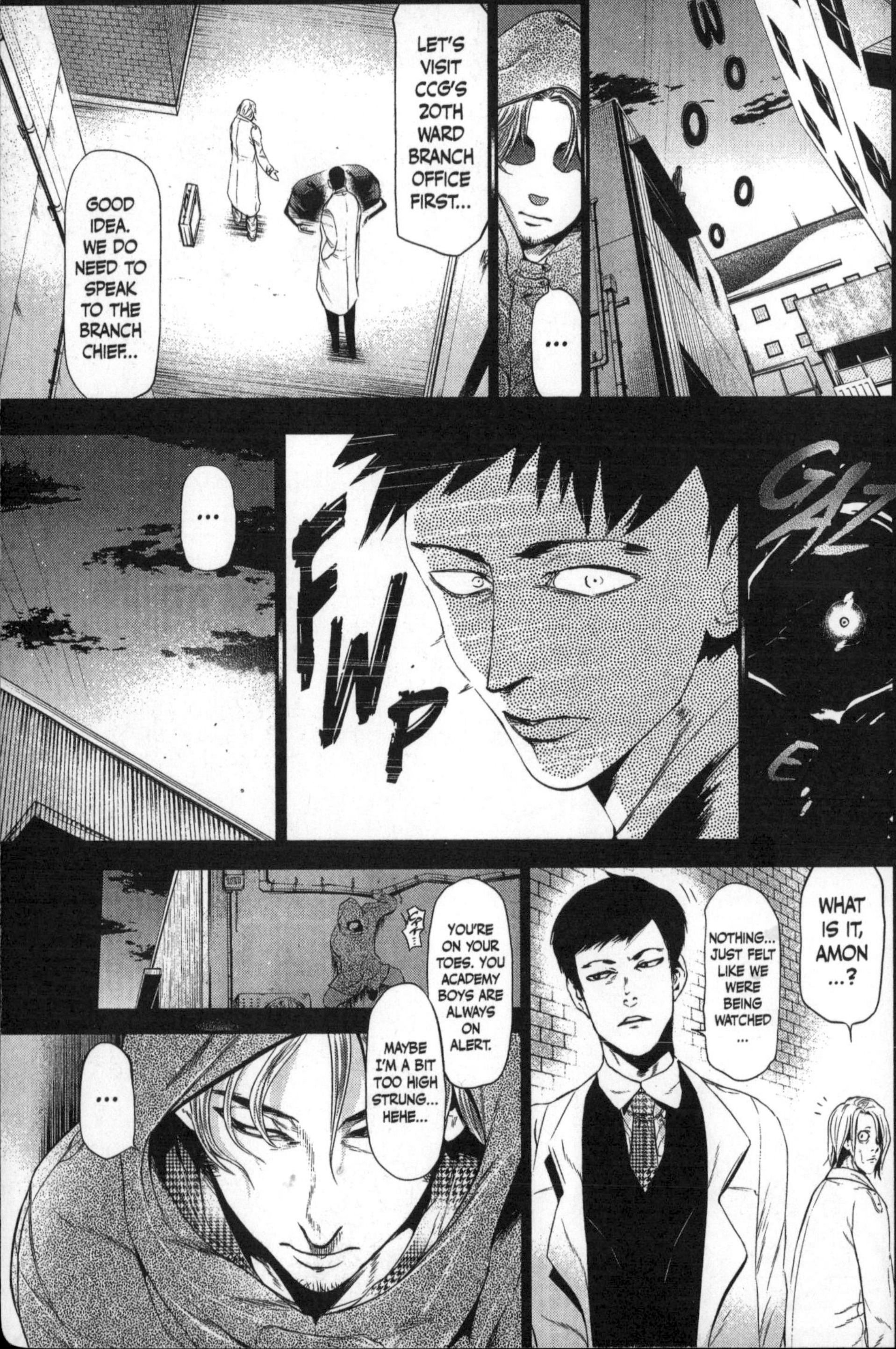
WOOOOO
...
LET'S VISIT CCG'S 20TH WARD BRANCH OFFICE FIRST...
GOOD IDEA. WE DO NEED TO SPEAK TO THE BRANCH CHIEF...
GAZE
FWP
...
WHAT IS IT, AMON ...?
NOTHING... JUST FELT LIKE WE WERE BEING WATCHED ...
YOU'RE ON YOUR TOES. YOU ACADEMY BOYS ARE ALWAYS ON ALERT.
MAYBE I'M A BIT TOO HIGH STRUNG... HEHE...
...

#011 MASK

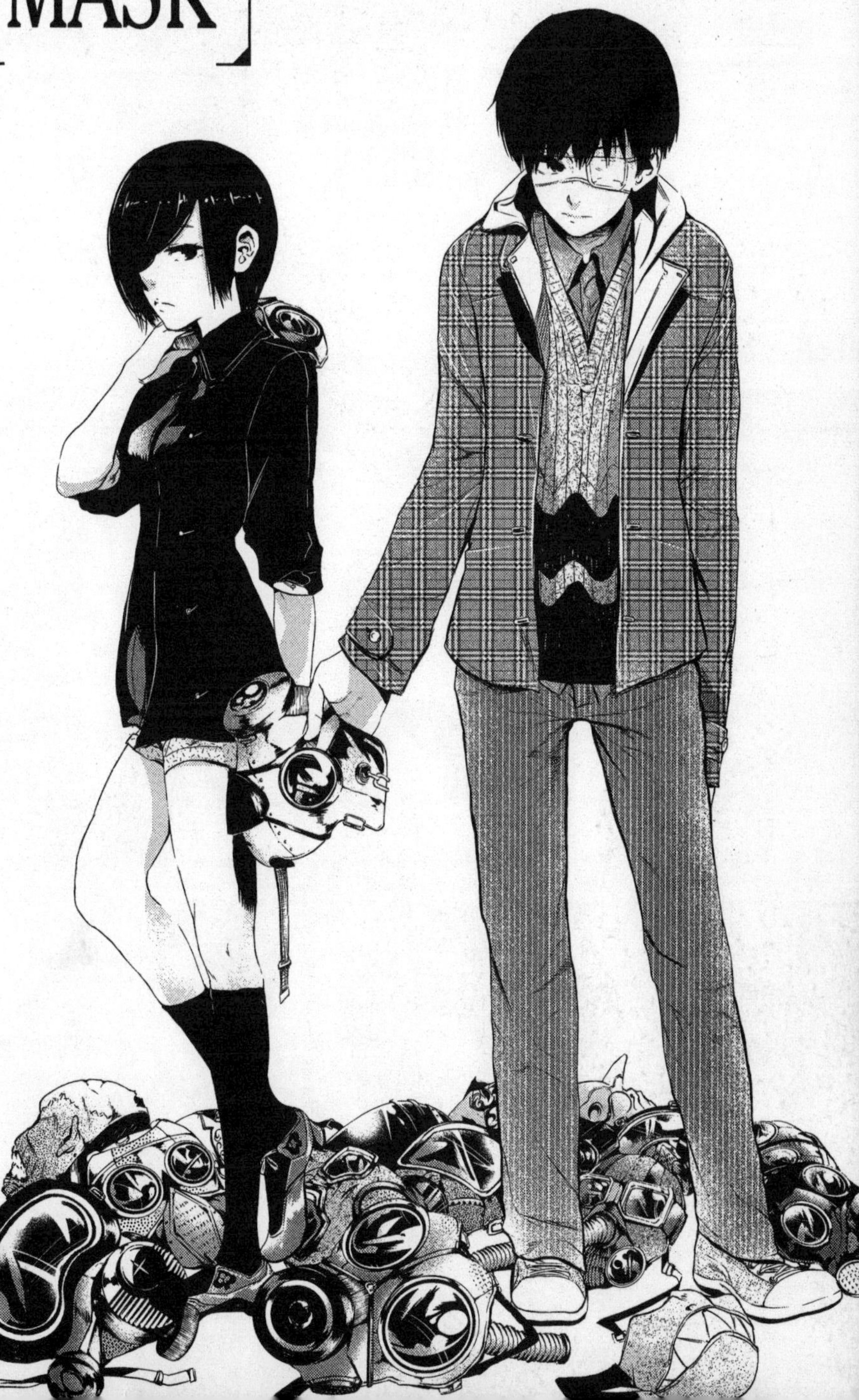

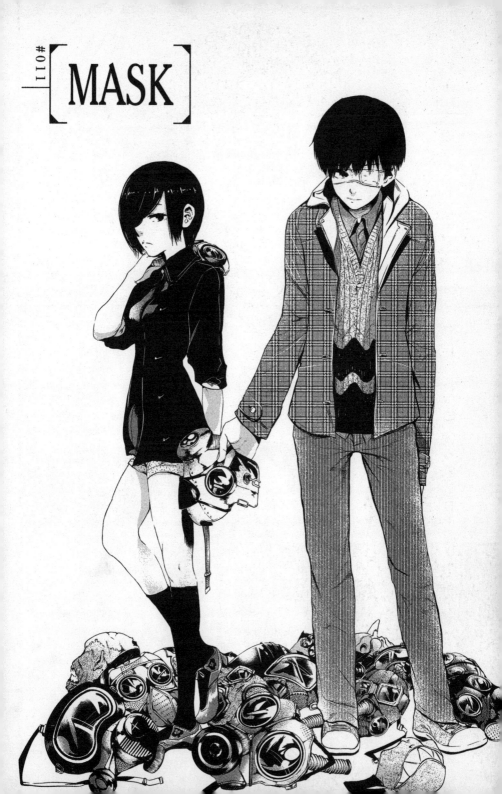

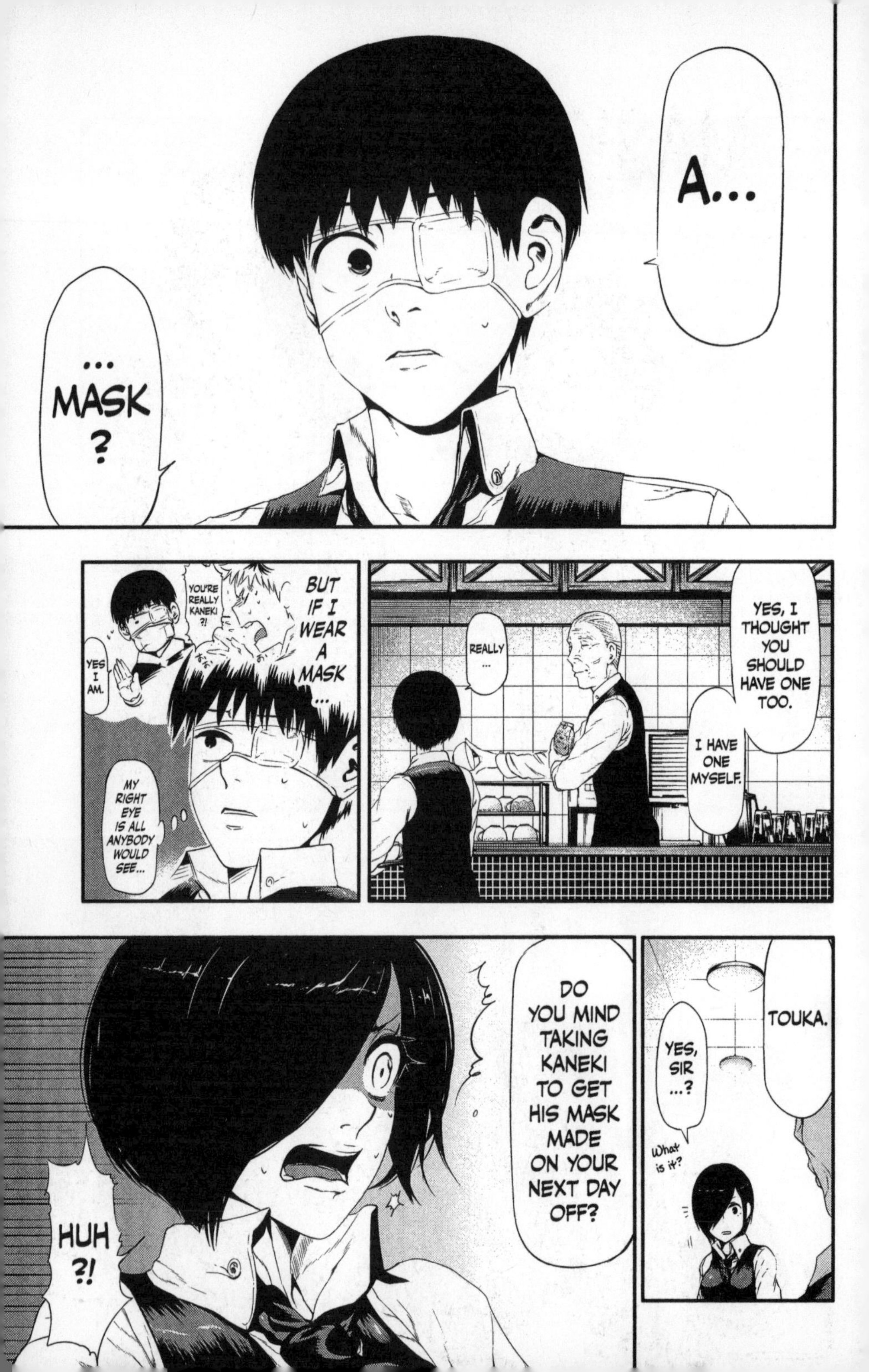
A...
... MASK ?
YES, I THOUGHT YOU SHOULD HAVE ONE TOO.
I HAVE ONE MYSELF.
REALLY ...
BUT IF I WEAR A MASK ...
YOU'RE REALLY KANEKI ?!
YES I AM.
MY RIGHT EYE IS ALL ANYBODY WOULD SEE...
TOUKA.
YES, SIR ...?
What is it?
DO YOU MIND TAKING KANEKI TO GET HIS MASK MADE ON YOUR NEXT DAY OFF?
HUH ?!

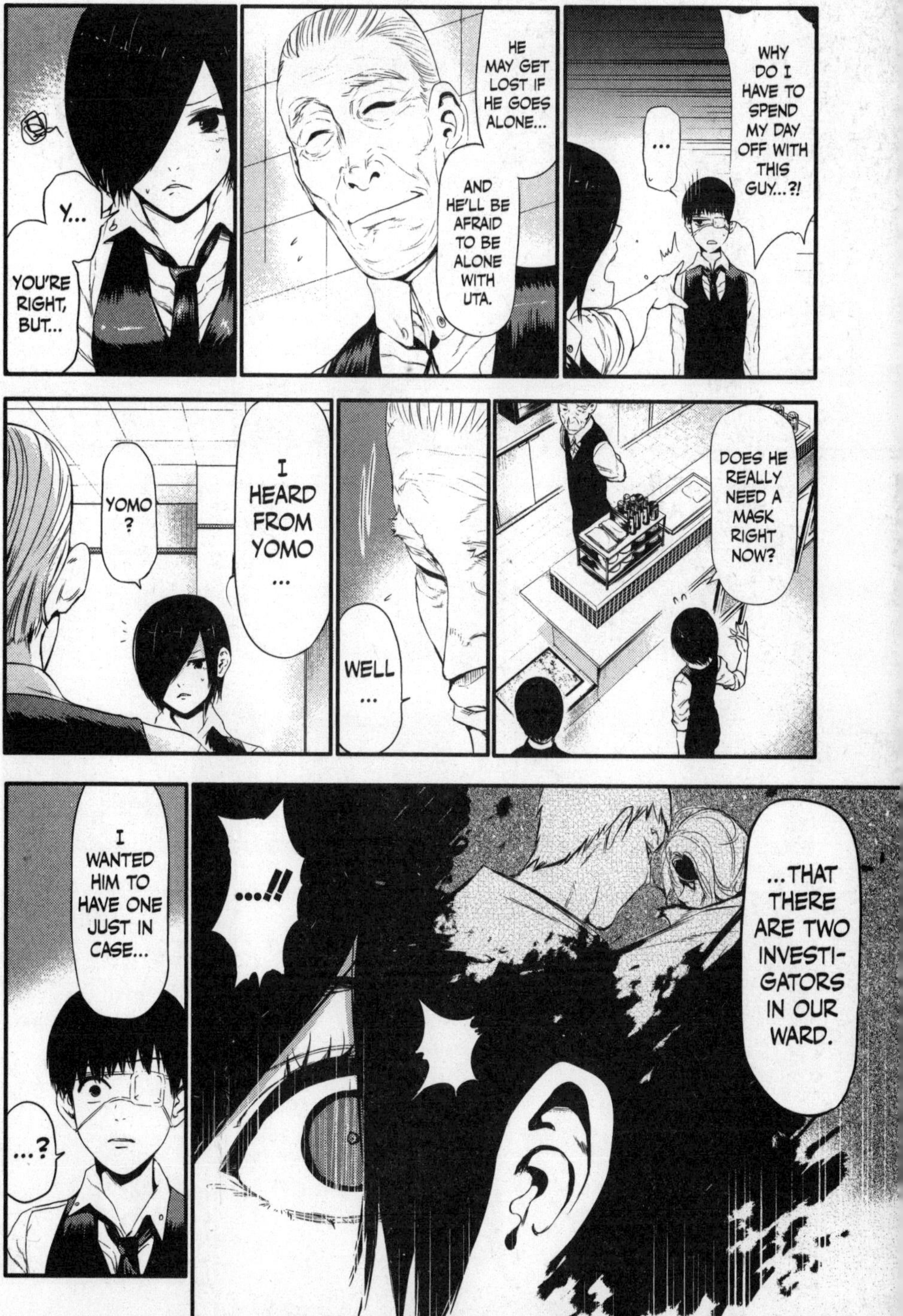
WHY DO I HAVE TO SPEND MY DAY OFF WITH THIS GUY...?!
...
HE MAY GET LOST IF HE GOES ALONE...
AND HE'LL BE AFRAID TO BE ALONE WITH UTA.
Y...
YOU'RE RIGHT, BUT...
DOES HE REALLY NEED A MASK RIGHT NOW?
WELL ...
I HEARD FROM YOMO ...
YOMO ?
...THAT THERE ARE TWO INVESTI-GATORS IN OUR WARD.
...!!
I WANTED HIM TO HAVE ONE JUST IN CASE...
...?

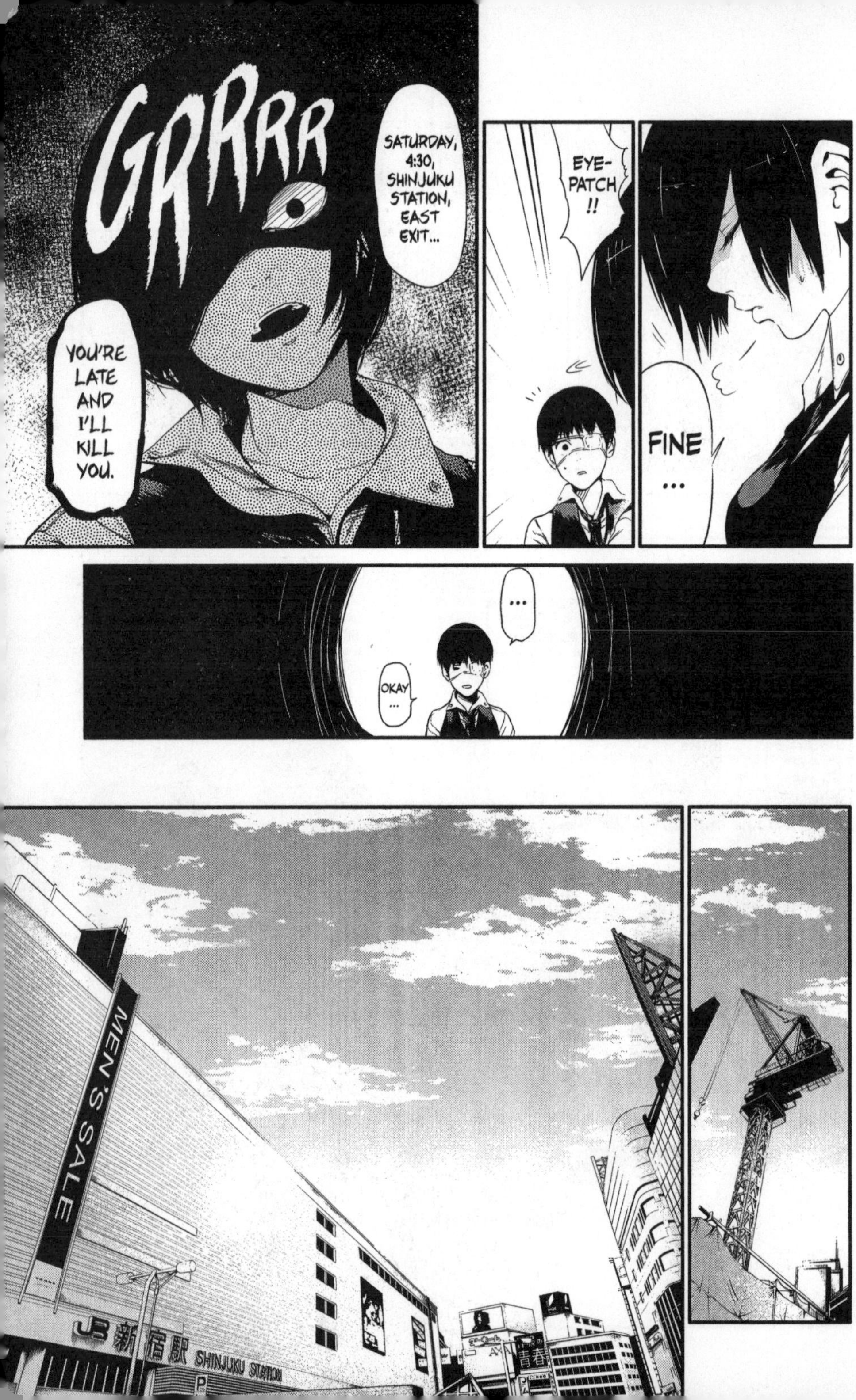
FINE ...
EYE-PATCH !!
SATURDAY, 4:30, SHINJUKU STATION, EAST EXIT...
GRRRR
YOU'RE LATE AND I'LL KILL YOU.
...
OKAY ...
MEN'S SALE
JR 新宿駅 SHINJUKU STATION
青春

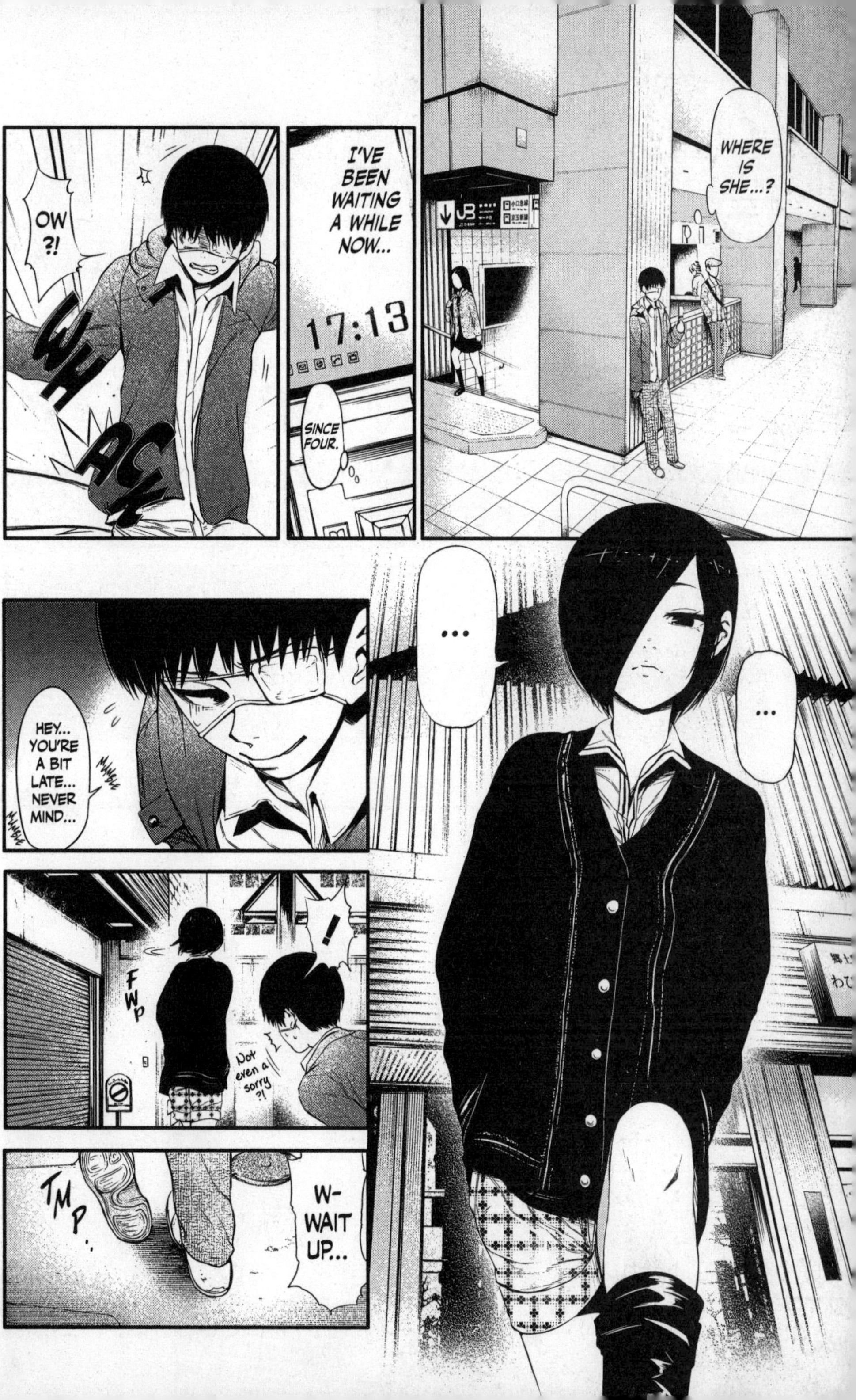
WHERE IS SHE...?
I'VE BEEN WAITING A WHILE NOW...
17:13
SINCE FOUR.
OW?!
WHACK
...
...
HEY... YOU'RE A BIT LATE... NEVER MIND...
!
FWP
Not even a sorry?!
W-WAIT UP...
TMP..

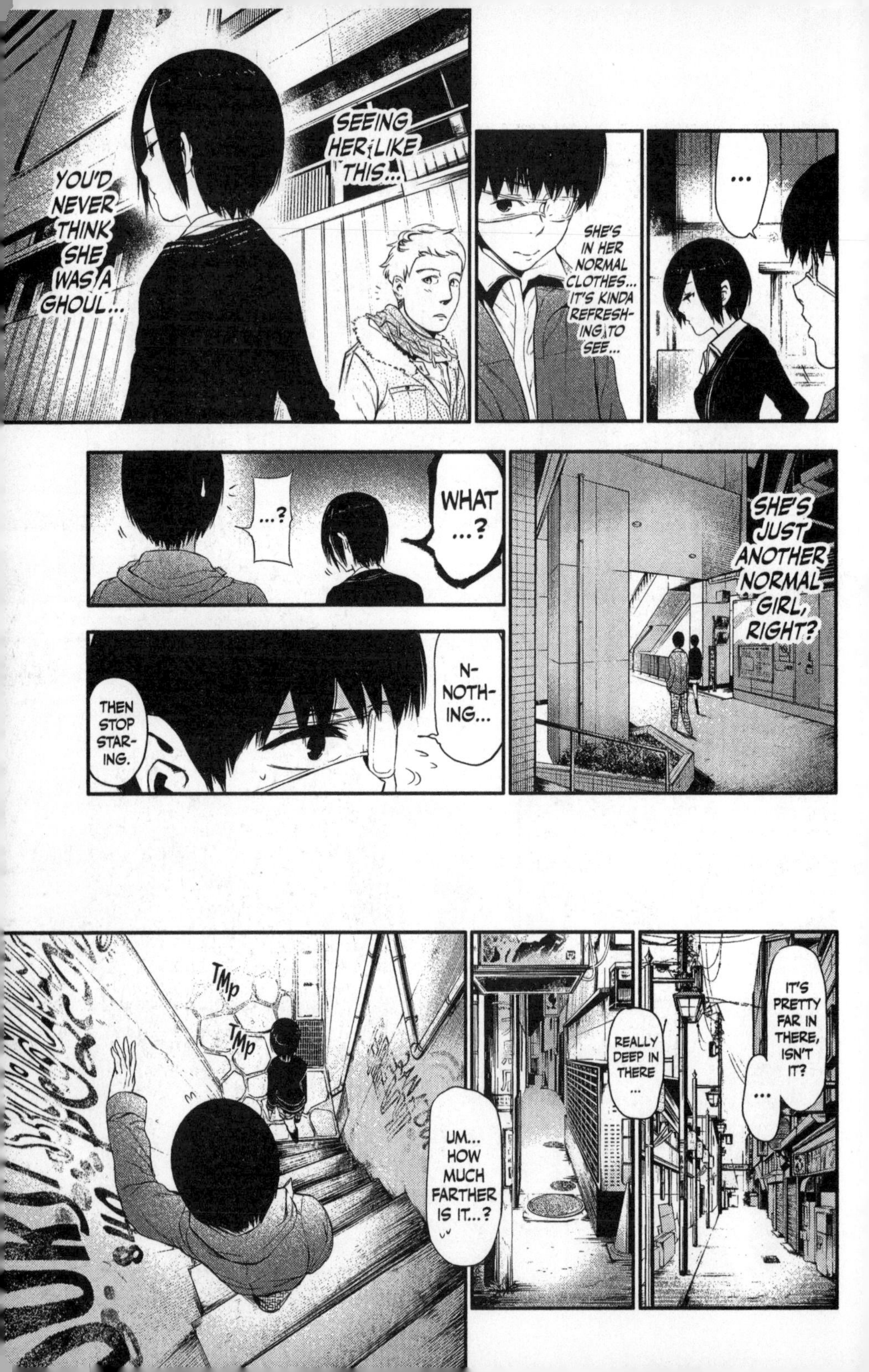
...
SHE'S IN HER NORMAL CLOTHES... IT'S KINDA REFRESHING TO SEE...
SEEING HER LIKE THIS...
YOU'D NEVER THINK SHE WAS A GHOUL...
SHE'S JUST ANOTHER NORMAL GIRL, RIGHT?
WHAT ...?
...?
N-NOTHING...
THEN STOP STARING.
IT'S PRETTY FAR IN THERE, ISN'T IT?
...
REALLY DEEP IN THERE ...
TMp
TMp
UM... HOW MUCH FARTHER IS IT...?

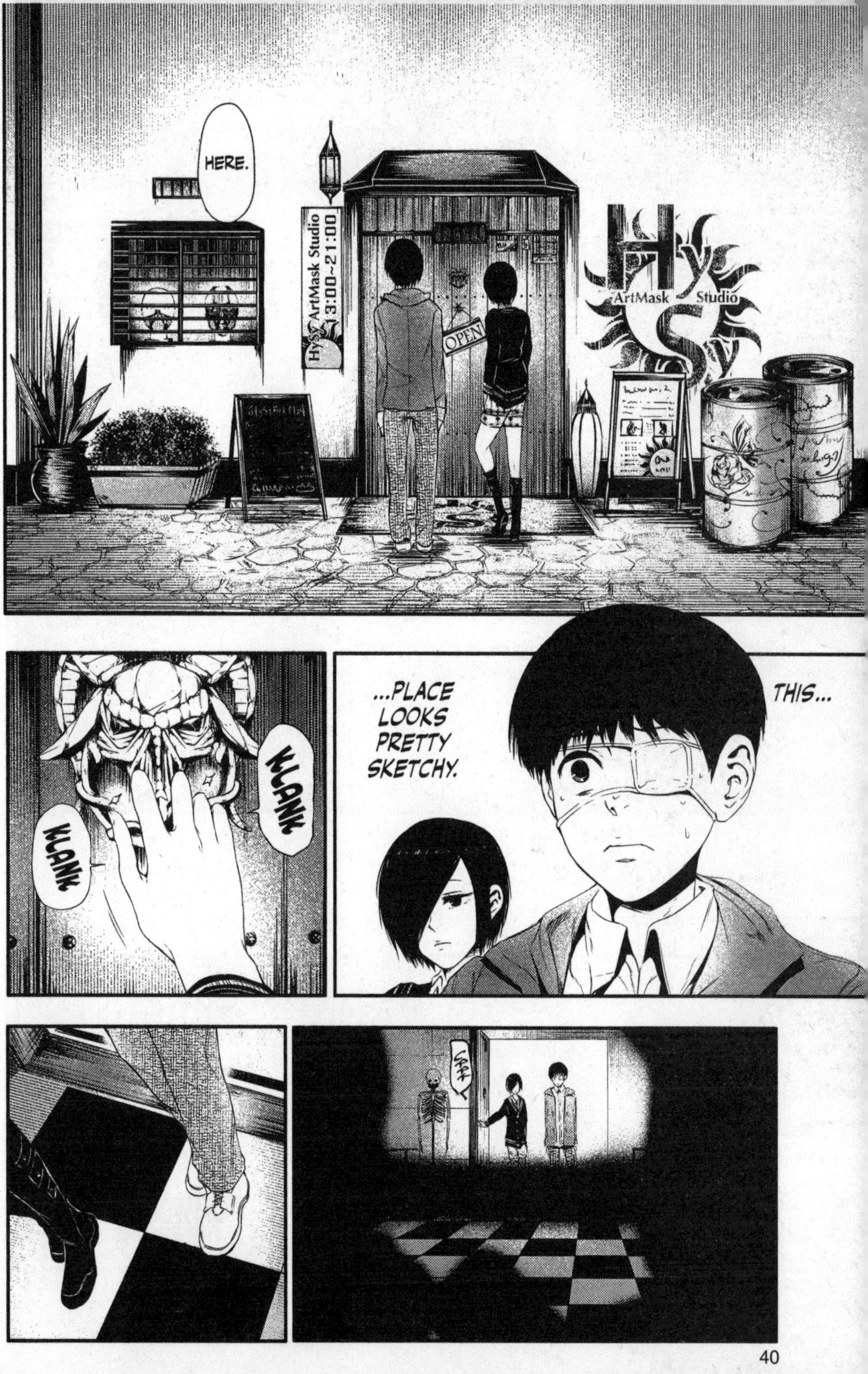
HERE.
HySy ArtMask Studio 13:00~21:00
OPEN
HySy ArtMask Studio
THIS...
...PLACE LOOKS PRETTY SKETCHY.
KLANK
KLANK

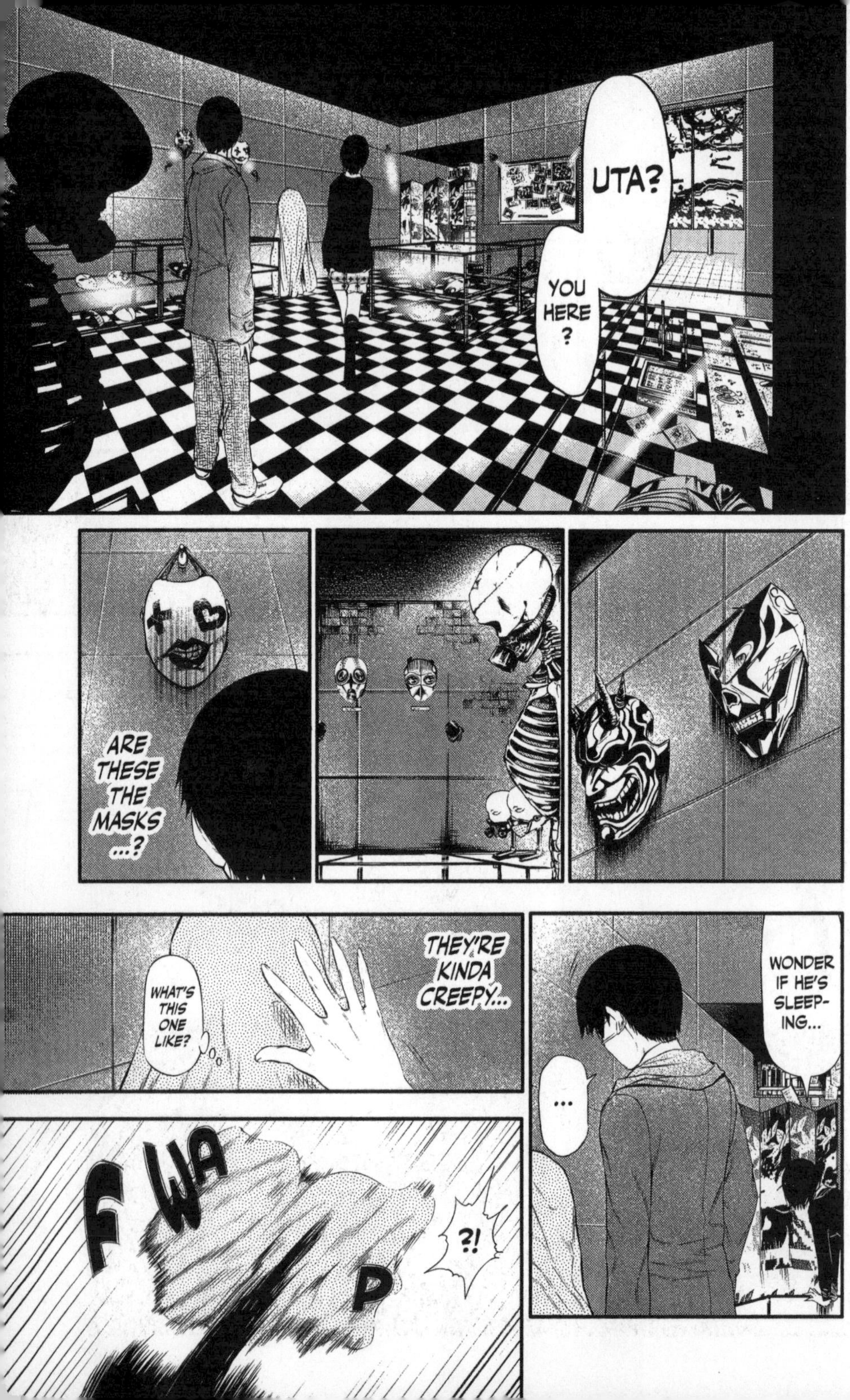
UTA?
YOU HERE?
ARE THESE THE MASKS ...?
WONDER IF HE'S SLEEP-ING...
...
THEY'RE KINDA CREEPY...
WHAT'S THIS ONE LIKE?
FWAP
?!

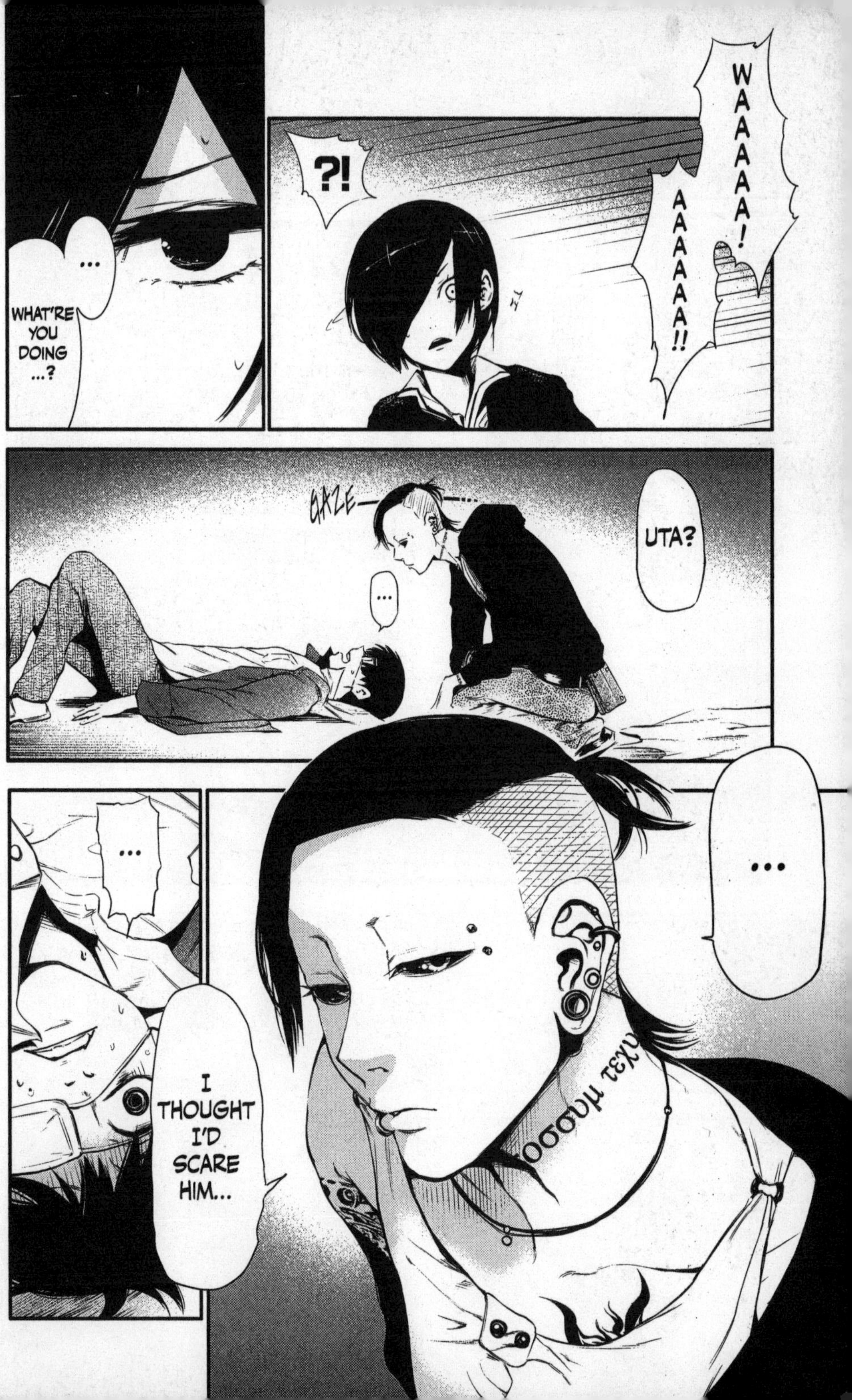
WAAAAAA!
AAAAAAA!!
?!
...
WHAT'RE YOU DOING ...?
UTA?
GAZE
...
...
I THOUGHT I'D SCARE HIM...
...

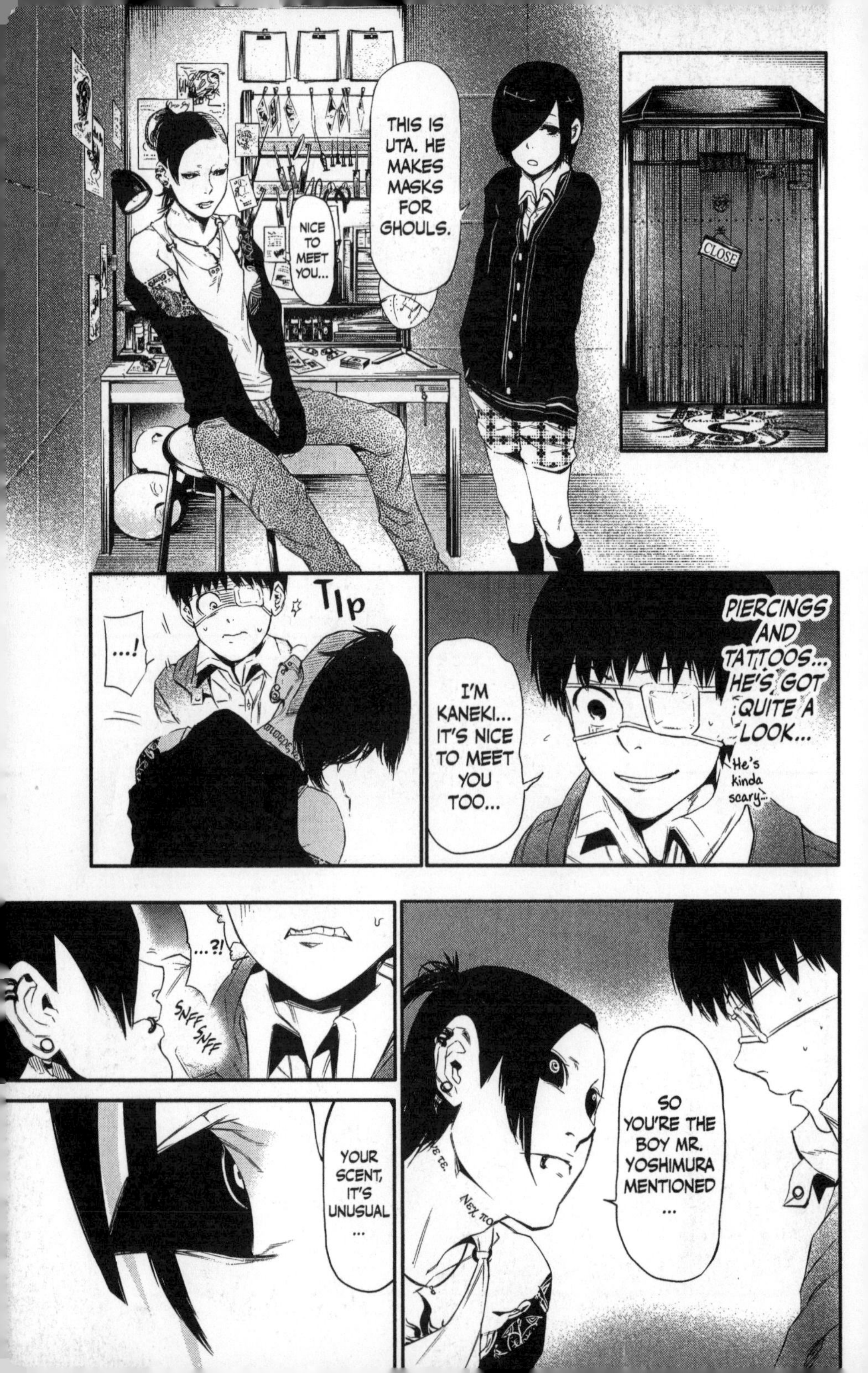
CLOSE
THIS IS UTA. HE MAKES MASKS FOR GHOULS.
NICE TO MEET YOU...
I'M KANEKI... IT'S NICE TO MEET YOU TOO...
PIERCINGS AND TATTOOS... HE'S GOT QUITE A LOOK...
He's kinda scary...
TIP
...!
SO YOU'RE THE BOY MR. YOSHIMURA MENTIONED...
...?!
SNFF SNFF
YOUR SCENT, IT'S UNUSUAL...

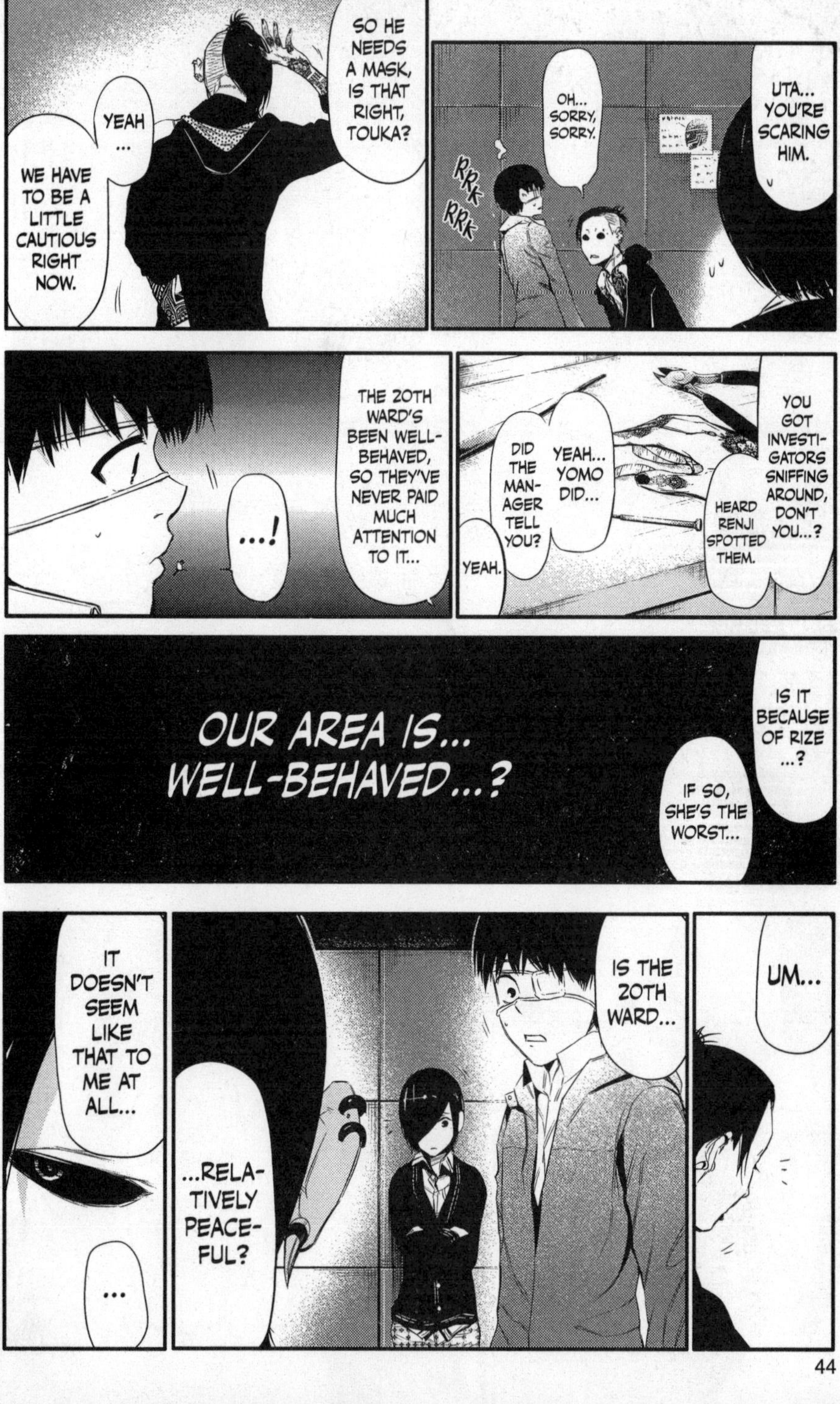
UTA... YOU'RE SCARING HIM.
OH... SORRY, SORRY.
RRK RRK
SO HE NEEDS A MASK, IS THAT RIGHT, TOUKA?
YEAH ...
WE HAVE TO BE A LITTLE CAUTIOUS RIGHT NOW.
YOU GOT INVESTIGATORS SNIFFING AROUND, DON'T YOU...?
HEARD RENJI SPOTTED THEM.
YEAH... YOMO DID...
DID THE MANAGER TELL YOU?
YEAH.
THE 20TH WARD'S BEEN WELL-BEHAVED, SO THEY'VE NEVER PAID MUCH ATTENTION TO IT...
...!
IS IT BECAUSE OF RIZE ...?
IF SO, SHE'S THE WORST...
OUR AREA IS... WELL-BEHAVED...?
UM...
IS THE 20TH WARD...
...RELATIVELY PEACEFUL?
IT DOESN'T SEEM LIKE THAT TO ME AT ALL...
...

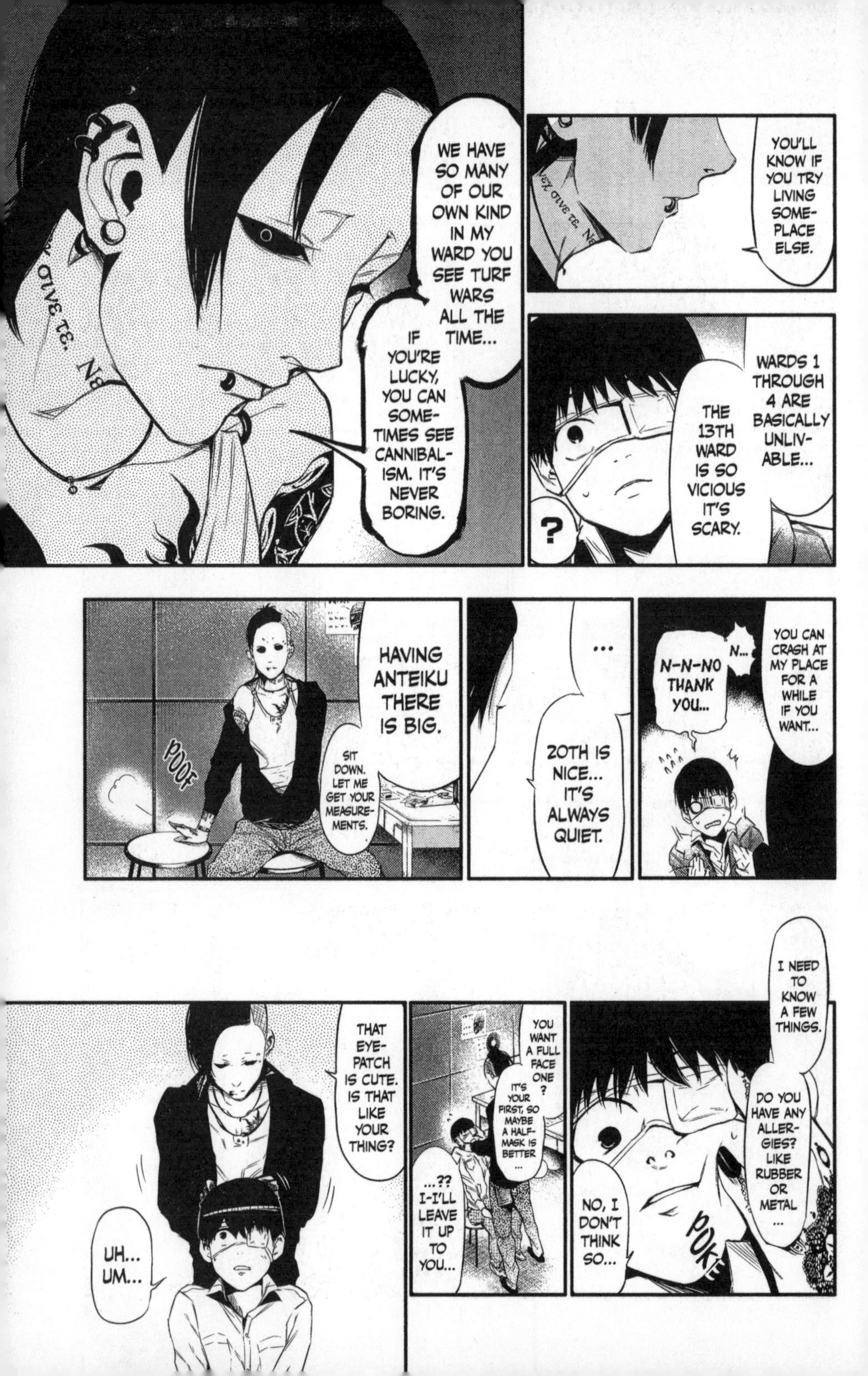
YOU'LL KNOW IF YOU TRY LIVING SOME-PLACE ELSE.
WARDS 1 THROUGH 4 ARE BASICALLY UNLIV-ABLE...
THE 13TH WARD IS SO VICIOUS IT'S SCARY.
?
WE HAVE SO MANY OF OUR OWN KIND IN MY WARD YOU SEE TURF WARS ALL THE TIME...
IF YOU'RE LUCKY, YOU CAN SOME-TIMES SEE CANNIBAL-ISM. IT'S NEVER BORING.
YOU CAN CRASH AT MY PLACE FOR A WHILE IF YOU WANT...
N...
N-N-NO THANK YOU...
...
20TH IS NICE... IT'S ALWAYS QUIET.
HAVING ANTEIKU THERE IS BIG.
SIT DOWN. LET ME GET YOUR MEASURE-MENTS.
POOF
I NEED TO KNOW A FEW THINGS.
DO YOU HAVE ANY ALLER-GIES? LIKE RUBBER OR METAL ...
NO, I DON'T THINK SO...
POKE
YOU WANT A FULL FACE ONE ?
IT'S YOUR FIRST, SO MAYBE A HALF-MASK IS BETTER ...
...?? I-I'LL LEAVE IT UP TO YOU...
THAT EYE-PATCH IS CUTE. IS THAT LIKE YOUR THING?
UH... UM...

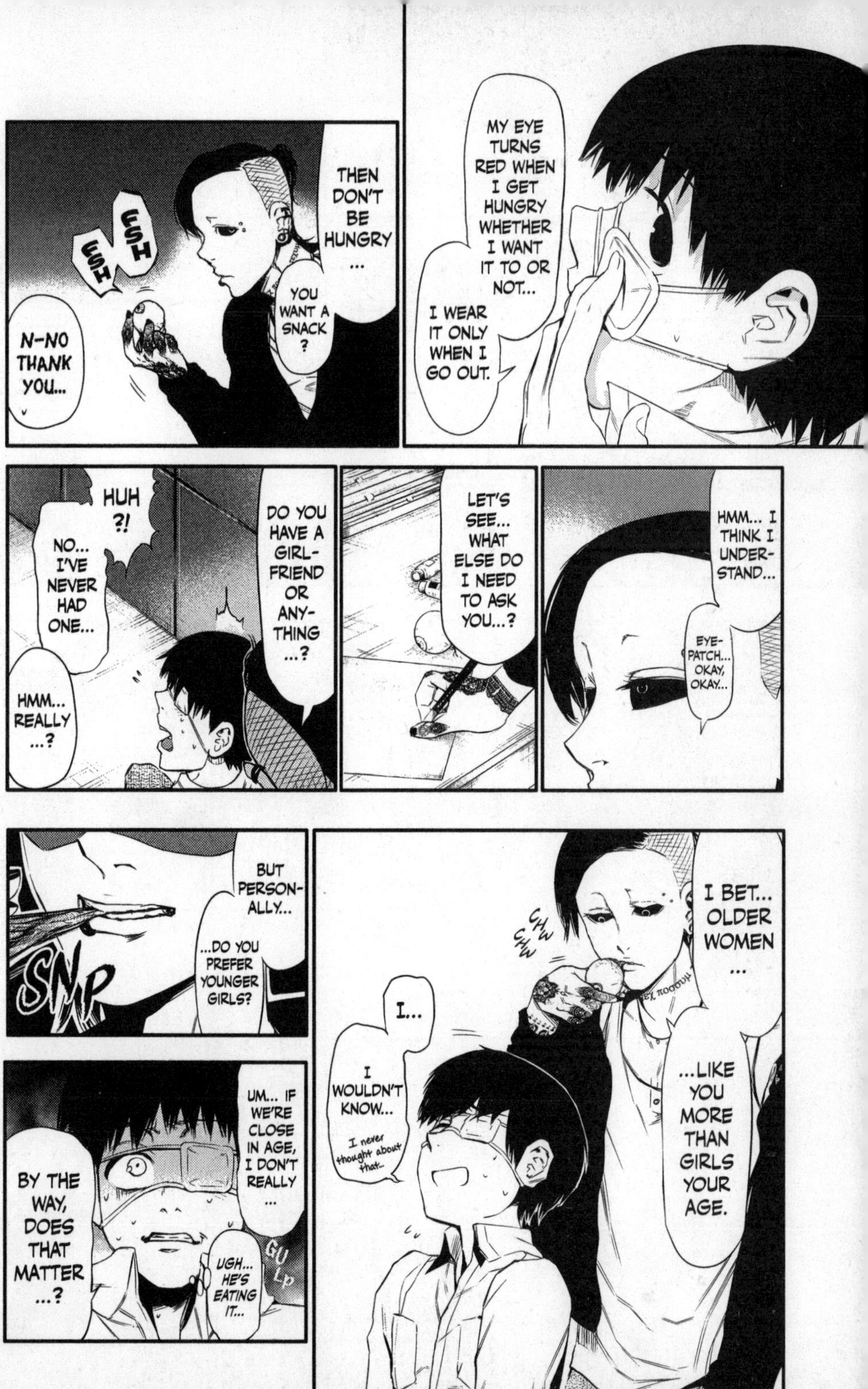
MY EYE TURNS RED WHEN I GET HUNGRY WHETHER I WANT IT TO OR NOT...
I WEAR IT ONLY WHEN I GO OUT.
THEN DON'T BE HUNGRY ...
YOU WANT A SNACK ?
FSH
FSH
N-NO THANK YOU...
HMM... I THINK I UNDER-STAND...
EYE-PATCH... OKAY, OKAY...
LET'S SEE... WHAT ELSE DO I NEED TO ASK YOU...?
DO YOU HAVE A GIRL-FRIEND OR ANY-THING ...?
HUH ?!
NO... I'VE NEVER HAD ONE...
HMM... REALLY ...?
I BET... OLDER WOMEN ...
CHW CHW
...LIKE YOU MORE THAN GIRLS YOUR AGE.
I...
I WOULDN'T KNOW...
I never thought about that...
SNP
BUT PERSON-ALLY...
...DO YOU PREFER YOUNGER GIRLS?
UM... IF WE'RE CLOSE IN AGE, I DON'T REALLY ...
UGH... HE'S EATING IT...
GULP
BY THE WAY, DOES THAT MATTER ...?

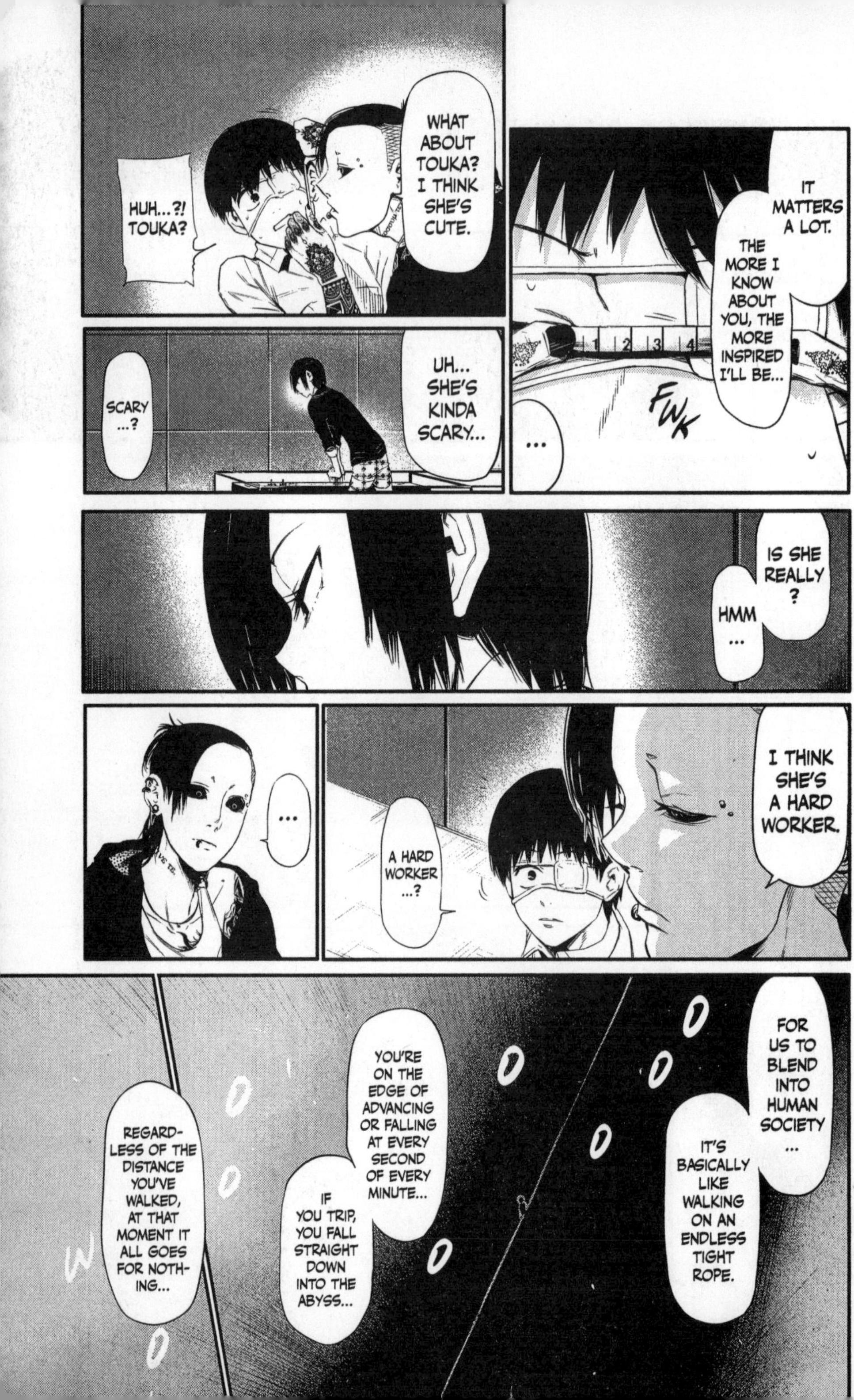
IT MATTERS A LOT.
THE MORE I KNOW ABOUT YOU, THE MORE INSPIRED I'LL BE...
FWK
...
WHAT ABOUT TOUKA? I THINK SHE'S CUTE.
HUH...?! TOUKA?
UH... SHE'S KINDA SCARY...
SCARY ...?
IS SHE REALLY ?
HMM ...
I THINK SHE'S A HARD WORKER.
A HARD WORKER ...?
...
FOR US TO BLEND INTO HUMAN SOCIETY ...
IT'S BASICALLY LIKE WALKING ON AN ENDLESS TIGHT ROPE.
YOU'RE ON THE EDGE OF ADVANCING OR FALLING AT EVERY SECOND OF EVERY MINUTE...
IF YOU TRIP, YOU FALL STRAIGHT DOWN INTO THE ABYSS...
REGARD-LESS OF THE DISTANCE YOU'VE WALKED, AT THAT MOMENT IT ALL GOES FOR NOTH-ING...

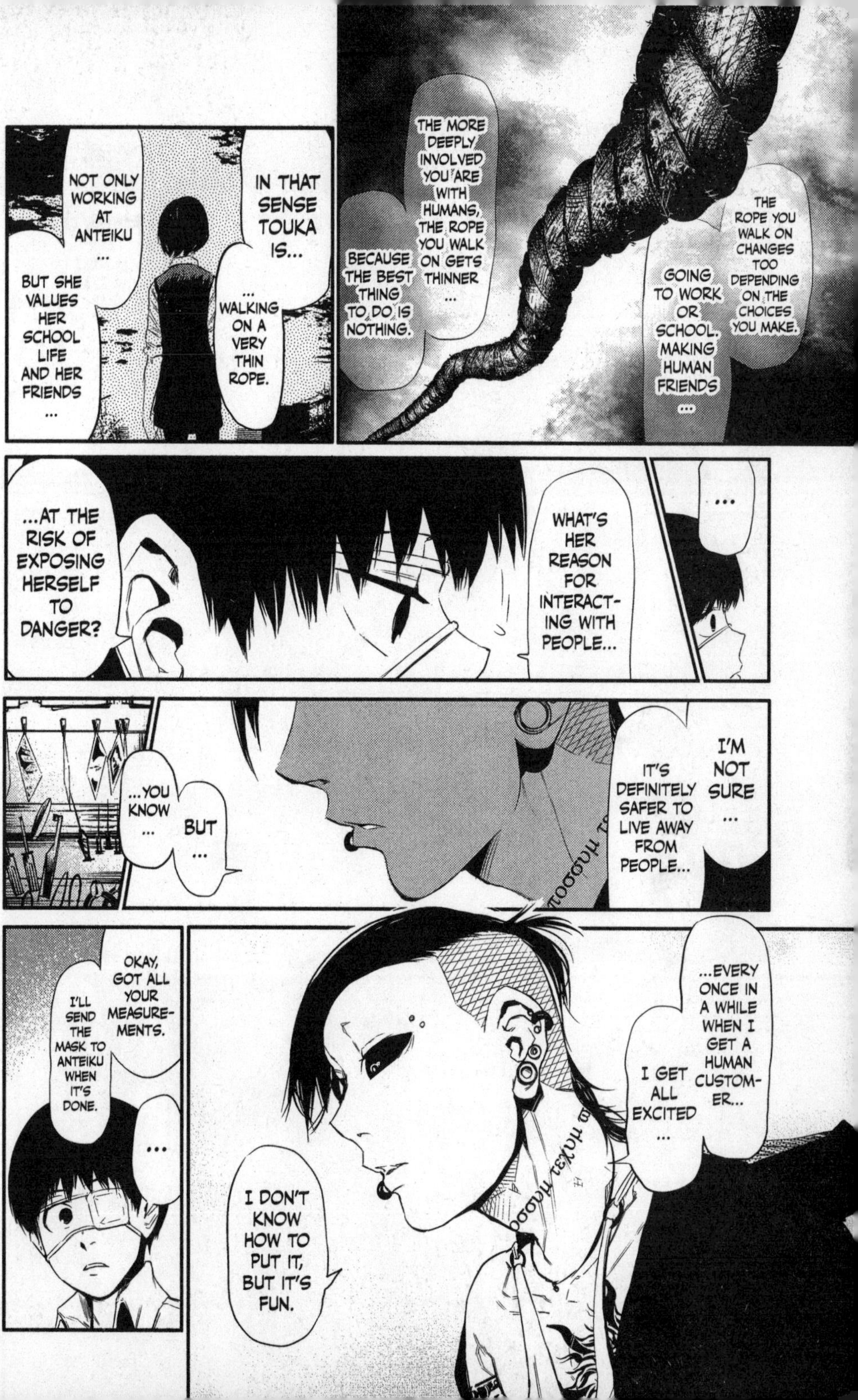
THE ROPE YOU WALK ON CHANGES TOO DEPENDING ON THE CHOICES YOU MAKE.
GOING TO WORK OR SCHOOL. MAKING HUMAN FRIENDS...
THE MORE DEEPLY INVOLVED YOU ARE WITH HUMANS, THE ROPE YOU WALK ON GETS THINNER...
BECAUSE THE BEST THING TO DO IS NOTHING.
IN THAT SENSE TOUKA IS...
...WALKING ON A VERY THIN ROPE.
NOT ONLY WORKING AT ANTEIKU...
BUT SHE VALUES HER SCHOOL LIFE AND HER FRIENDS...
...
WHAT'S HER REASON FOR INTERACTING WITH PEOPLE...
...AT THE RISK OF EXPOSING HERSELF TO DANGER?
I'M NOT SURE...
IT'S DEFINITELY SAFER TO LIVE AWAY FROM PEOPLE...
...YOU KNOW...
BUT...
...EVERY ONCE IN A WHILE WHEN I GET A HUMAN CUSTOMER...
I GET ALL EXCITED...
I DON'T KNOW HOW TO PUT IT, BUT IT'S FUN.
OKAY, GOT ALL YOUR MEASUREMENTS.
I'LL SEND THE MASK TO ANTEIKU WHEN IT'S DONE.
...

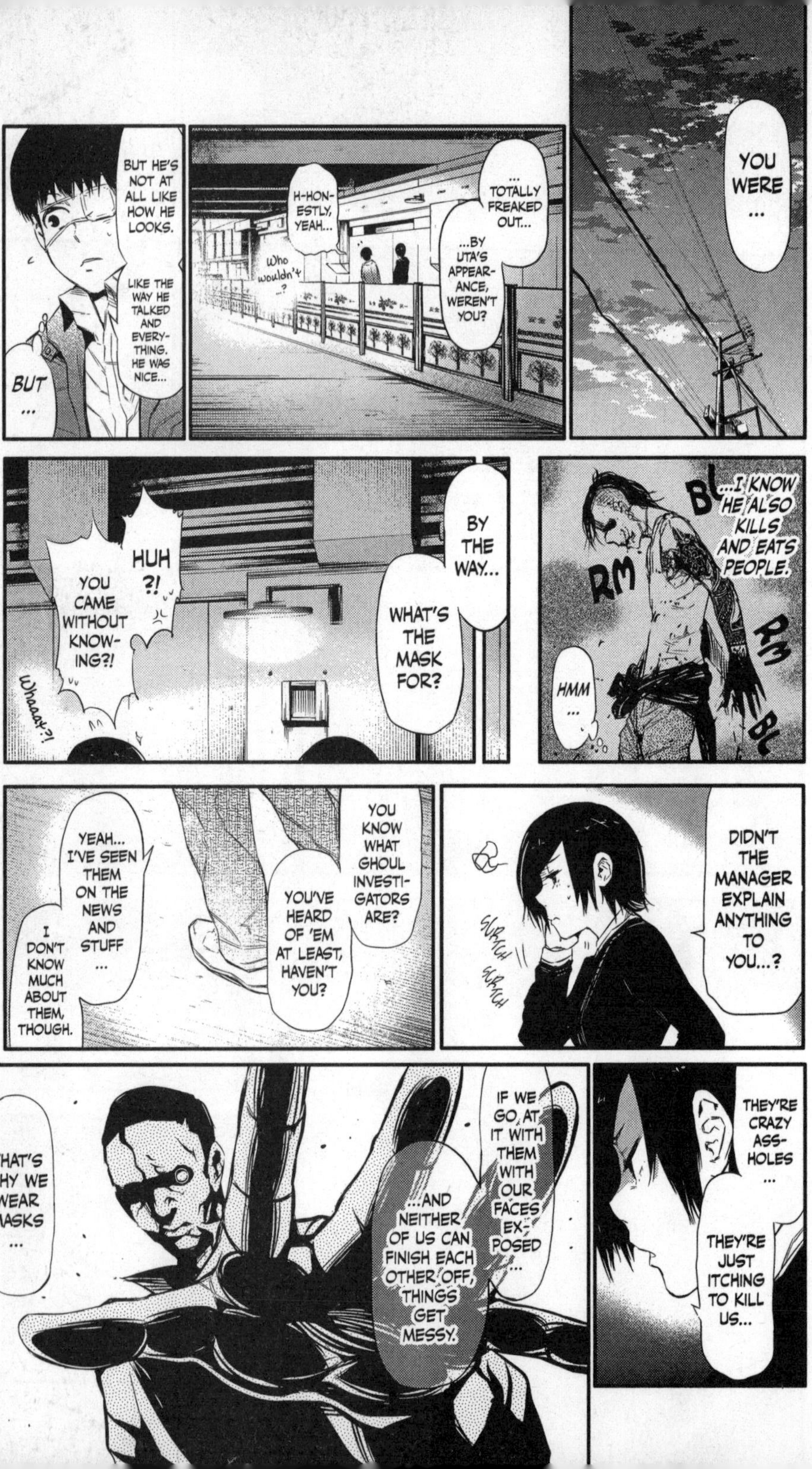
YOU WERE ...
... TOTALLY FREAKED OUT...
...BY UTA'S APPEARANCE, WEREN'T YOU?
H-HONESTLY, YEAH...
Who wouldn't ...?
BUT HE'S NOT AT ALL LIKE HOW HE LOOKS.
LIKE THE WAY HE TALKED AND EVERYTHING. HE WAS NICE...
BUT ...
...I KNOW HE ALSO KILLS AND EATS PEOPLE.
BL
RM
RM
BL
HMM ...
BY THE WAY...
WHAT'S THE MASK FOR?
HUH ?!
YOU CAME WITHOUT KNOWING?!
Whaaat?!
DIDN'T THE MANAGER EXPLAIN ANYTHING TO YOU...?
SCRITCH
SCRITCH
YOU KNOW WHAT GHOUL INVESTIGATORS ARE?
YOU'VE HEARD OF 'EM AT LEAST, HAVEN'T YOU?
YEAH... I'VE SEEN THEM ON THE NEWS AND STUFF ...
I DON'T KNOW MUCH ABOUT THEM, THOUGH.
THEY'RE CRAZY ASSHOLES ...
THEY'RE JUST ITCHING TO KILL US...
IF WE GO AT IT WITH THEM WITH OUR FACES EXPOSED ...
...AND NEITHER OF US CAN FINISH EACH OTHER OFF, THINGS GET MESSY.
THAT'S WHY WE WEAR MASKS ...

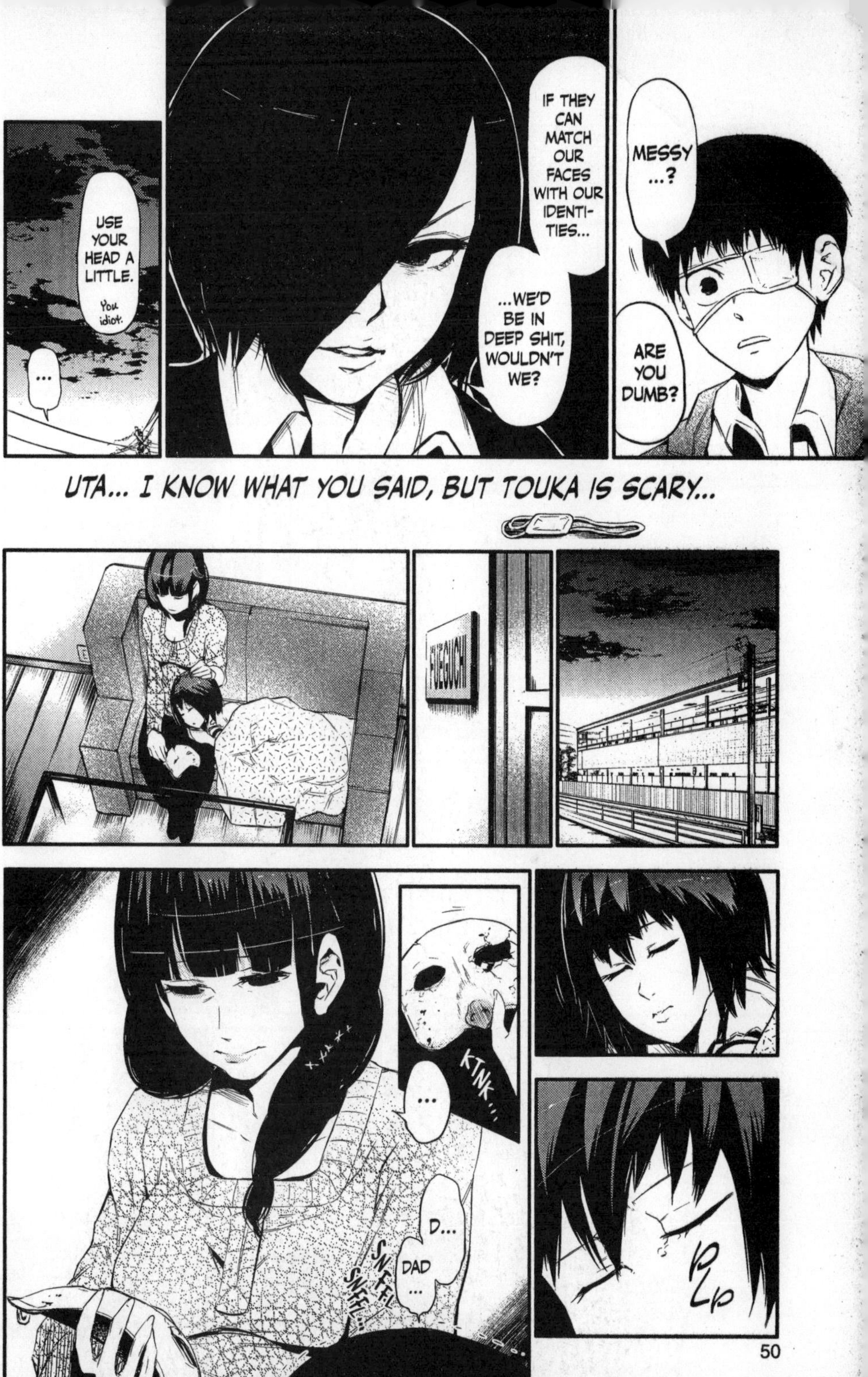
MESSY ...?
ARE YOU DUMB?
IF THEY CAN MATCH OUR FACES WITH OUR IDENTI-TIES...
...WE'D BE IN DEEP SHIT, WOULDN'T WE?
USE YOUR HEAD A LITTLE.
You idiot.
...
UTA... I KNOW WHAT YOU SAID, BUT TOUKA IS SCARY...
FUEGUCHI
KTNK...
...
D... DAD ...
SNIFF SNIFF...

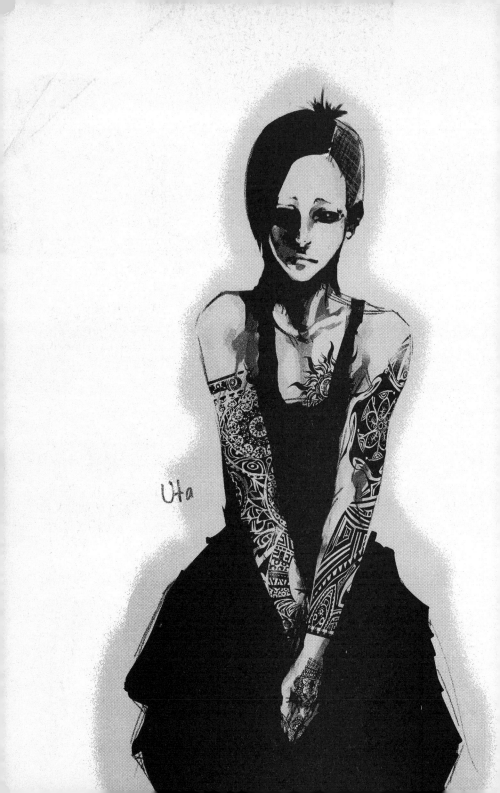

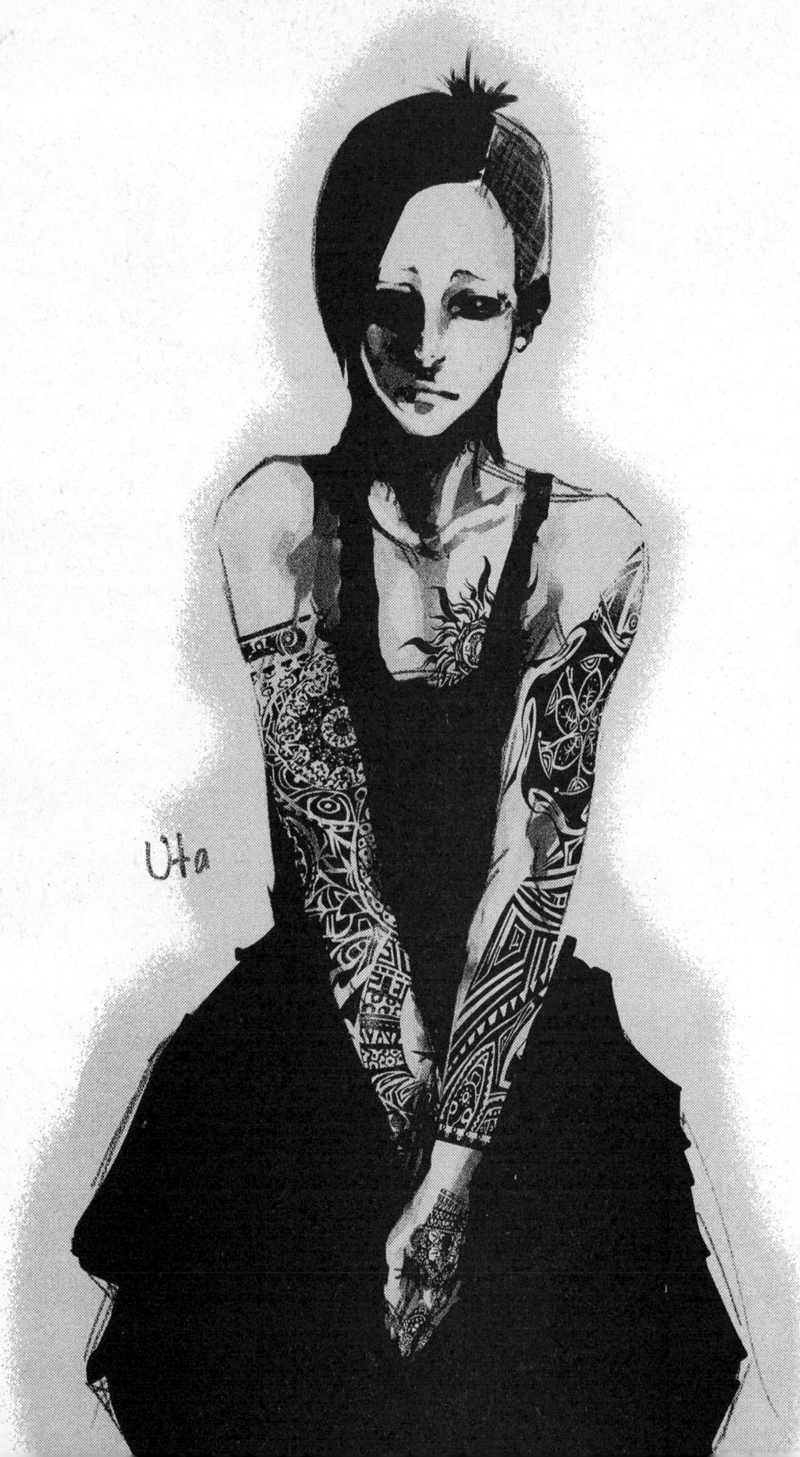
Uta

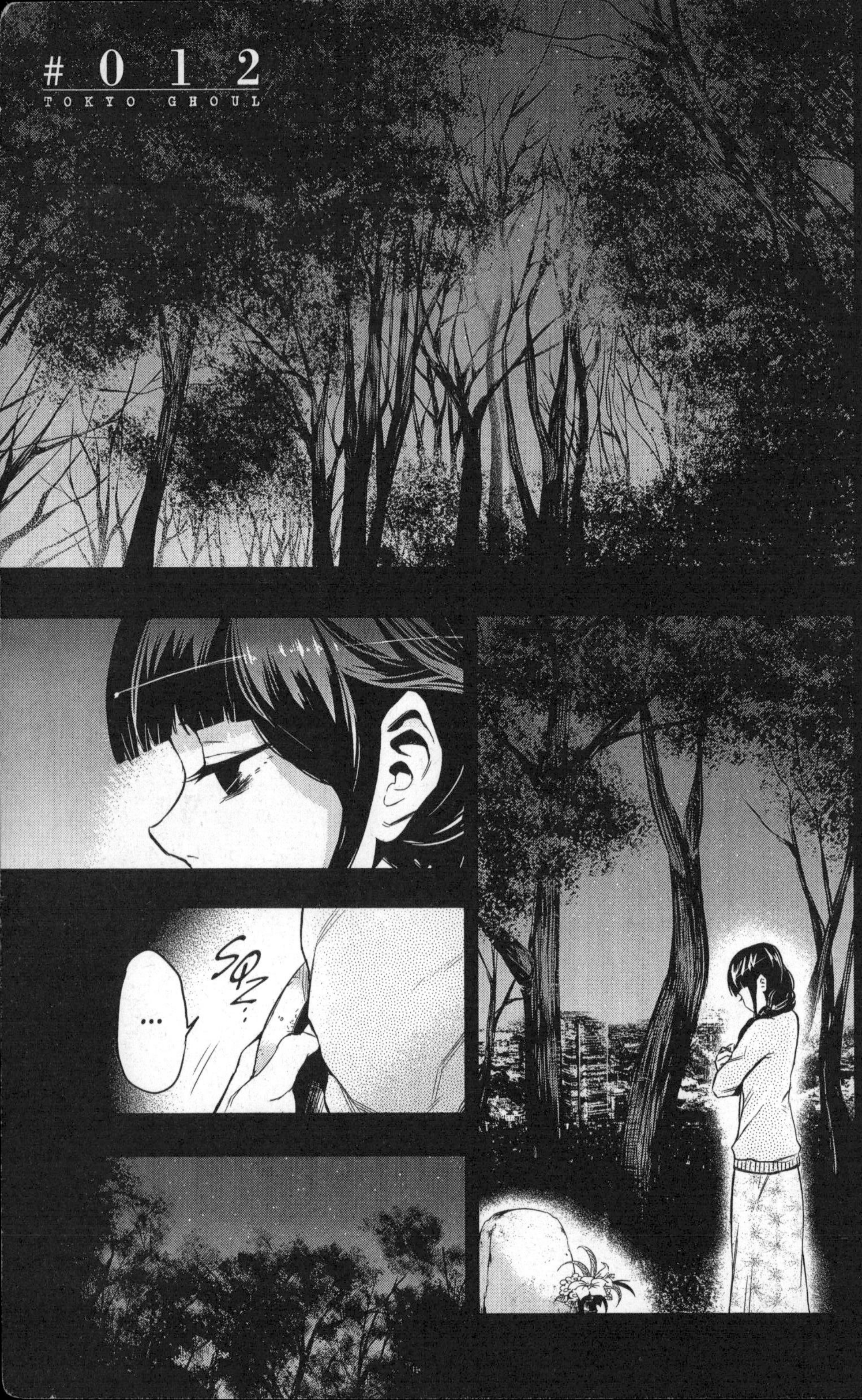
#012
TOKYO GHOUL
SQZ
...

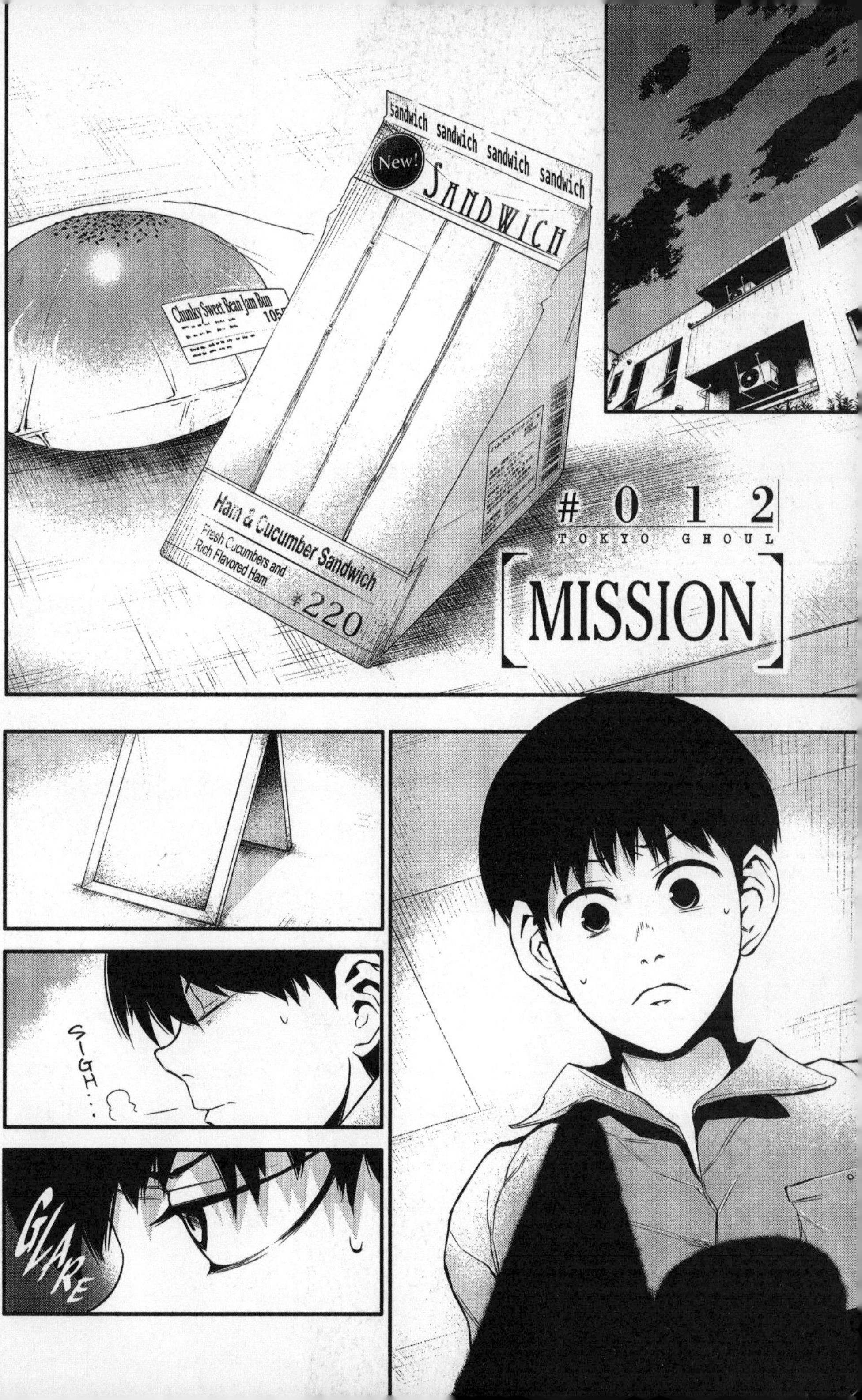
sandwich sandwich sandwich sandwich
New!
SANDWICH
Chunky Sweet Bean Jam Bun
105
Ham & Cucumber Sandwich
Fresh Cucumbers and Rich Flavored Ham
¥220
#012
TOKYO GHOUL
MISSION
SIGH...
GLARE

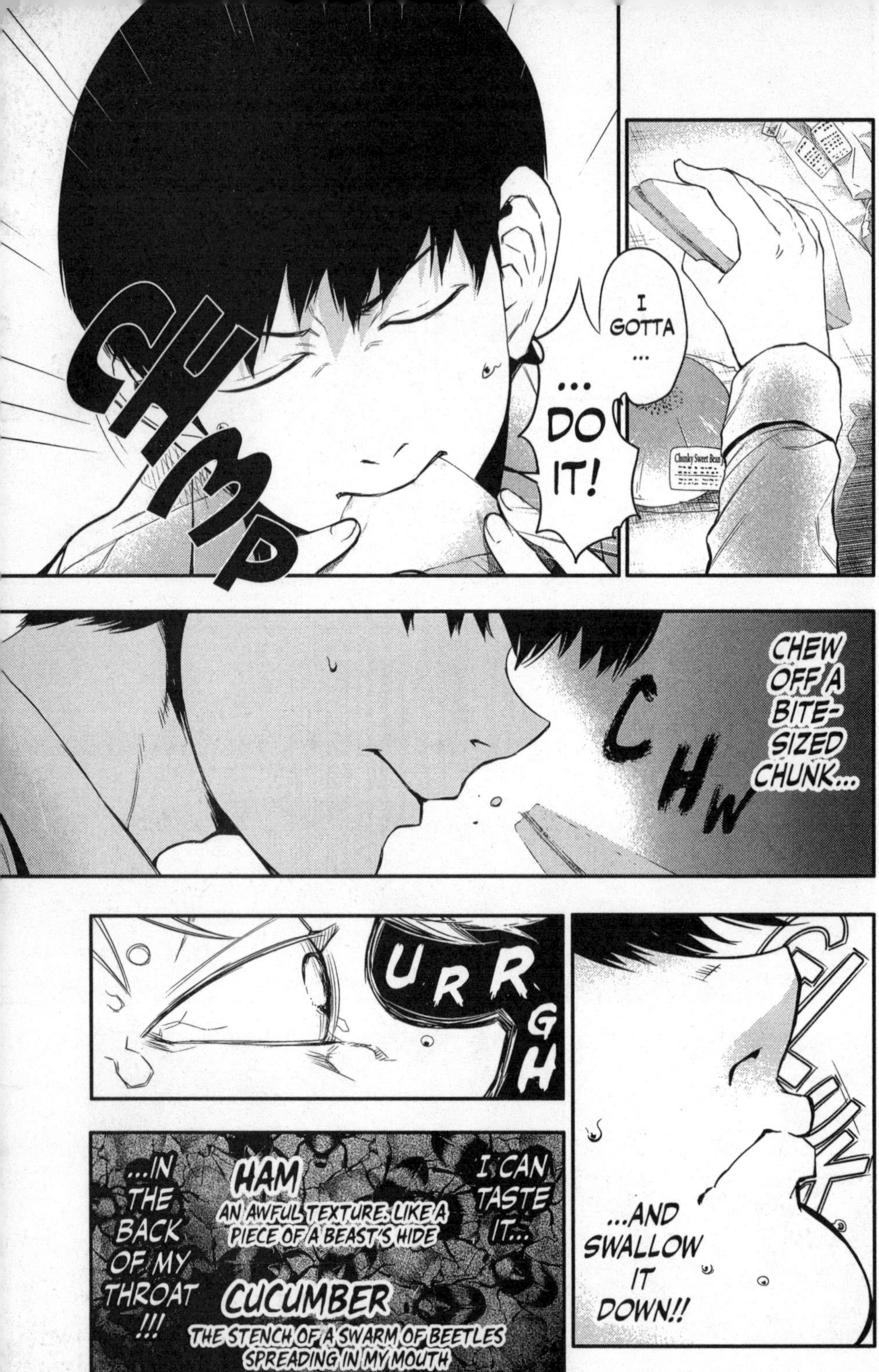
Chunky Sweet Bean
I GOTTA ...
... DO IT!
CHMP
CHEW OFF A BITE-SIZED CHUNK...
CHW
...AND SWALLOW IT DOWN!!
URRGH
I CAN TASTE IT...
HAM
AN AWFUL TEXTURE. LIKE A PIECE OF A BEAST'S HIDE
CUCUMBER
THE STENCH OF A SWARM OF BEETLES SPREADING IN MY MOUTH
...IN THE BACK OF MY THROAT!!!

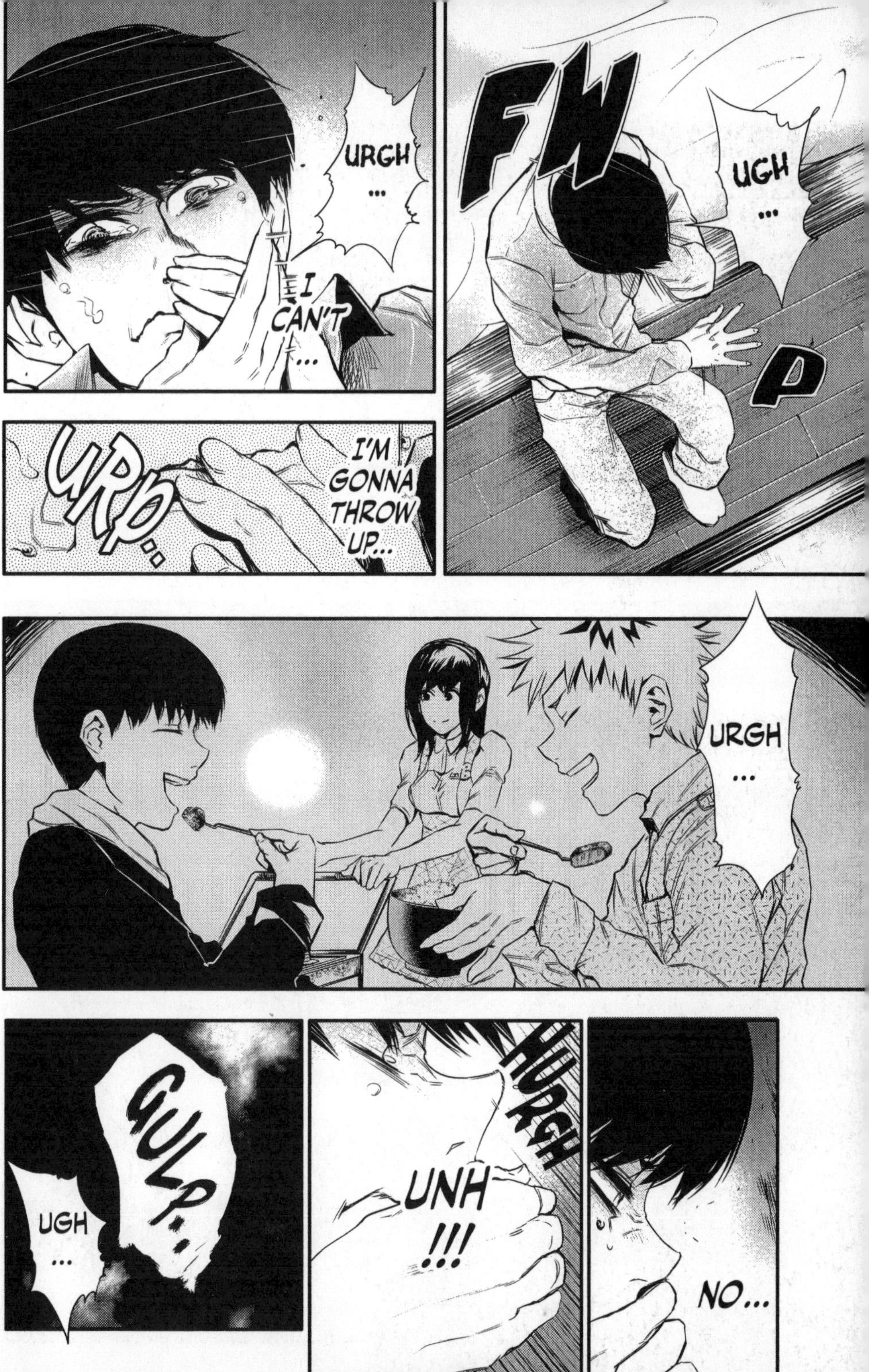
UGH ...
FW
P
URGH ...
I CAN'T ...
I'M GONNA THROW UP...
URP...
URGH ...
NO...
HURGH
UNH !!!
GULP..
UGH ...

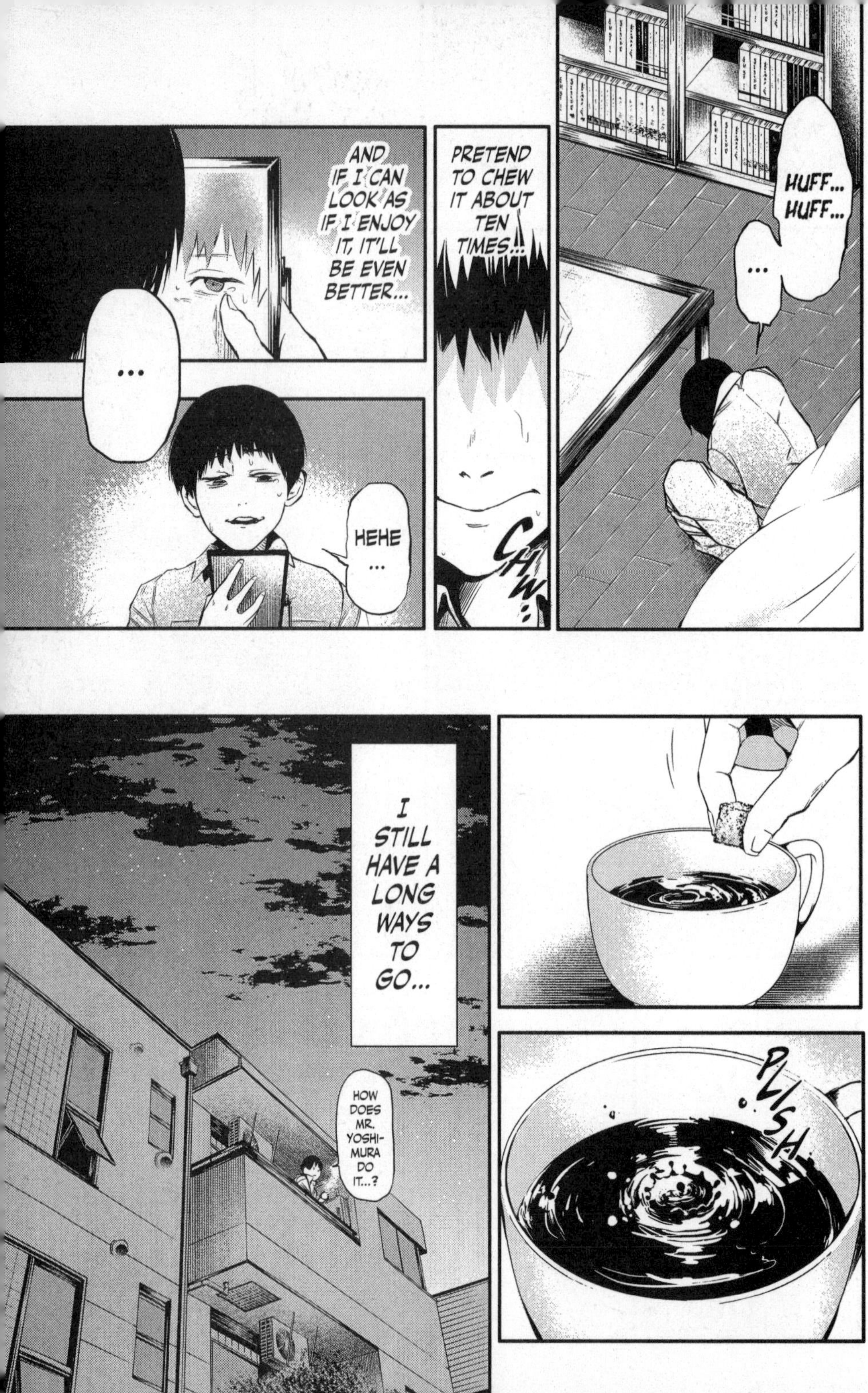
HUFF... HUFF...
...
PRETEND TO CHEW IT ABOUT TEN TIMES...
CHW...
AND IF I CAN LOOK AS IF I ENJOY IT, IT'LL BE EVEN BETTER...
...
HEHE ...
PLISH
I STILL HAVE A LONG WAYS TO GO...
HOW DOES MR. YOSHIMURA DO IT...?

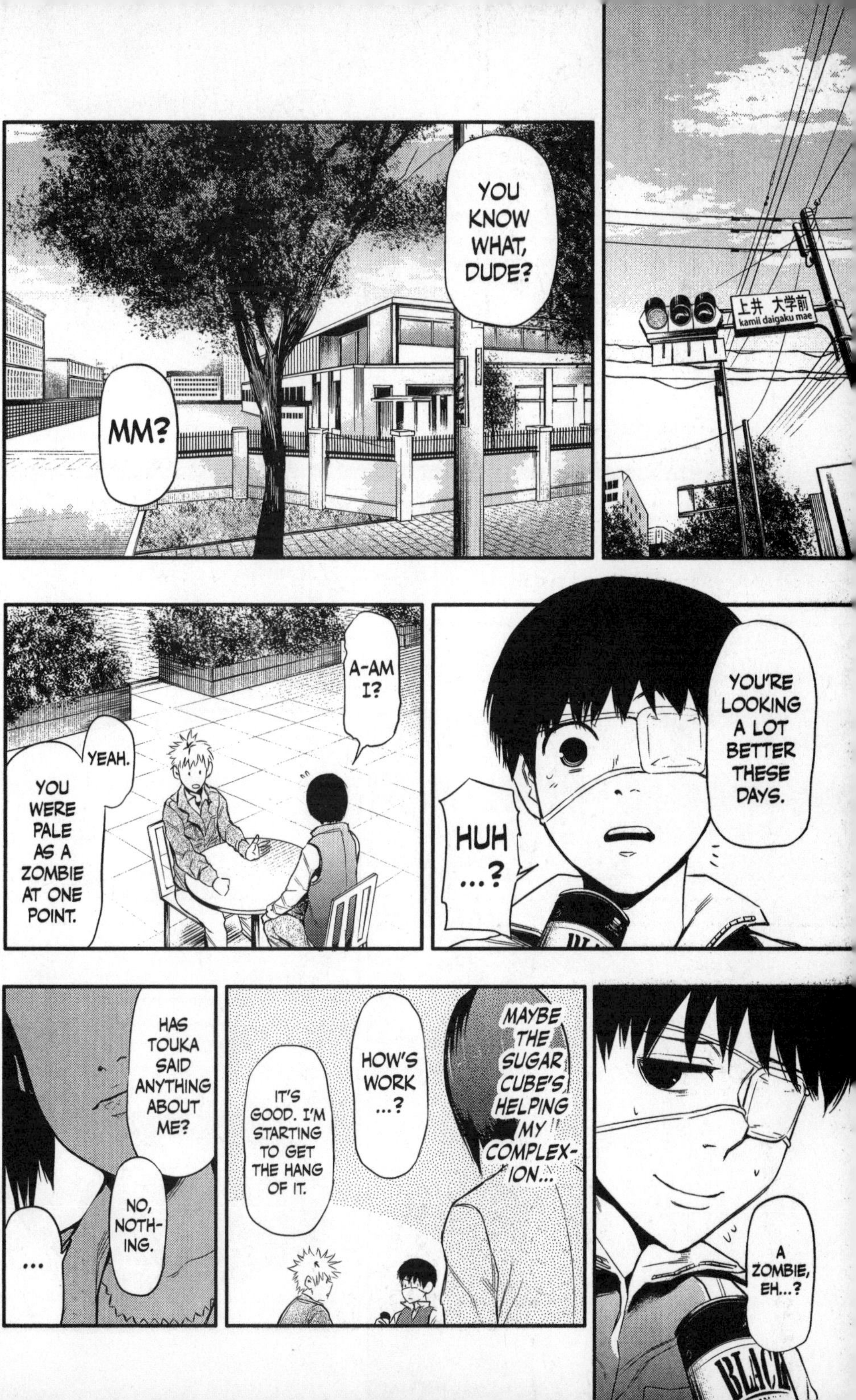
上井 大学前
kamii daigaku mae
YOU KNOW WHAT, DUDE?
MM?
YOU'RE LOOKING A LOT BETTER THESE DAYS.
HUH ...?
A-AM I?
YEAH.
YOU WERE PALE AS A ZOMBIE AT ONE POINT.
A ZOMBIE, EH...?
MAYBE THE SUGAR CUBE'S HELPING MY COMPLEX-ION...
HOW'S WORK ...?
IT'S GOOD. I'M STARTING TO GET THE HANG OF IT.
HAS TOUKA SAID ANYTHING ABOUT ME?
NO, NOTH-ING.
...

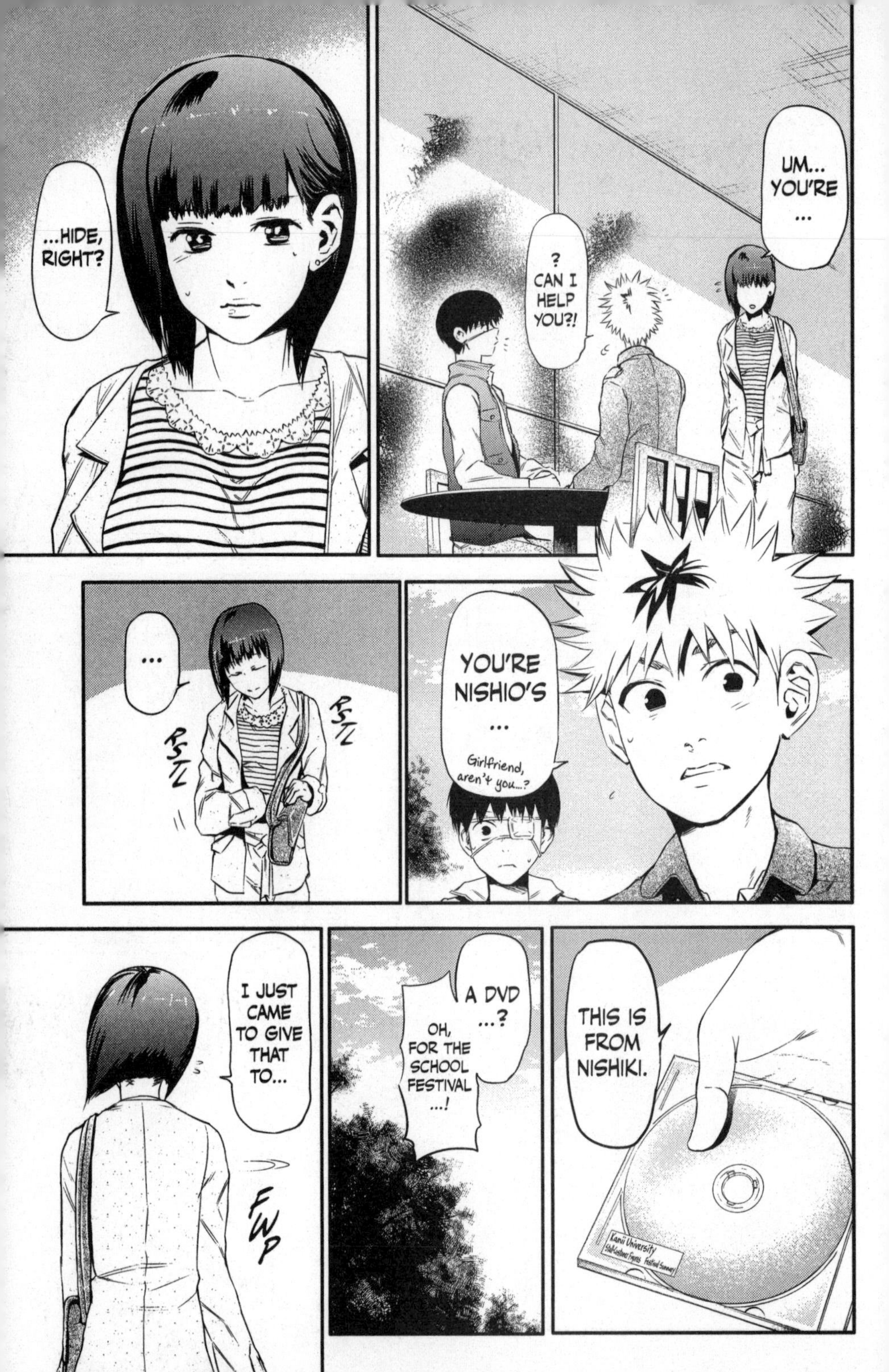
UM... YOU'RE ...
? CAN I HELP YOU?!
...HIDE, RIGHT?
YOU'RE NISHIO'S ...
Girlfriend, aren't you...?
...
RSTL
RSTL
THIS IS FROM NISHIKI.
Kamii University
A DVD ...?
OH, FOR THE SCHOOL FESTIVAL ...!
I JUST CAME TO GIVE THAT TO...
FWP

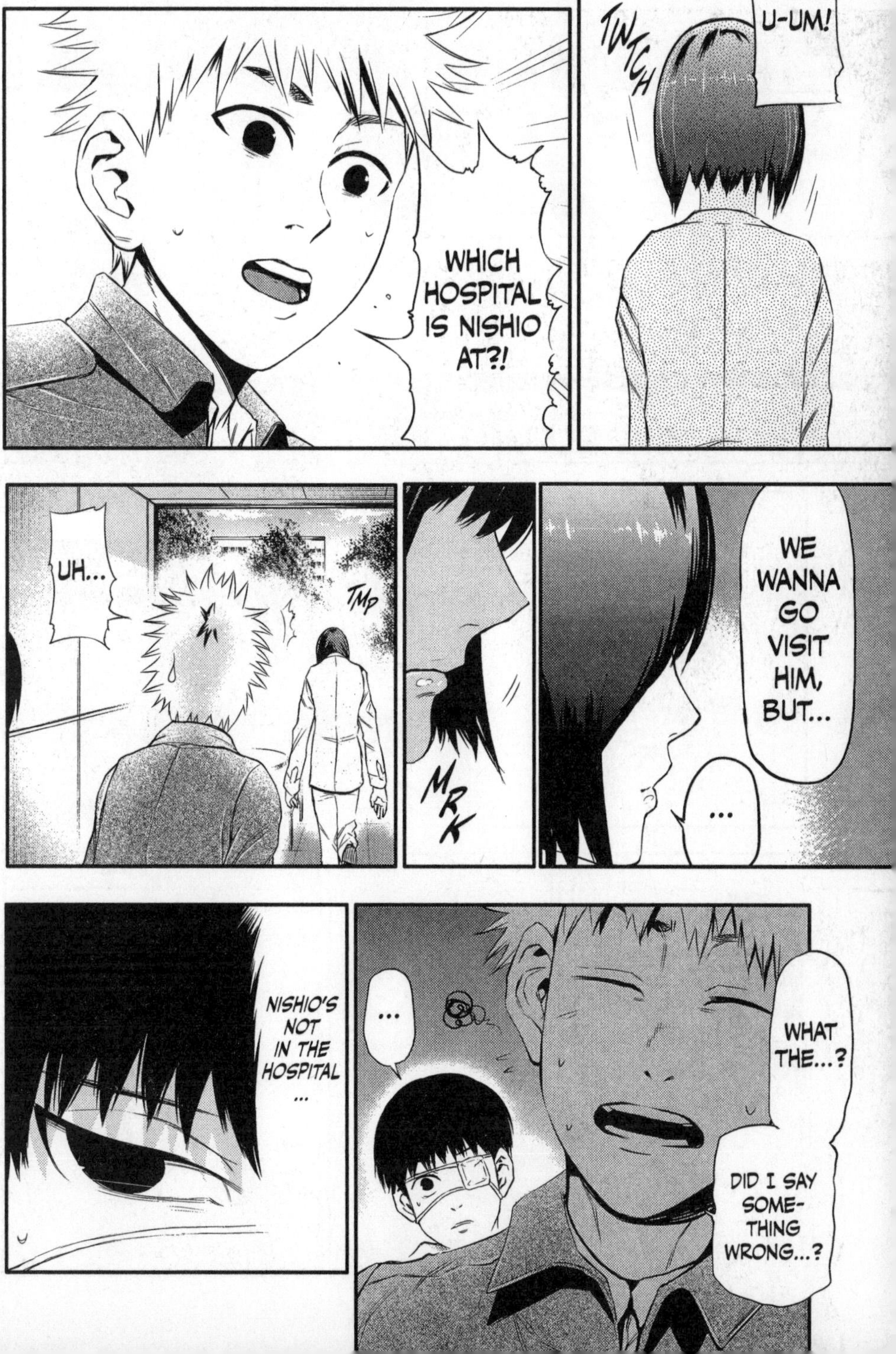
U-UM!
TWITCH
WHICH HOSPITAL IS NISHIO AT?!
WE WANNA GO VISIT HIM, BUT...
...
MRK
TMP
UH...
WHAT THE...?
...
DID I SAY SOME-THING WRONG...?
NISHIO'S NOT IN THE HOSPITAL...

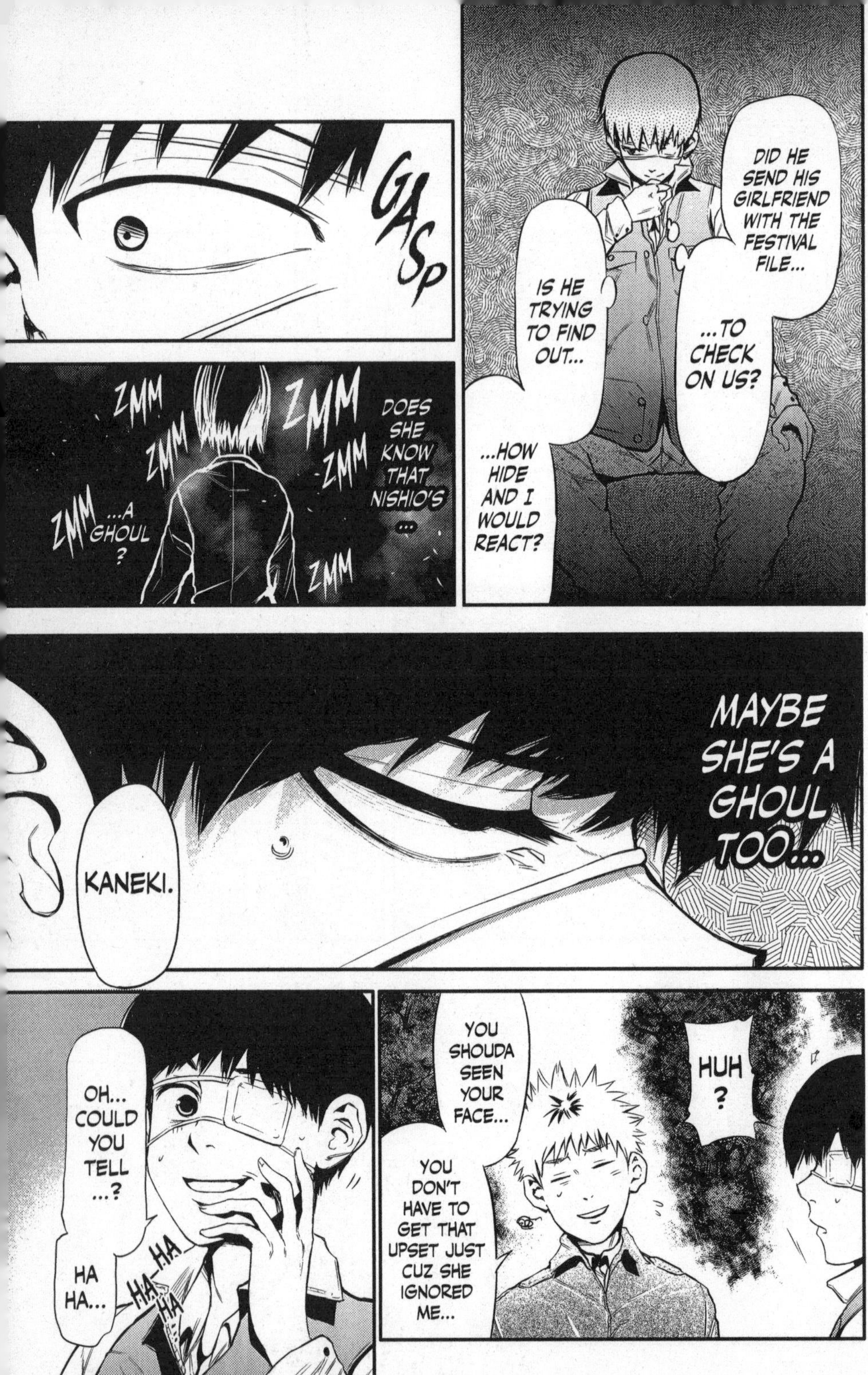
DID HE SEND HIS GIRLFRIEND WITH THE FESTIVAL FILE...
...TO CHECK ON US?
IS HE TRYING TO FIND OUT...
...HOW HIDE AND I WOULD REACT?
GASP
ZMM ZMM ZMM ZMM ZMM ZMM
DOES SHE KNOW THAT NISHIO'S ...
...A GHOUL ?
MAYBE SHE'S A GHOUL TOO...
KANEKI.
HUH ?
YOU SHOUDA SEEN YOUR FACE...
YOU DON'T HAVE TO GET THAT UPSET JUST CUZ SHE IGNORED ME...
OH... COULD YOU TELL ...?
HA HA...
HA HA HA HA

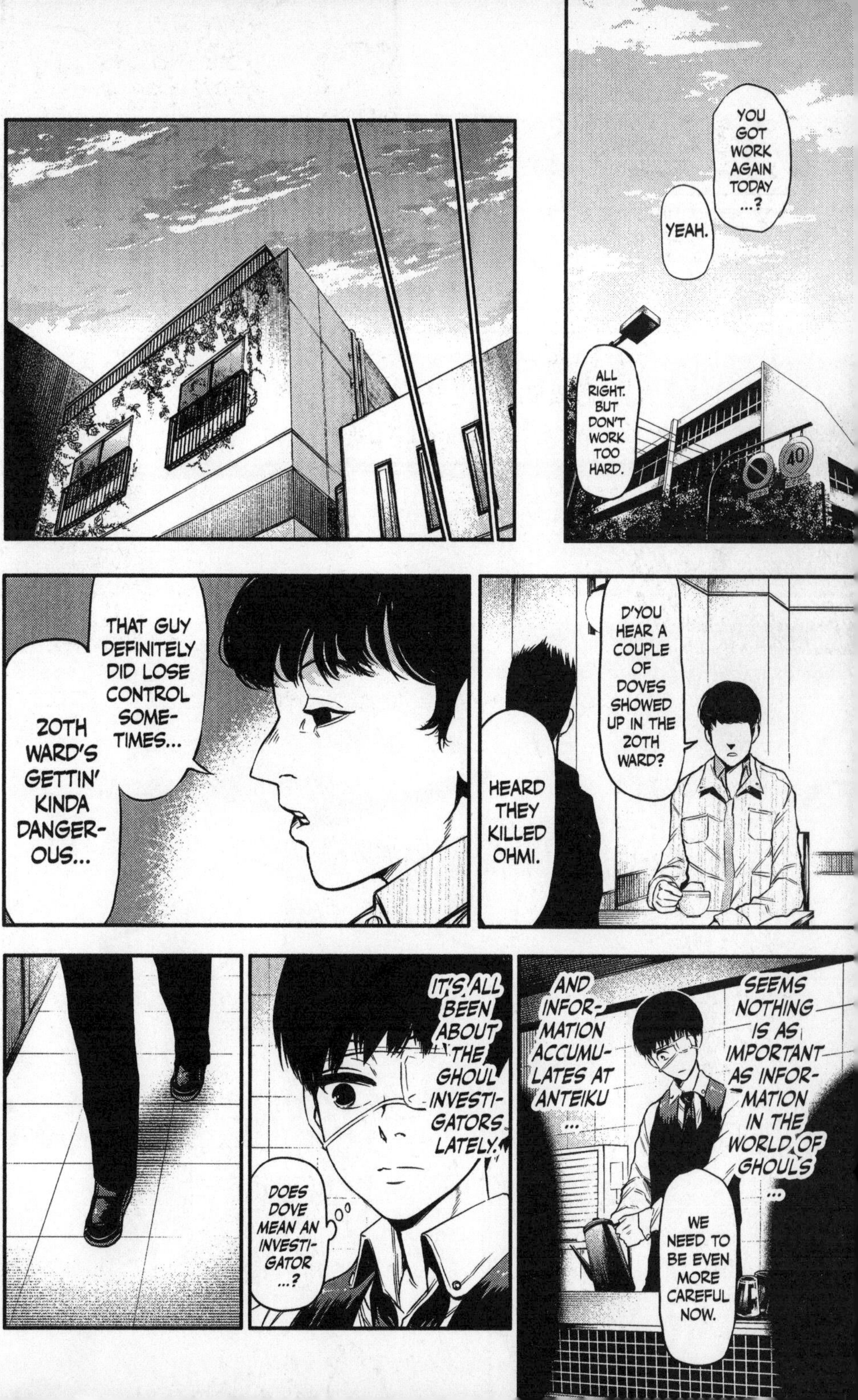
YOU GOT WORK AGAIN TODAY ...?
YEAH.
ALL RIGHT. BUT DON'T WORK TOO HARD.
D'YOU HEAR A COUPLE OF DOVES SHOWED UP IN THE 20TH WARD?
HEARD THEY KILLED OHMI.
THAT GUY DEFINITELY DID LOSE CONTROL SOMETIMES...
20TH WARD'S GETTIN' KINDA DANGEROUS...
SEEMS NOTHING IS AS IMPORTANT AS INFORMATION IN THE WORLD OF GHOULS...
AND INFORMATION ACCUMULATES AT ANTEIKU...
WE NEED TO BE EVEN MORE CAREFUL NOW.
IT'S ALL BEEN ABOUT THE GHOUL INVESTIGATORS LATELY.
DOES DOVE MEAN AN INVESTIGATOR...?

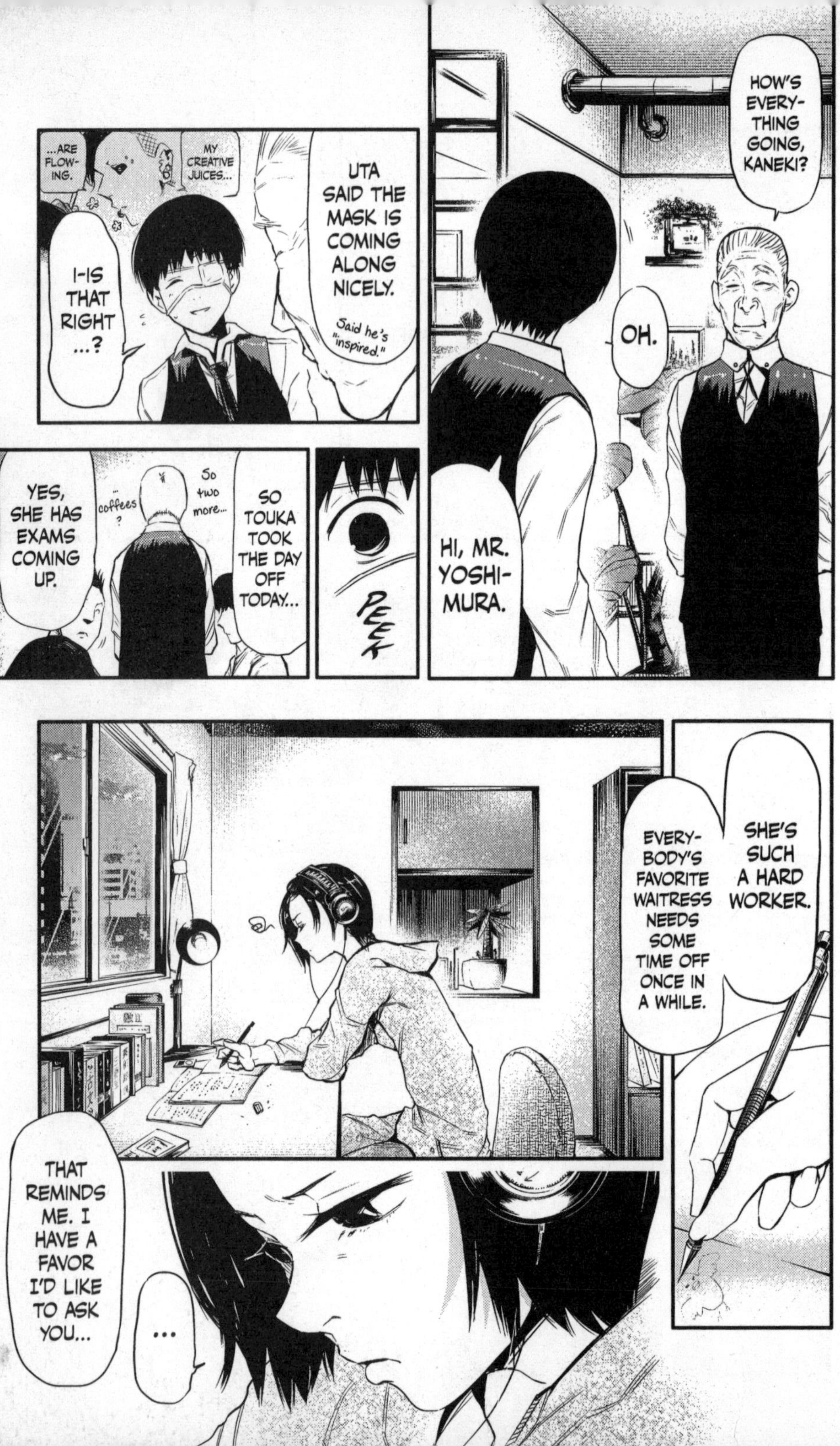
HOW'S EVERYTHING GOING, KANEKI?
OH.
HI, MR. YOSHIMURA.
UTA SAID THE MASK IS COMING ALONG NICELY.
Said he's "inspired."
MY CREATIVE JUICES...
...ARE FLOWING.
I-IS THAT RIGHT ...?
PEEK
SO TOUKA TOOK THE DAY OFF TODAY...
So two more...
...coffees?
YES, SHE HAS EXAMS COMING UP.
SHE'S SUCH A HARD WORKER.
EVERYBODY'S FAVORITE WAITRESS NEEDS SOME TIME OFF ONCE IN A WHILE.
THAT REMINDS ME. I HAVE A FAVOR I'D LIKE TO ASK YOU...
...

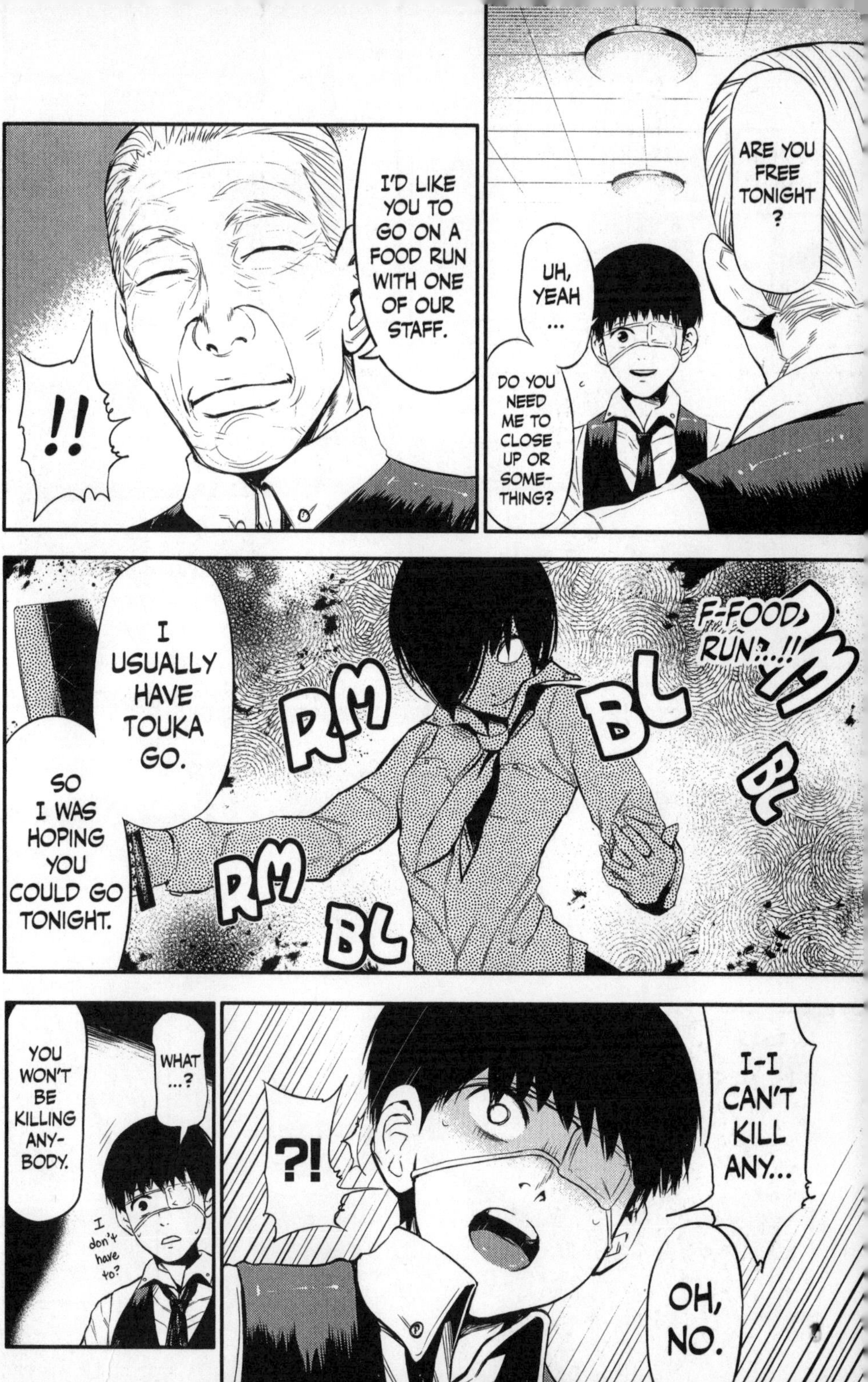
ARE YOU FREE TONIGHT?
UH, YEAH...
DO YOU NEED ME TO CLOSE UP OR SOME-THING?
I'D LIKE YOU TO GO ON A FOOD RUN WITH ONE OF OUR STAFF.
!!
F-FOOD RUN?...!!
RM BL
BL
RM
I USUALLY HAVE TOUKA GO.
SO I WAS HOPING YOU COULD GO TONIGHT.
RM
BL
I-I CAN'T KILL ANY...
OH, NO.
?!
WHAT...?
YOU WON'T BE KILLING ANY-BODY.
I don't have to?

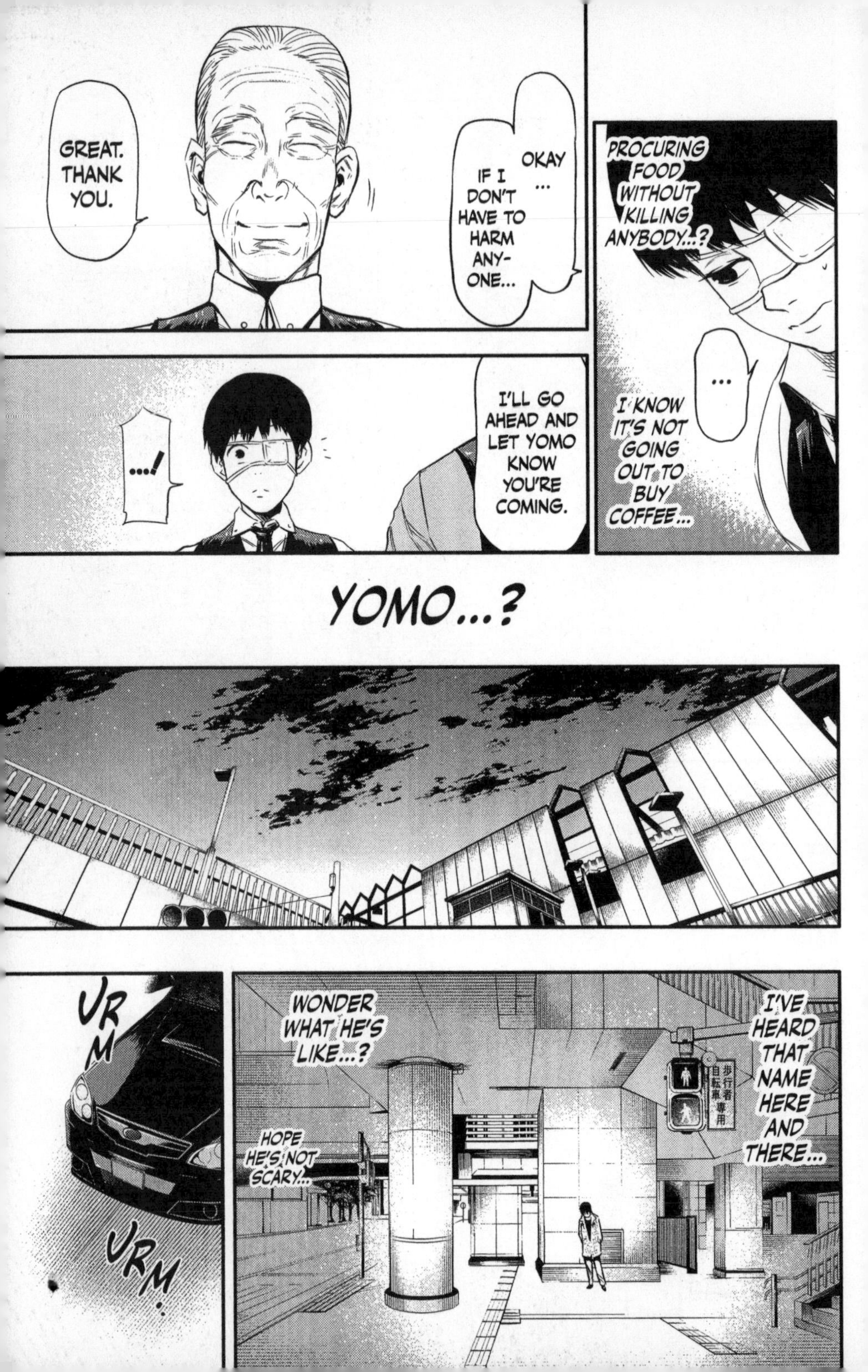
PROCURING FOOD WITHOUT KILLING ANYBODY...?
...
I KNOW IT'S NOT GOING OUT TO BUY COFFEE...
OKAY ... IF I DON'T HAVE TO HARM ANY-ONE...
GREAT. THANK YOU.
I'LL GO AHEAD AND LET YOMO KNOW YOU'RE COMING.
...!
YOMO...?
I'VE HEARD THAT NAME HERE AND THERE...
歩行者自転車専用
WONDER WHAT HE'S LIKE...?
HOPE HE'S NOT SCARY...
VRM
VRM.

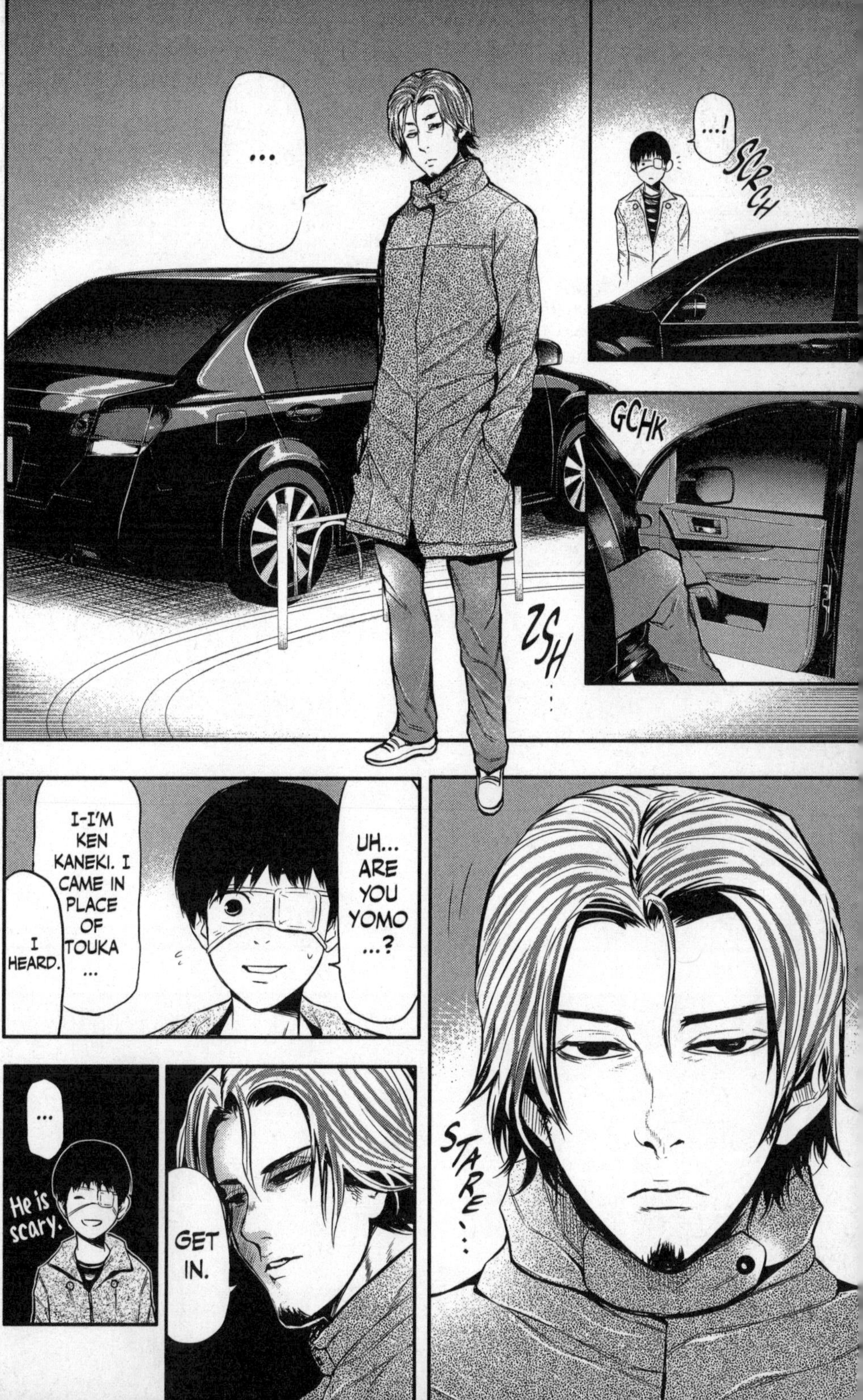
...!
SCRCH
GCHK
ZSH...
...
STARE...
UH... ARE YOU YOMO...?
I-I'M KEN KANEKI. I CAME IN PLACE OF TOUKA...
I HEARD.
GET IN.
...
He is scary.

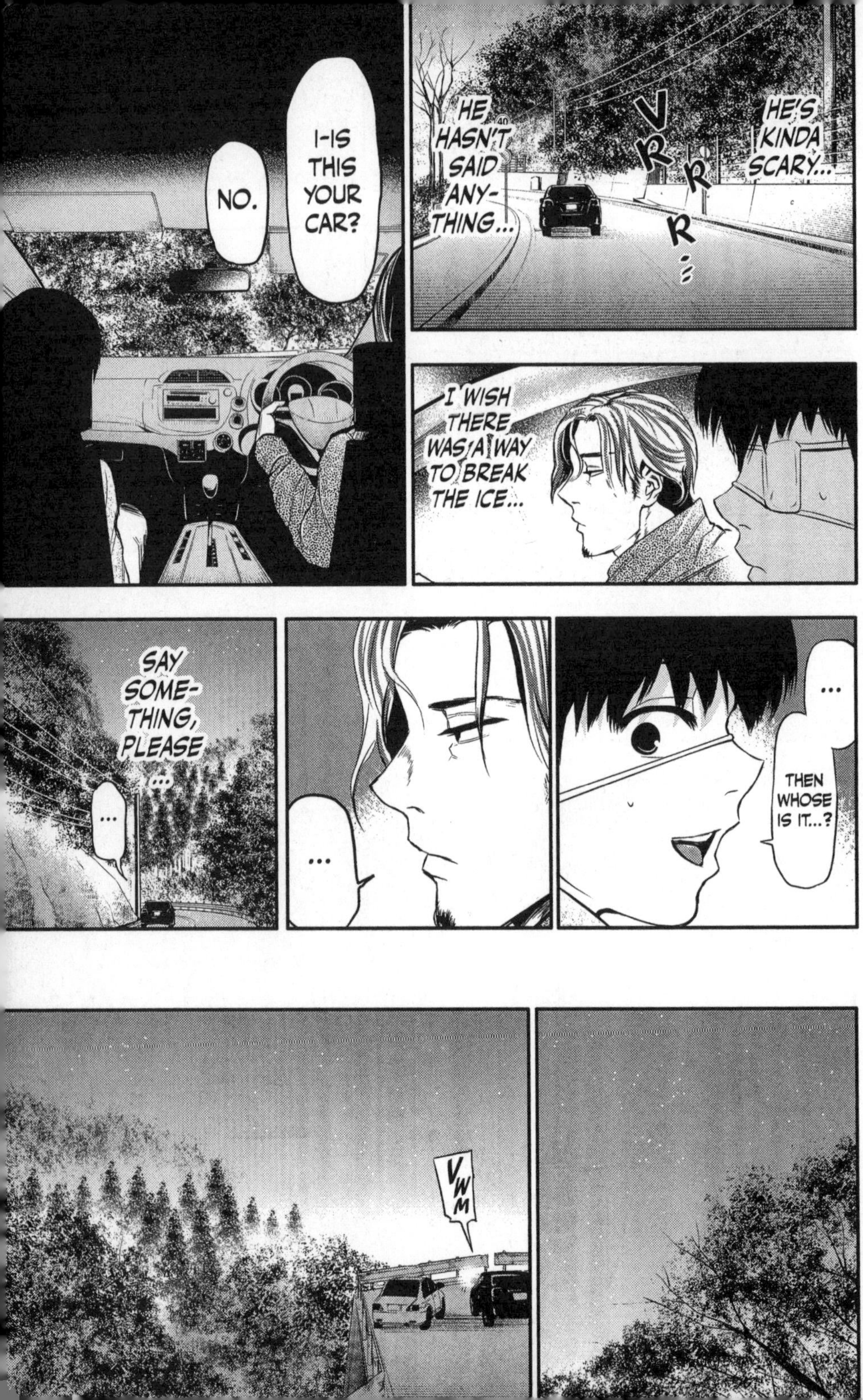
HE'S KINDA SCARY...
VRRR...
HE HASN'T SAID ANYTHING...
I WISH THERE WAS A WAY TO BREAK THE ICE...
I-IS THIS YOUR CAR?
NO.
...
THEN WHOSE IS IT...?
...
SAY SOMETHING, PLEASE...
...
VWM

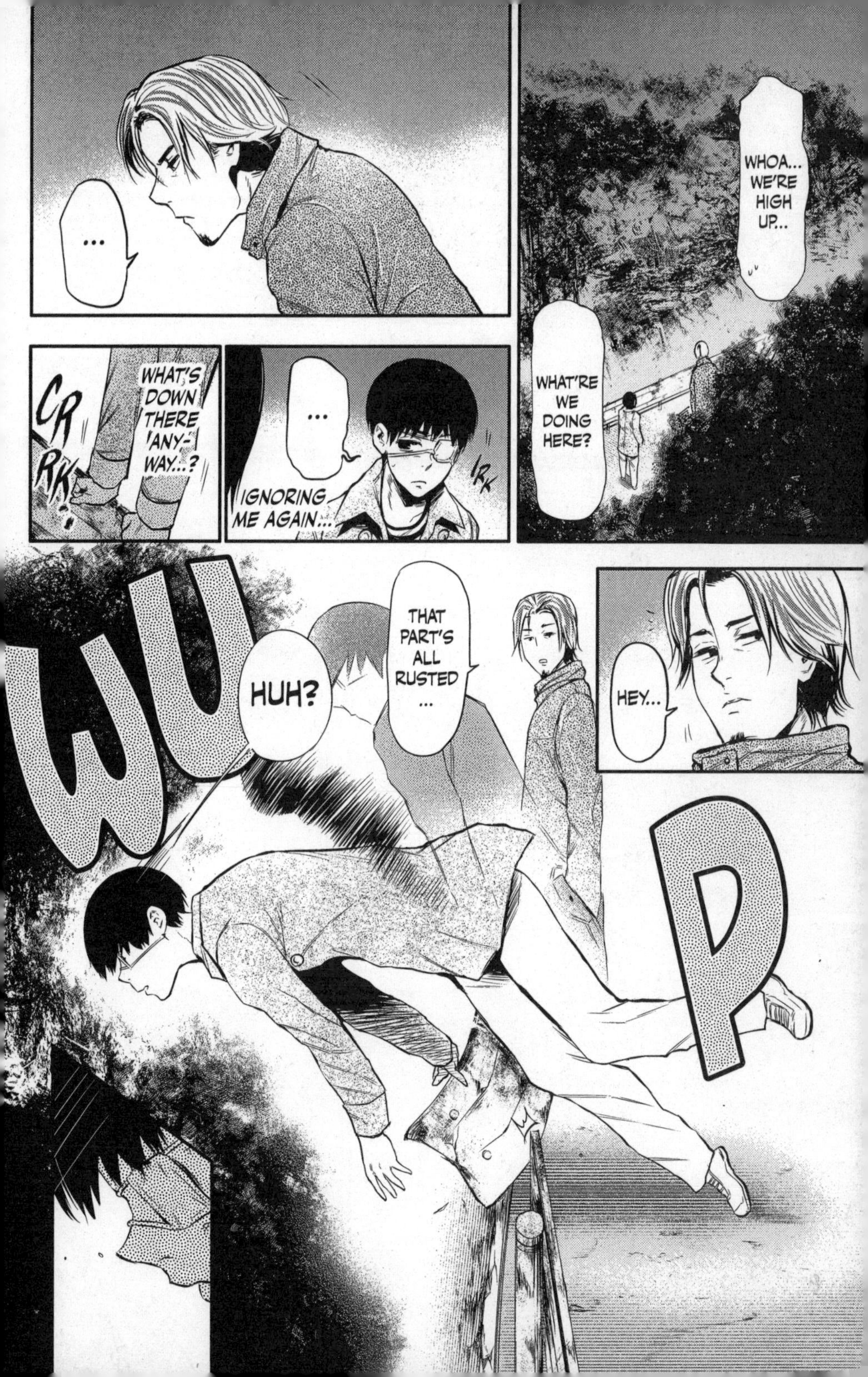
WHOA... WE'RE HIGH UP...
WHAT'RE WE DOING HERE?
...
...
IGNORING ME AGAIN...
IRK
WHAT'S DOWN THERE ANY-WAY...?
CRRK
HEY...
THAT PART'S ALL RUSTED...
HUH?
WU
P

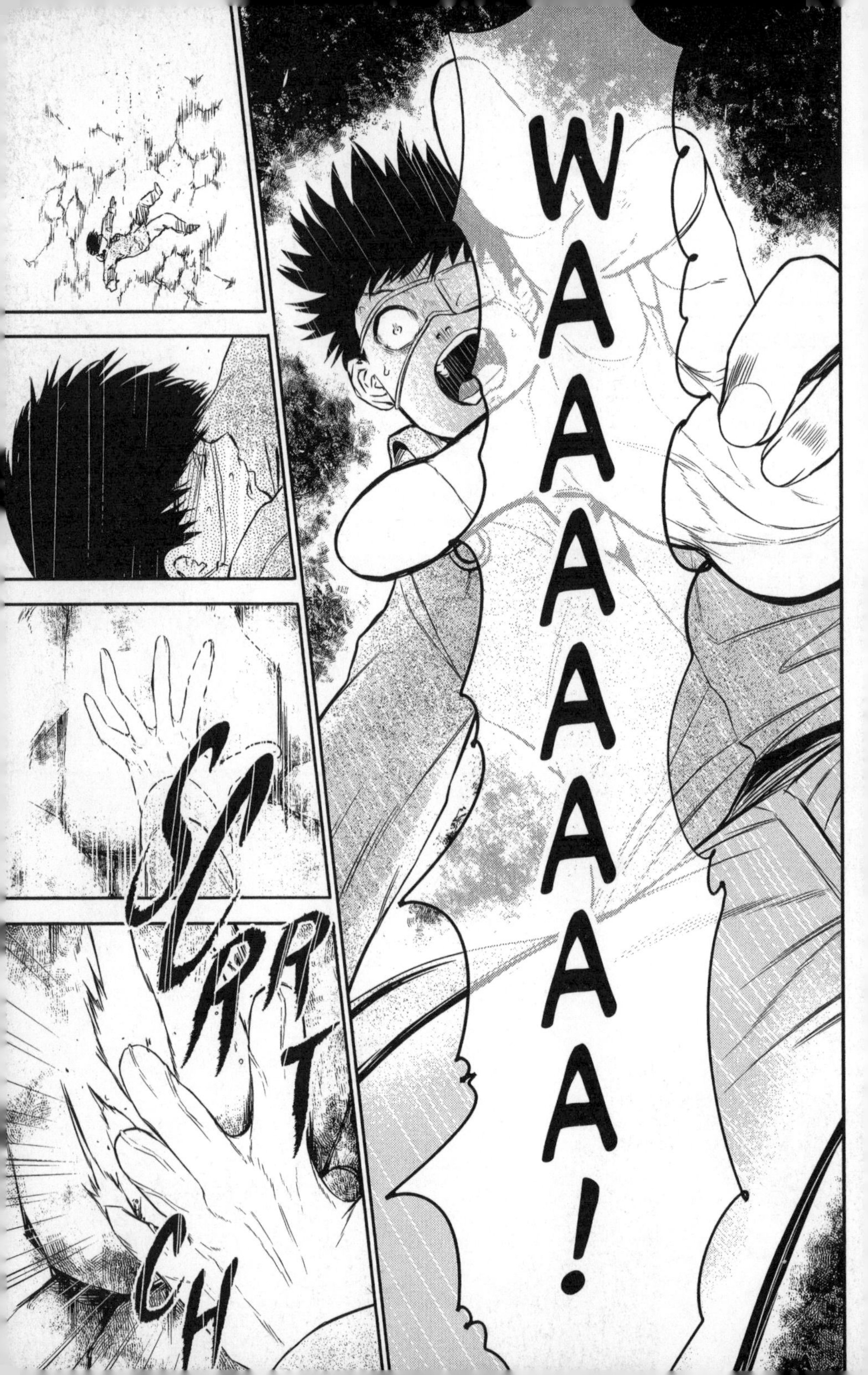
WAAAAAAAA!
SCRRTCH

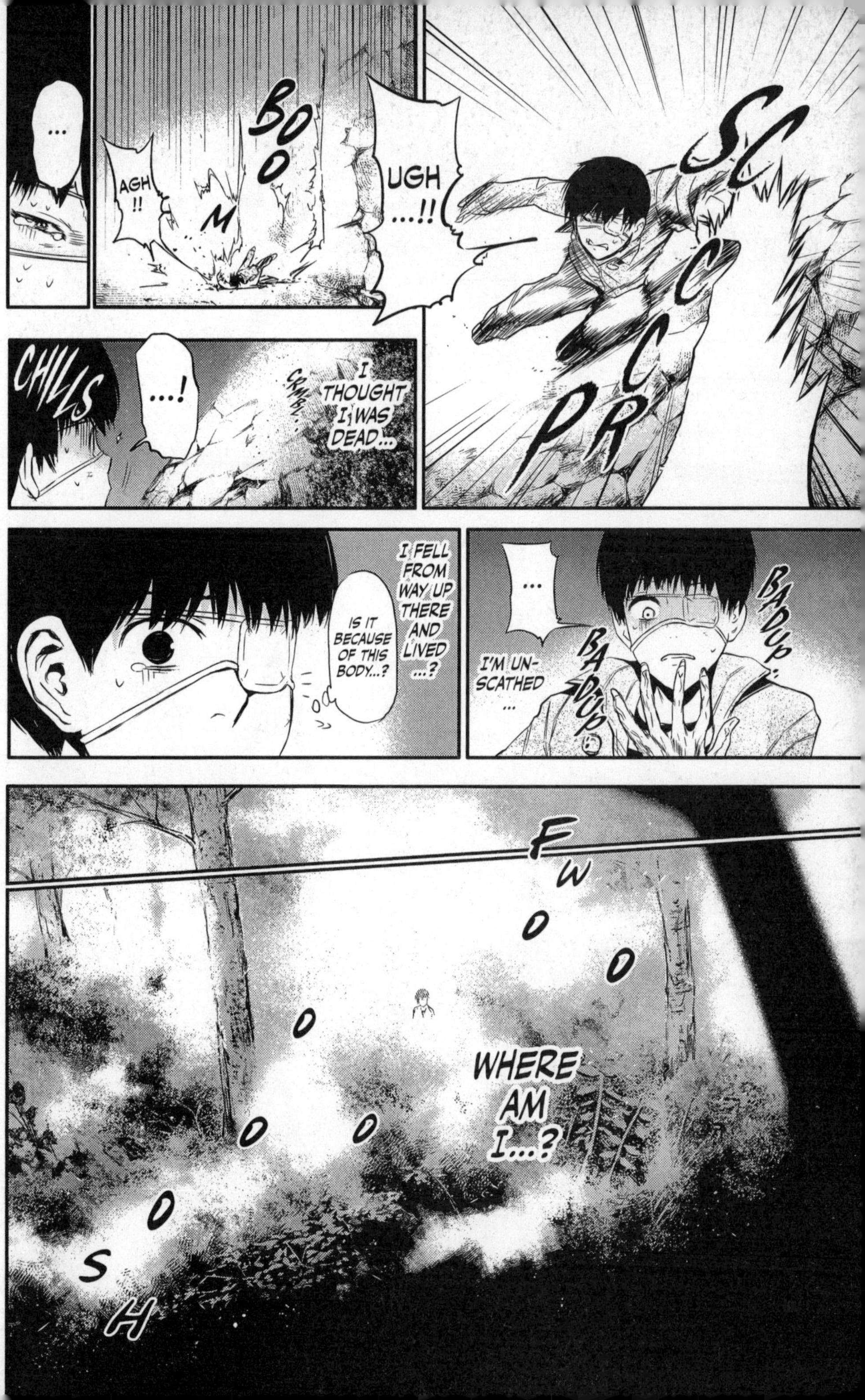
SCCCPR
UGH ...!!
BOOM
AGH !!
...
I THOUGHT I WAS DEAD...
CRMBL
...!
CHILLS
BADUP BADUP
...
I'M UN-SCATHED ...
I FELL FROM WAY UP THERE AND LIVED ...?
IS IT BECAUSE OF THIS BODY...?
FWOOOOOOSH
WHERE AM I...?

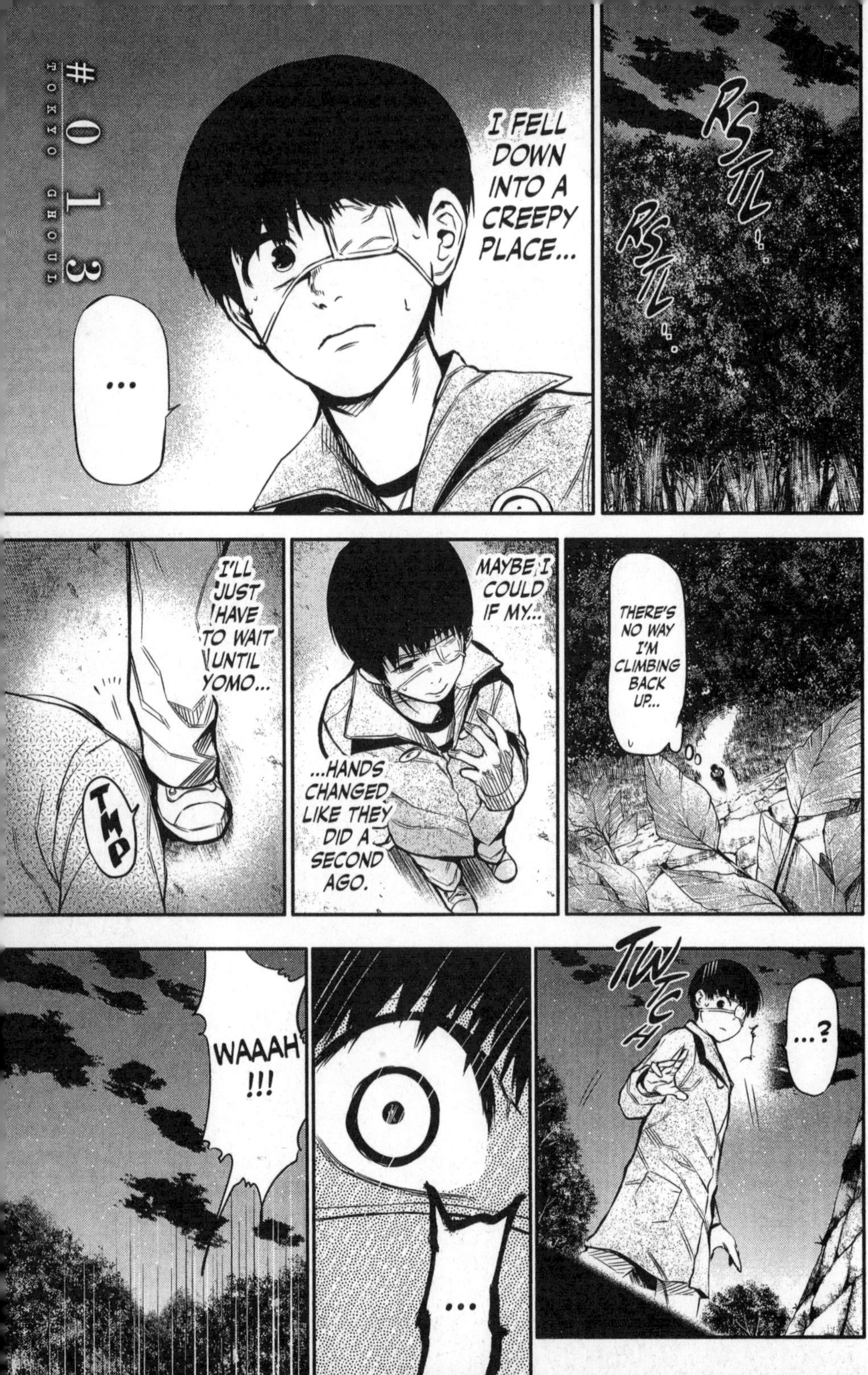
RSTL
RSTL
I FELL DOWN INTO A CREEPY PLACE...
#013 TOKYO GHOUL
...
THERE'S NO WAY I'M CLIMBING BACK UP...
MAYBE I COULD IF MY...
...HANDS CHANGED LIKE THEY DID A SECOND AGO.
I'LL JUST HAVE TO WAIT UNTIL YOMO...
TMP
TWITCH
...?
...
WAAAH !!!

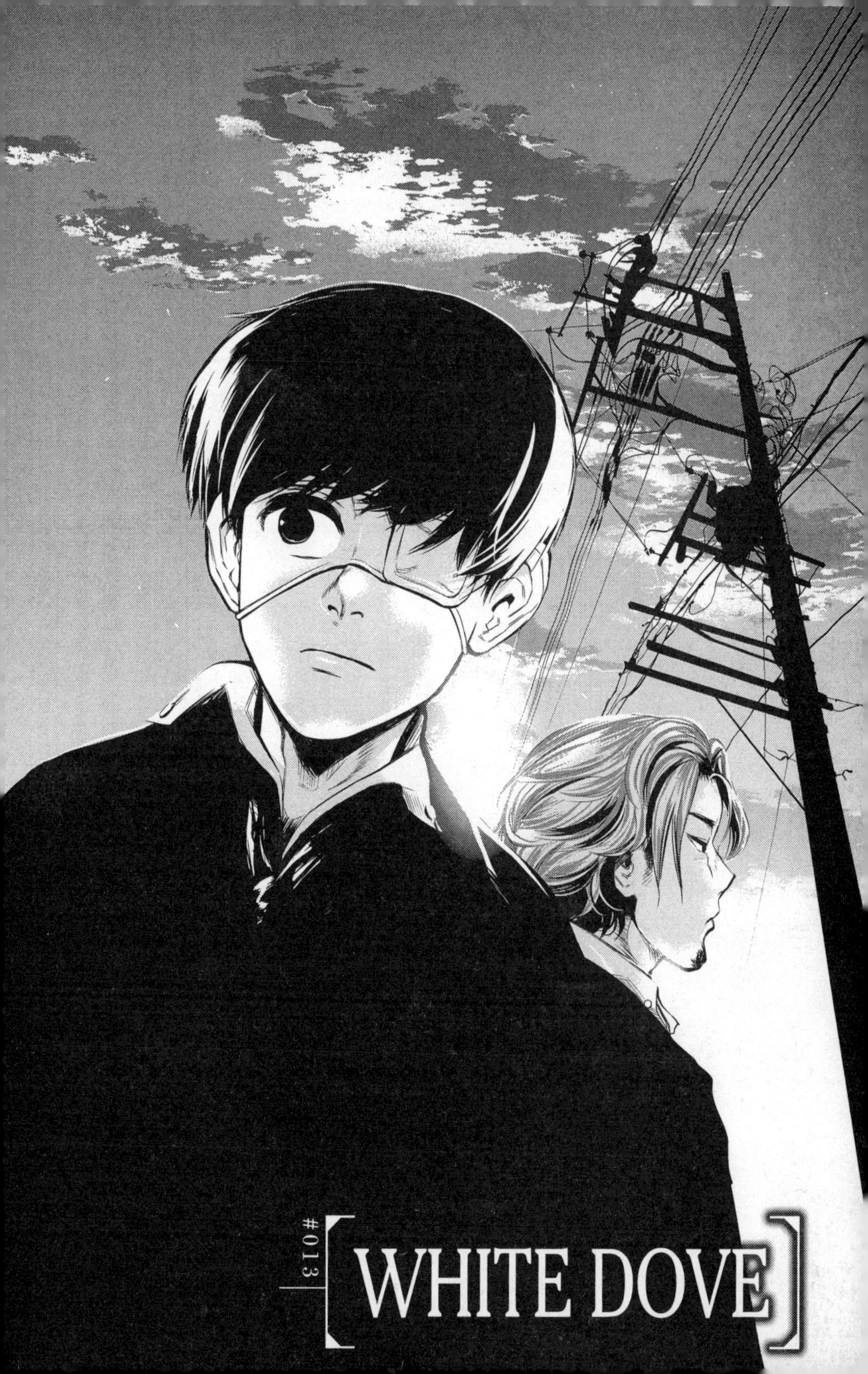
#013
WHITE DOVE

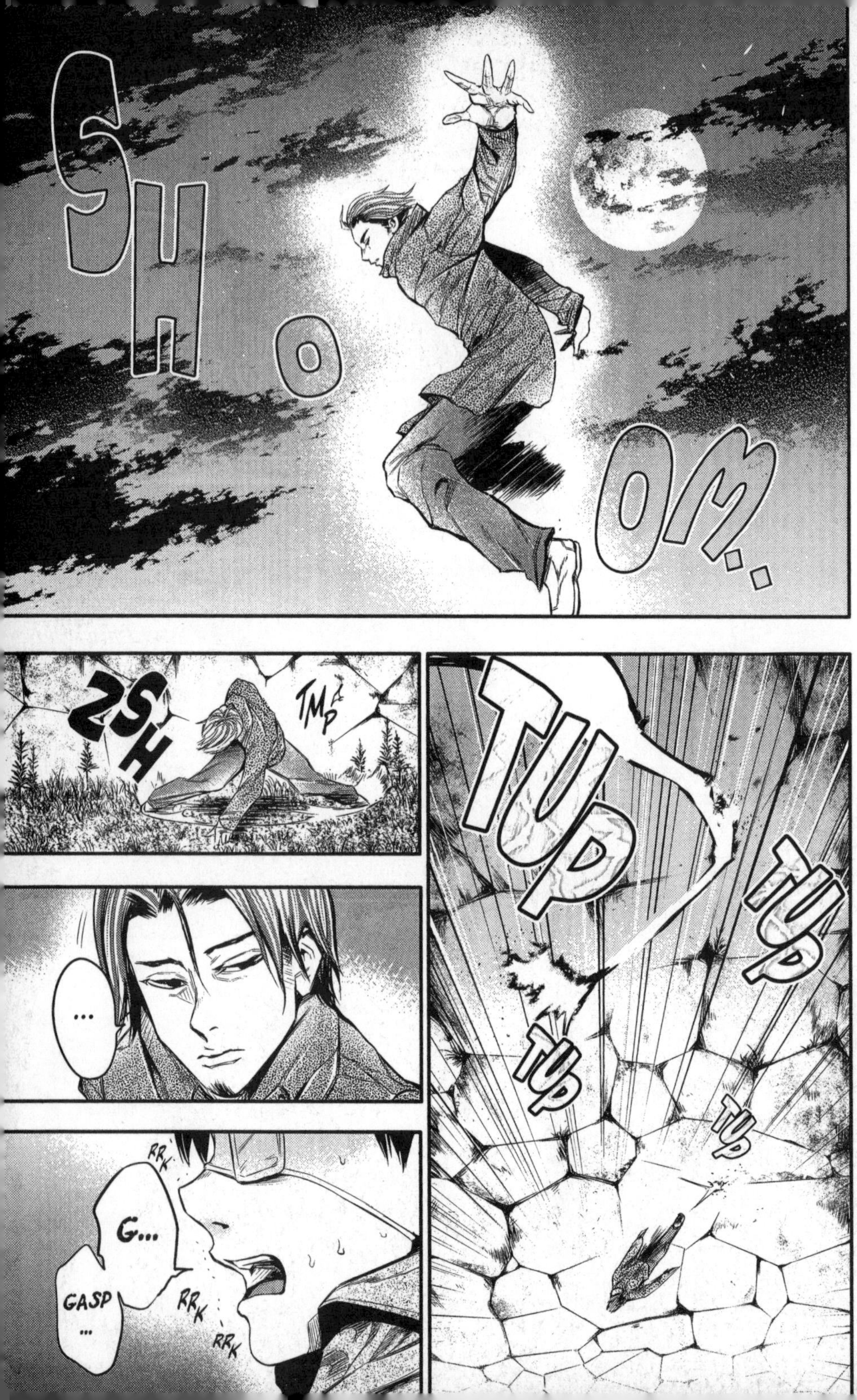
SHOOM..
TUP
TUP
TUP
TUP
ZSH
TMP
...
RRK
G...
RRK
RRK
GASP ...

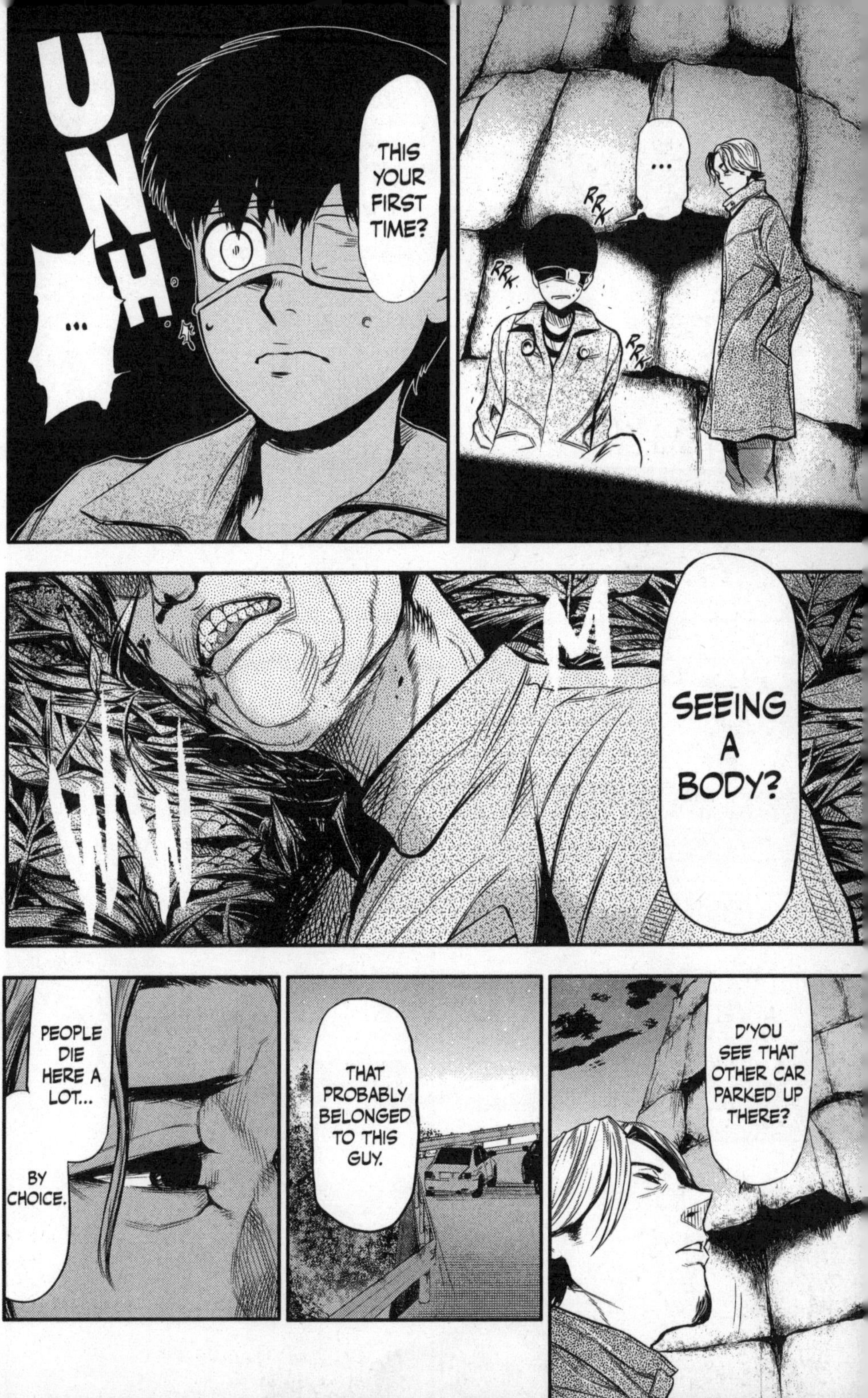
...
RRK
RRK
RRK
THIS YOUR FIRST TIME?
UNH
...
SEEING A BODY?
M
WW
D'YOU SEE THAT OTHER CAR PARKED UP THERE?
THAT PROBABLY BELONGED TO THIS GUY.
PEOPLE DIE HERE A LOT...
BY CHOICE.

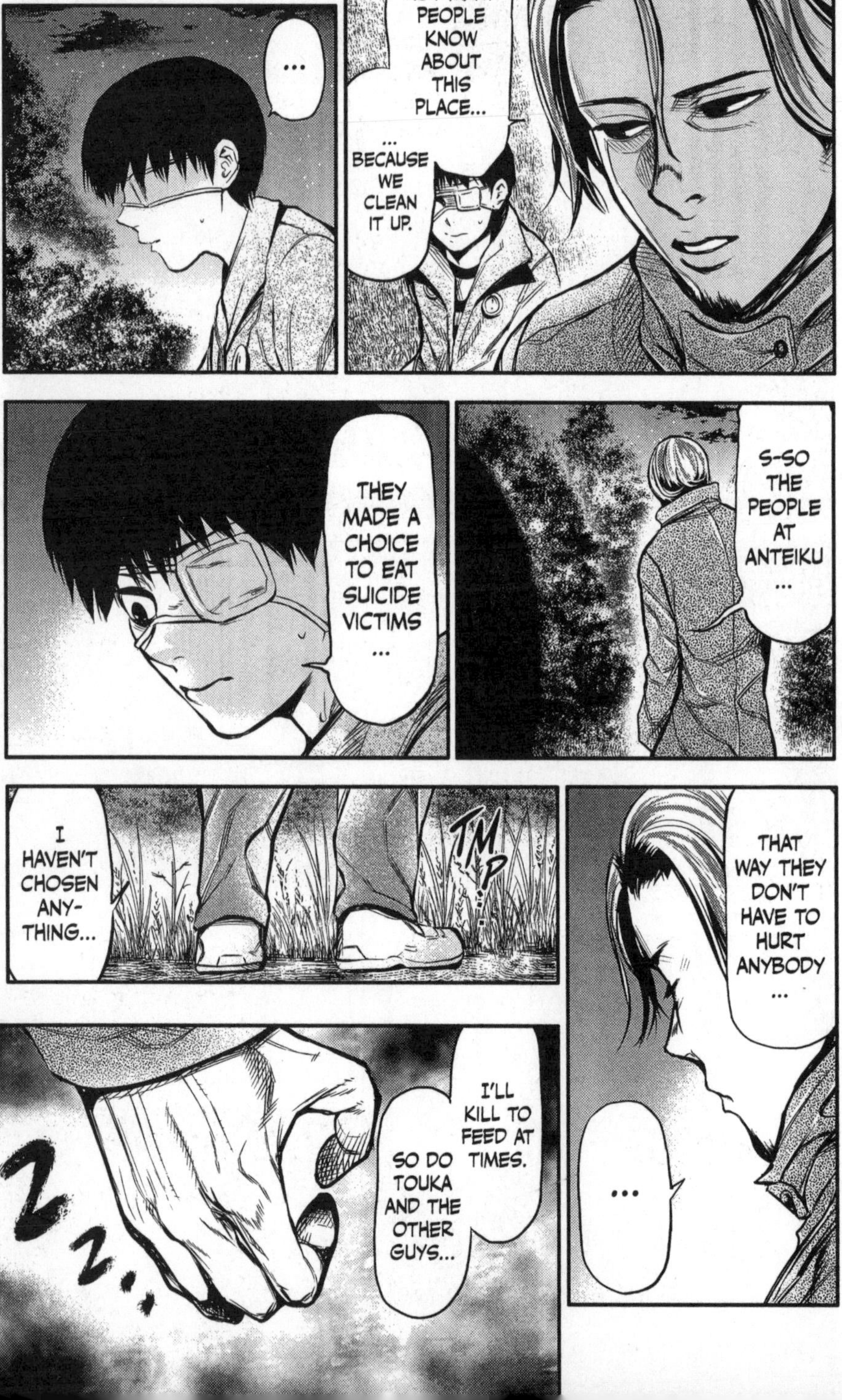
NOT MANY PEOPLE KNOW ABOUT THIS PLACE...
... BECAUSE WE CLEAN IT UP.
...
S-SO THE PEOPLE AT ANTEIKU ...
THEY MADE A CHOICE TO EAT SUICIDE VICTIMS ...
THAT WAY THEY DON'T HAVE TO HURT ANYBODY ...
...
TMP
I HAVEN'T CHOSEN ANY-THING...
I'LL KILL TO FEED AT TIMES.
SO DO TOUKA AND THE OTHER GUYS...
ZZ..

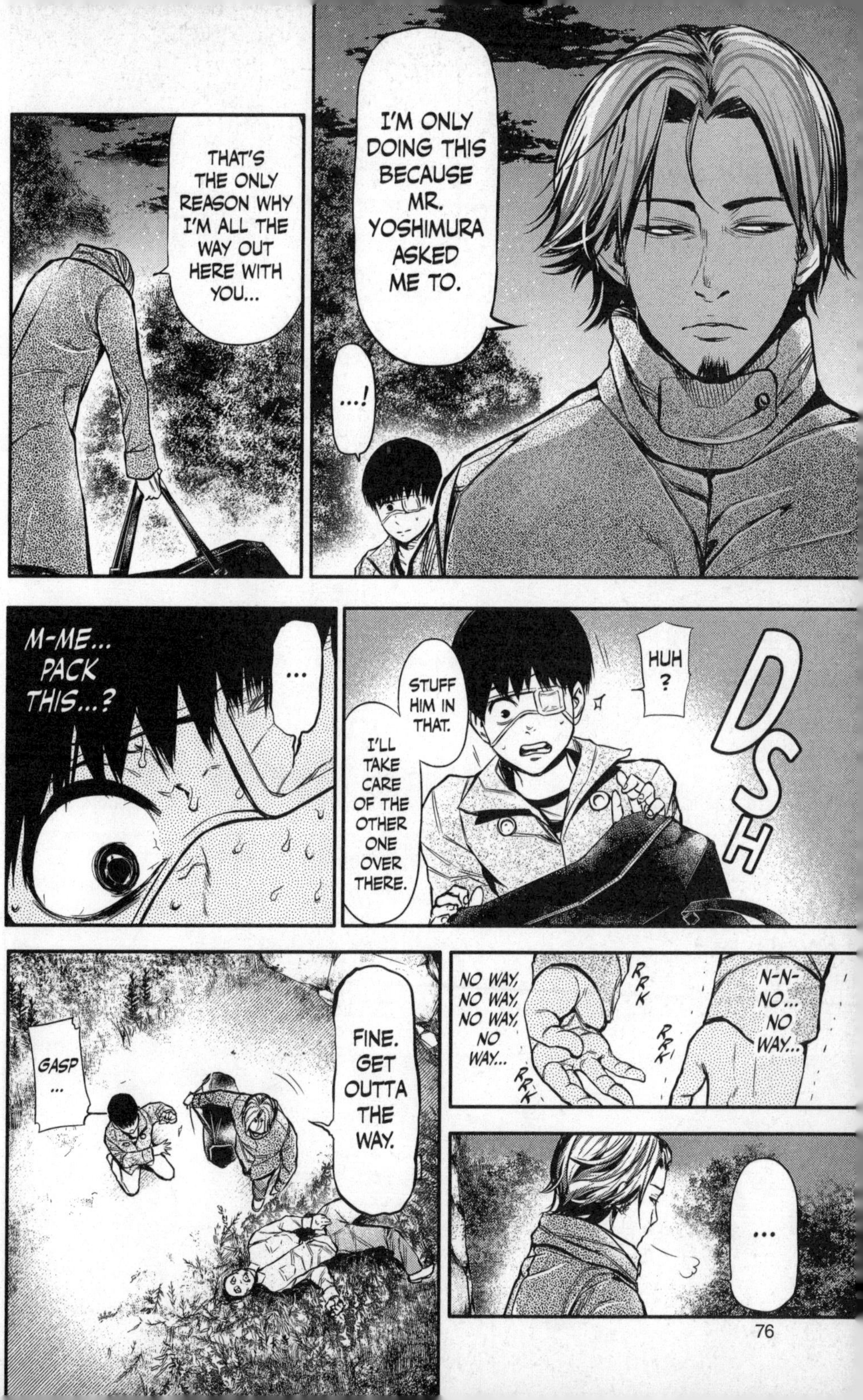

I'M ONLY DOING THIS BECAUSE MR. YOSHIMURA ASKED ME TO.
...!
THAT'S THE ONLY REASON WHY I'M ALL THE WAY OUT HERE WITH YOU...
DSH
HUH ?
STUFF HIM IN THAT.
I'LL TAKE CARE OF THE OTHER ONE OVER THERE.
...
M-ME... PACK THIS...?
N-N-NO... NO WAY...
RRK
RRK
NO WAY, NO WAY, NO WAY, NO WAY...
RRK
...
FINE. GET OUTTA THE WAY.
GASP ...

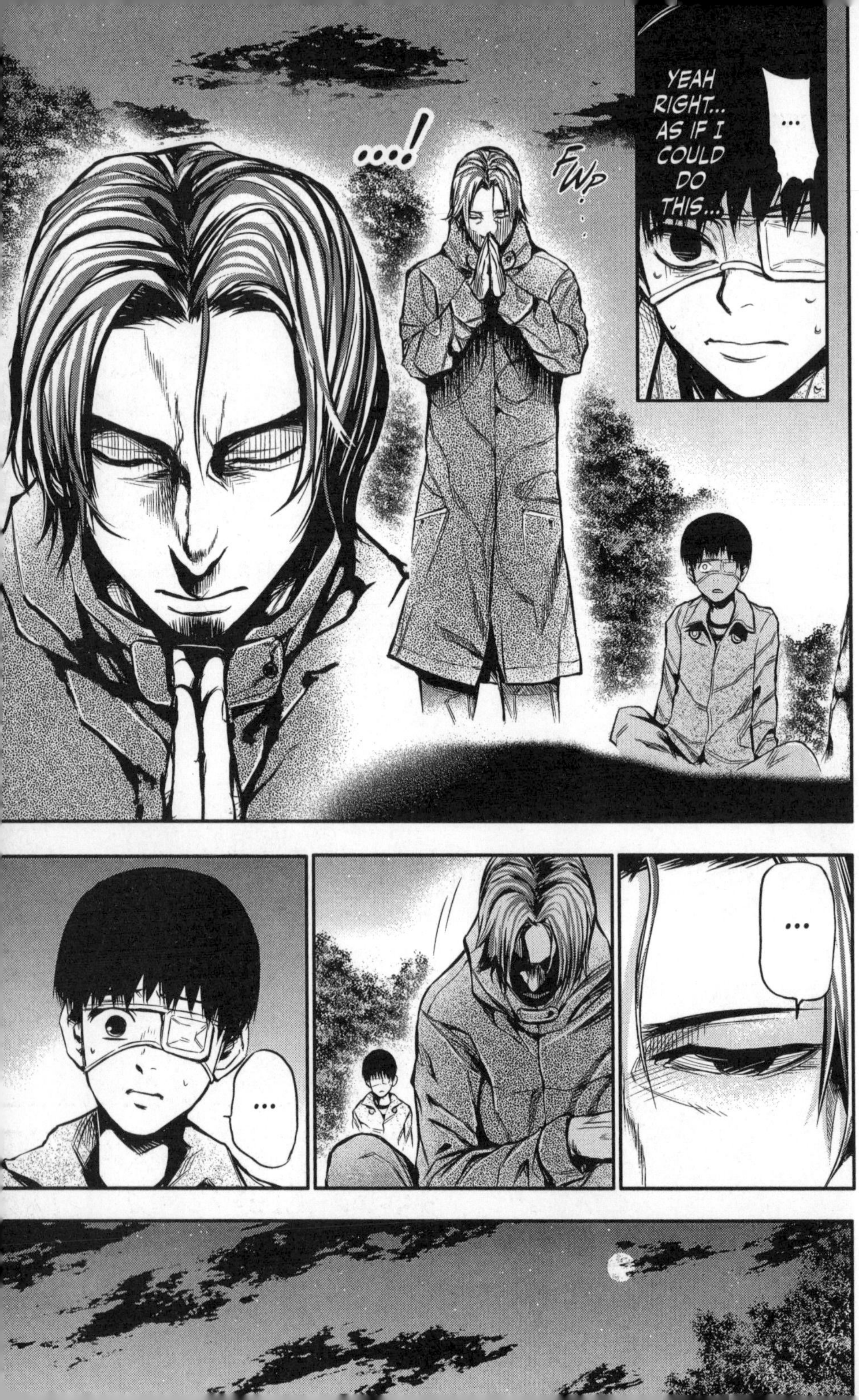
...
YEAH RIGHT... AS IF I COULD DO THIS...
FWP
...!
...
...

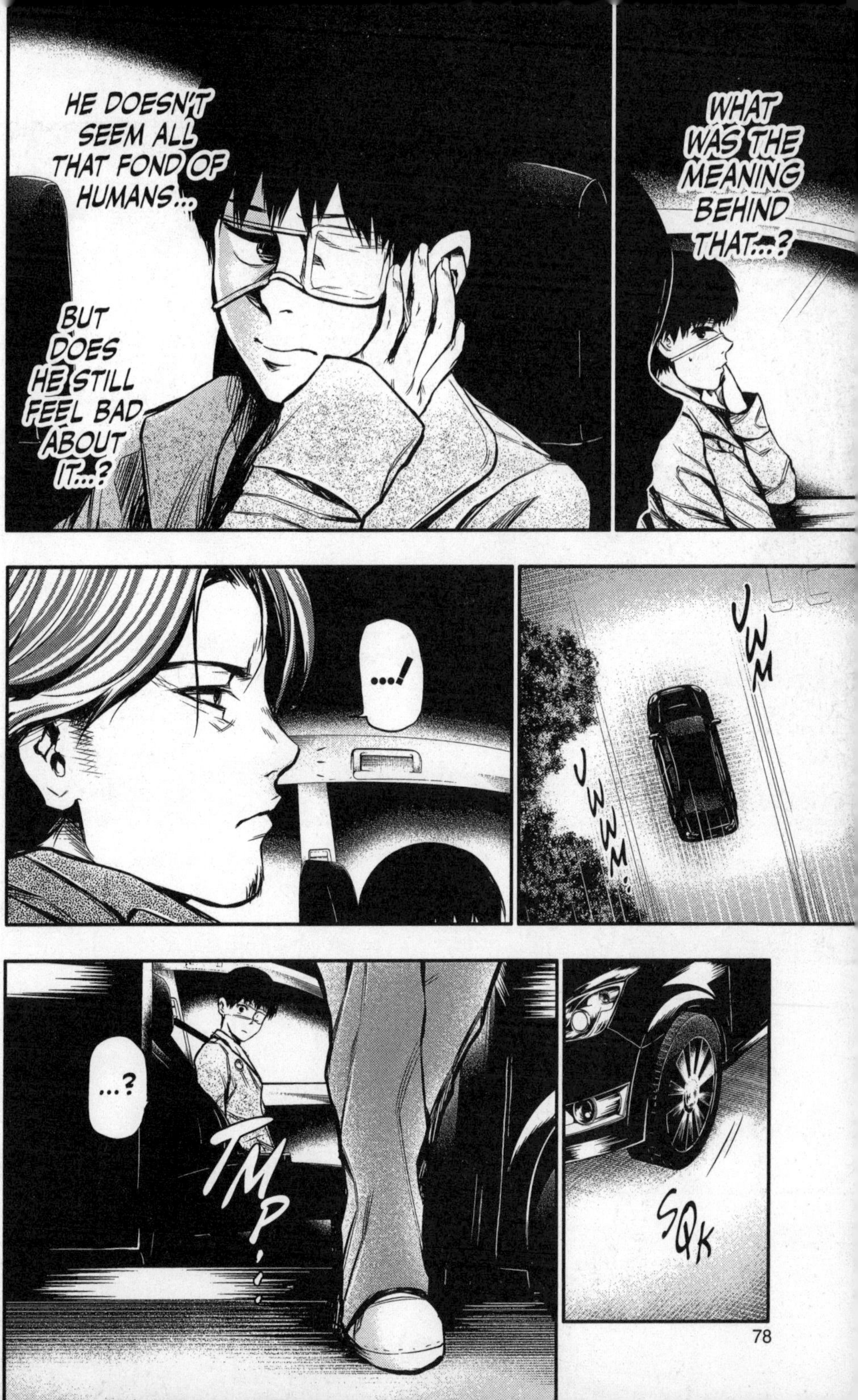
WHAT WAS THE MEANING BEHIND THAT...?
HE DOESN'T SEEM ALL THAT FOND OF HUMANS...
BUT DOES HE STILL FEEL BAD ABOUT IT...?
JWWM
JWWWM
...!
SQK
...?
TMP

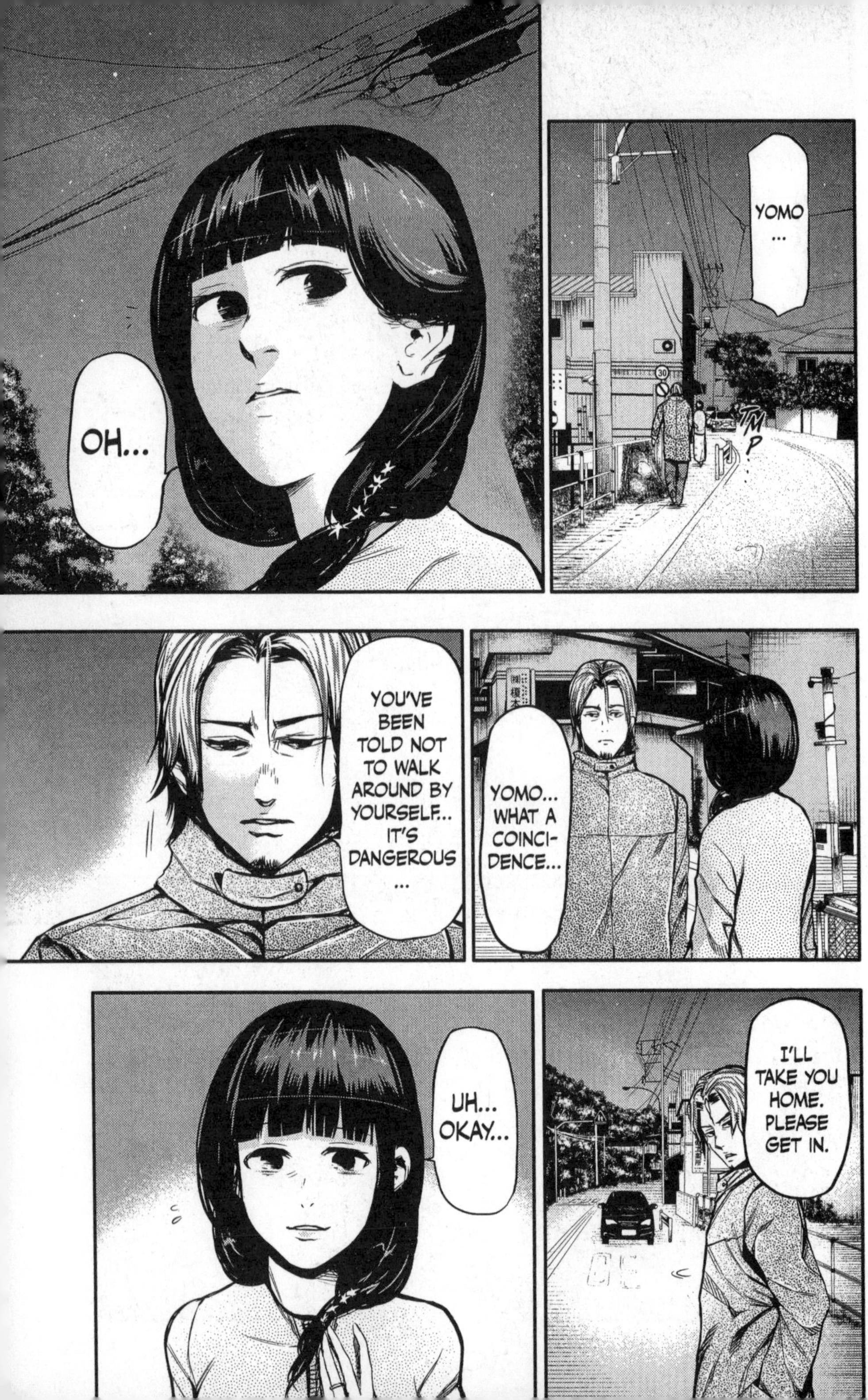
YOMO ...
TMP
OH...
YOMO... WHAT A COINCIDENCE...
YOU'VE BEEN TOLD NOT TO WALK AROUND BY YOURSELF... IT'S DANGEROUS ...
I'LL TAKE YOU HOME. PLEASE GET IN.
UH... OKAY...

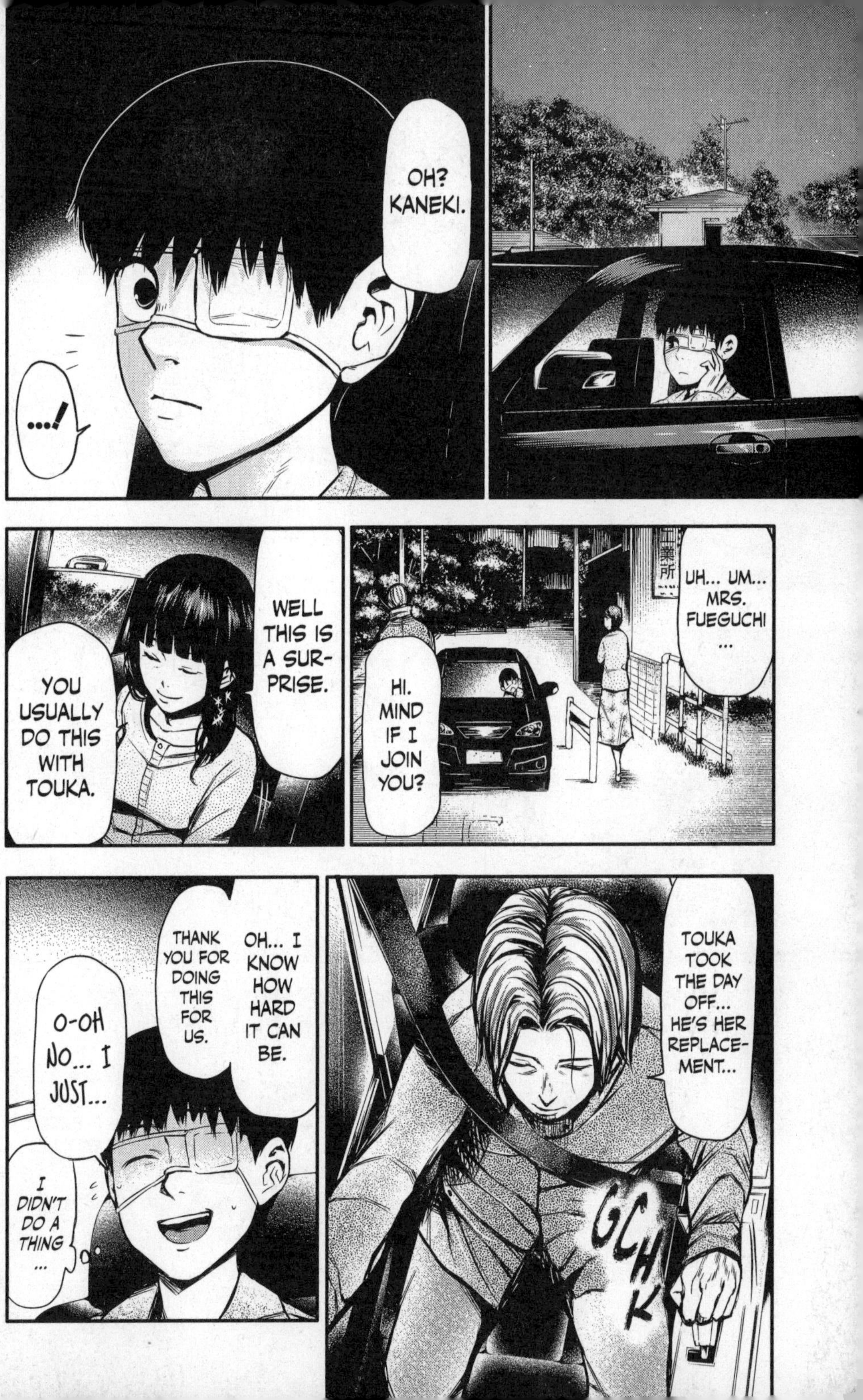
OH? KANEKI.
...!
UH... UM... MRS. FUEGUCHI ...
HI. MIND IF I JOIN YOU?
WELL THIS IS A SUR-PRISE.
YOU USUALLY DO THIS WITH TOUKA.
TOUKA TOOK THE DAY OFF... HE'S HER REPLACE-MENT...
GCHK
OH... I KNOW HOW HARD IT CAN BE.
THANK YOU FOR DOING THIS FOR US.
O-OH NO... I JUST...
I DIDN'T DO A THING ...

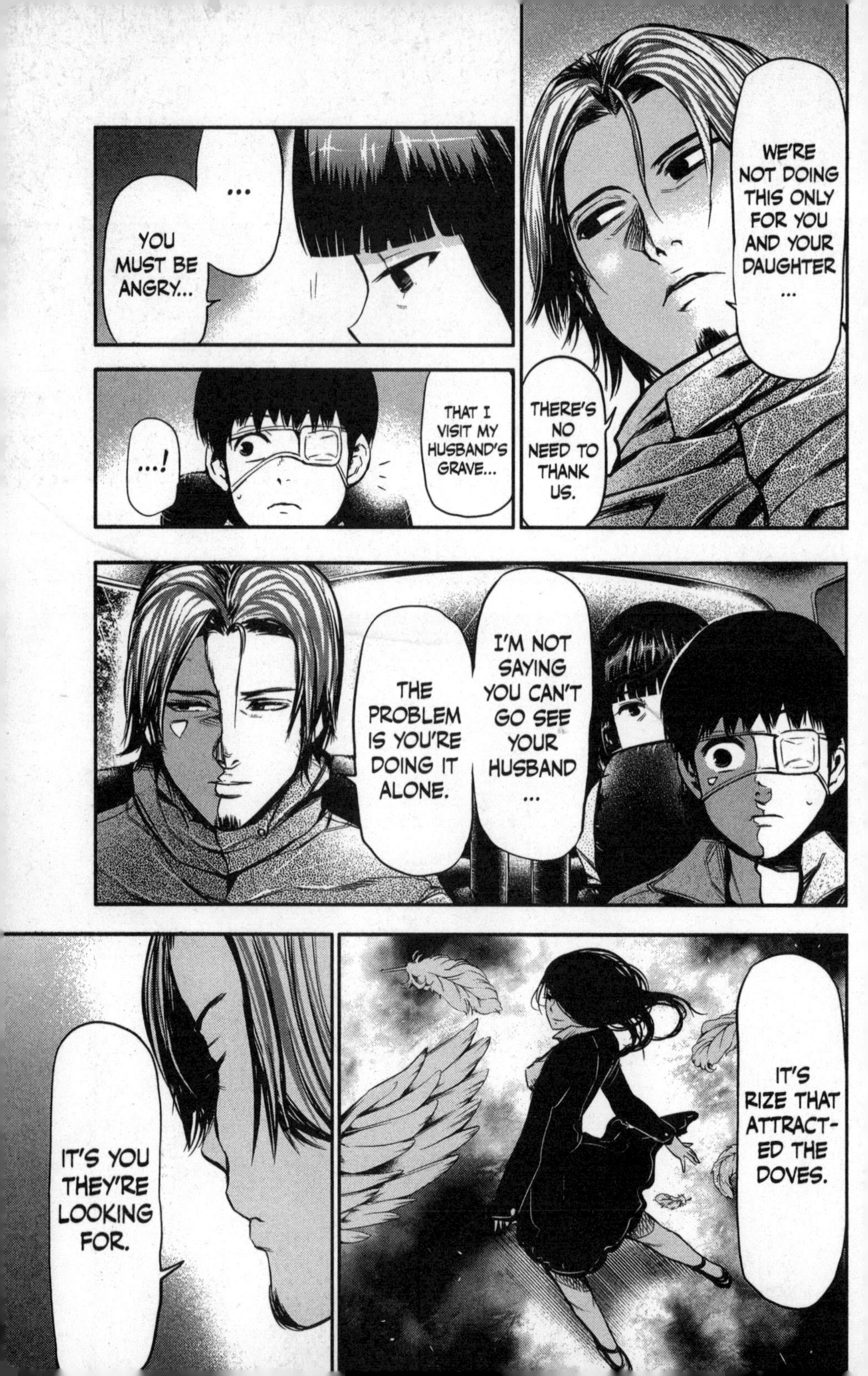
WE'RE NOT DOING THIS ONLY FOR YOU AND YOUR DAUGHTER ...
THERE'S NO NEED TO THANK US.
... YOU MUST BE ANGRY...
THAT I VISIT MY HUSBAND'S GRAVE...
...!
I'M NOT SAYING YOU CAN'T GO SEE YOUR HUSBAND ...
THE PROBLEM IS YOU'RE DOING IT ALONE.
IT'S RIZE THAT ATTRACT-ED THE DOVES.
IT'S YOU THEY'RE LOOKING FOR.

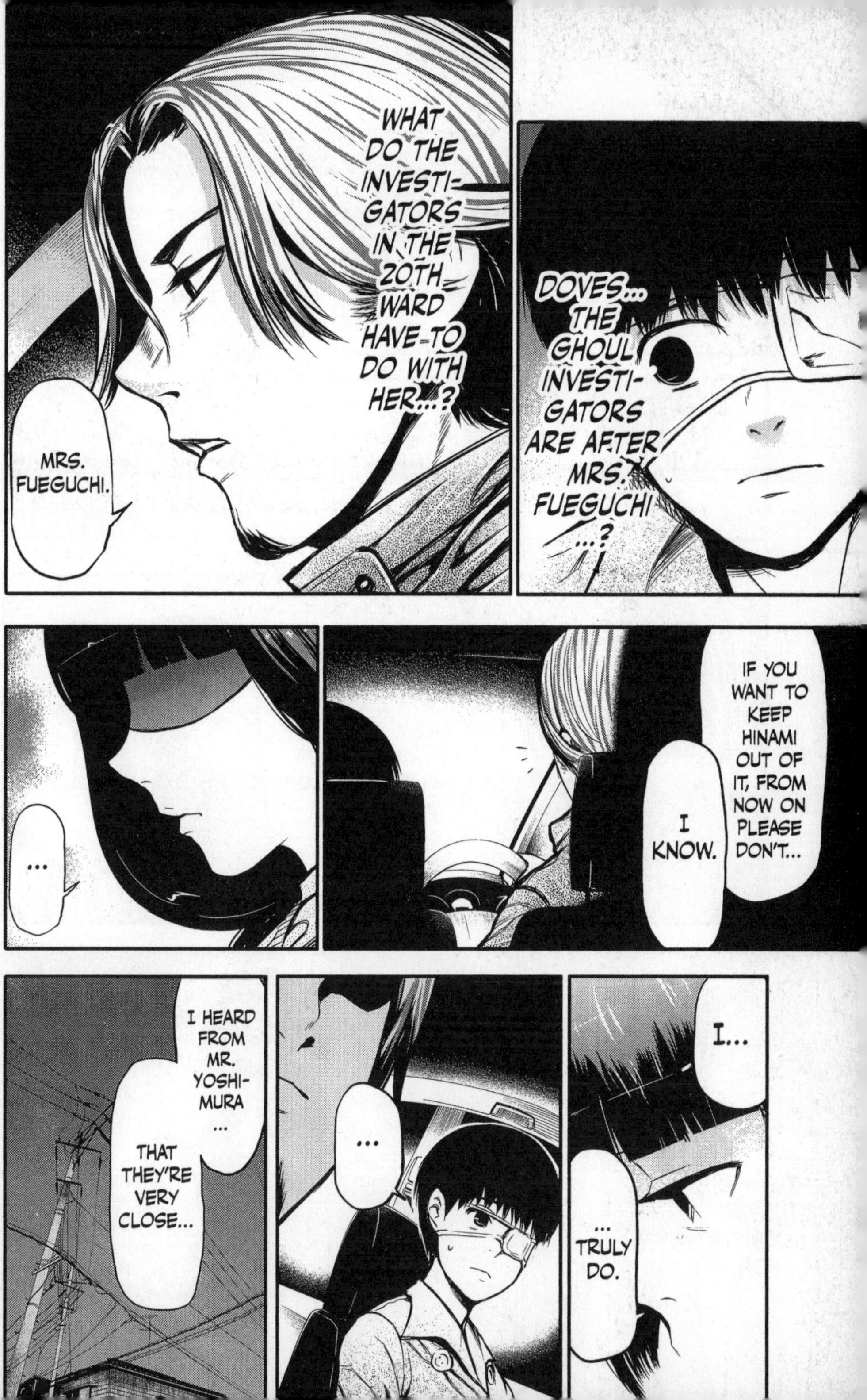
DOVES... THE GHOUL INVESTIGATORS ARE AFTER MRS. FUEGUCHI ...?
WHAT DO THE INVESTIGATORS IN THE 20TH WARD HAVE TO DO WITH HER...?
MRS. FUEGUCHI.
IF YOU WANT TO KEEP HINAMI OUT OF IT, FROM NOW ON PLEASE DON'T...
I KNOW.
...
I...
... TRULY DO.
...
I HEARD FROM MR. YOSHIMURA ...
THAT THEY'RE VERY CLOSE...

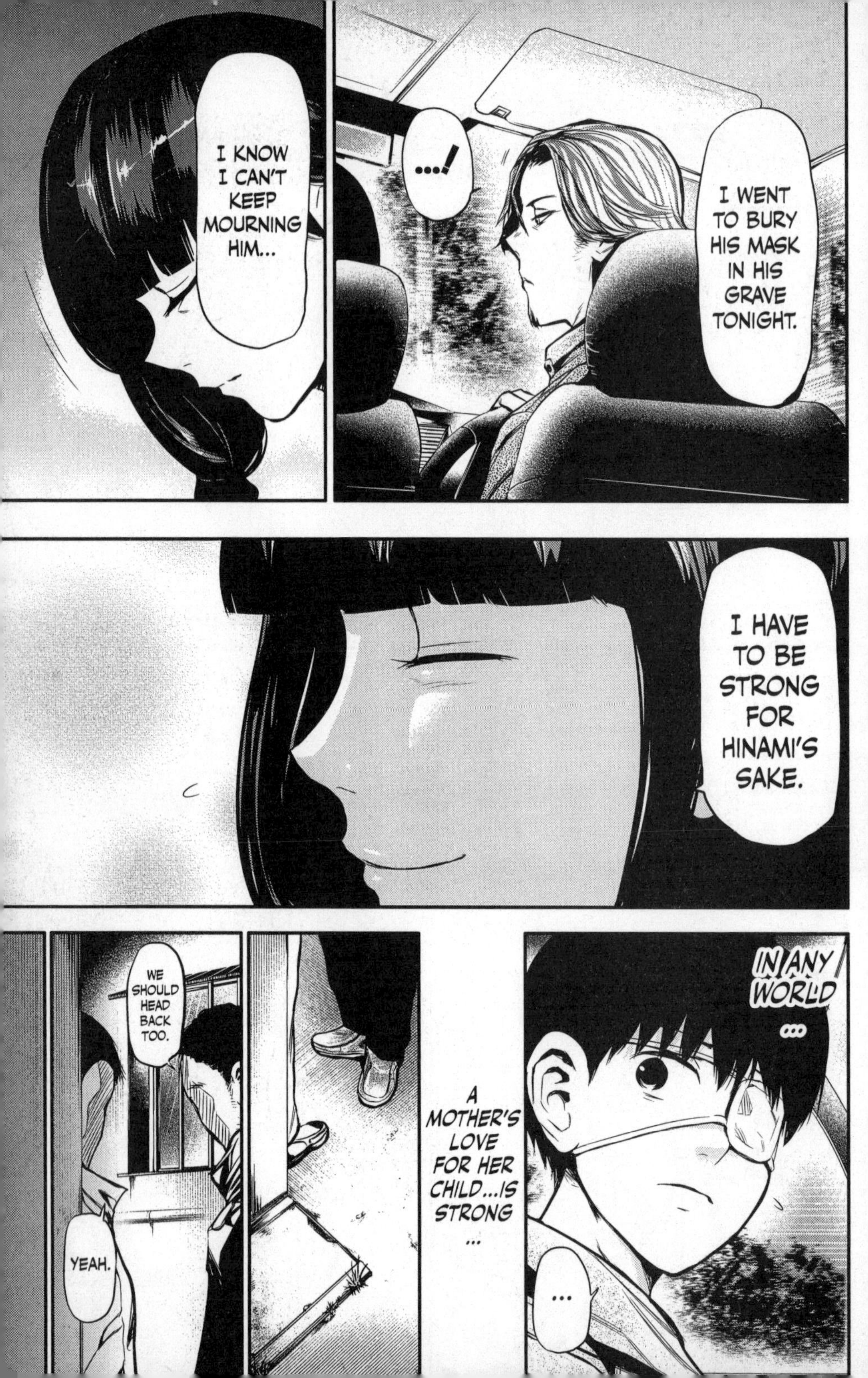
I WENT TO BURY HIS MASK IN HIS GRAVE TONIGHT.
...!
I KNOW I CAN'T KEEP MOURNING HIM...
I HAVE TO BE STRONG FOR HINAMI'S SAKE.
IN ANY WORLD...
A MOTHER'S LOVE FOR HER CHILD...IS STRONG...
...
WE SHOULD HEAD BACK TOO.
YEAH.

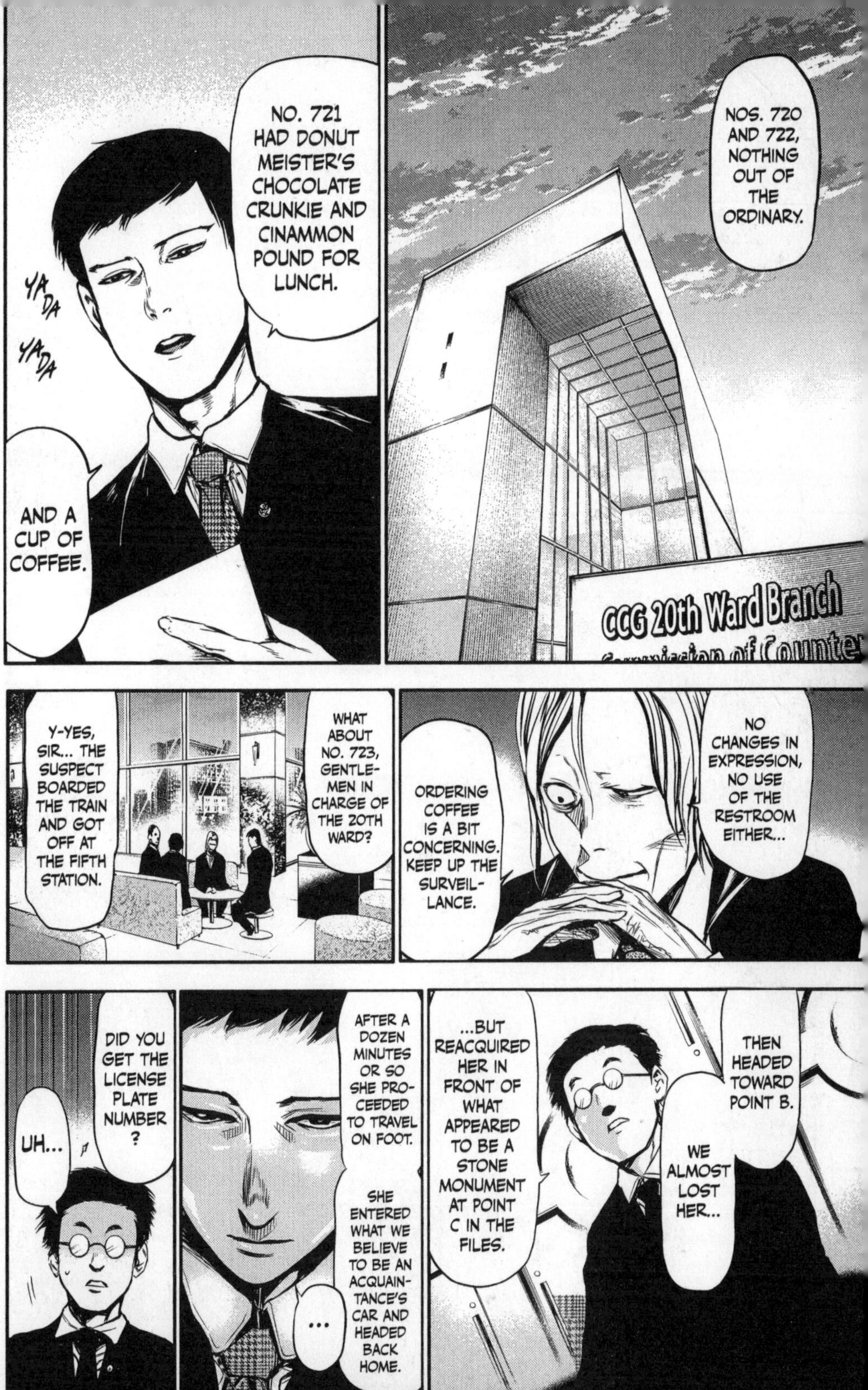
NOS. 720 AND 722, NOTHING OUT OF THE ORDINARY.
CCG 20th Ward Branch
NO. 721 HAD DONUT MEISTER'S CHOCOLATE CRUNKIE AND CINAMMON POUND FOR LUNCH.
YADA YADA
AND A CUP OF COFFEE.
NO CHANGES IN EXPRESSION, NO USE OF THE RESTROOM EITHER...
ORDERING COFFEE IS A BIT CONCERNING. KEEP UP THE SURVEIL-LANCE.
WHAT ABOUT NO. 723, GENTLE-MEN IN CHARGE OF THE 20TH WARD?
Y-YES, SIR... THE SUSPECT BOARDED THE TRAIN AND GOT OFF AT THE FIFTH STATION.
THEN HEADED TOWARD POINT B.
WE ALMOST LOST HER...
...BUT REACQUIRED HER IN FRONT OF WHAT APPEARED TO BE A STONE MONUMENT AT POINT C IN THE FILES.
AFTER A DOZEN MINUTES OR SO SHE PRO-CEEDED TO TRAVEL ON FOOT.
SHE ENTERED WHAT WE BELIEVE TO BE AN ACQUAIN-TANCE'S CAR AND HEADED BACK HOME.
...
DID YOU GET THE LICENSE PLATE NUMBER?
UH...

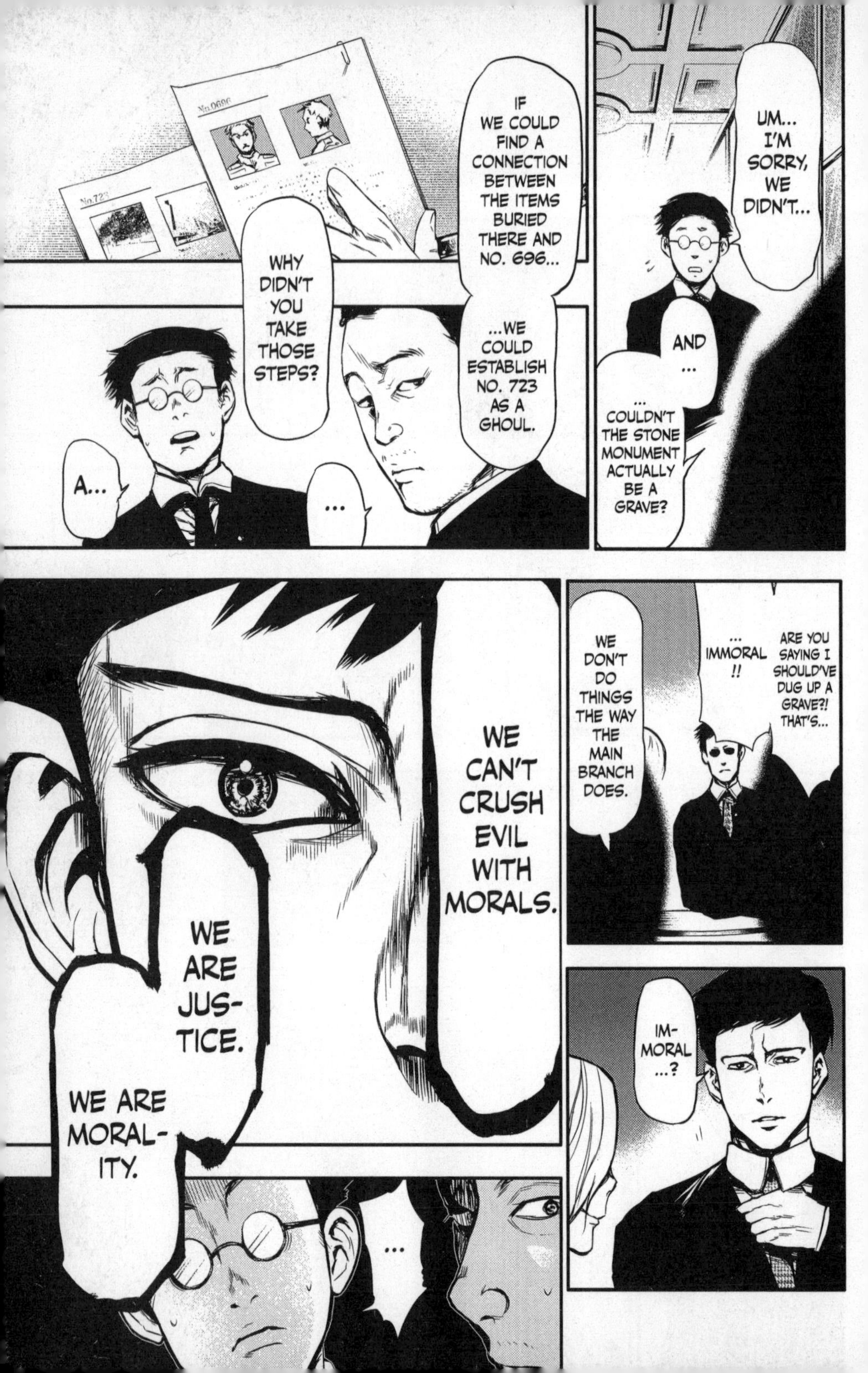

UM... I'M SORRY, WE DIDN'T...
AND...
...COULDN'T THE STONE MONUMENT ACTUALLY BE A GRAVE?
IF WE COULD FIND A CONNECTION BETWEEN THE ITEMS BURIED THERE AND NO. 696...
...WE COULD ESTABLISH NO. 723 AS A GHOUL.
WHY DIDN'T YOU TAKE THOSE STEPS?
...
A...
ARE YOU SAYING I SHOULD'VE DUG UP A GRAVE?! THAT'S...
...IMMORAL!!
WE DON'T DO THINGS THE WAY THE MAIN BRANCH DOES.
IM-MORAL...?
WE CAN'T CRUSH EVIL WITH MORALS.
WE ARE JUS-TICE.
WE ARE MORAL-ITY.
...

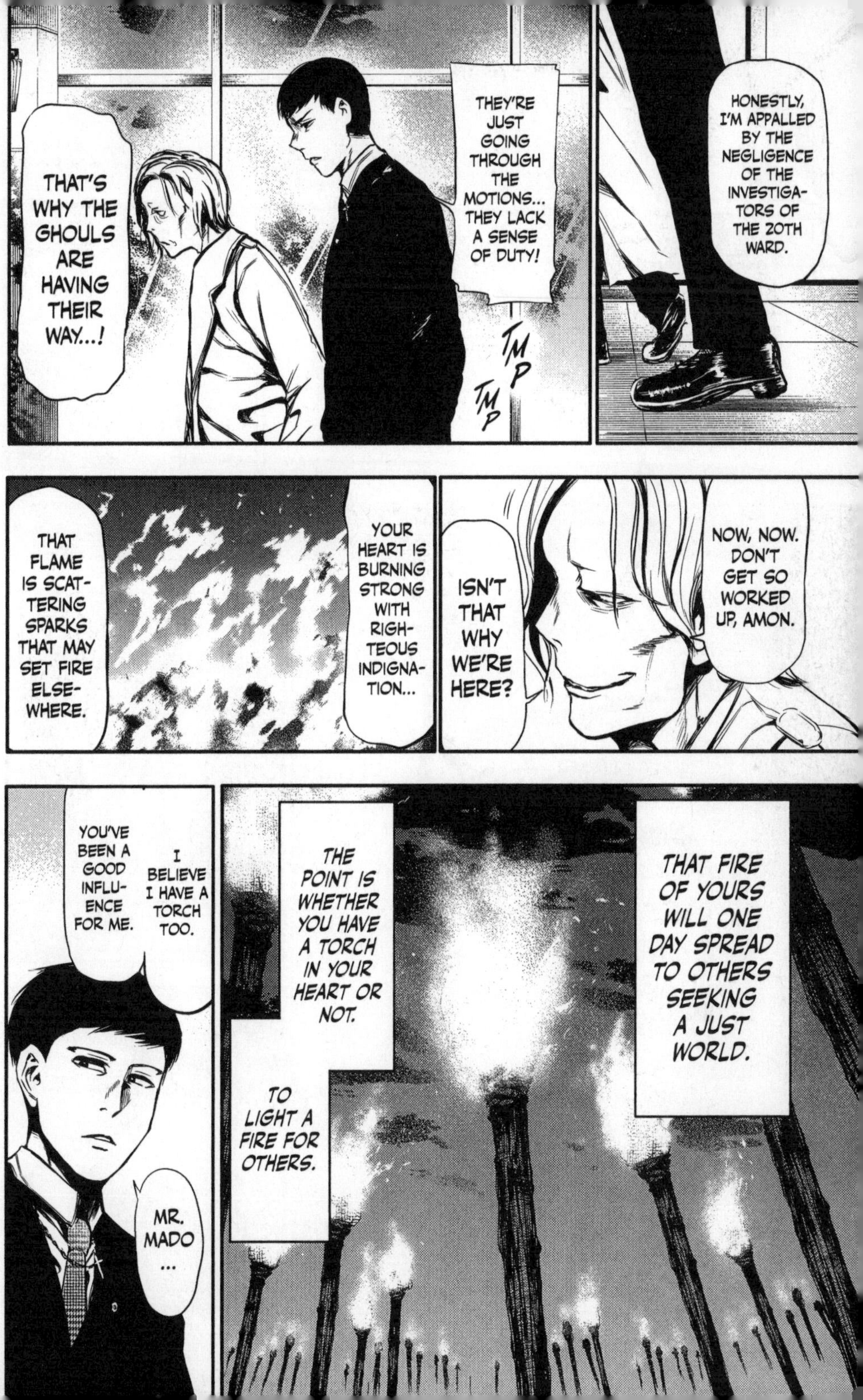
HONESTLY, I'M APPALLED BY THE NEGLIGENCE OF THE INVESTIGATORS OF THE 20TH WARD.
THEY'RE JUST GOING THROUGH THE MOTIONS... THEY LACK A SENSE OF DUTY!
TMP TMP
THAT'S WHY THE GHOULS ARE HAVING THEIR WAY...!
NOW, NOW. DON'T GET SO WORKED UP, AMON.
ISN'T THAT WHY WE'RE HERE?
YOUR HEART IS BURNING STRONG WITH RIGHTEOUS INDIGNATION...
THAT FLAME IS SCATTERING SPARKS THAT MAY SET FIRE ELSEWHERE.
THAT FIRE OF YOURS WILL ONE DAY SPREAD TO OTHERS SEEKING A JUST WORLD.
THE POINT IS WHETHER YOU HAVE A TORCH IN YOUR HEART OR NOT.
TO LIGHT A FIRE FOR OTHERS.
I BELIEVE I HAVE A TORCH TOO.
YOU'VE BEEN A GOOD INFLUENCE FOR ME.
MR. MADO ...

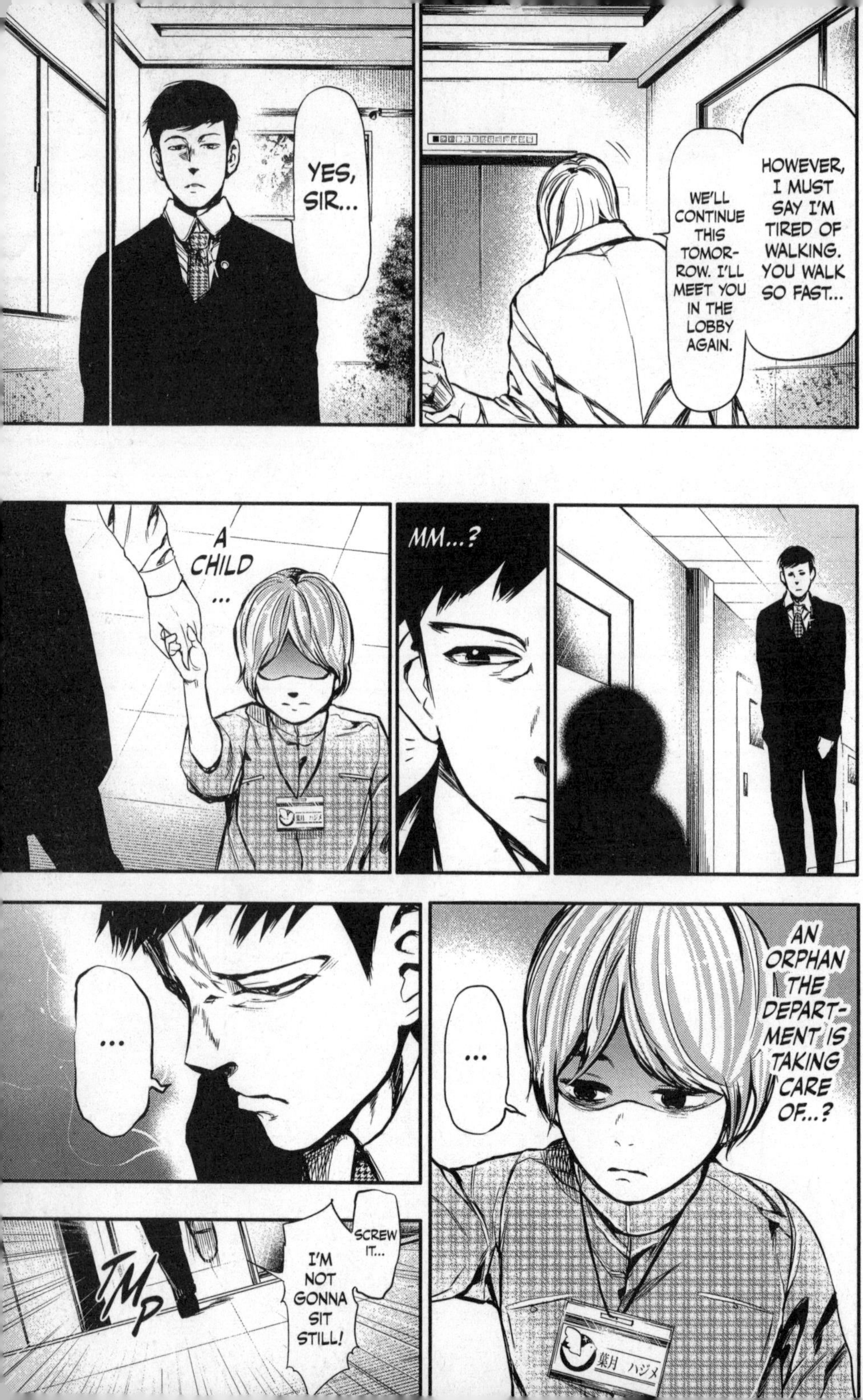
HOWEVER, I MUST SAY I'M TIRED OF WALKING. YOU WALK SO FAST...
WE'LL CONTINUE THIS TOMORROW. I'LL MEET YOU IN THE LOBBY AGAIN.
YES, SIR...
MM...?
A CHILD ...
AN ORPHAN THE DEPARTMENT IS TAKING CARE OF...?
...
巣月 ハジメ
...
SCREW IT...
I'M NOT GONNA SIT STILL!
TMP

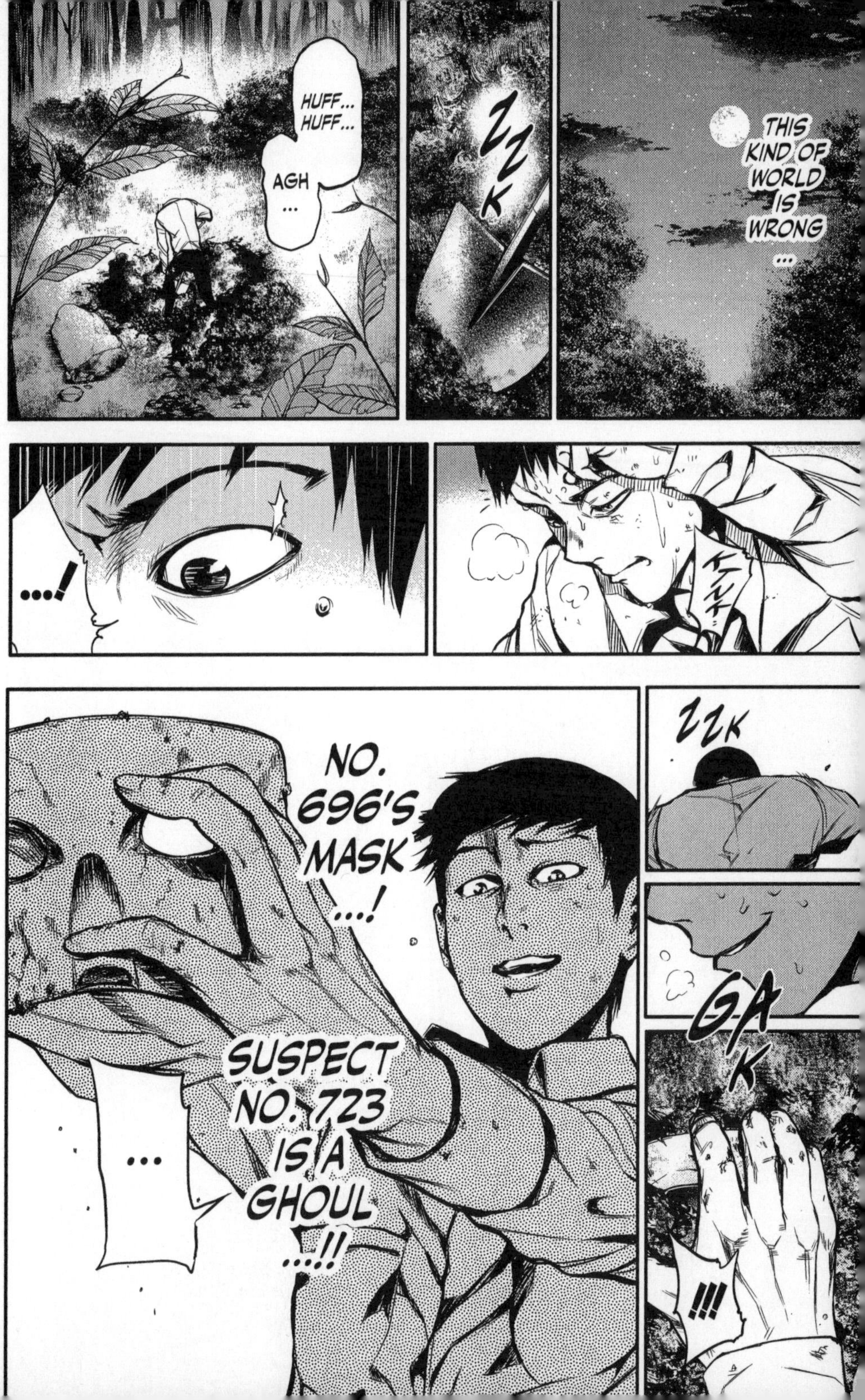
THIS KIND OF WORLD IS WRONG ...
ZZZK
HUFF... HUFF...
AGH ...
...!
ZZK
GAK
!!!
NO. 696'S MASK ...!
SUSPECT NO. 723 IS A GHOUL ...!!
...

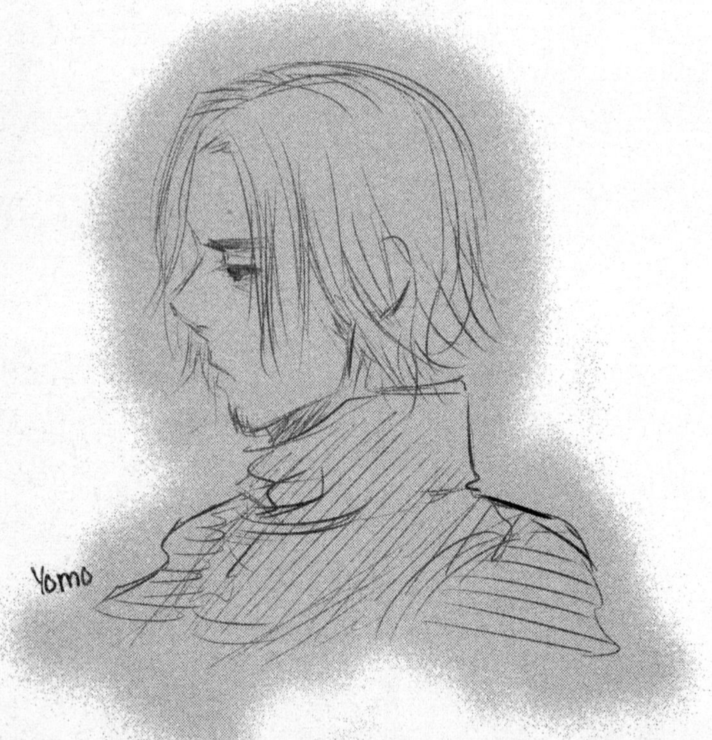
Yomo

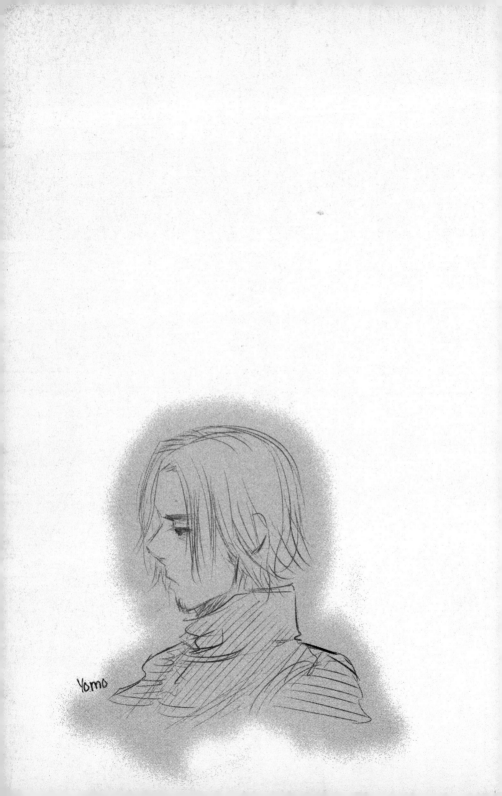

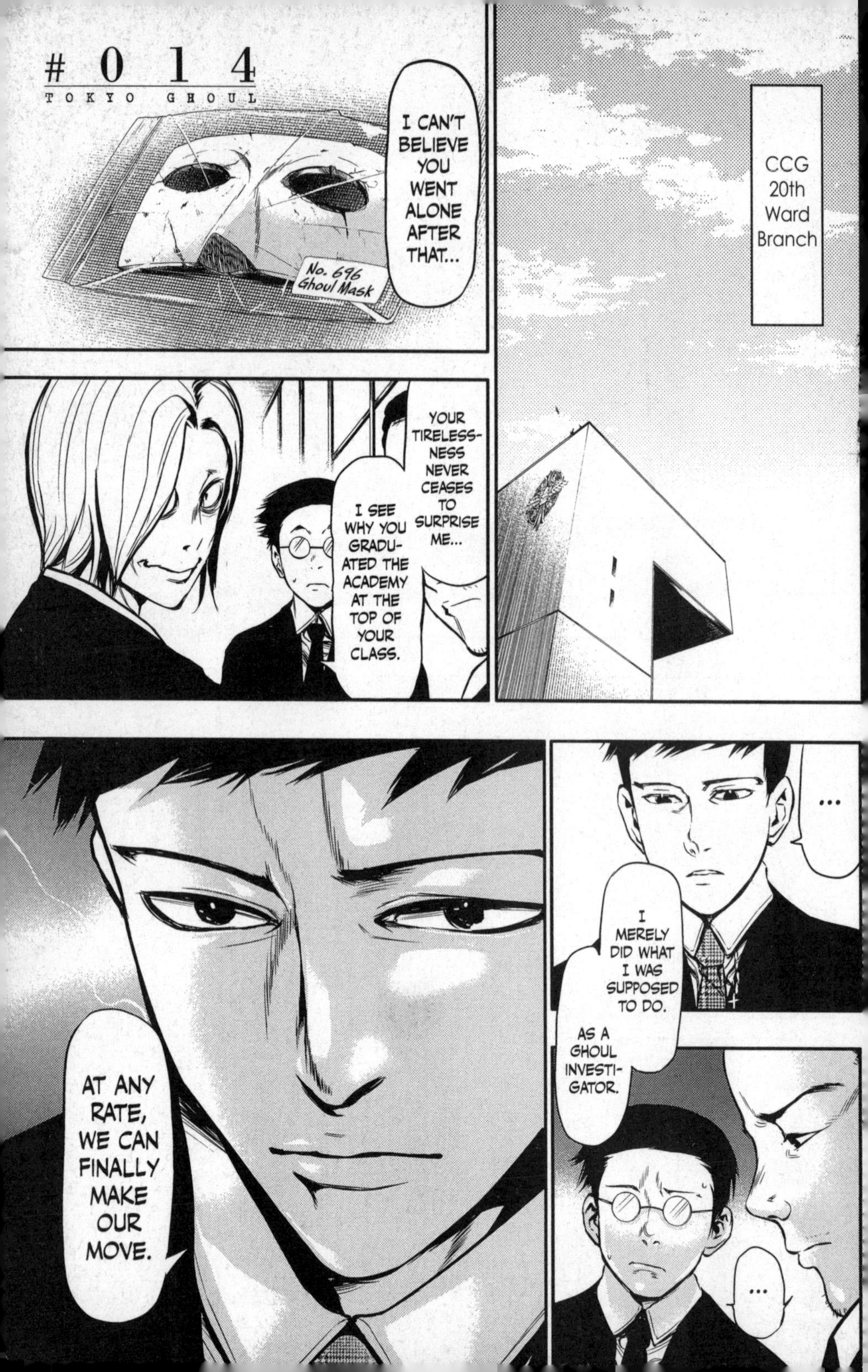
CCG 20th Ward Branch
#014
TOKYO GHOUL
I CAN'T BELIEVE YOU WENT ALONE AFTER THAT...
No. 696 Ghoul Mask
YOUR TIRELESSNESS NEVER CEASES TO SURPRISE ME...
I SEE WHY YOU GRADUATED THE ACADEMY AT THE TOP OF YOUR CLASS.
...
I MERELY DID WHAT I WAS SUPPOSED TO DO.
AS A GHOUL INVESTIGATOR.
...
AT ANY RATE, WE CAN FINALLY MAKE OUR MOVE.

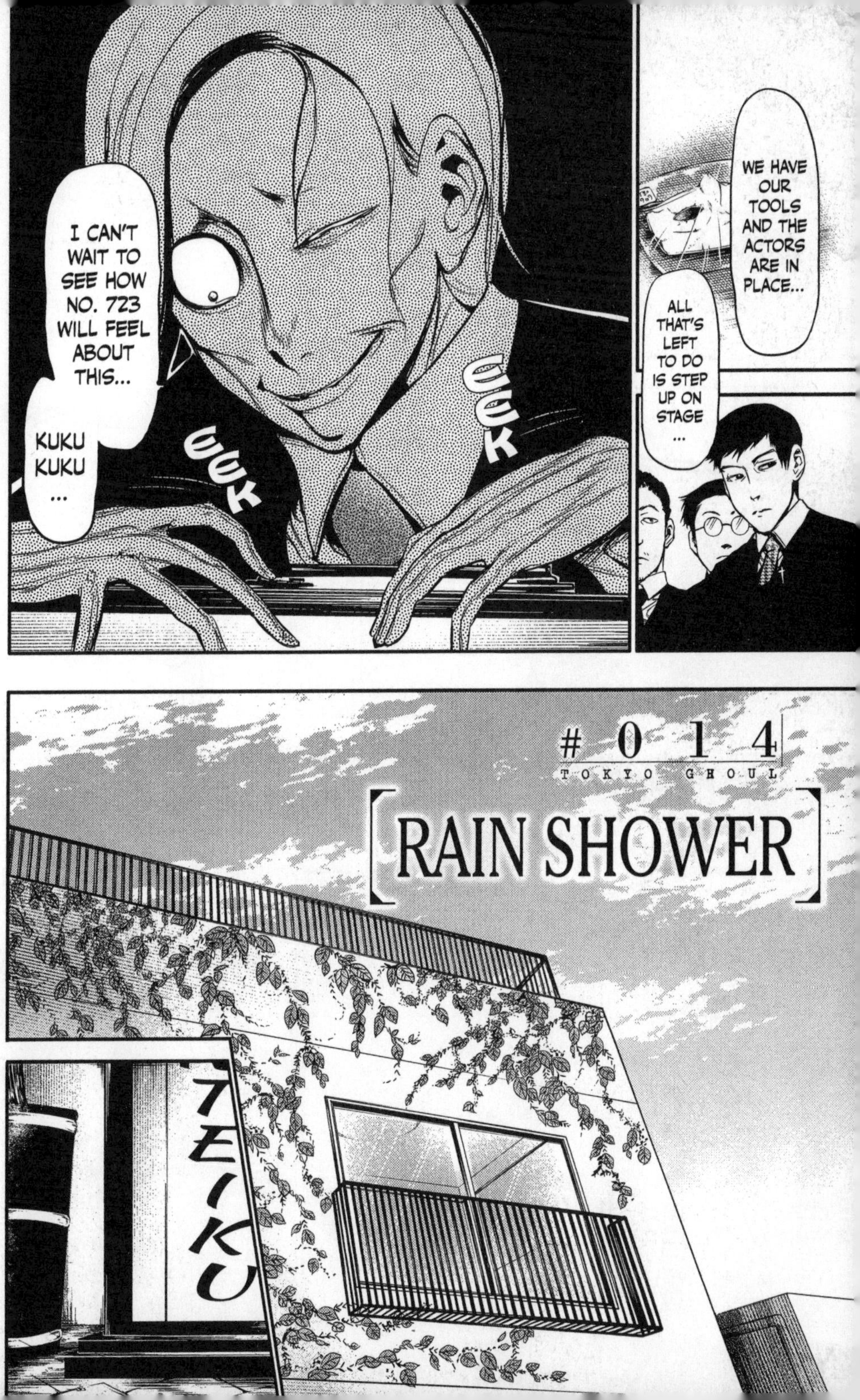
WE HAVE OUR TOOLS AND THE ACTORS ARE IN PLACE...
ALL THAT'S LEFT TO DO IS STEP UP ON STAGE ...
I CAN'T WAIT TO SEE HOW NO. 723 WILL FEEL ABOUT THIS...
KUKU KUKU ...
EEK
EEK
#014
TOKYO GHOUL
[RAIN SHOWER]
TEIKU

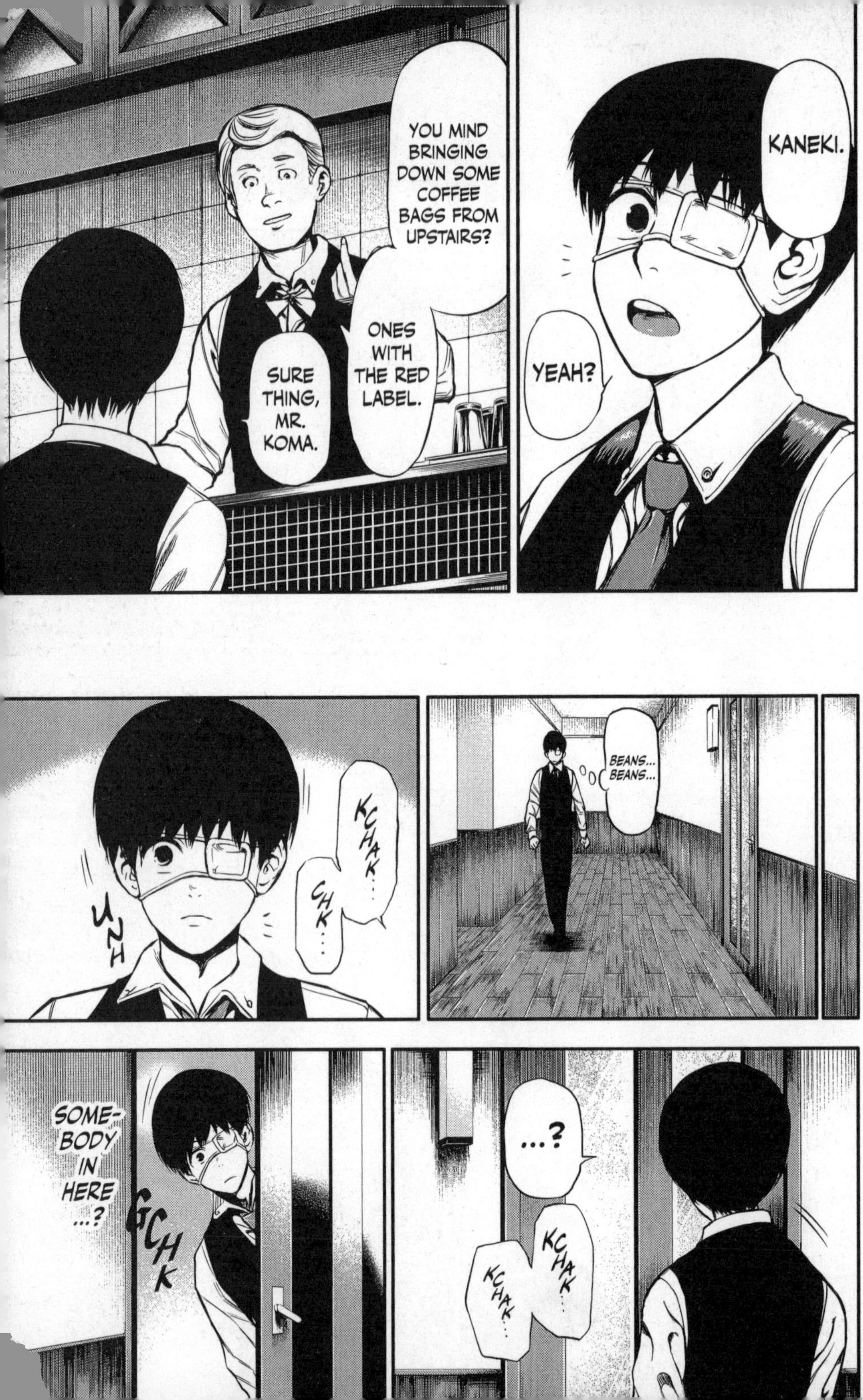
KANEKI.
YEAH?
YOU MIND BRINGING DOWN SOME COFFEE BAGS FROM UPSTAIRS?
ONES WITH THE RED LABEL.
SURE THING, MR. KOMA.
BEANS... BEANS...
KCHAK...
CHK...
UNH
...?
KCHAK...
KCHAK...
SOME-BODY IN HERE ...?
GCHK

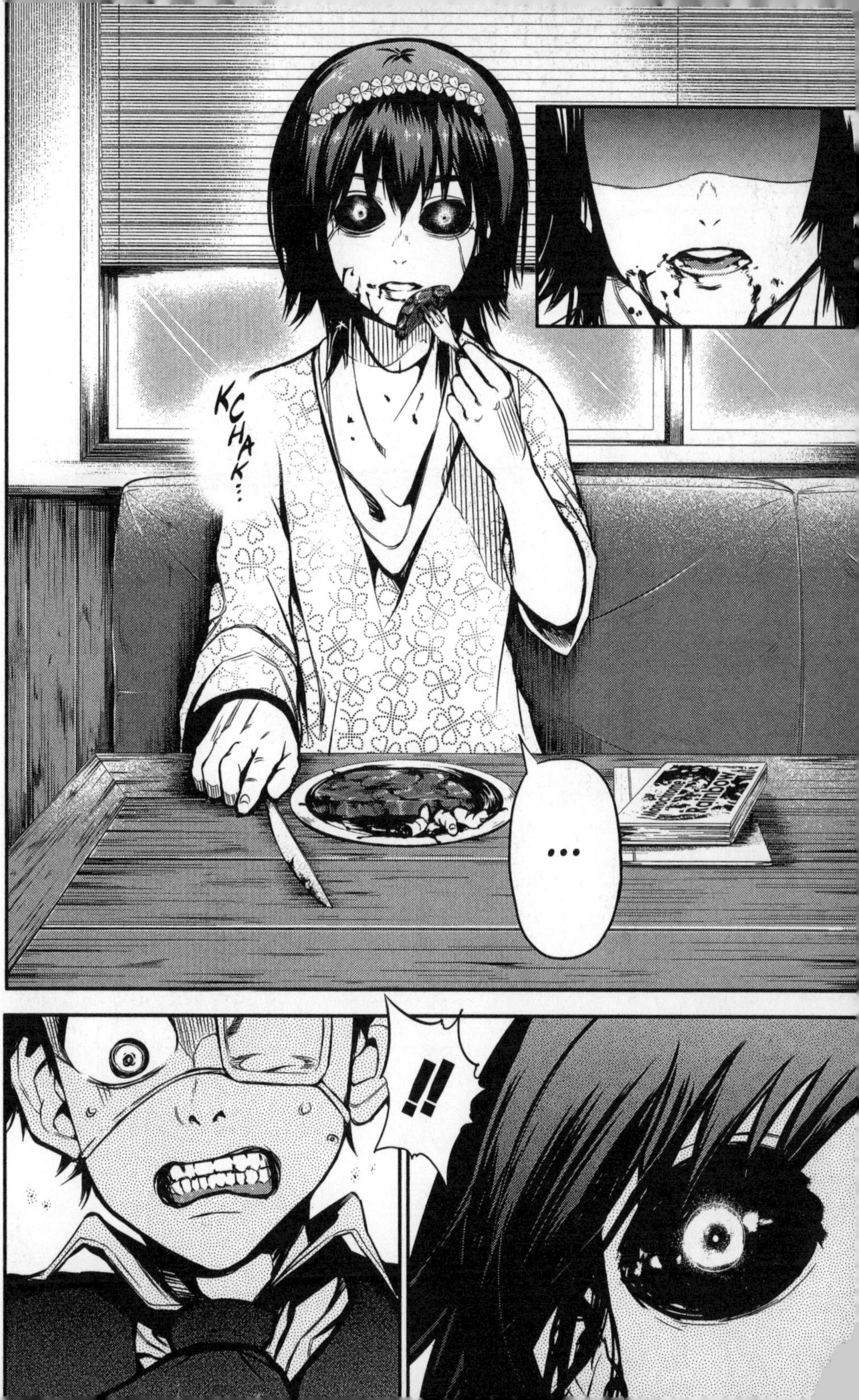
KCHAK...
...
!!

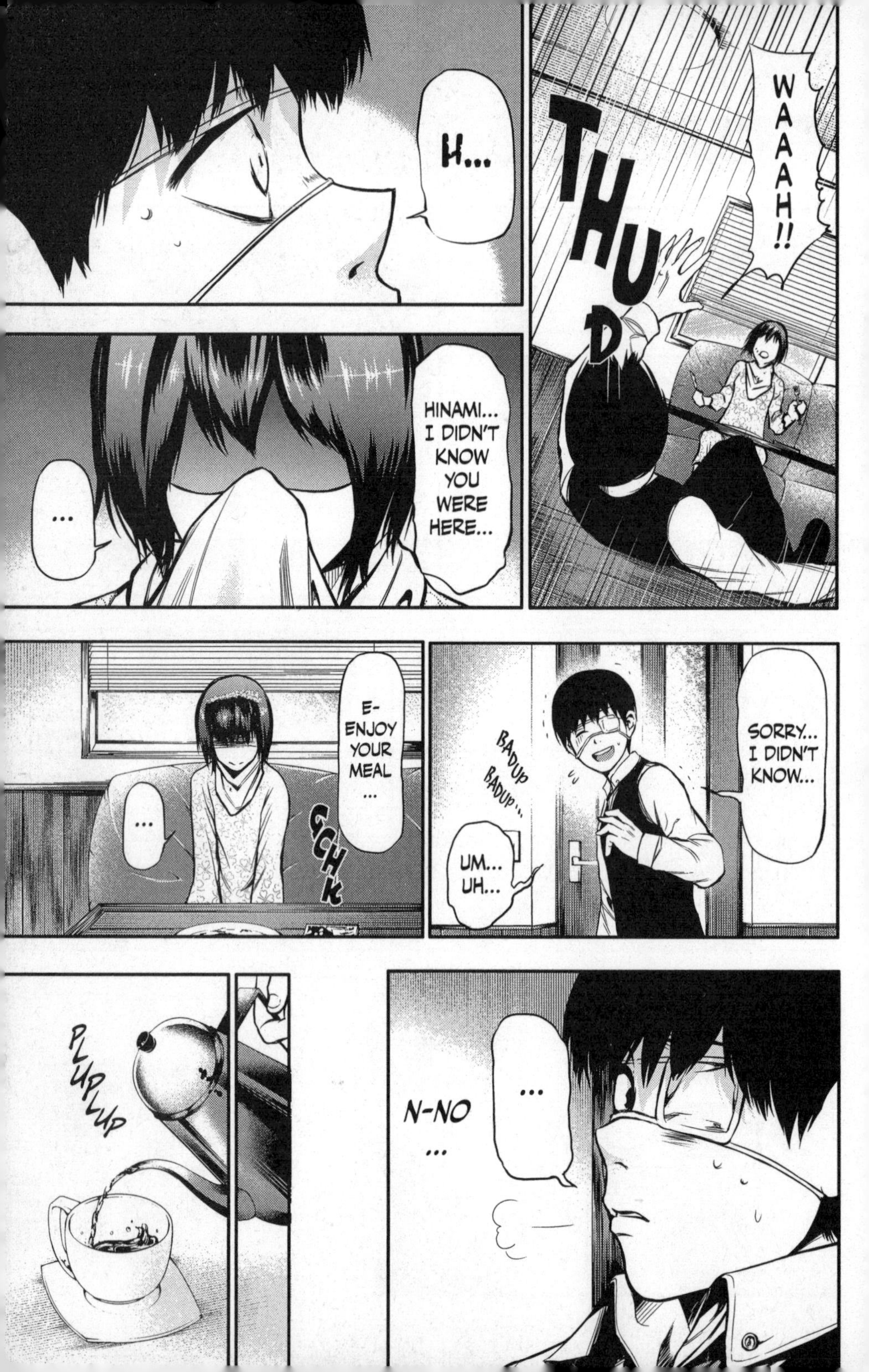
WAAAAH!!
THUD
H...
HINAMI... I DIDN'T KNOW YOU WERE HERE...
...
SORRY... I DIDN'T KNOW...
BADUP BADUP...
UM... UH...
E- ENJOY YOUR MEAL ...
GCHK
...
...
N-NO ...
PLUPLUP

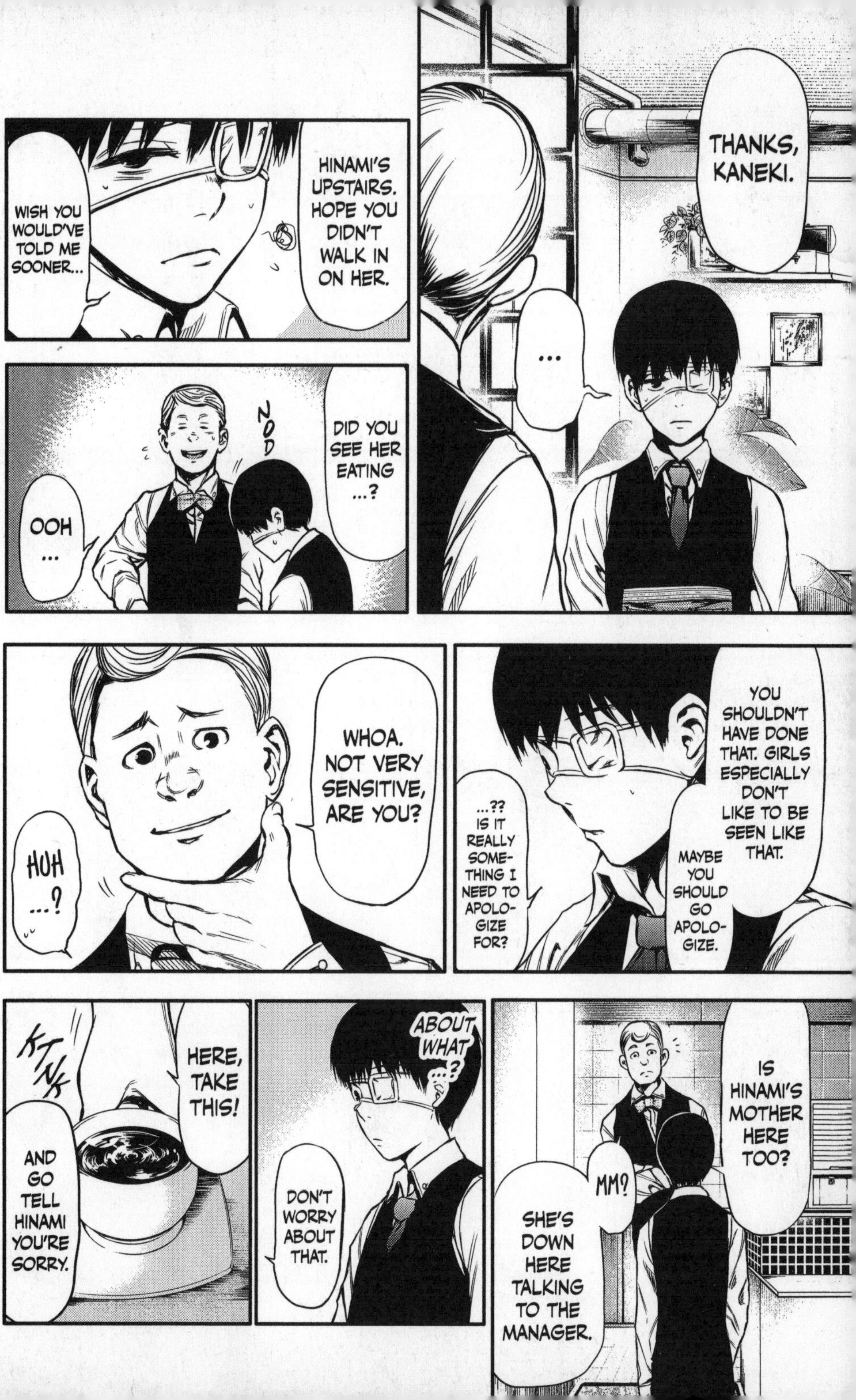
THANKS, KANEKI.
...
HINAMI'S UPSTAIRS. HOPE YOU DIDN'T WALK IN ON HER.
WISH YOU WOULD'VE TOLD ME SOONER...
DID YOU SEE HER EATING ...?
NOD
OOH ...
YOU SHOULDN'T HAVE DONE THAT. GIRLS ESPECIALLY DON'T LIKE TO BE SEEN LIKE THAT.
MAYBE YOU SHOULD GO APOLOGIZE.
...?? IS IT REALLY SOMETHING I NEED TO APOLOGIZE FOR?
WHOA. NOT VERY SENSITIVE, ARE YOU?
HUH ...?
IS HINAMI'S MOTHER HERE TOO?
MM?
SHE'S DOWN HERE TALKING TO THE MANAGER.
ABOUT WHAT ...?
DON'T WORRY ABOUT THAT.
KTINK
HERE, TAKE THIS!
AND GO TELL HINAMI YOU'RE SORRY.

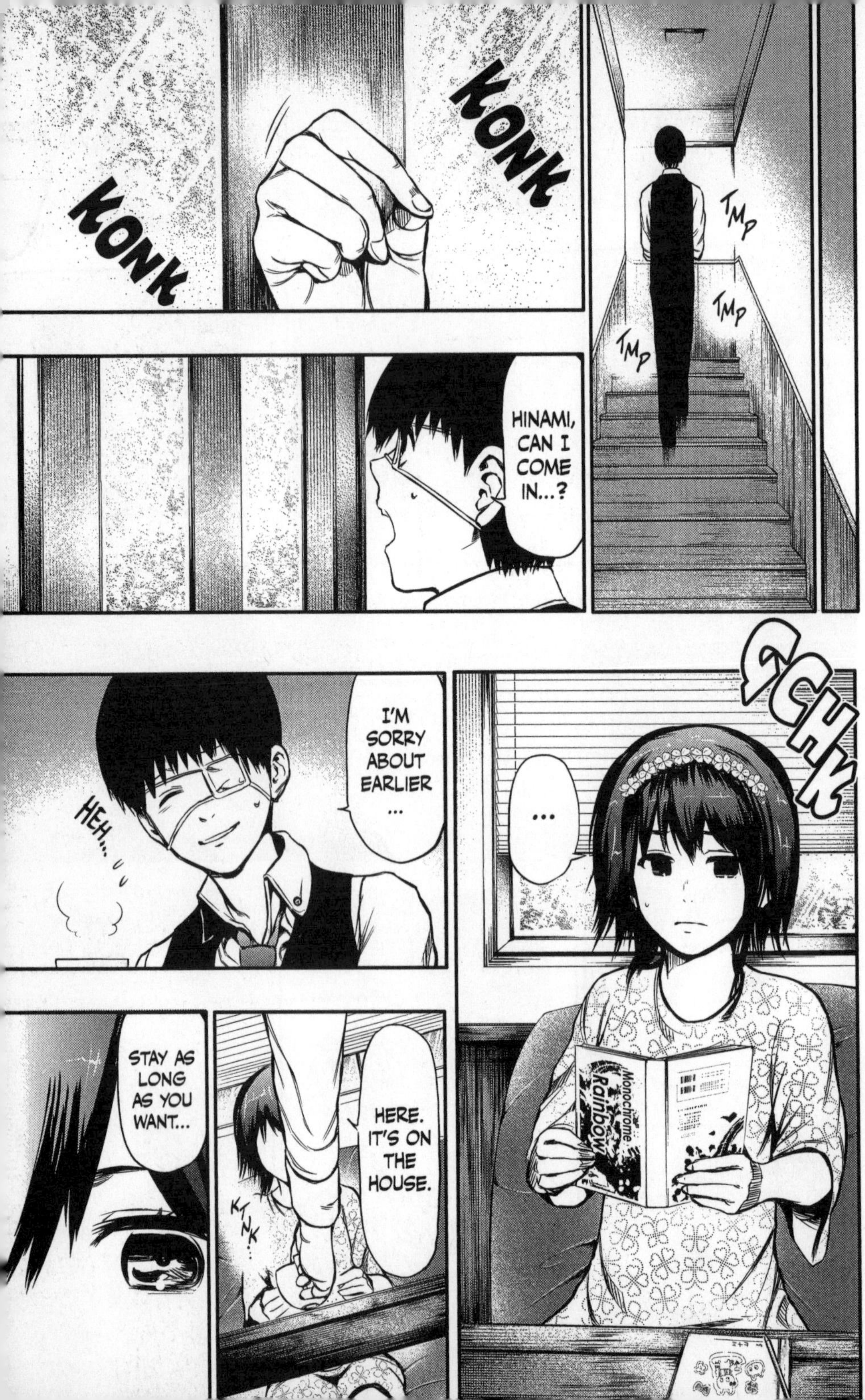
TMP
TMP
TMP
KONK
KONK
HINAMI, CAN I COME IN...?
GCHK
...
Monochrome Rainbow
I'M SORRY ABOUT EARLIER ...
HEH...
HERE. IT'S ON THE HOUSE.
KTINK...
STAY AS LONG AS YOU WANT...

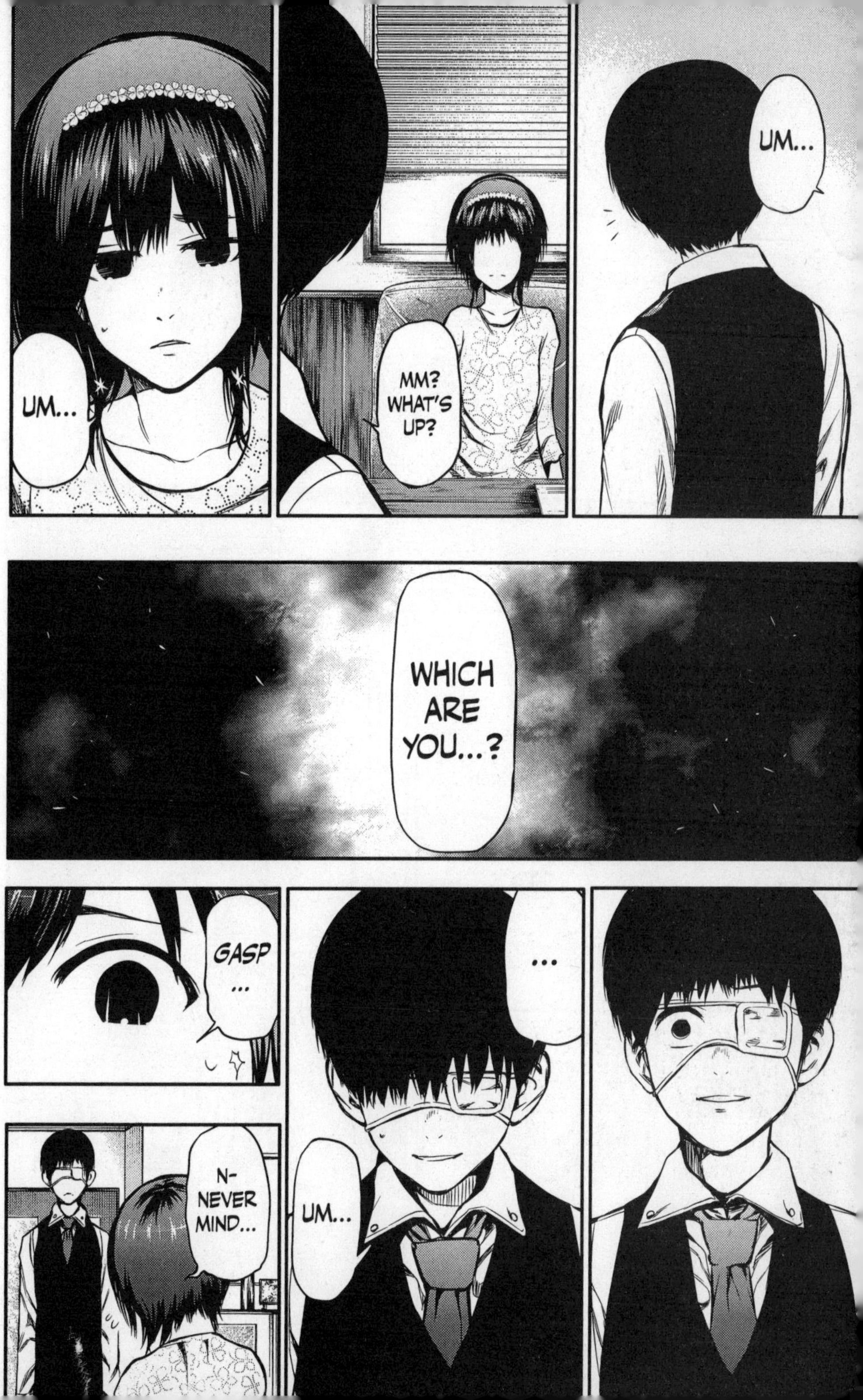
UM...
MM? WHAT'S UP?
UM...
WHICH ARE YOU...?
...
UM...
GASP ...
N- NEVER MIND...

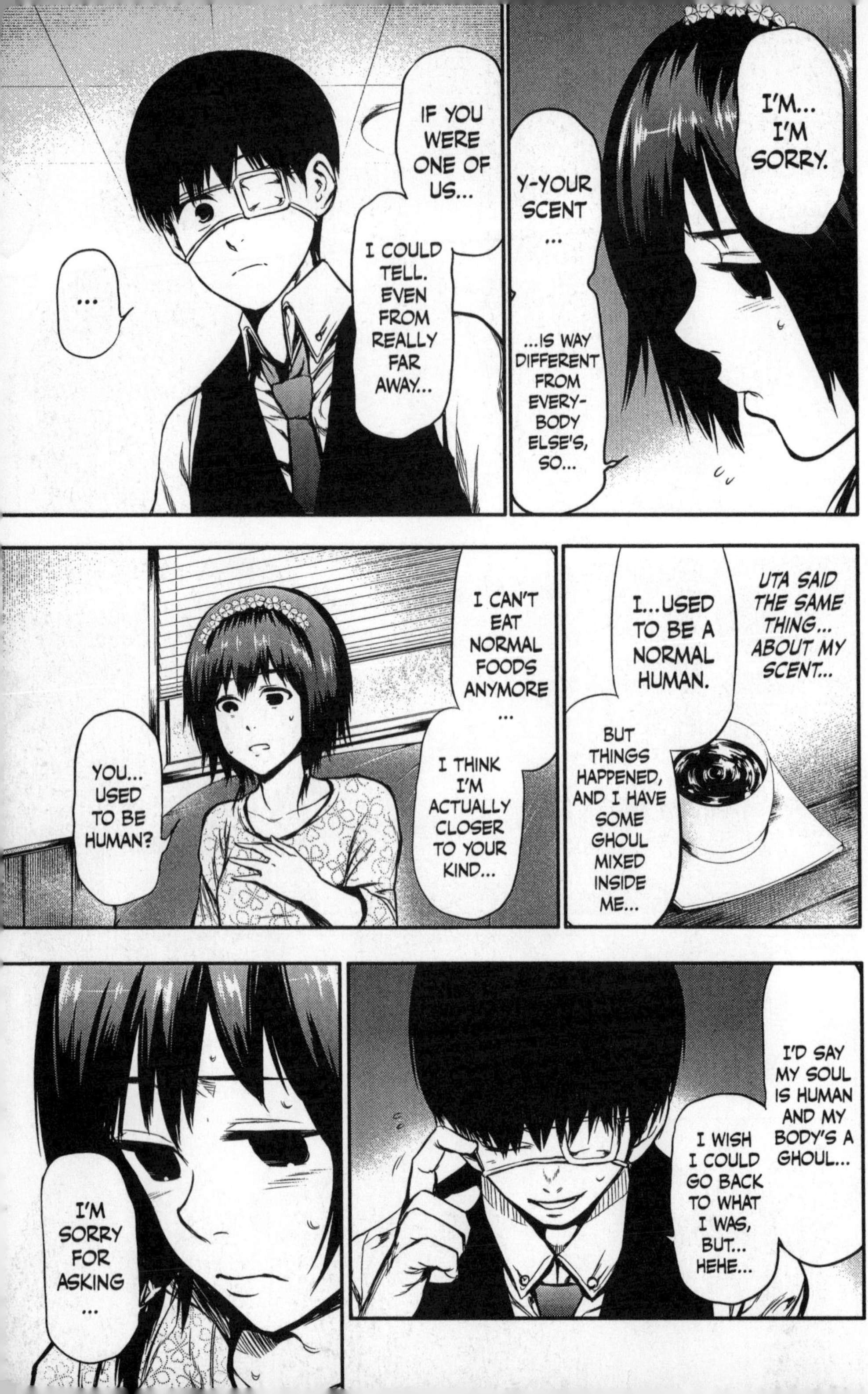
I'M... I'M SORRY.
Y-YOUR SCENT ...
...IS WAY DIFFERENT FROM EVERY-BODY ELSE'S, SO...
IF YOU WERE ONE OF US...
I COULD TELL. EVEN FROM REALLY FAR AWAY...
...
UTA SAID THE SAME THING... ABOUT MY SCENT...
I...USED TO BE A NORMAL HUMAN.
BUT THINGS HAPPENED, AND I HAVE SOME GHOUL MIXED INSIDE ME...
I CAN'T EAT NORMAL FOODS ANYMORE ...
I THINK I'M ACTUALLY CLOSER TO YOUR KIND...
YOU... USED TO BE HUMAN?
I'D SAY MY SOUL IS HUMAN AND MY BODY'S A GHOUL...
I WISH I COULD GO BACK TO WHAT I WAS, BUT... HEHE...
I'M SORRY FOR ASKING ...

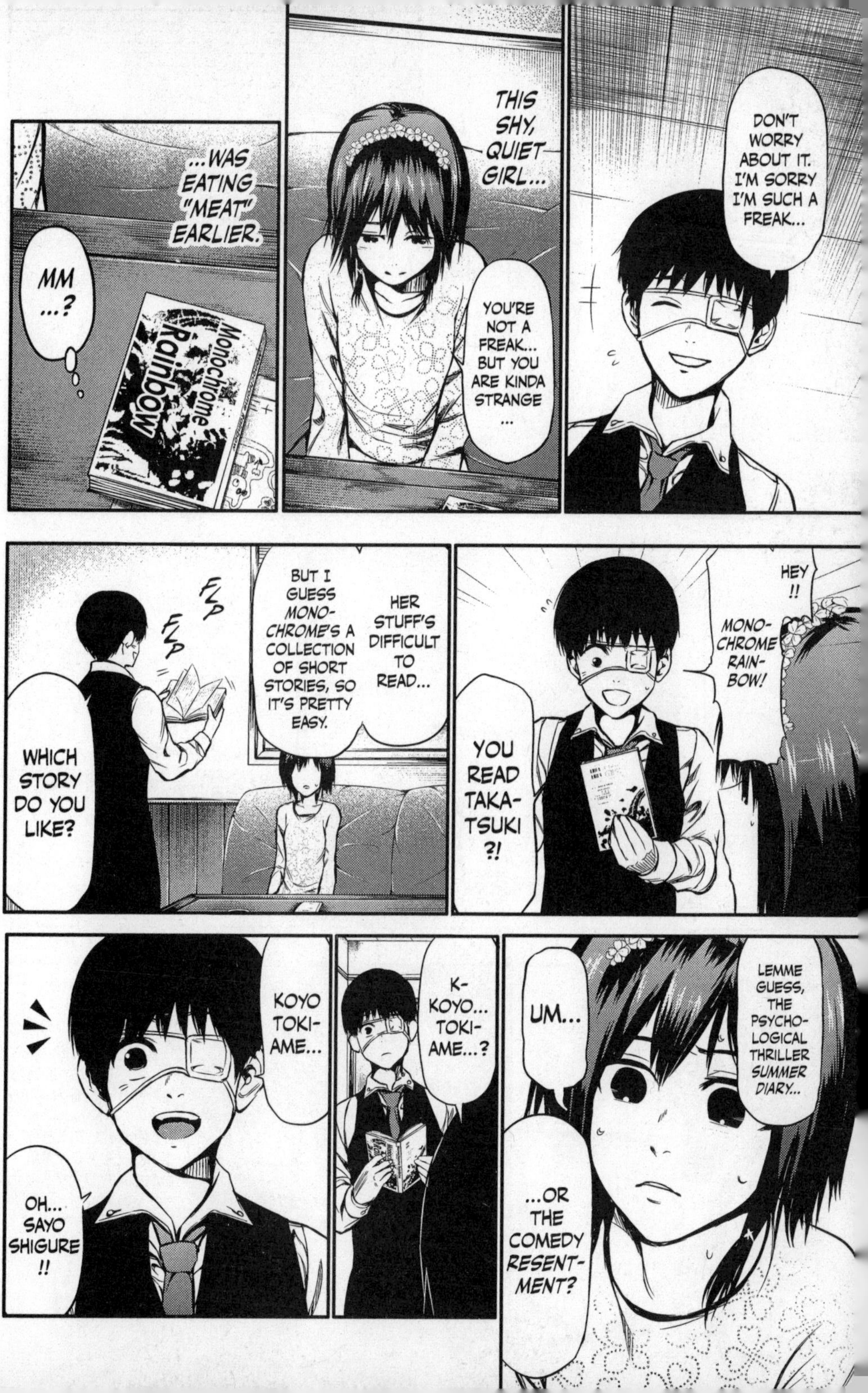
DON'T WORRY ABOUT IT. I'M SORRY I'M SUCH A FREAK...
THIS SHY, QUIET GIRL...
YOU'RE NOT A FREAK... BUT YOU ARE KINDA STRANGE ...
...WAS EATING "MEAT" EARLIER.
MM ...?
Monochrome Rainbow
HEY !!
MONO-CHROME RAIN-BOW!
YOU READ TAKA-TSUKI ?!
HER STUFF'S DIFFICULT TO READ...
BUT I GUESS MONO-CHROME'S A COLLECTION OF SHORT STORIES, SO IT'S PRETTY EASY.
FLP
FLP
WHICH STORY DO YOU LIKE?
LEMME GUESS, THE PSYCHO-LOGICAL THRILLER SUMMER DIARY...
UM...
...OR THE COMEDY RESENT-MENT?
K-KOYO... TOKI-AME...?
KOYO TOKI-AME...
OH... SAYO SHIGURE !!

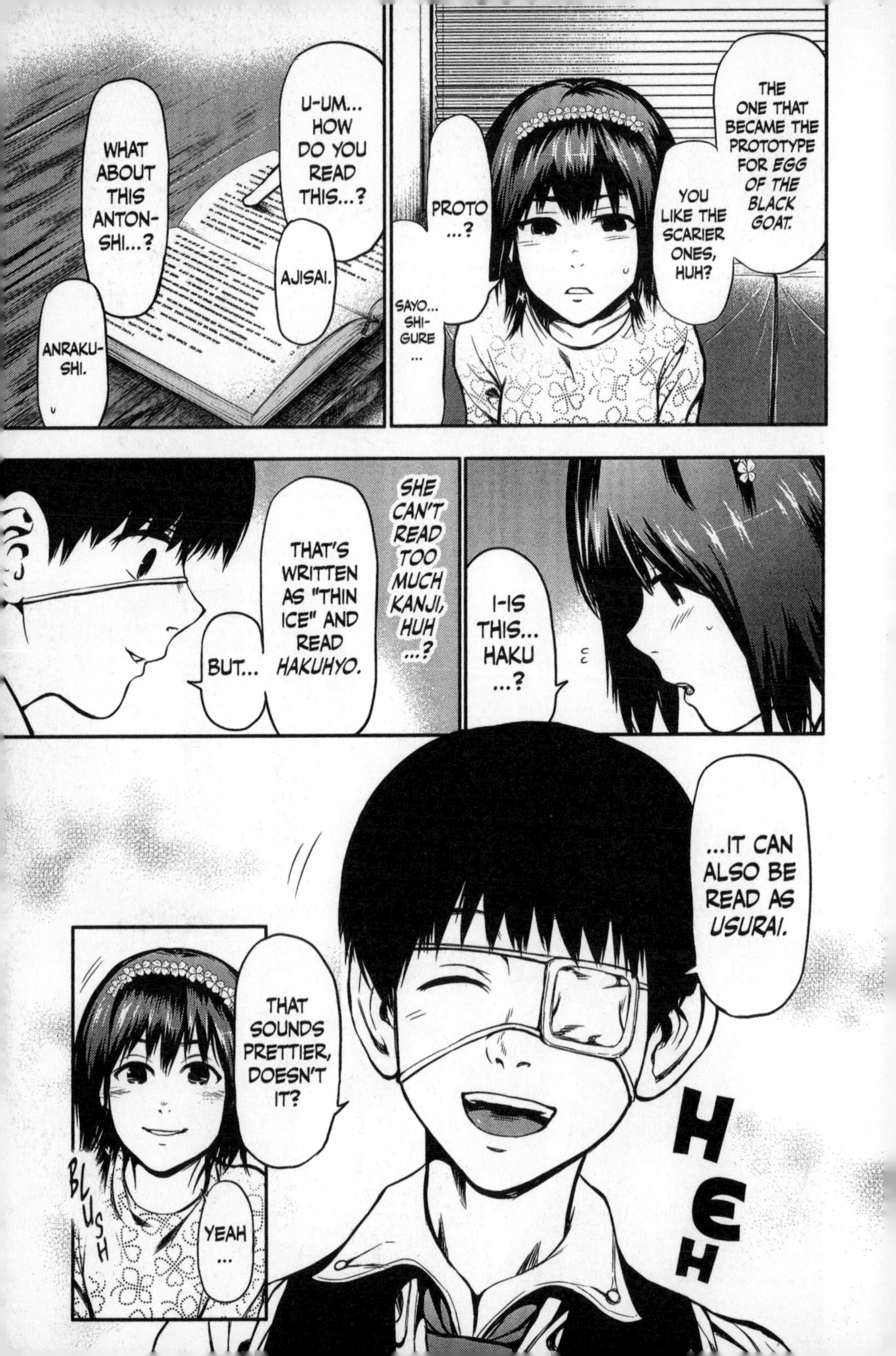
THE ONE THAT BECAME THE PROTOTYPE FOR EGG OF THE BLACK GOAT.
YOU LIKE THE SCARIER ONES, HUH?
PROTO...?
SAYO... SHI-GURE...
U-UM... HOW DO YOU READ THIS...?
AJISAI.
WHAT ABOUT THIS ANTON-SHI...?
ANRAKU-SHI.
I-IS THIS... HAKU...?
SHE CAN'T READ TOO MUCH KANJI, HUH...?
THAT'S WRITTEN AS "THIN ICE" AND READ HAKUHYO.
BUT...
...IT CAN ALSO BE READ AS USURAI.
HEH
THAT SOUNDS PRETTIER, DOESN'T IT?
BLUSH
YEAH...

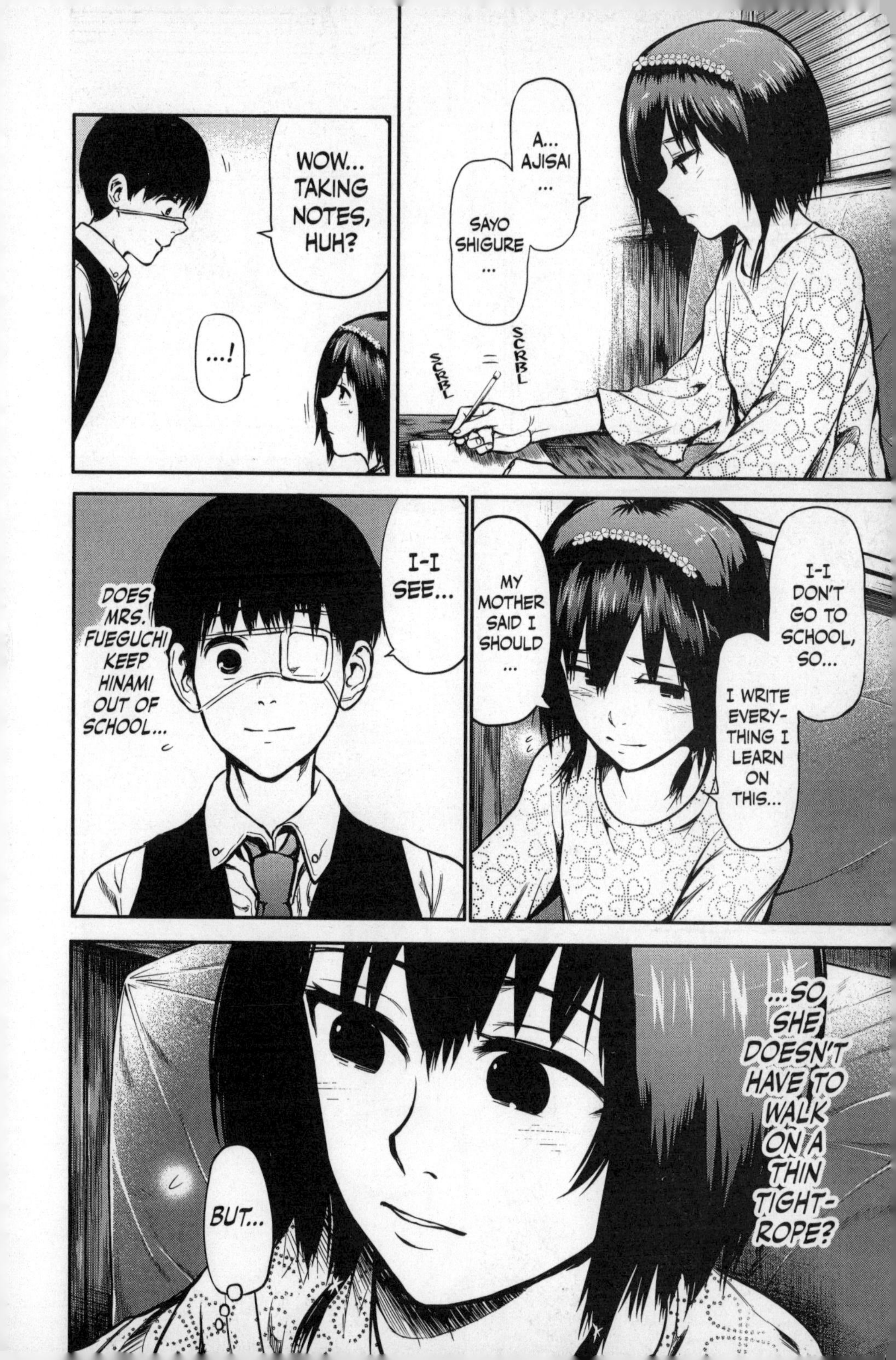

A... AJISAI ...
SAYO SHIGURE ...
SCRBL
SCRBL
WOW... TAKING NOTES, HUH?
...!
I-I DON'T GO TO SCHOOL, SO...
I WRITE EVERY-THING I LEARN ON THIS...
MY MOTHER SAID I SHOULD ...
I-I SEE...
DOES MRS. FUEGUCHI KEEP HINAMI OUT OF SCHOOL...
...SO SHE DOESN'T HAVE TO WALK ON A THIN TIGHT-ROPE?
BUT...

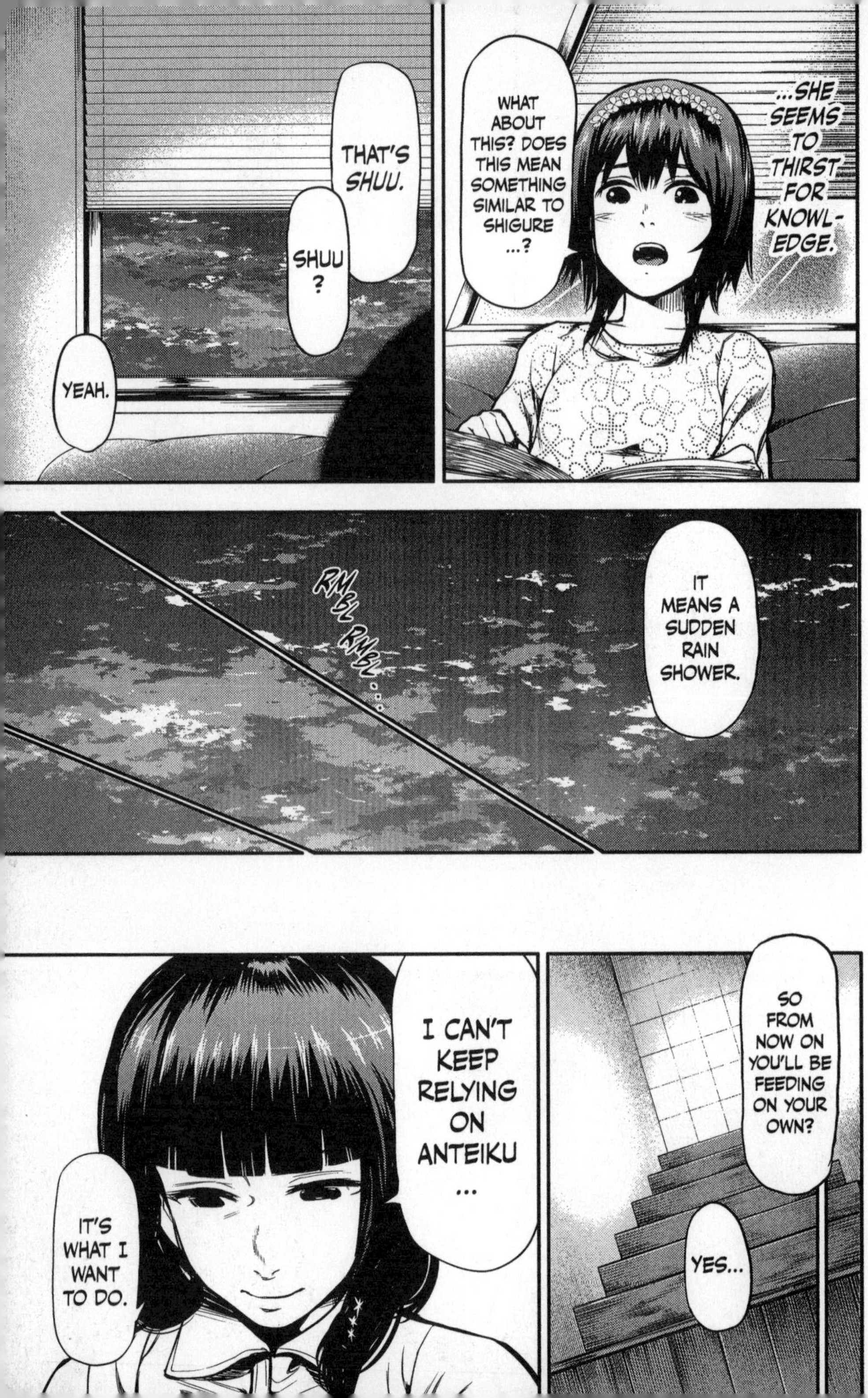
...SHE SEEMS TO THIRST FOR KNOWL-EDGE.
WHAT ABOUT THIS? DOES THIS MEAN SOMETHING SIMILAR TO SHIGURE ...?
THAT'S SHUU.
SHUU ?
YEAH.
IT MEANS A SUDDEN RAIN SHOWER.
RMBL RMBL...
SO FROM NOW ON YOU'LL BE FEEDING ON YOUR OWN?
YES...
I CAN'T KEEP RELYING ON ANTEIKU ...
IT'S WHAT I WANT TO DO.

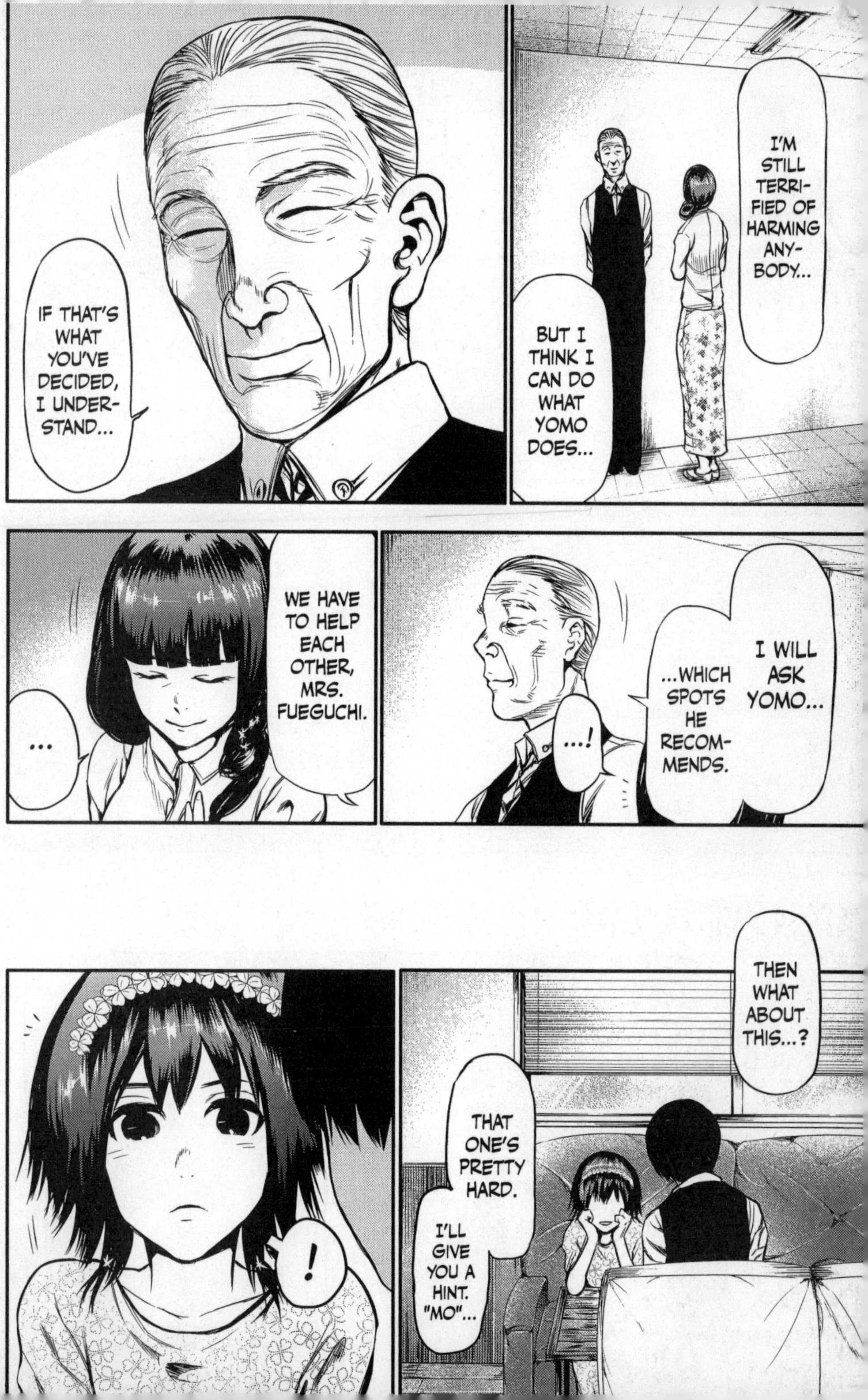
I'M STILL TERRIFIED OF HARMING ANYBODY...
BUT I THINK I CAN DO WHAT YOMO DOES...
IF THAT'S WHAT YOU'VE DECIDED, I UNDERSTAND...
I WILL ASK YOMO...
...WHICH SPOTS HE RECOMMENDS.
...!
WE HAVE TO HELP EACH OTHER, MRS. FUEGUCHI.
...
THEN WHAT ABOUT THIS...?
THAT ONE'S PRETTY HARD.
I'LL GIVE YOU A HINT. "MO"...
!

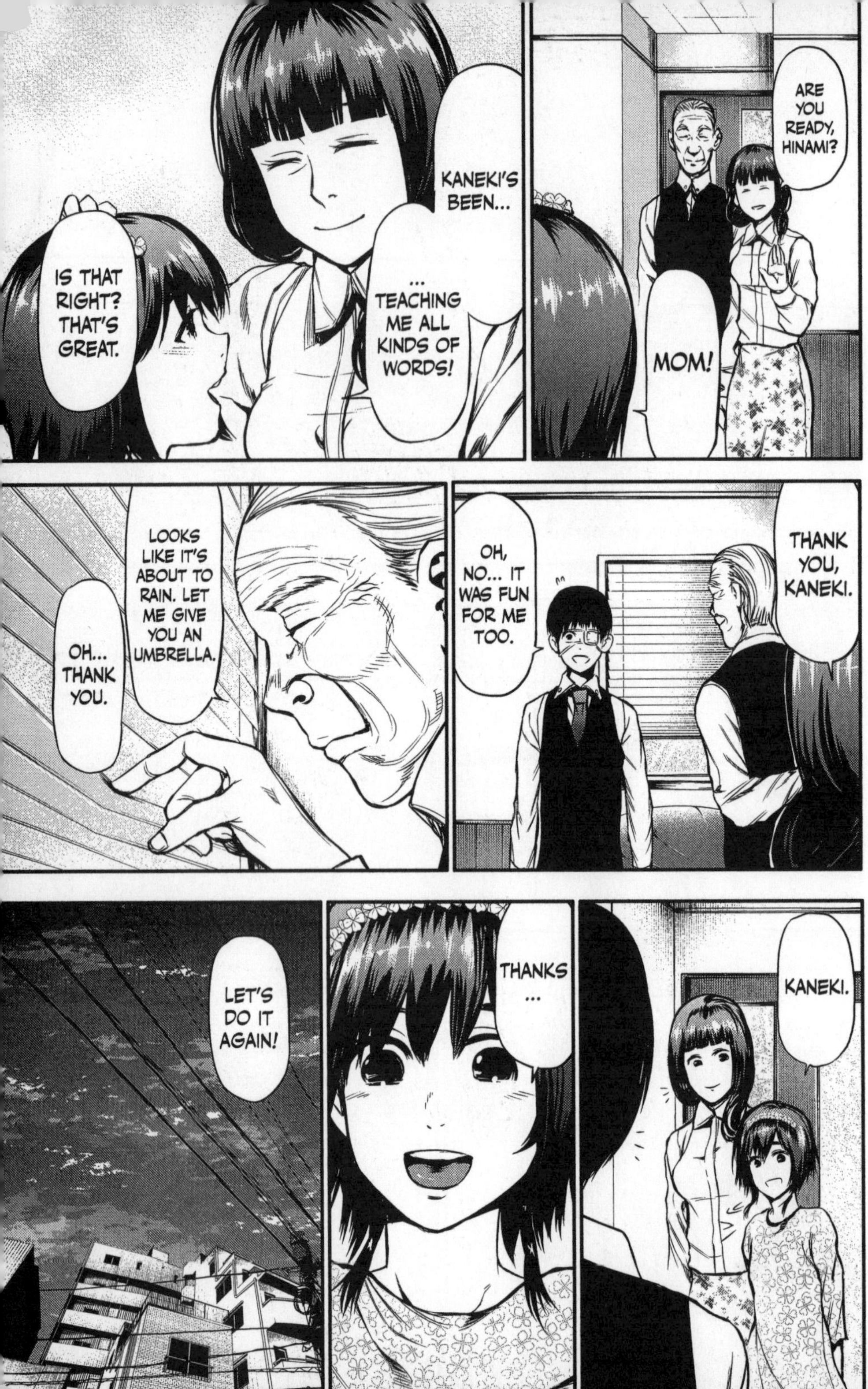
ARE YOU READY, HINAMI?
MOM!
KANEKI'S BEEN...
... TEACHING ME ALL KINDS OF WORDS!
IS THAT RIGHT? THAT'S GREAT.
THANK YOU, KANEKI.
OH, NO... IT WAS FUN FOR ME TOO.
LOOKS LIKE IT'S ABOUT TO RAIN. LET ME GIVE YOU AN UMBRELLA.
OH... THANK YOU.
KANEKI.
THANKS ...
LET'S DO IT AGAIN!

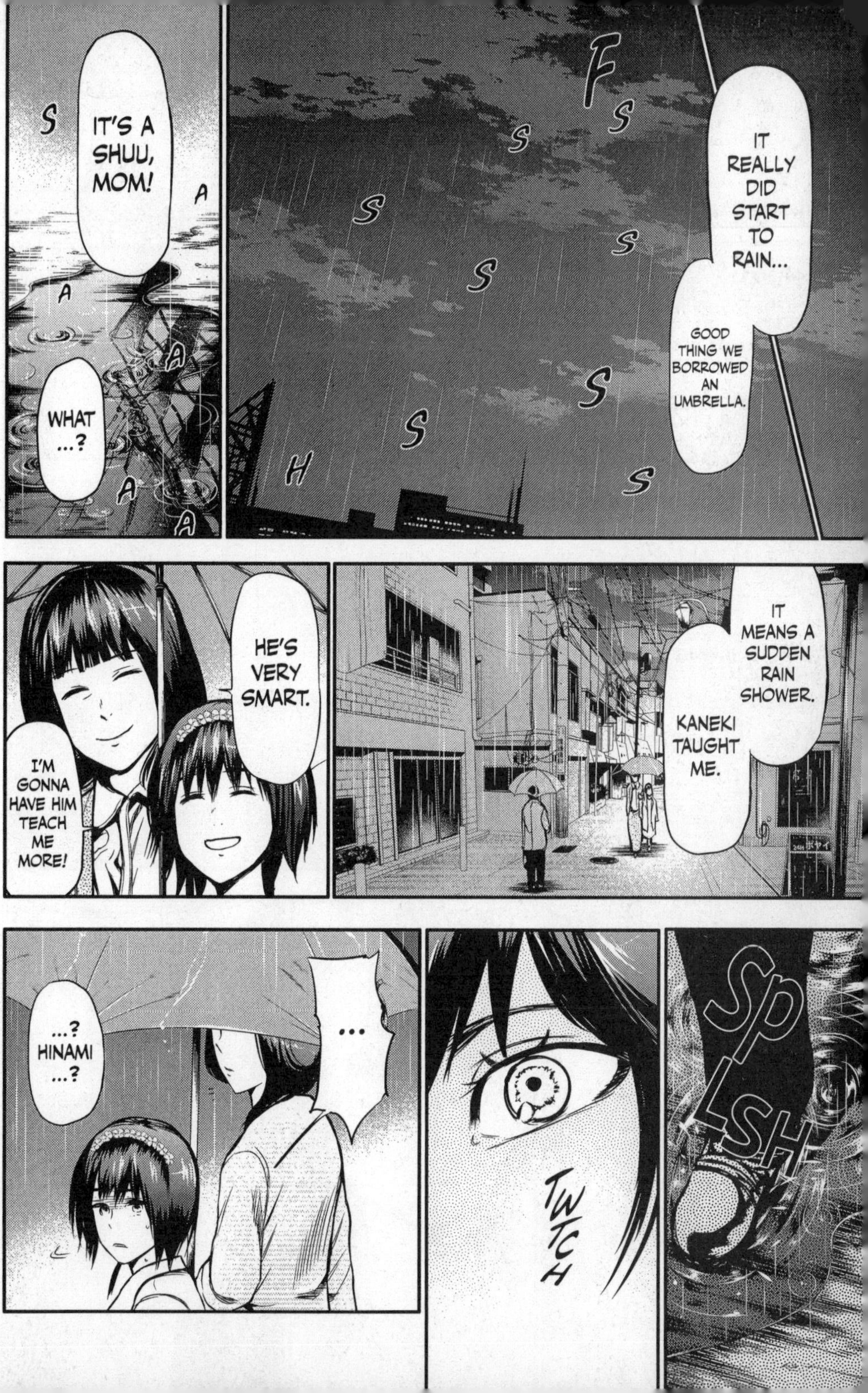
IT REALLY DID START TO RAIN...
GOOD THING WE BORROWED AN UMBRELLA.
FSSSSSSSSH
IT'S A SHUU, MOM!
SAAAAA
WHAT ...?
IT MEANS A SUDDEN RAIN SHOWER.
KANEKI TAUGHT ME.
HE'S VERY SMART.
I'M GONNA HAVE HIM TEACH ME MORE!
SPLSH
TWTCH
...
...? HINAMI ...?

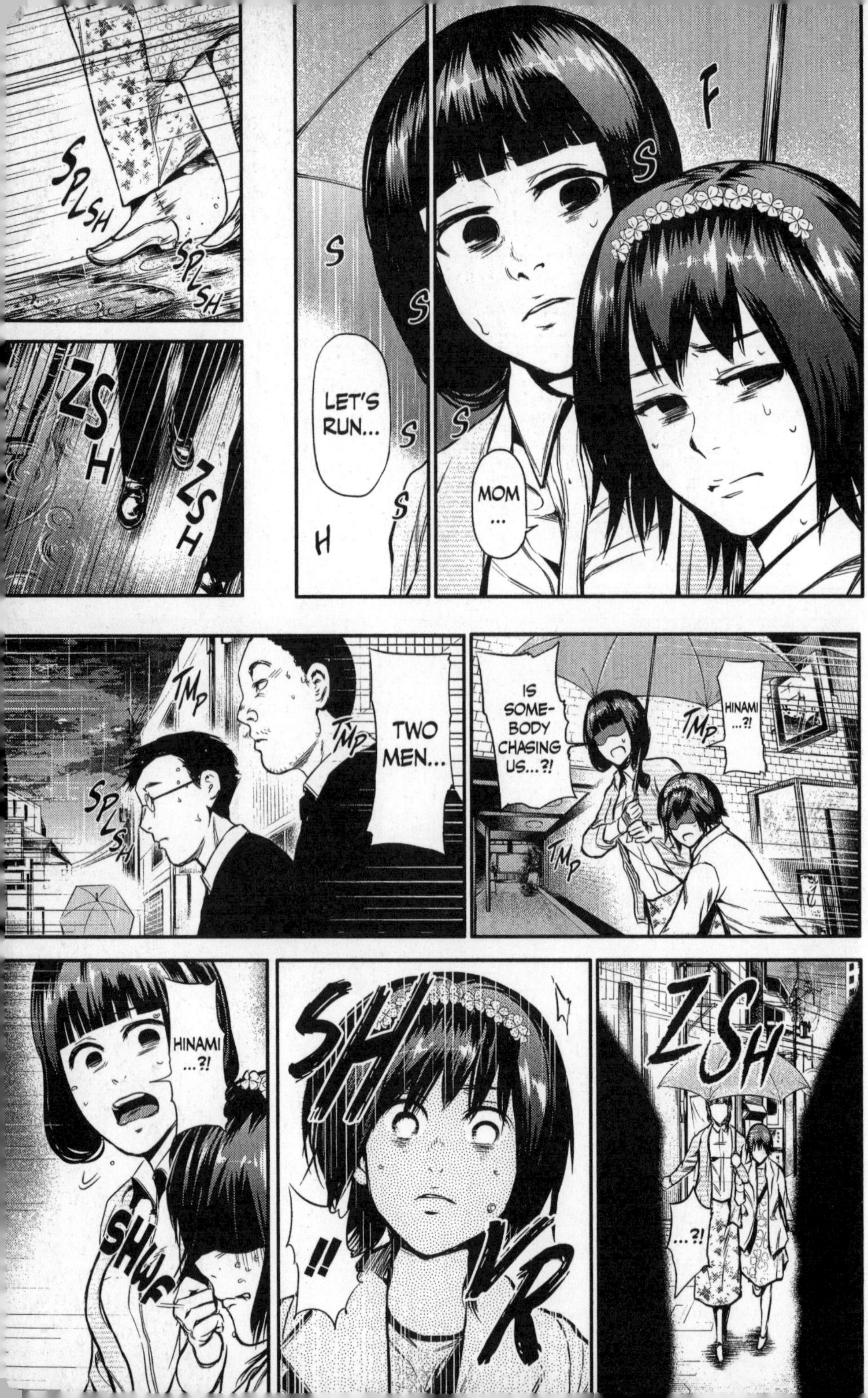

F
S
S
MOM ...
LET'S RUN...
S
S
S
S
S
H
SPLSH
SPLSH
ZSH
ZSH
IS SOME-BODY CHASING US...?!
HINAMI ...?!
TMP
TMP
TWO MEN...
TMP
TMP
SPLSH
ZSH
...?!
SH
!!
VR
HINAMI ...?!
SHWF

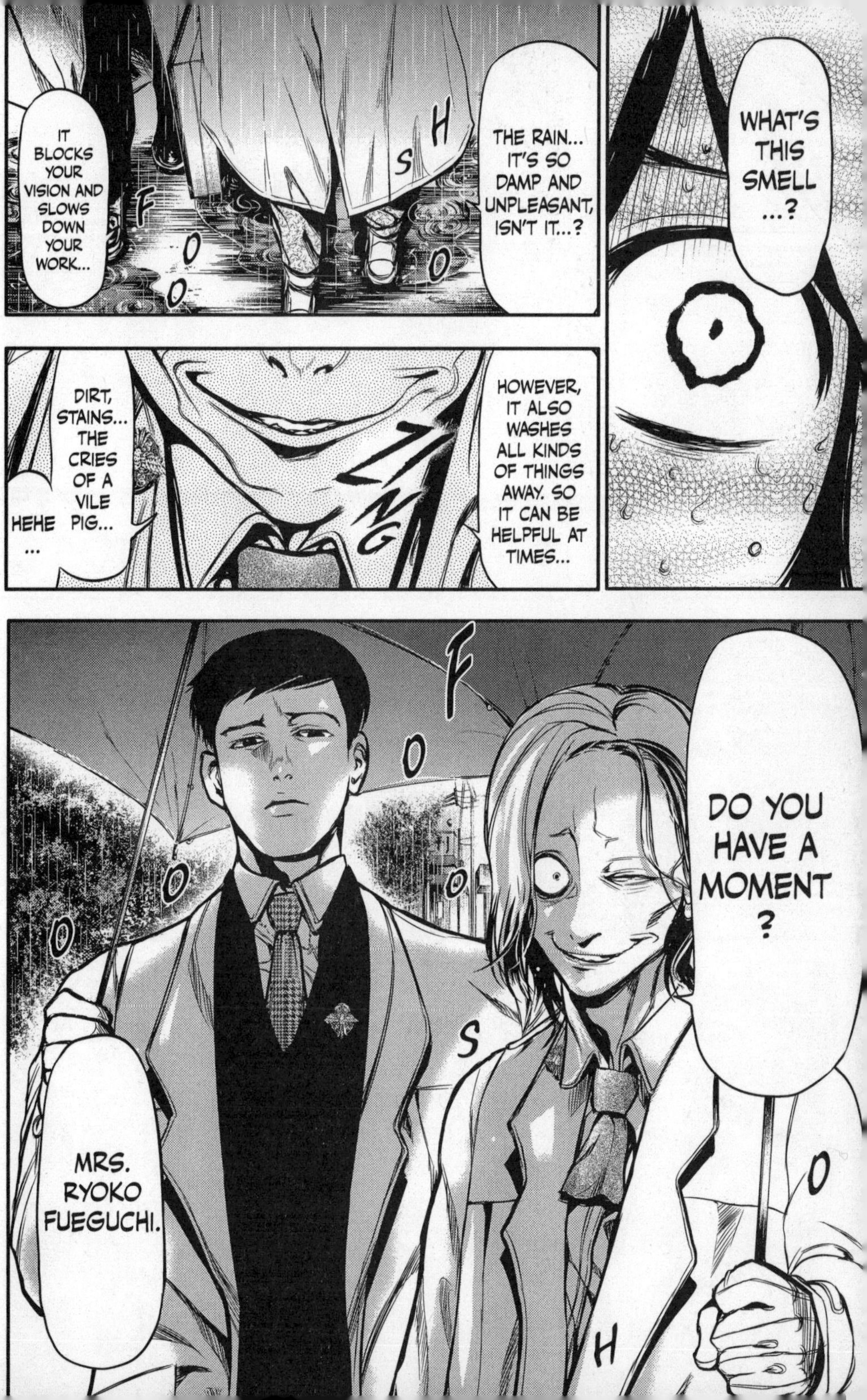
WHAT'S THIS SMELL ...?
THE RAIN... IT'S SO DAMP AND UNPLEASANT, ISN'T IT...?
SH
FOOO
IT BLOCKS YOUR VISION AND SLOWS DOWN YOUR WORK...
HOWEVER, IT ALSO WASHES ALL KINDS OF THINGS AWAY. SO IT CAN BE HELPFUL AT TIMES...
ZING
DIRT, STAINS... THE CRIES OF A VILE PIG...
HEHE ...
DO YOU HAVE A MOMENT?
FOOOO
SH
MRS. RYOKO FUEGUCHI.

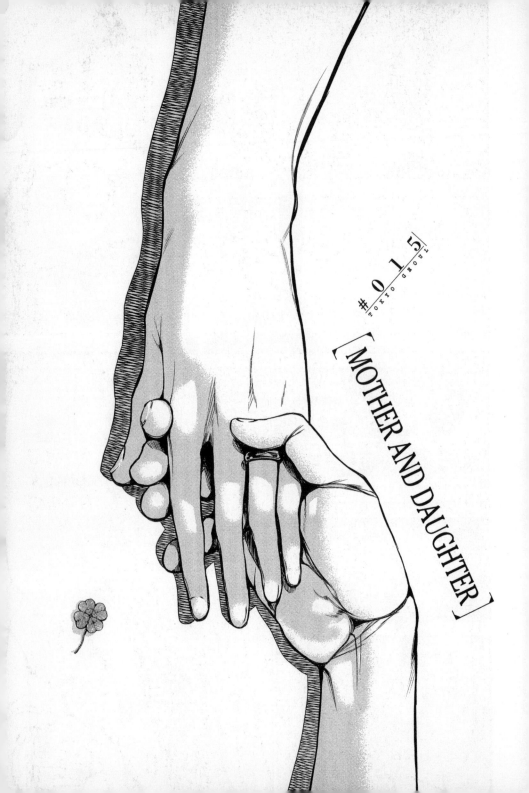

#015 _tokyo ghoul_

[MOTHER AND DAUGHTER]

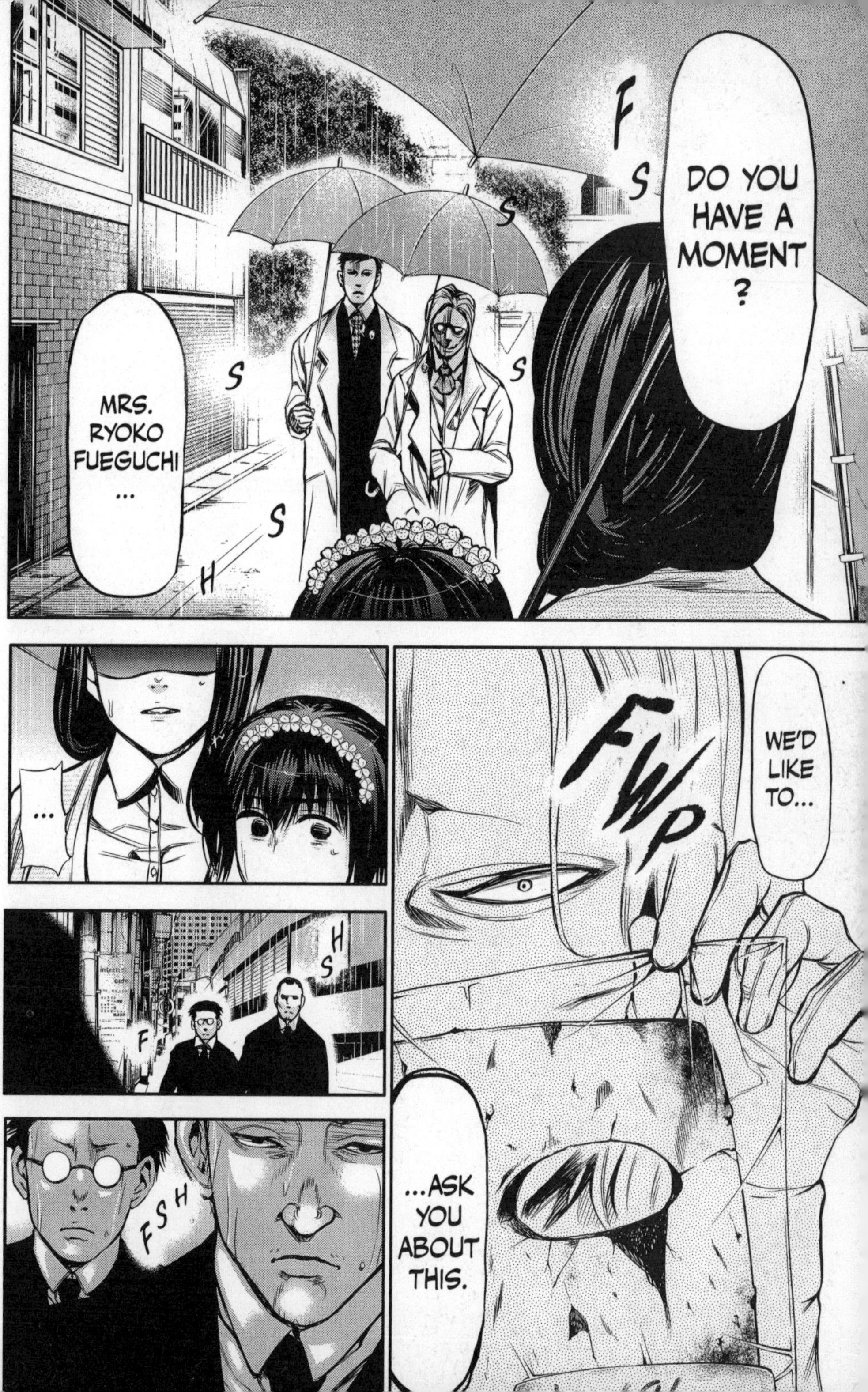
FSSSSSH
DO YOU HAVE A MOMENT?
MRS. RYOKO FUEGUCHI...
WE'D LIKE TO...
FWP
...ASK YOU ABOUT THIS.
...
FSH
FSH

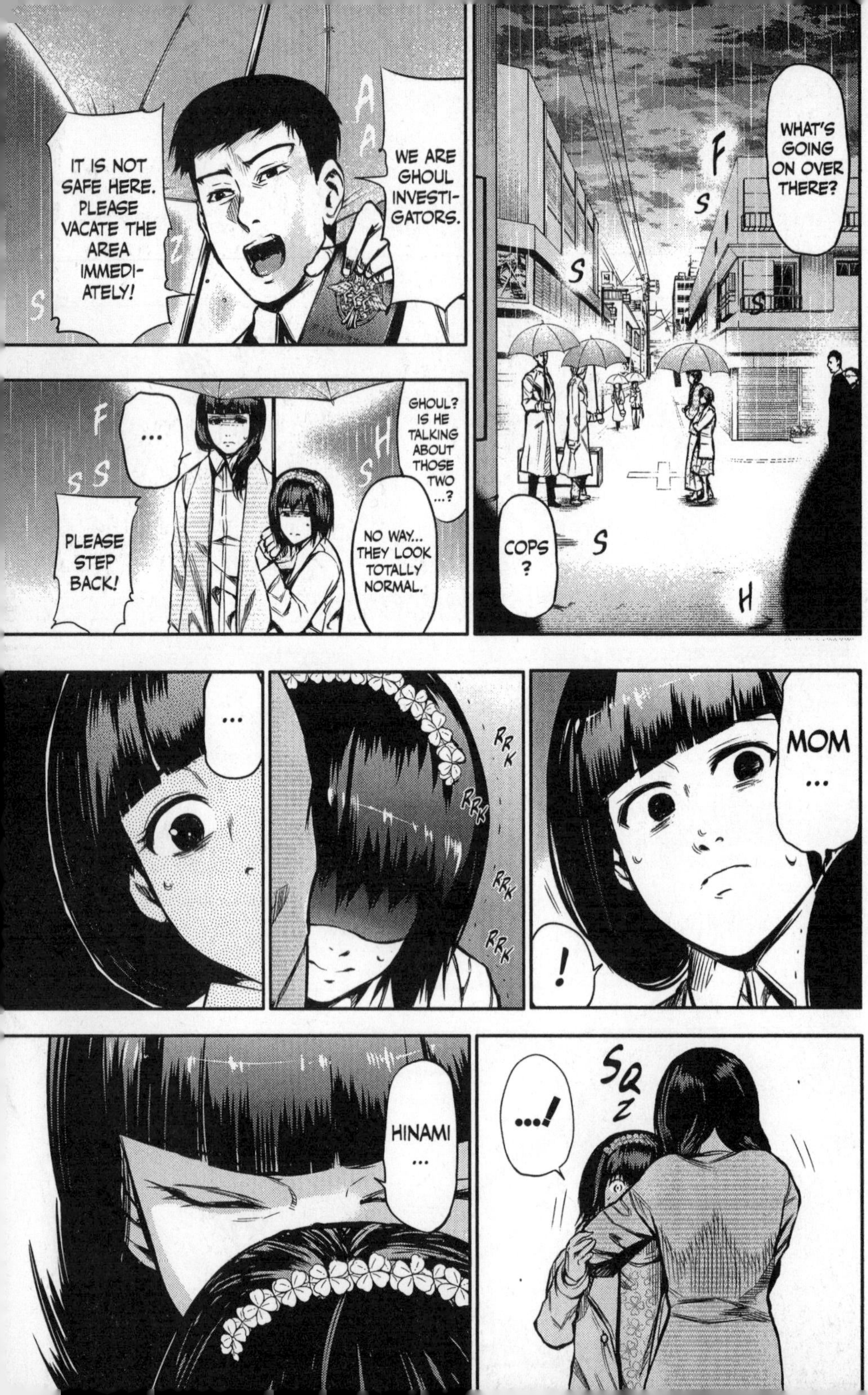
WHAT'S GOING ON OVER THERE?
FSSSSH
COPS?
AA
WE ARE GHOUL INVESTIGATORS.
IT IS NOT SAFE HERE. PLEASE VACATE THE AREA IMMEDIATELY!
ZS
GHOUL? IS HE TALKING ABOUT THOSE TWO ...?
NO WAY... THEY LOOK TOTALLY NORMAL.
SH
...
FSS
PLEASE STEP BACK!
MOM ...
!
RRK RRK RRK RRK
...
SQZ
...!
HINAMI ...

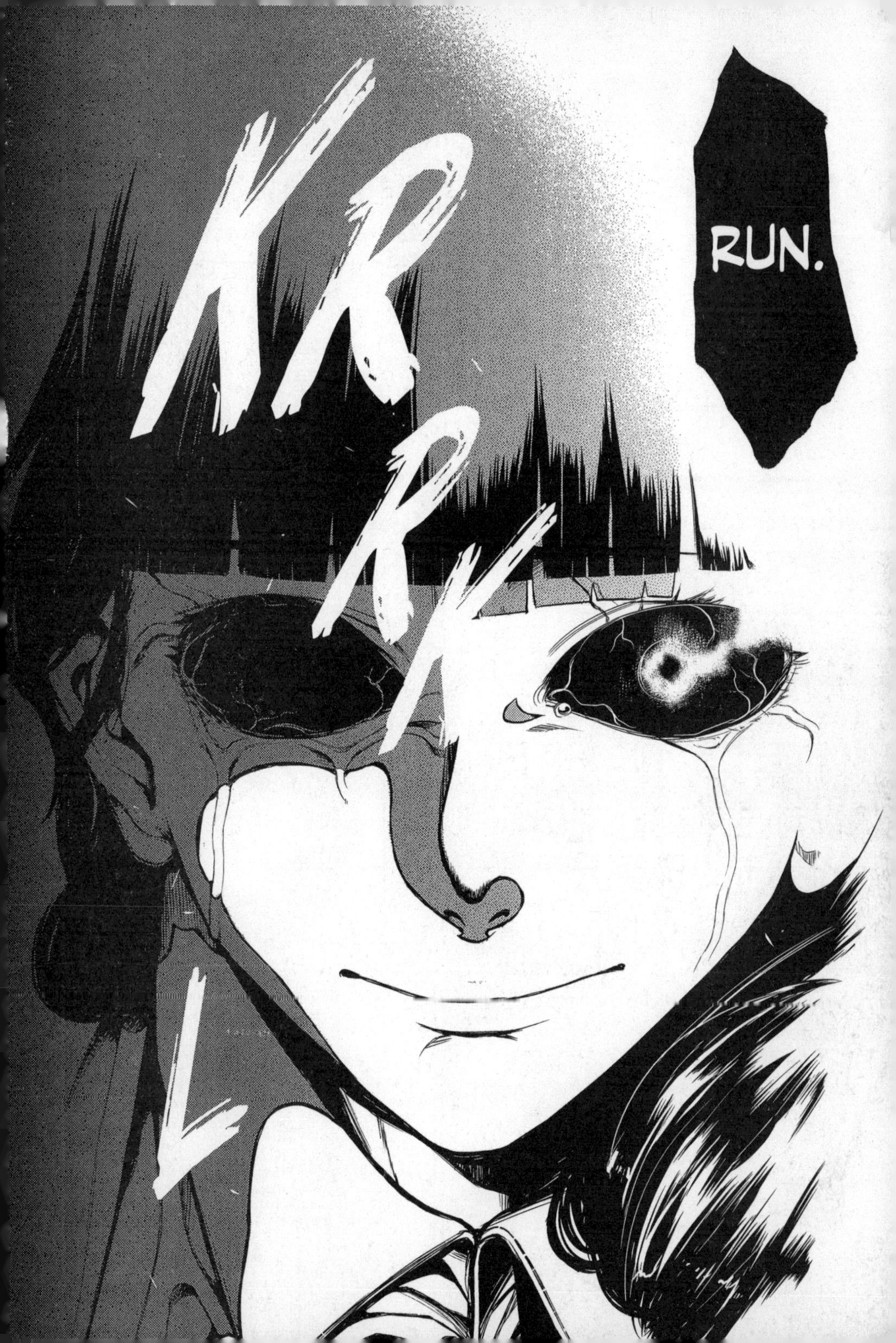
RUN.
KRRK

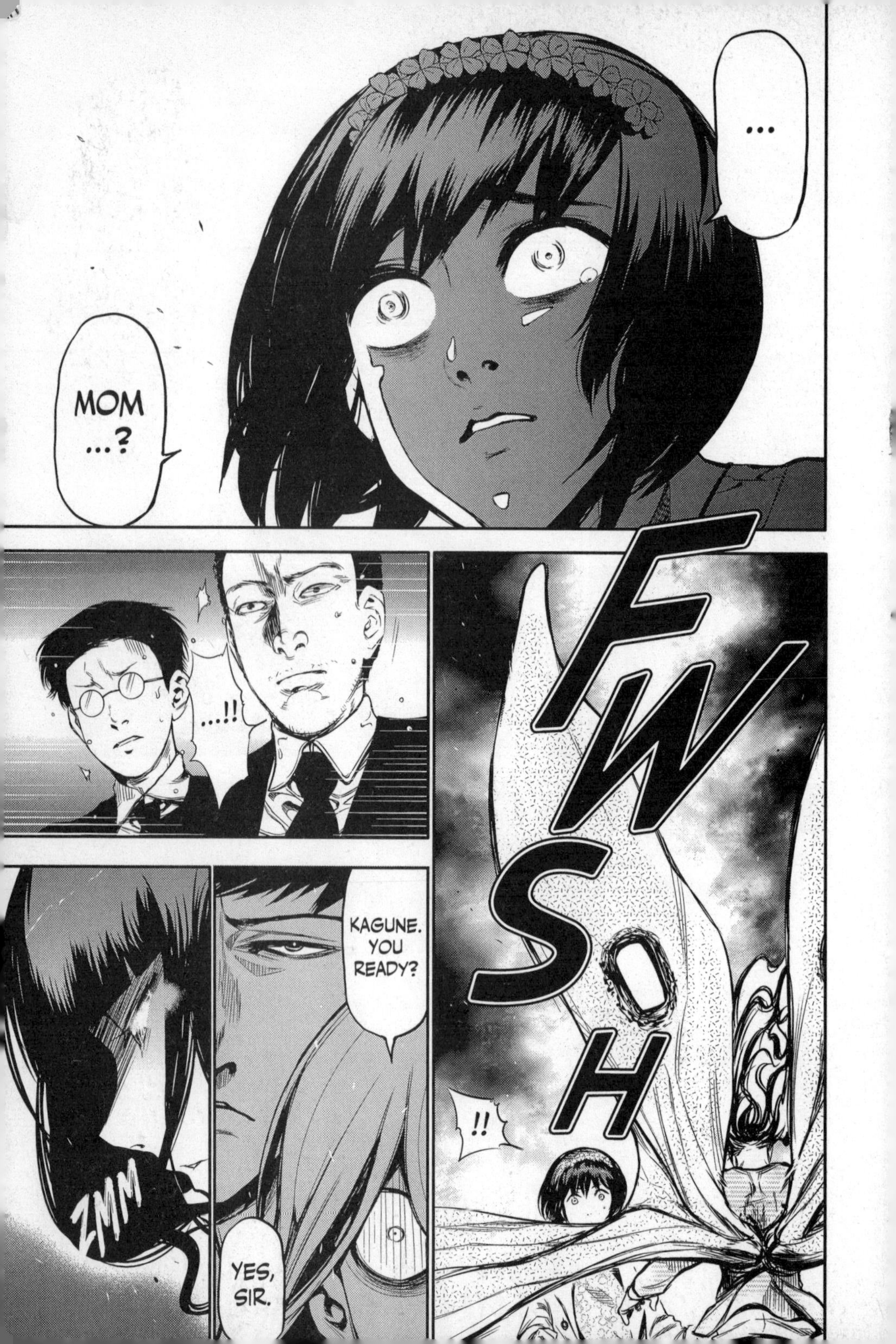
...
MOM ...?
FWSH
!!
...!!
KAGUNE. YOU READY?
YES, SIR.
ZMM

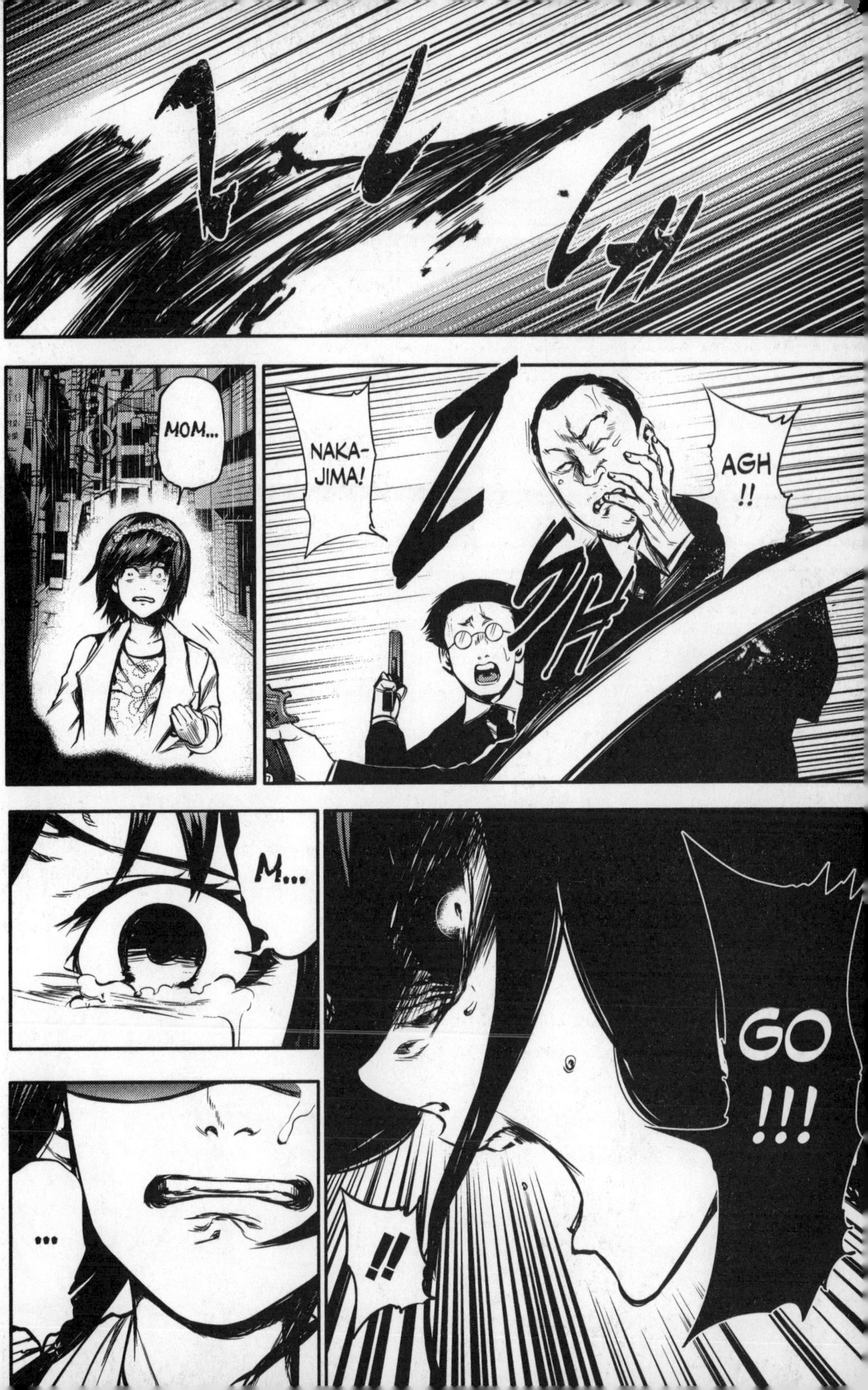
AGH !!
NAKA-JIMA!
MOM...
GO !!!
!!
M...
...

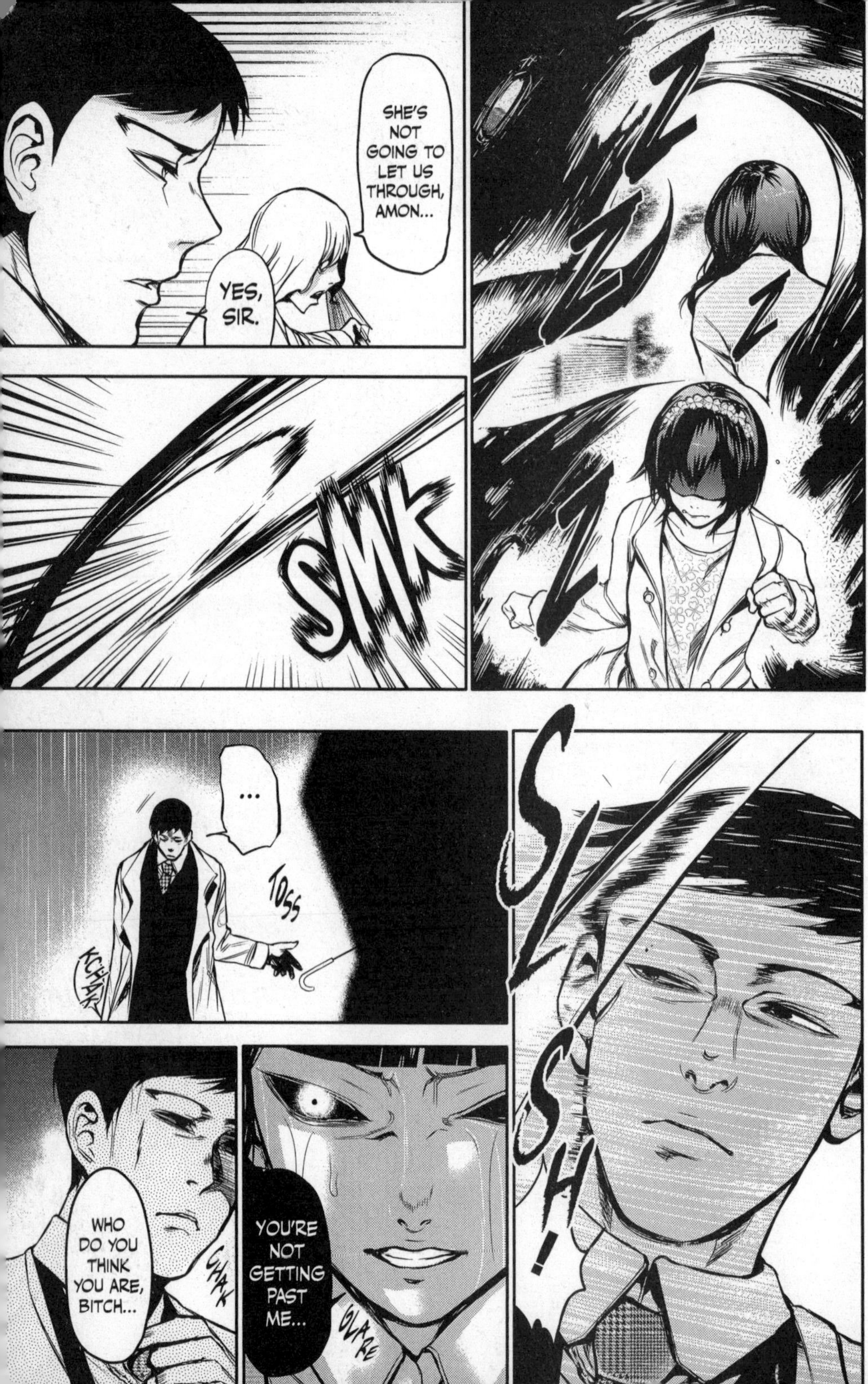
SHE'S NOT GOING TO LET US THROUGH, AMON...
YES, SIR.
SMK
...
TOSS
KCHAK
YOU'RE NOT GETTING PAST ME...
GLARE
WHO DO YOU THINK YOU ARE, BITCH...
CHAK

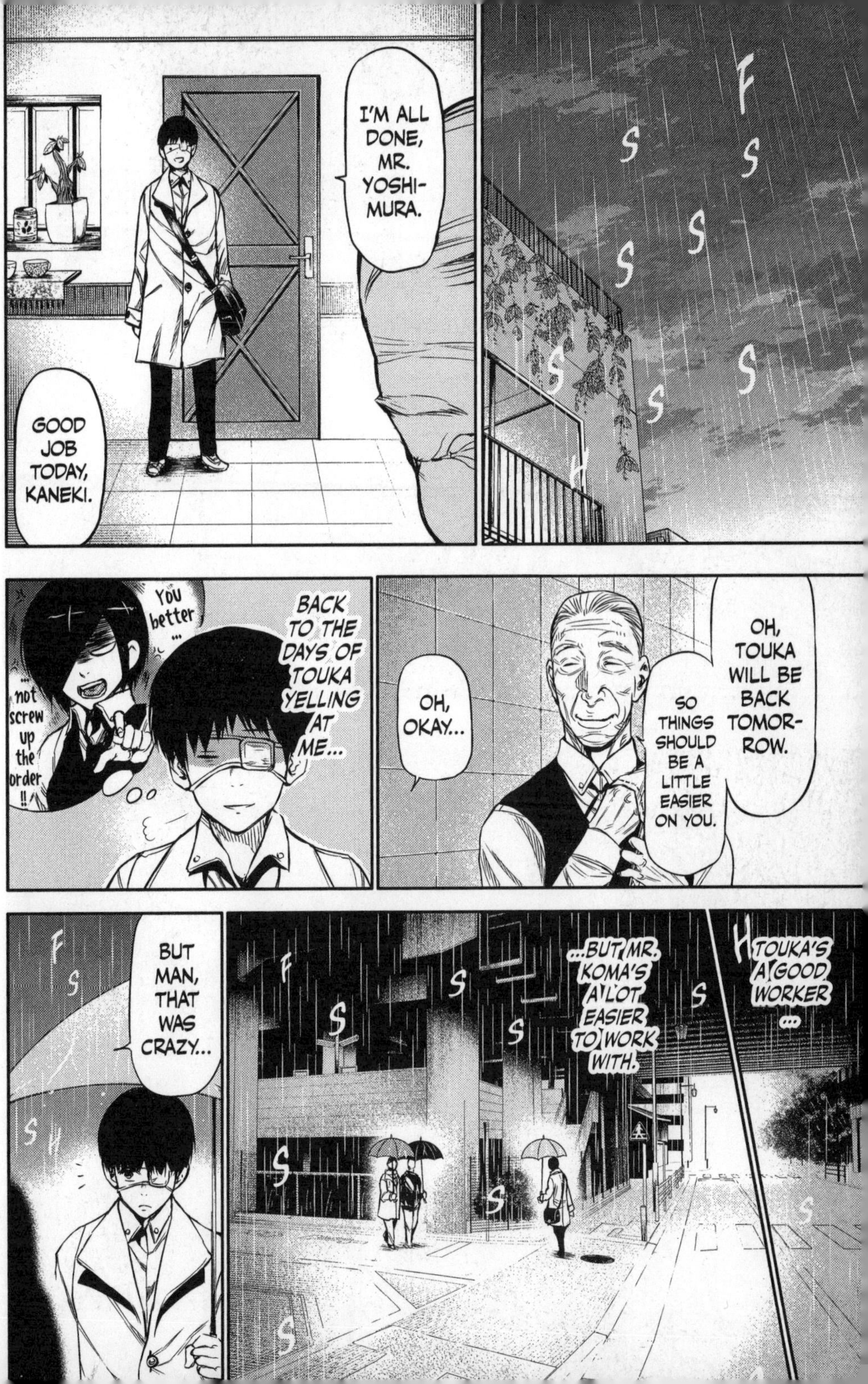
FSSSSSSH
I'M ALL DONE, MR. YOSHIMURA.
GOOD JOB TODAY, KANEKI.
OH, TOUKA WILL BE BACK TOMORROW.
SO THINGS SHOULD BE A LITTLE EASIER ON YOU.
OH, OKAY...
BACK TO THE DAYS OF TOUKA YELLING AT ME...
You better...
...not screw up the order!!
TOUKA'S A GOOD WORKER...
...BUT MR. KOMA'S A LOT EASIER TO WORK WITH.
FSSSSSH
BUT MAN, THAT WAS CRAZY...
FSSH

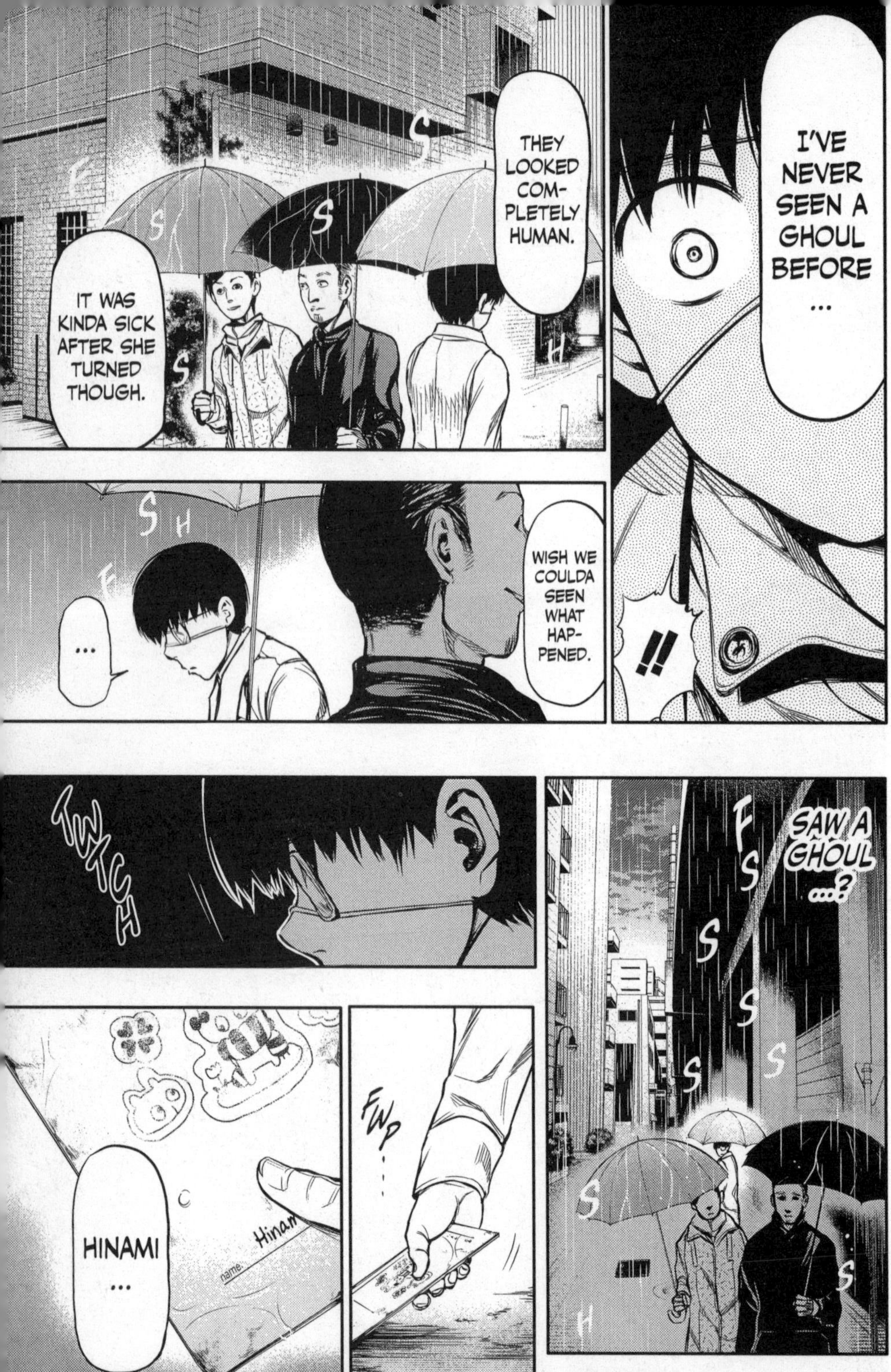
I'VE NEVER SEEN A GHOUL BEFORE ...
!!
THEY LOOKED COM-PLETELY HUMAN.
IT WAS KINDA SICK AFTER SHE TURNED THOUGH.
WISH WE COULDA SEEN WHAT HAP-PENED.
...
SAW A GHOUL ...?
TWITCH
FWP...
HINAMI ...
name: Hinam

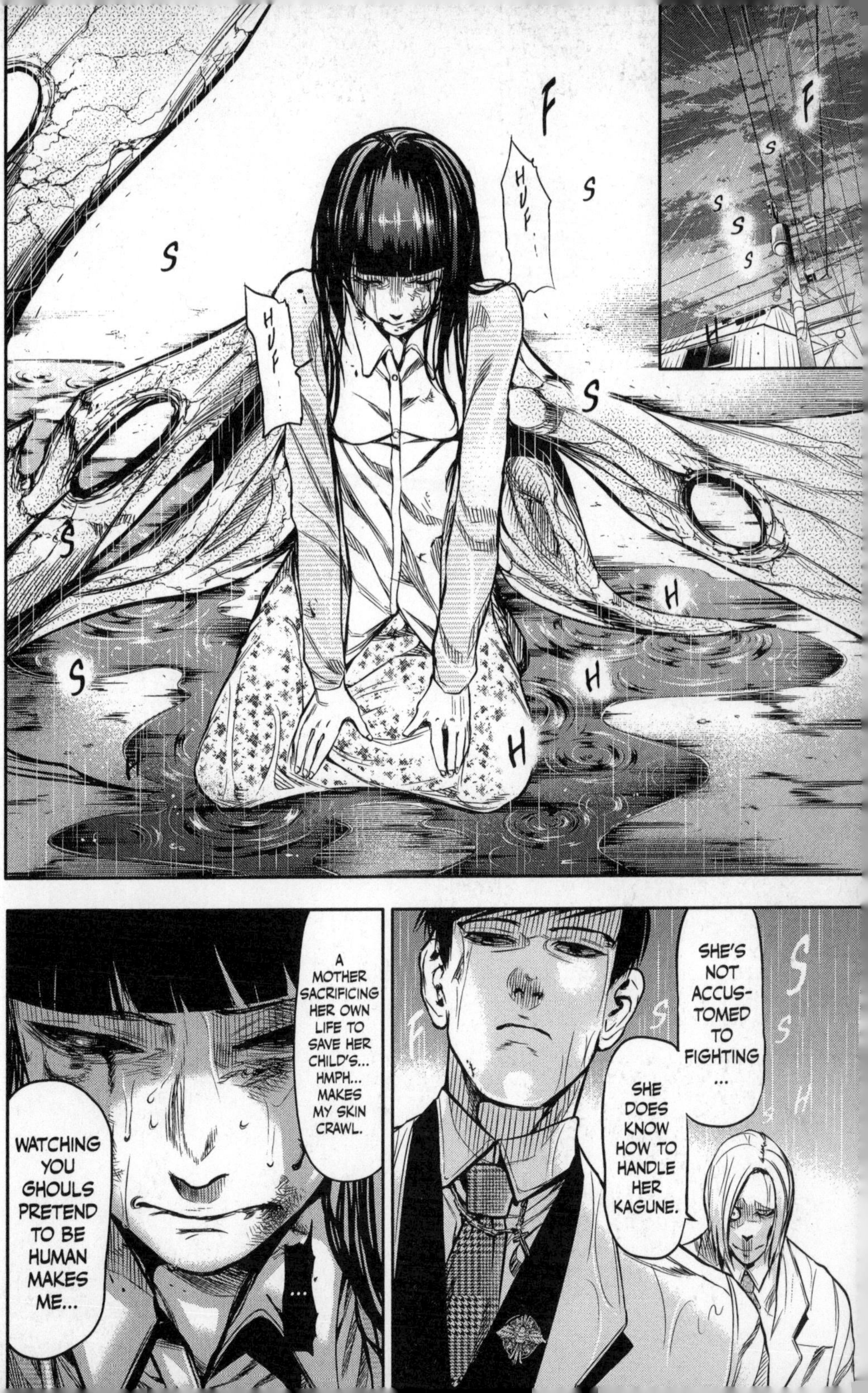

F
S
S
S
S
H
F
S
HUFF...
HUFF...
S
S
S
S
H
H
H
SHE'S NOT ACCUS-TOMED TO FIGHTING...
SHE DOES KNOW HOW TO HANDLE HER KAGUNE.
S
S
H
A MOTHER SACRIFICING HER OWN LIFE TO SAVE HER CHILD'S... HMPH... MAKES MY SKIN CRAWL.
WATCHING YOU GHOULS PRETEND TO BE HUMAN MAKES ME...
...

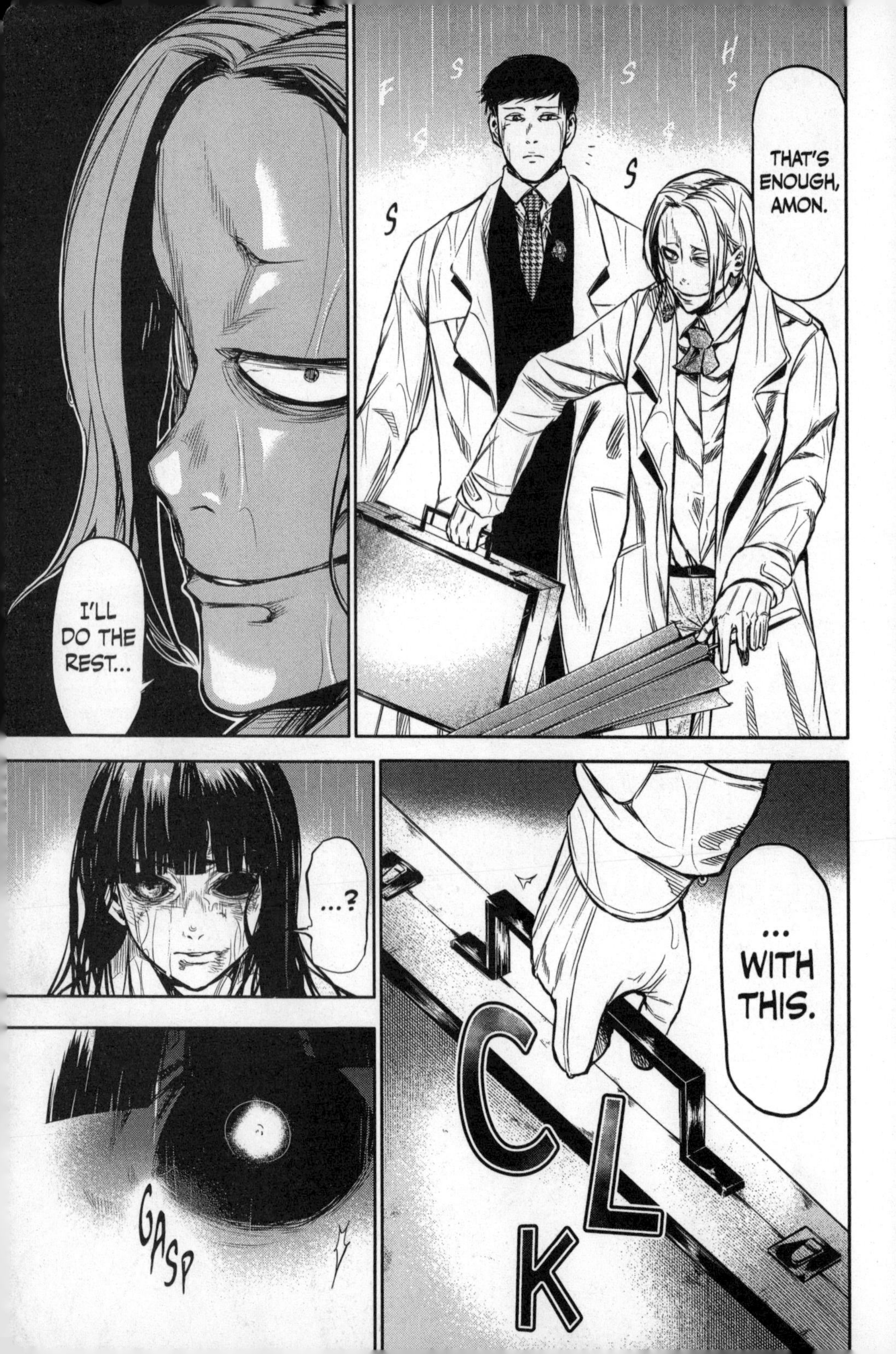
THAT'S ENOUGH, AMON.
I'LL DO THE REST...
... WITH THIS.
CLK
...?
GASP

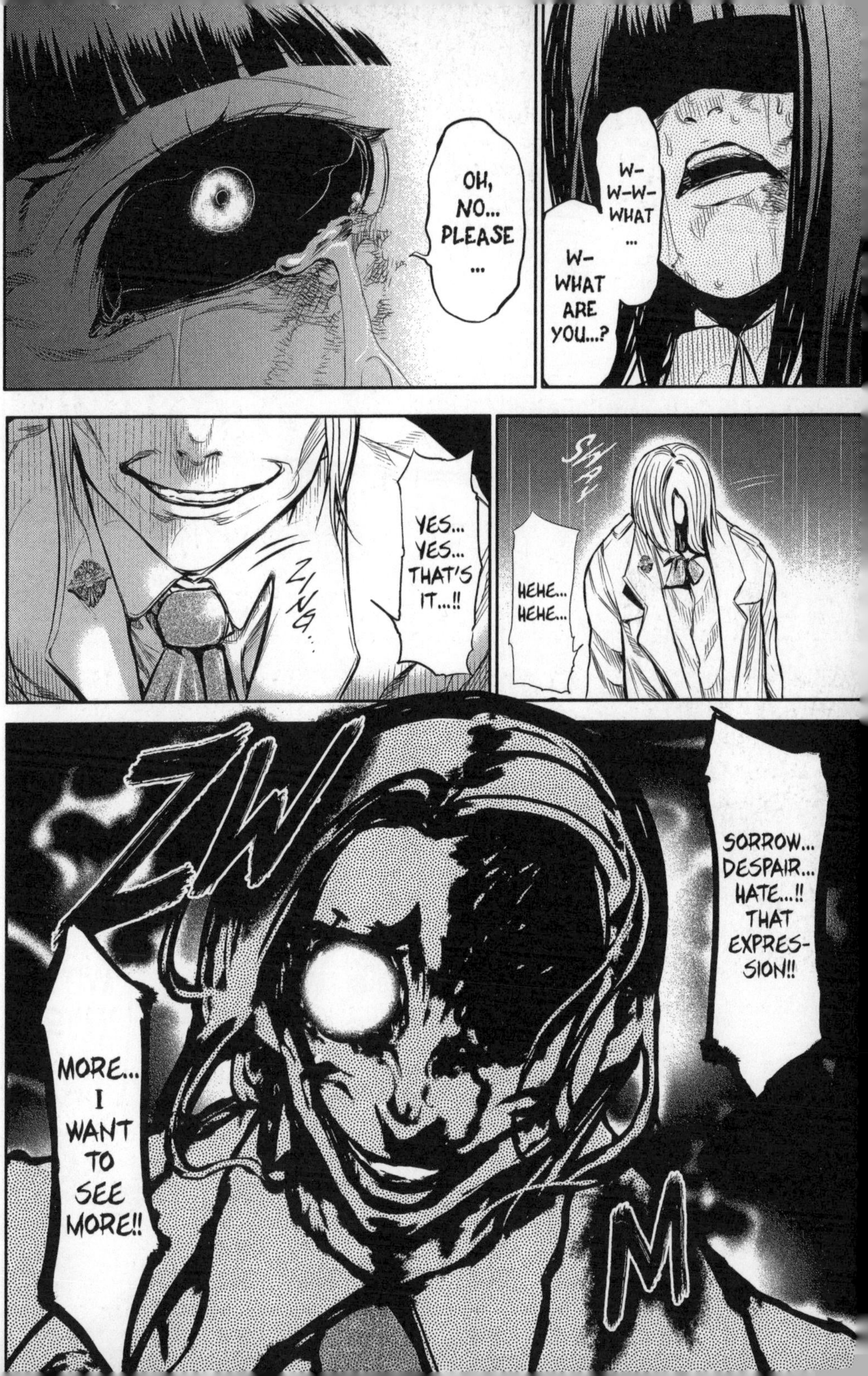
W- W-W-WHAT ...
W- WHAT ARE YOU...?
OH, NO... PLEASE ...
HEHE... HEHE...
YES... YES... THAT'S IT...!!
ZING...
SORROW... DESPAIR... HATE...!! THAT EXPRES- SION!!
ZW
M
MORE... I WANT TO SEE MORE!!

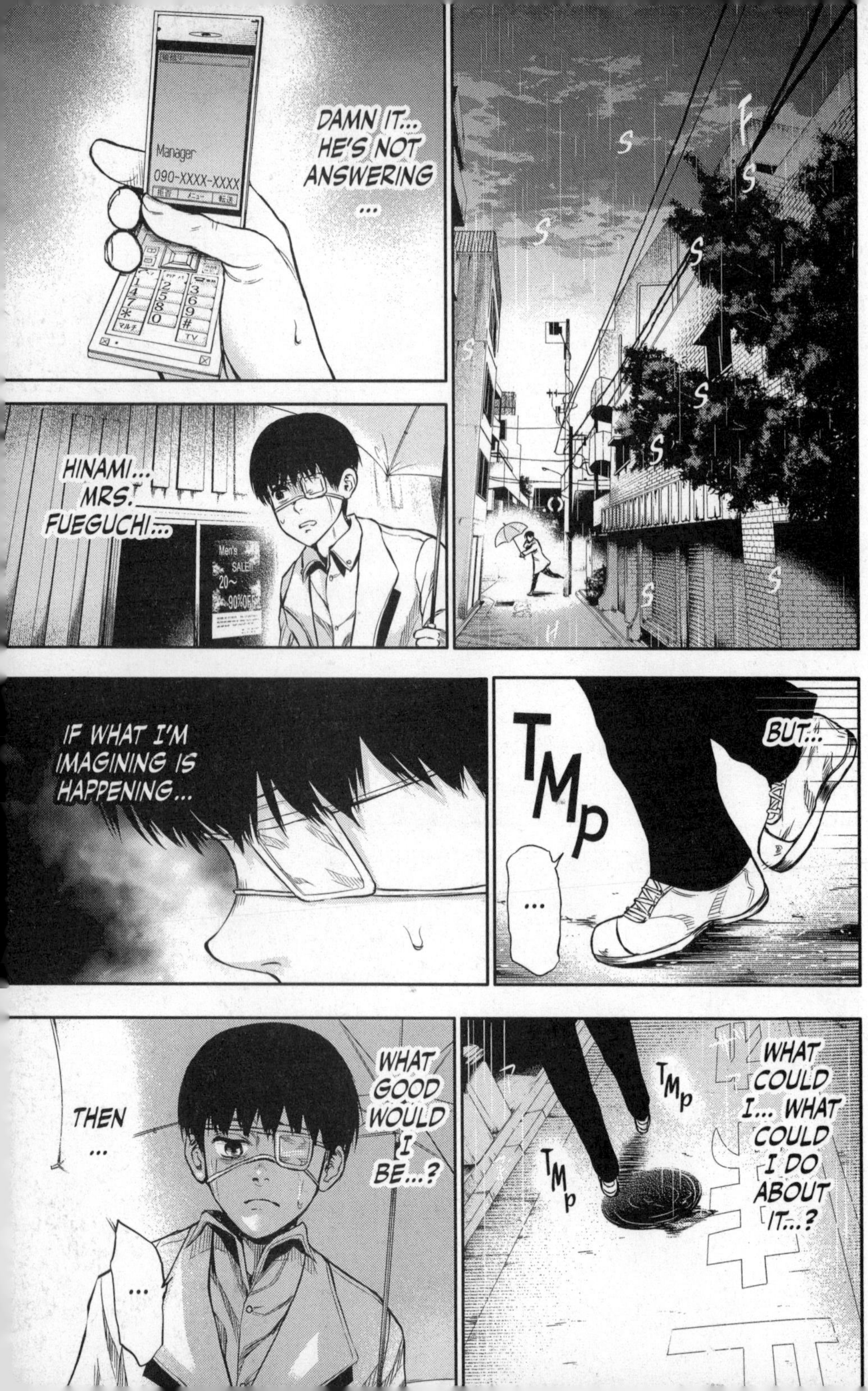

Manager
090-XXXX-XXXX
DAMN IT... HE'S NOT ANSWERING...
HINAMI... MRS. FUEGUCHI...
Men's SALE!! 20~90%OFF
BUT...
TMP
...
IF WHAT I'M IMAGINING IS HAPPENING...
WHAT COULD I... WHAT COULD I DO ABOUT IT...?
TMp
TMp
WHAT GOOD WOULD I BE...?
THEN...
...

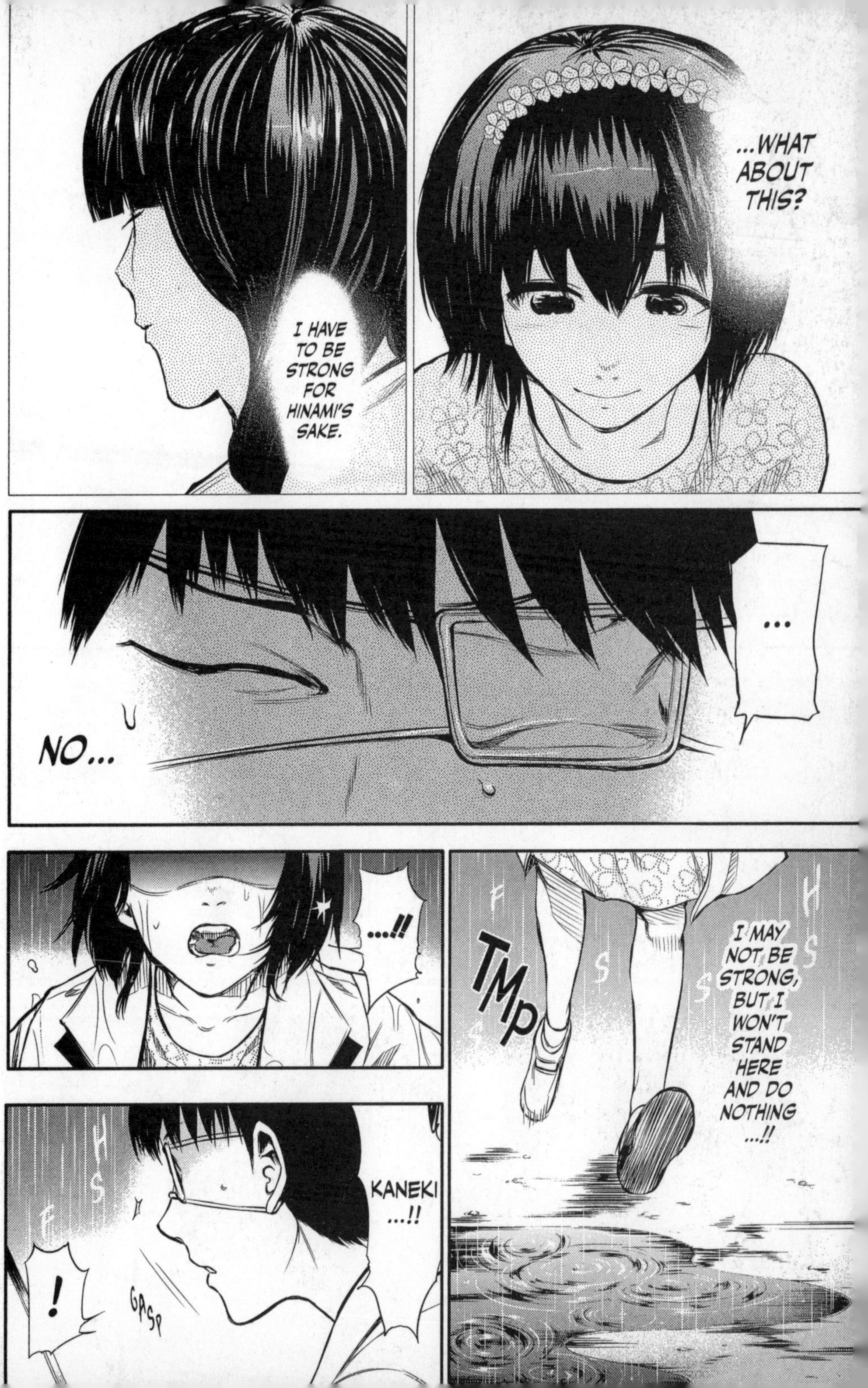
...WHAT ABOUT THIS?
I HAVE TO BE STRONG FOR HINAMI'S SAKE.
...
NO...
HSS
FSS
TMP
I MAY NOT BE STRONG, BUT I WON'T STAND HERE AND DO NOTHING ...!!
...!!
KANEKI ...!!
HSS
FSS
!
GASP

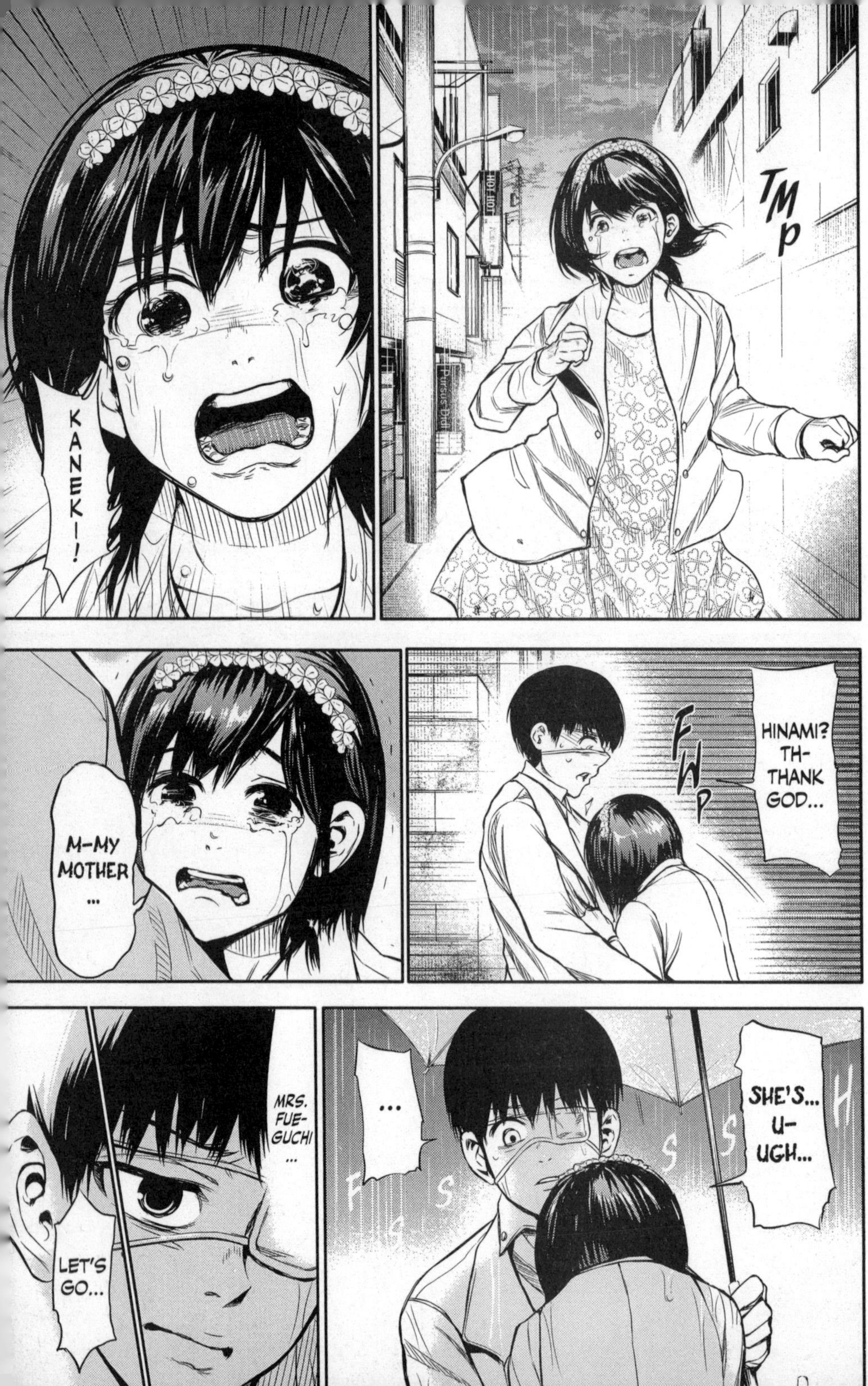
TMP
KANEKI!!
FWP
HINAMI? TH-THANK GOD...
M-MY MOTHER ...
SHE'S... U-UGH...
FSSSSH
...
MRS. FUEGUCHI ...
LET'S GO...

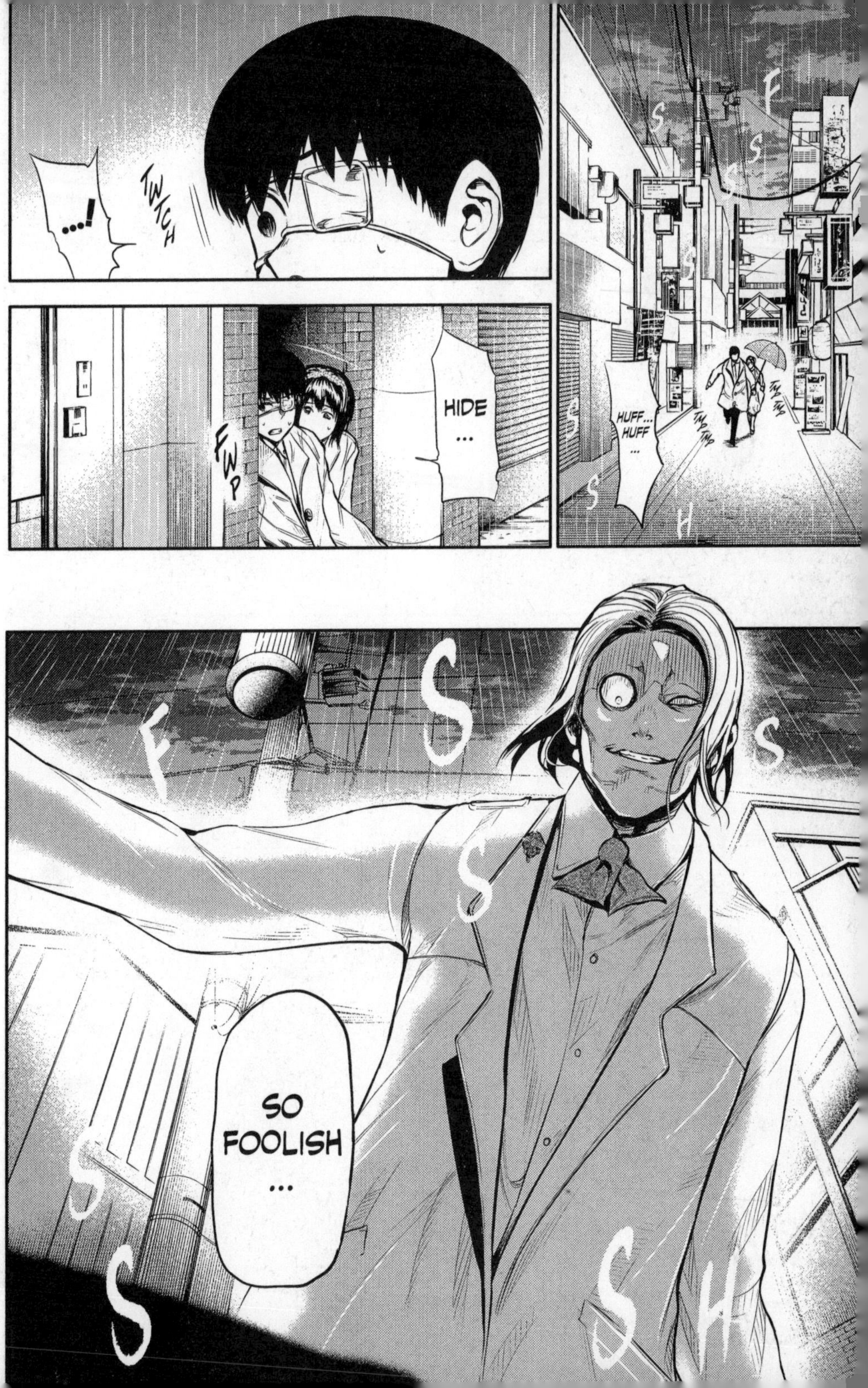

HUFF... HUFF ...
TMP TMP
TMP TMP
TWITCH
...!
HIDE ...
FWP
SO FOOLISH ...

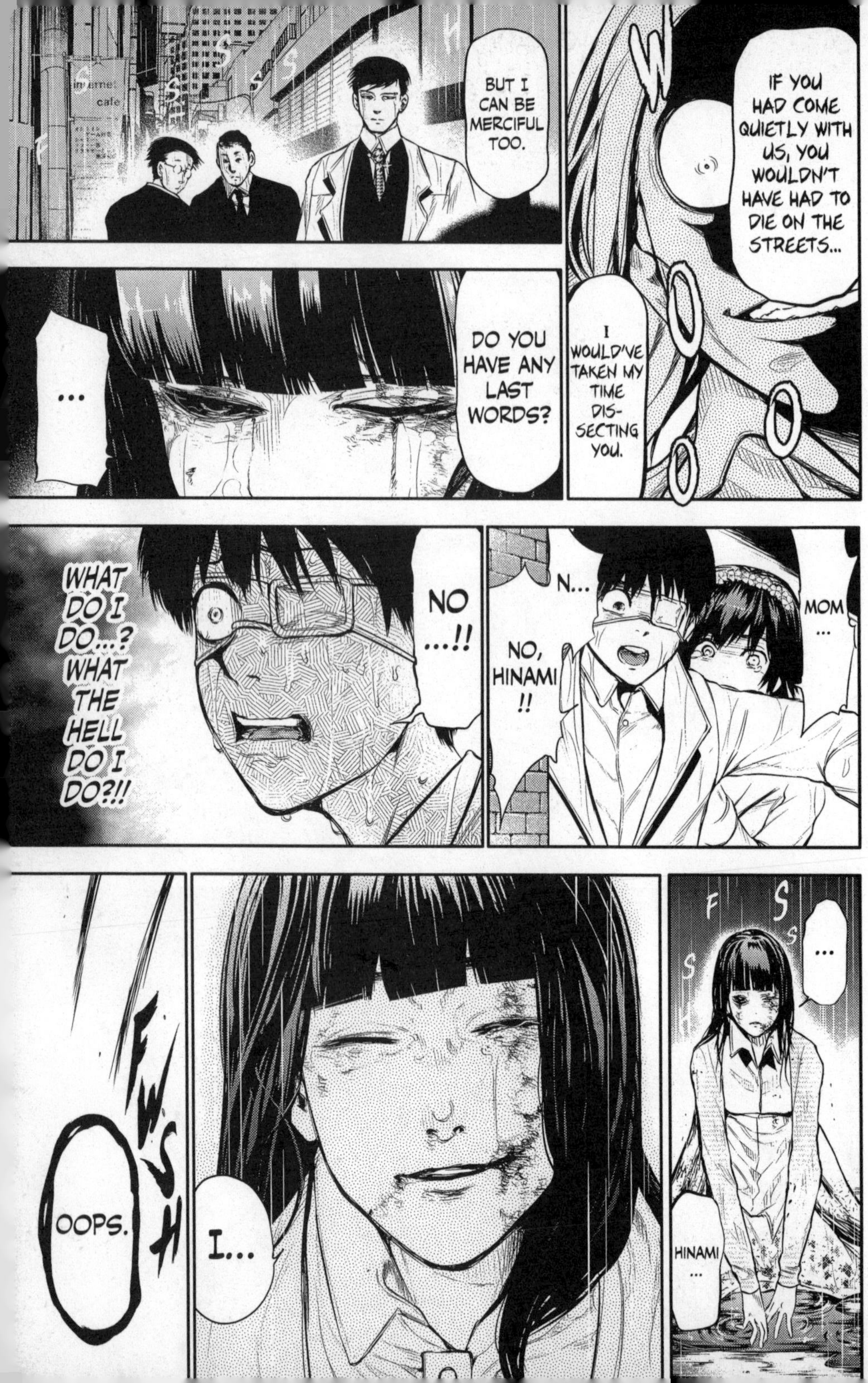
IF YOU HAD COME QUIETLY WITH US, YOU WOULDN'T HAVE HAD TO DIE ON THE STREETS...
I WOULD'VE TAKEN MY TIME DIS-SECTING YOU.
FSSSSSH
internet cafe
BUT I CAN BE MERCIFUL TOO.
DO YOU HAVE ANY LAST WORDS?
...
MOM...
N...
NO, HINAMI!!
NO...!!
WHAT DO I DO...? WHAT THE HELL DO I DO?!!
FSSSH
...
HINAMI...
I...
FWSH
OOPS.

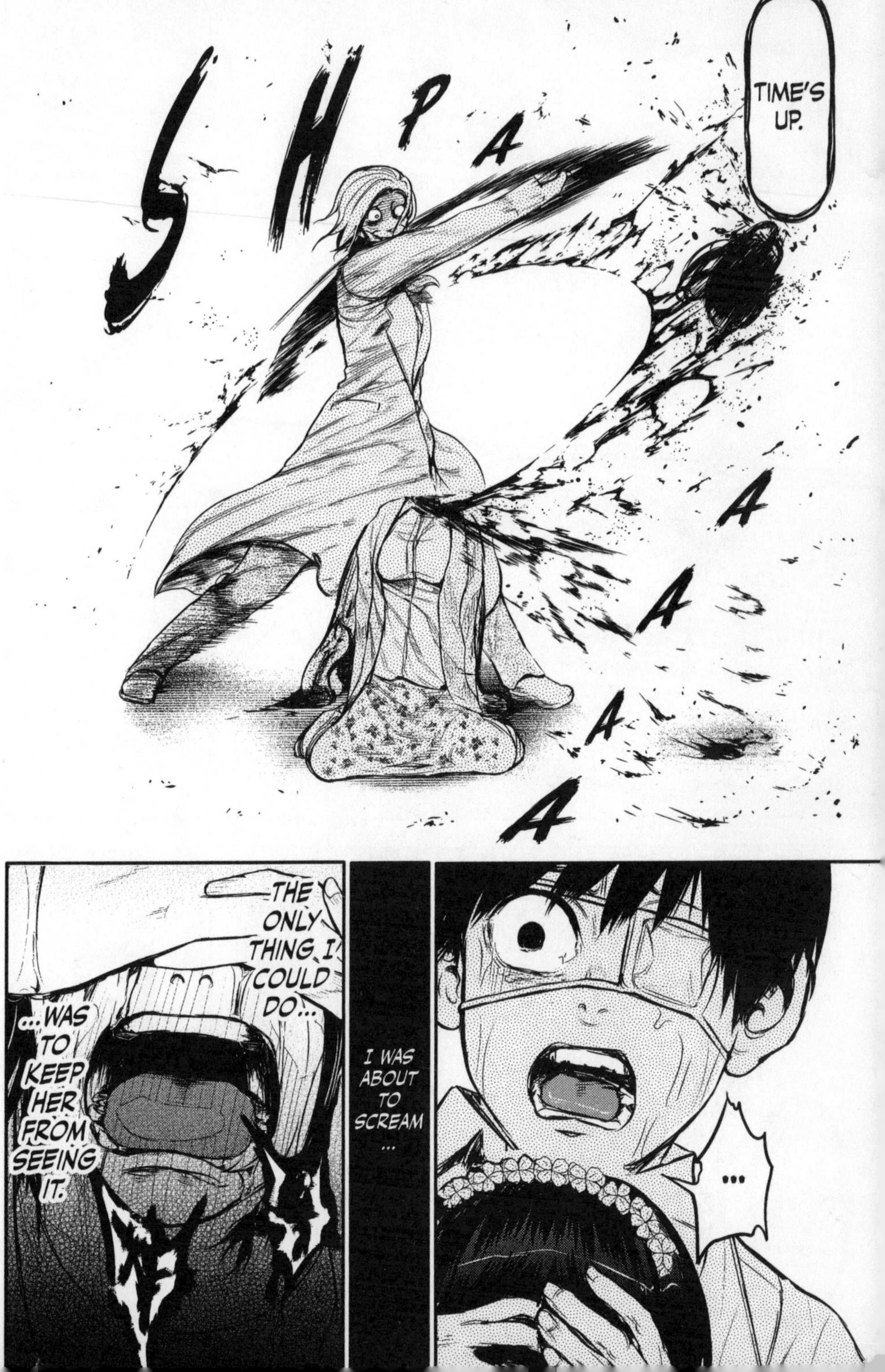
TIME'S UP.
SHPAAAAA
...
I WAS ABOUT TO SCREAM ...
THE ONLY THING I COULD DO...
...WAS TO KEEP HER FROM SEEING IT.

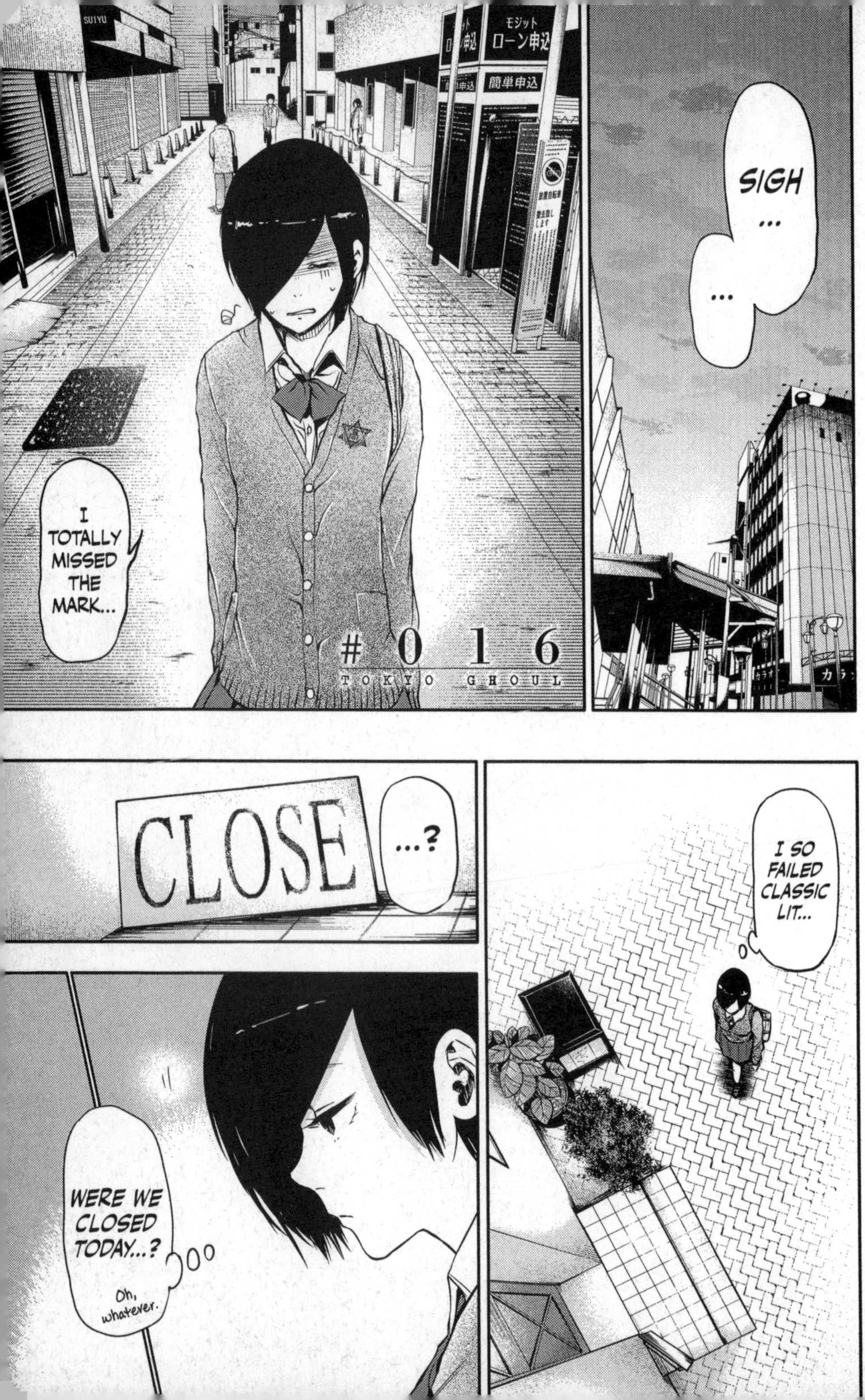
SIGH ...
...
SUIYU
モジット
ローン申込
簡単申込
I TOTALLY MISSED THE MARK...
#016
TOKYO GHOUL
I SO FAILED CLASSIC LIT...
CLOSE
...?
WERE WE CLOSED TODAY...?
Oh, whatever.

#016 [CONFINEMENT]

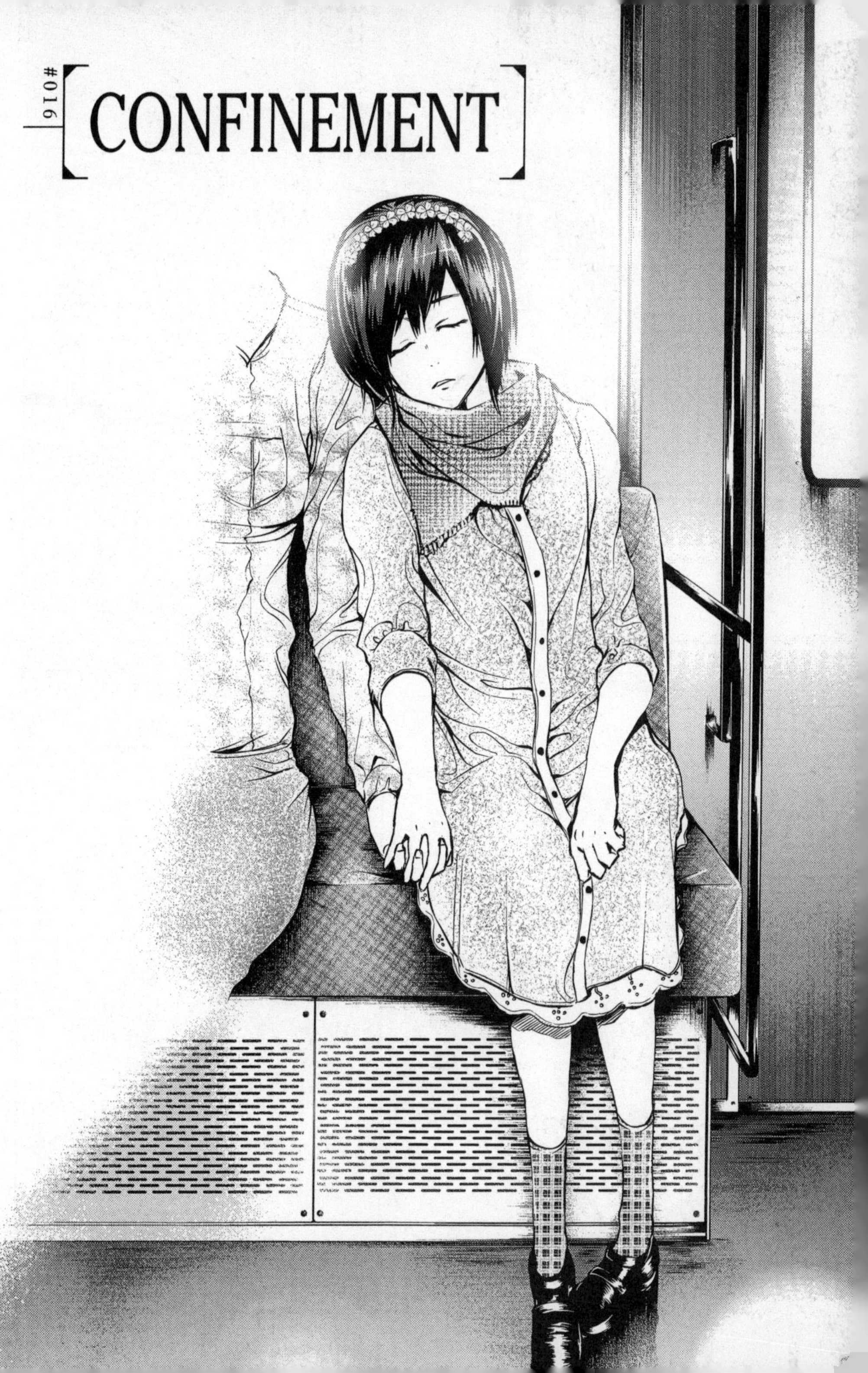

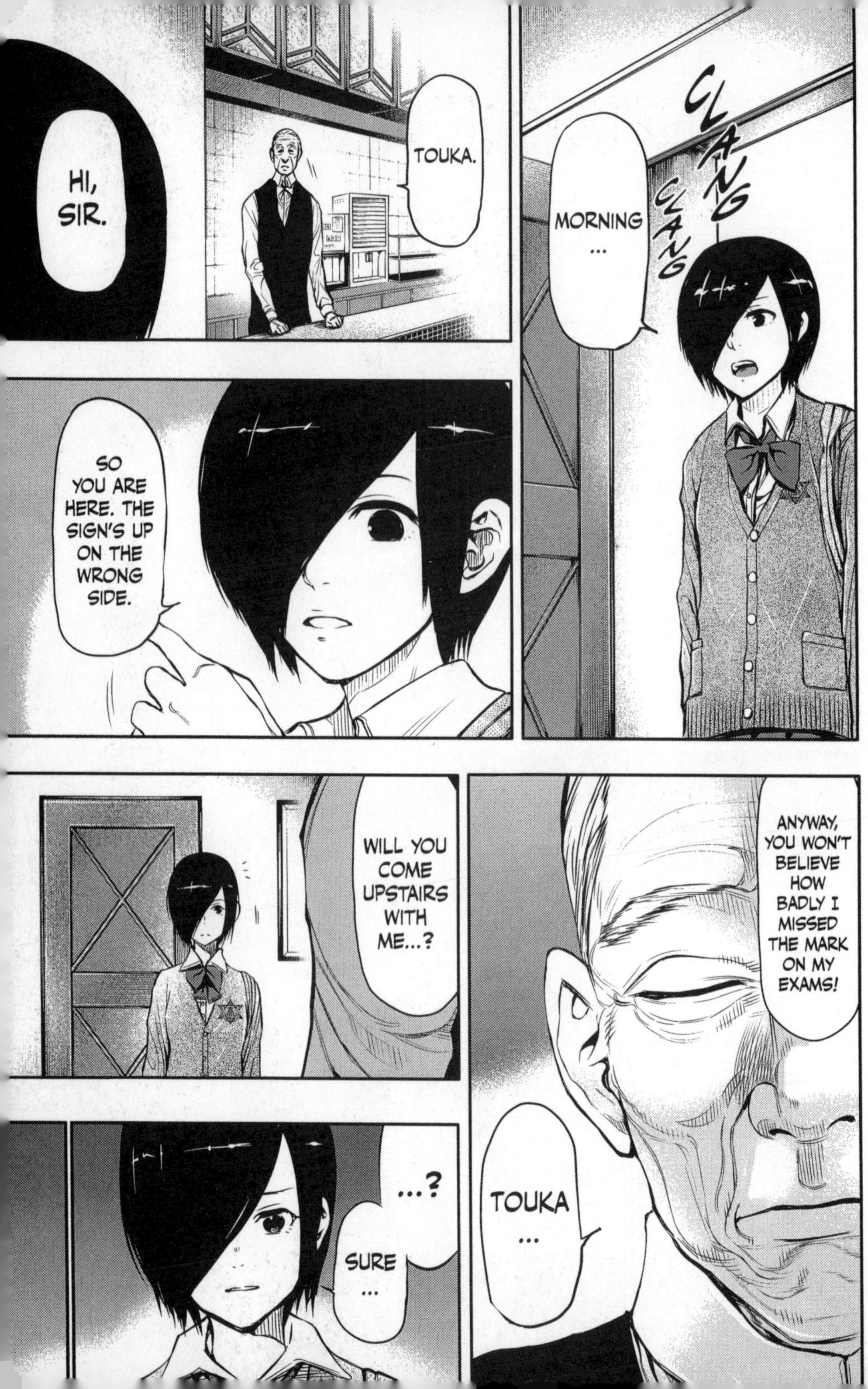

CLANG
CLANG
MORNING ...
TOUKA.
HI, SIR.
SO YOU ARE HERE. THE SIGN'S UP ON THE WRONG SIDE.
ANYWAY, YOU WON'T BELIEVE HOW BADLY I MISSED THE MARK ON MY EXAMS!
TOUKA ...
WILL YOU COME UPSTAIRS WITH ME...?
...?
SURE ...

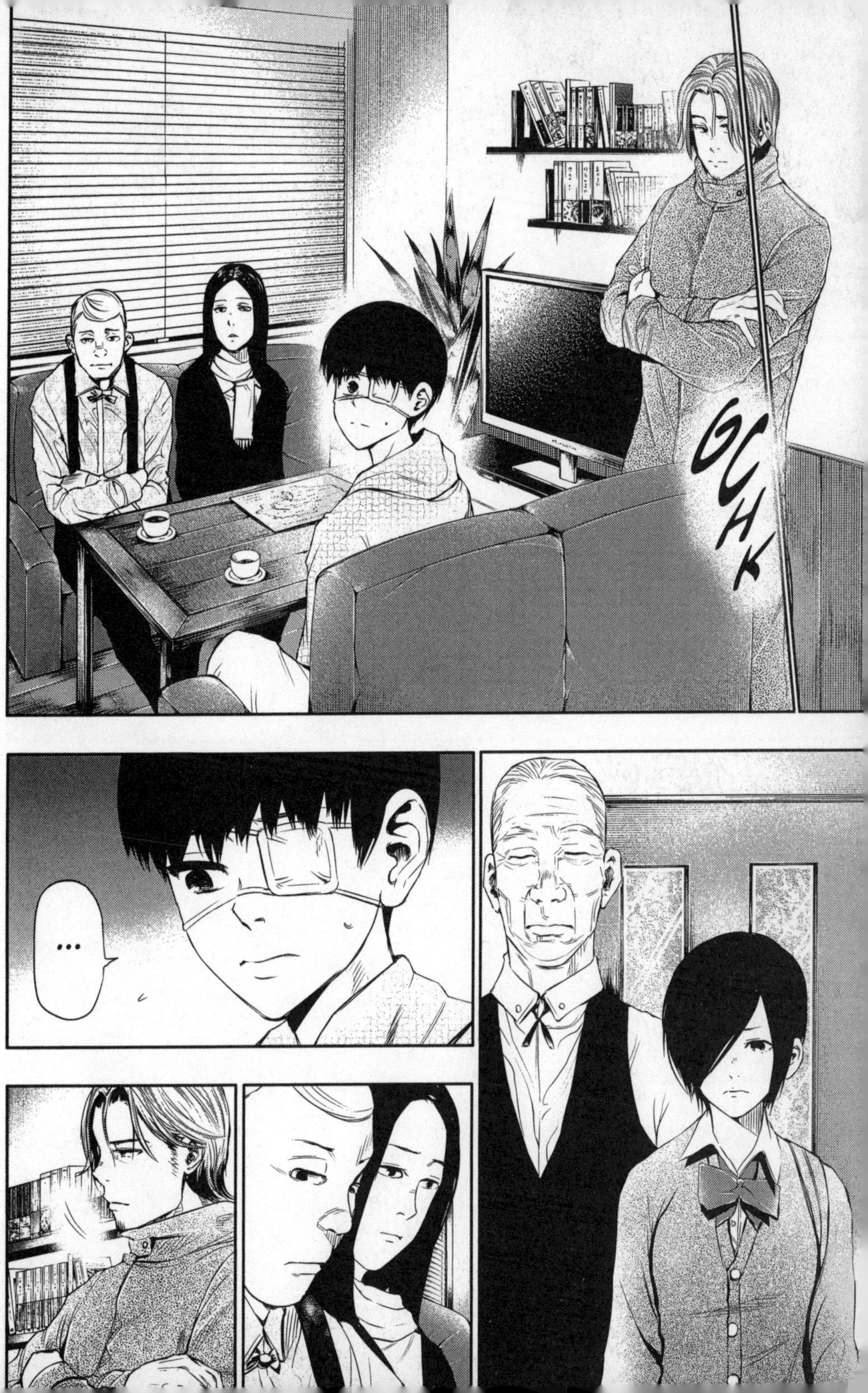
GCHK
...

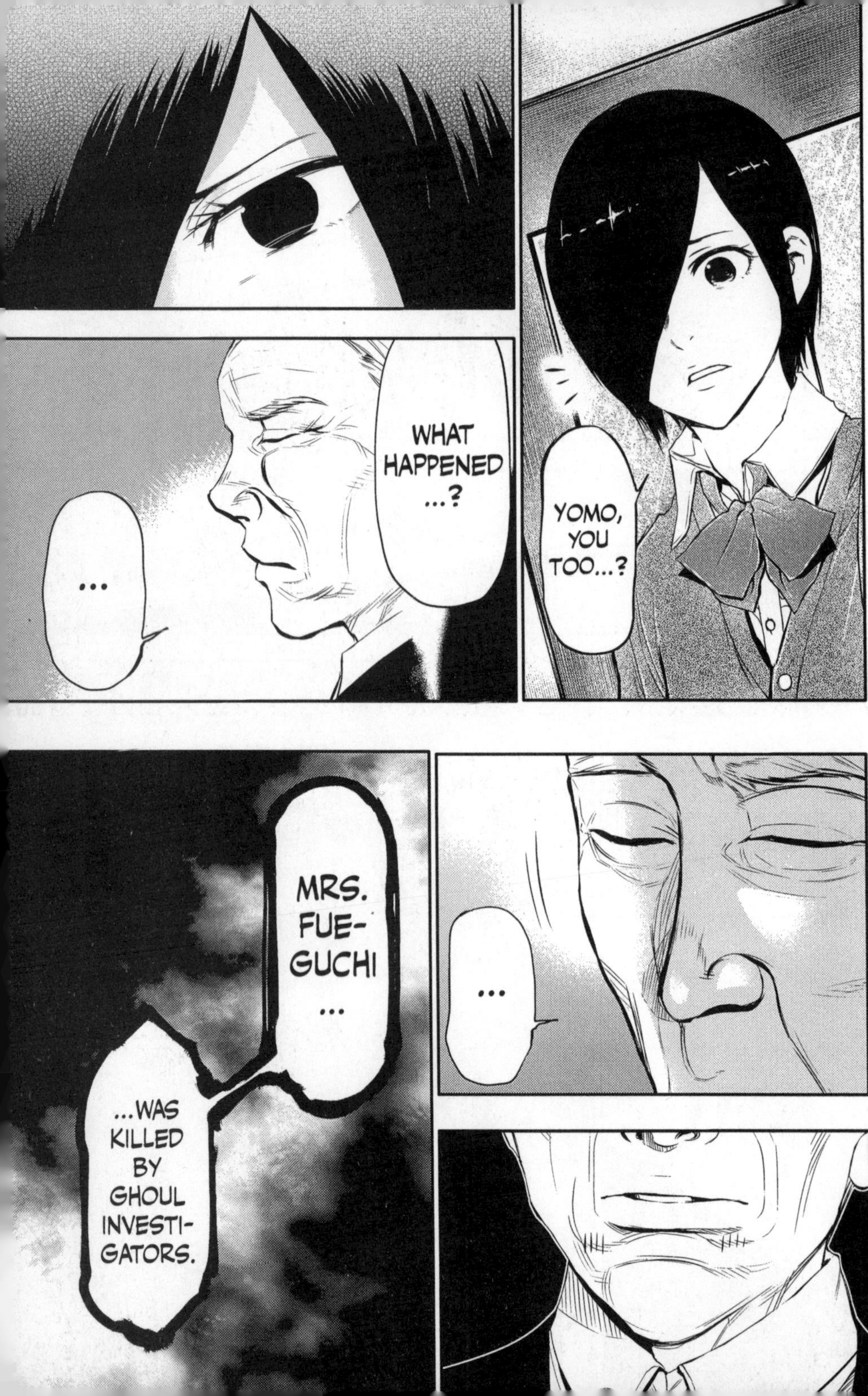
YOMO, YOU TOO...?
WHAT HAPPENED ...?
...
...
MRS. FUE-GUCHI ...
...WAS KILLED BY GHOUL INVESTI-GATORS.

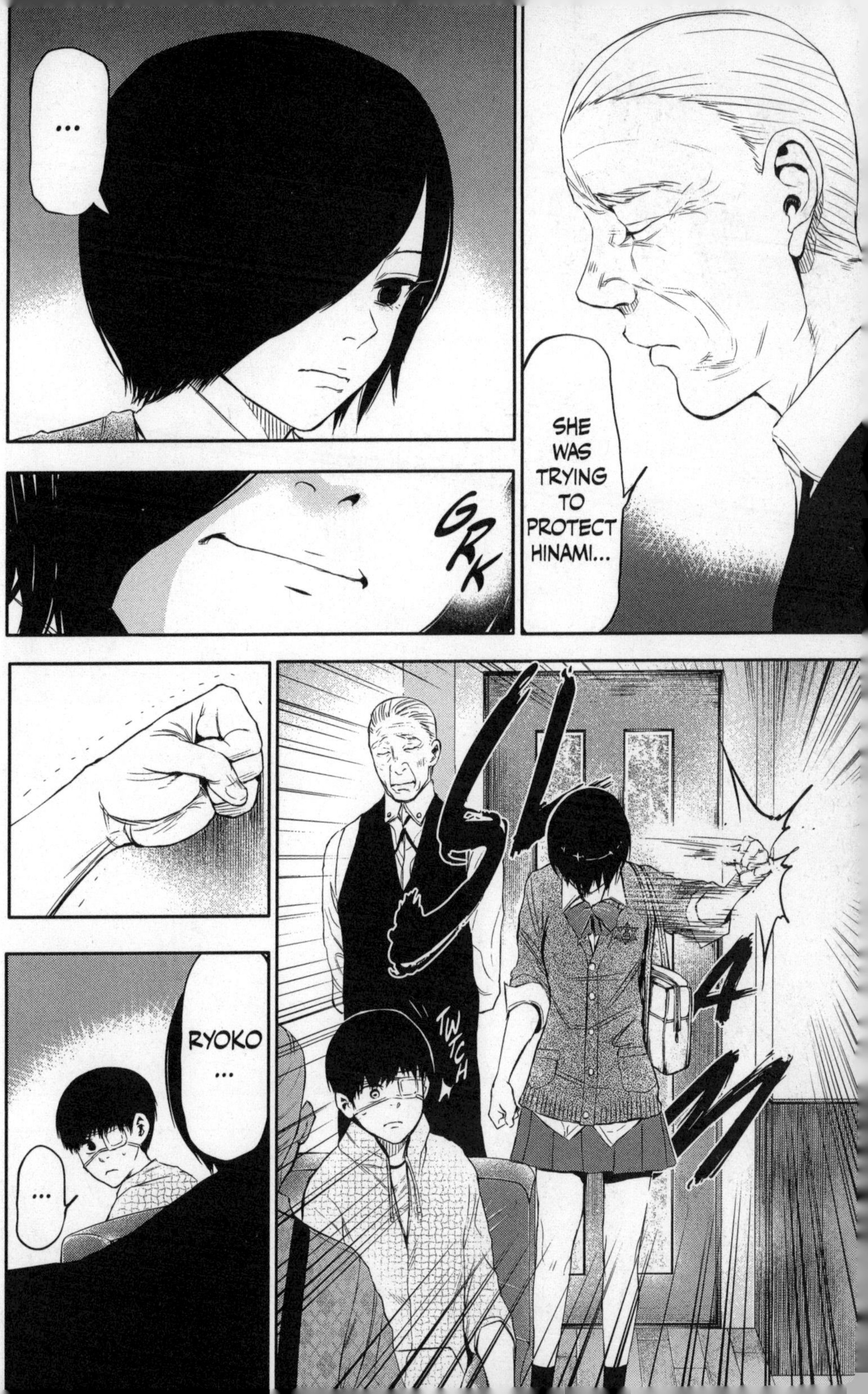
SHE WAS TRYING TO PROTECT HINAMI...
...
GRK
SLAM
TWITCH
RYOKO ...
...

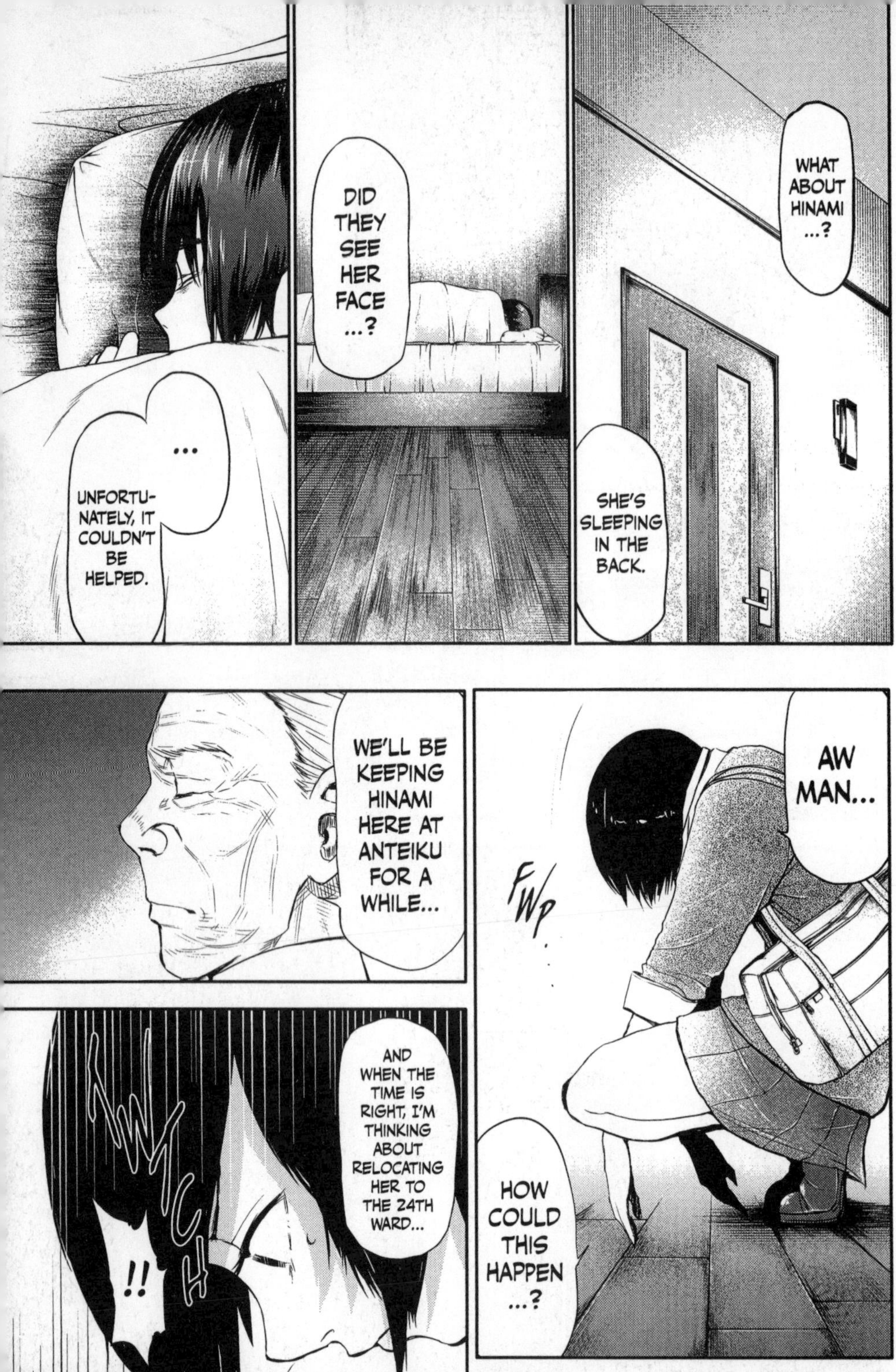
WHAT ABOUT HINAMI ...?
SHE'S SLEEPING IN THE BACK.
DID THEY SEE HER FACE ...?
...
UNFORTU-NATELY, IT COULDN'T BE HELPED.
AW MAN...
FWP
HOW COULD THIS HAPPEN ...?
WE'LL BE KEEPING HINAMI HERE AT ANTEIKU FOR A WHILE...
AND WHEN THE TIME IS RIGHT, I'M THINKING ABOUT RELOCATING HER TO THE 24TH WARD...
KWUCH
!!

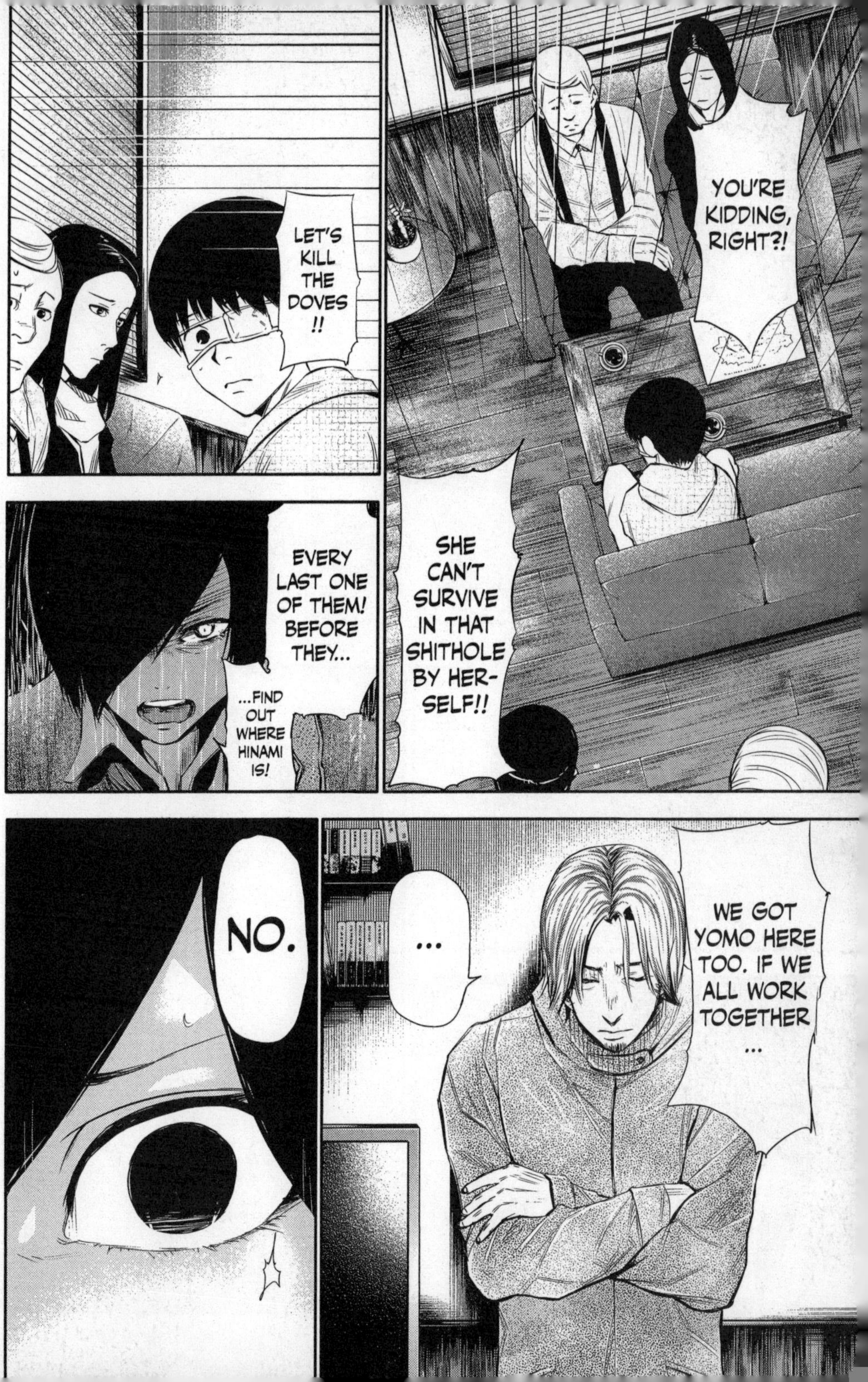
YOU'RE KIDDING, RIGHT?!
SHE CAN'T SURVIVE IN THAT SHITHOLE BY HER-SELF!!
LET'S KILL THE DOVES !!
EVERY LAST ONE OF THEM! BEFORE THEY...
...FIND OUT WHERE HINAMI IS!
WE GOT YOMO HERE TOO. IF WE ALL WORK TOGETHER ...
...
NO.

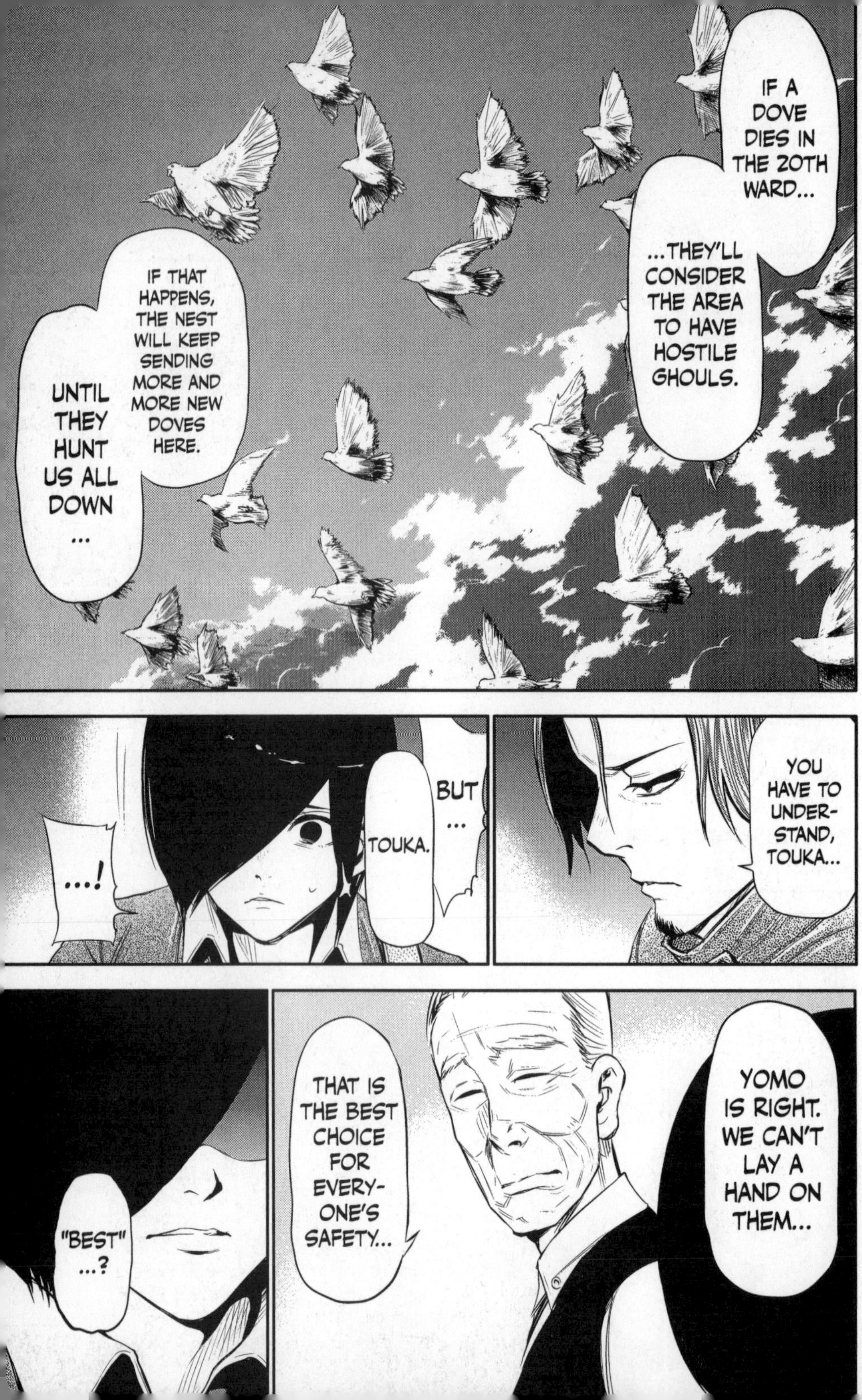
IF A DOVE DIES IN THE 20TH WARD...
...THEY'LL CONSIDER THE AREA TO HAVE HOSTILE GHOULS.
IF THAT HAPPENS, THE NEST WILL KEEP SENDING MORE AND MORE NEW DOVES HERE.
UNTIL THEY HUNT US ALL DOWN...
YOU HAVE TO UNDER-STAND, TOUKA...
BUT...
TOUKA.
...!
YOMO IS RIGHT. WE CAN'T LAY A HAND ON THEM...
THAT IS THE BEST CHOICE FOR EVERY-ONE'S SAFETY...
"BEST"...?

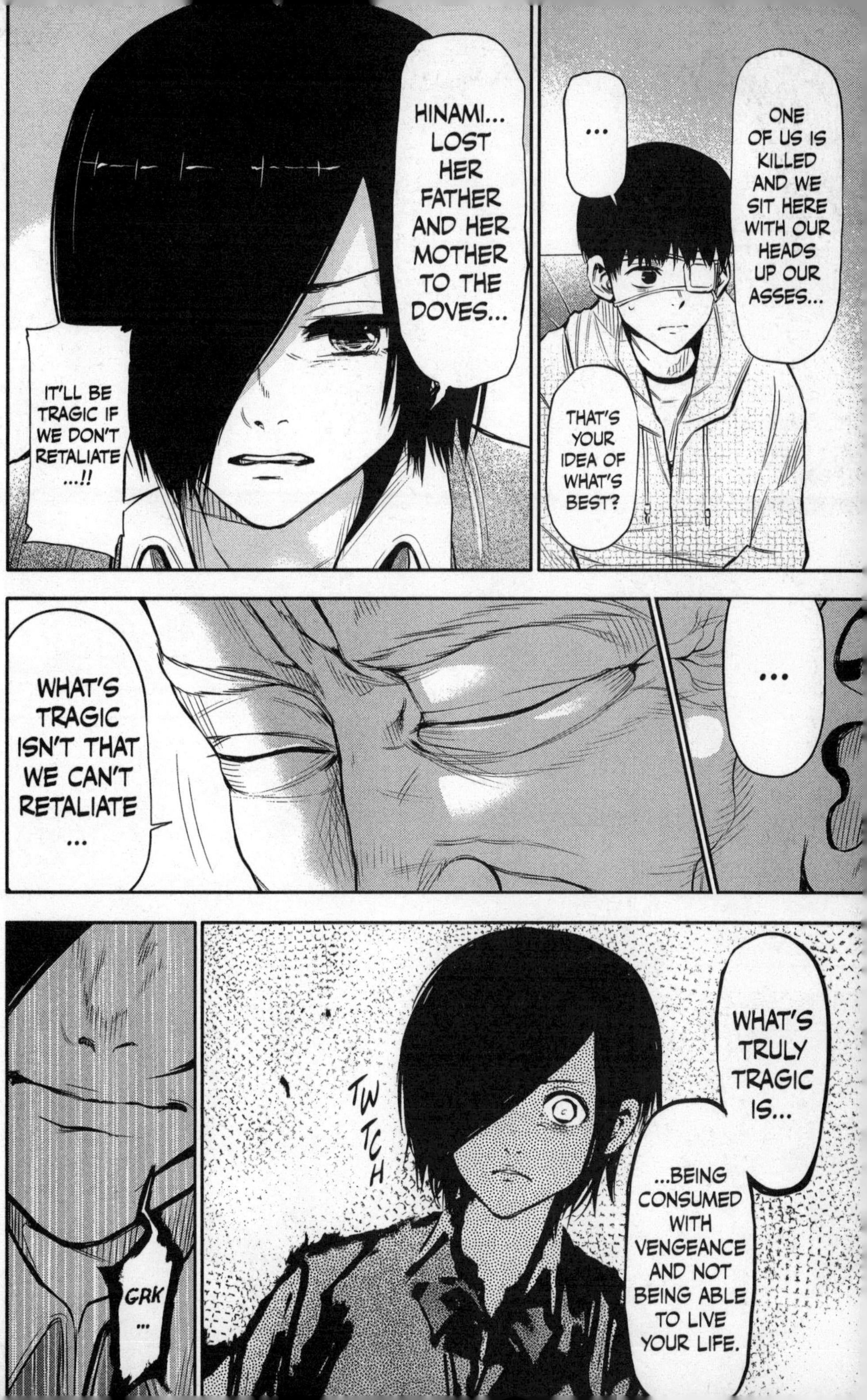
ONE OF US IS KILLED AND WE SIT HERE WITH OUR HEADS UP OUR ASSES...
...
THAT'S YOUR IDEA OF WHAT'S BEST?
HINAMI... LOST HER FATHER AND HER MOTHER TO THE DOVES...
IT'LL BE TRAGIC IF WE DON'T RETALIATE ...!!
...
WHAT'S TRAGIC ISN'T THAT WE CAN'T RETALIATE ...
WHAT'S TRULY TRAGIC IS...
...BEING CONSUMED WITH VENGEANCE AND NOT BEING ABLE TO LIVE YOUR LIFE.
TWITCH
GRK ...

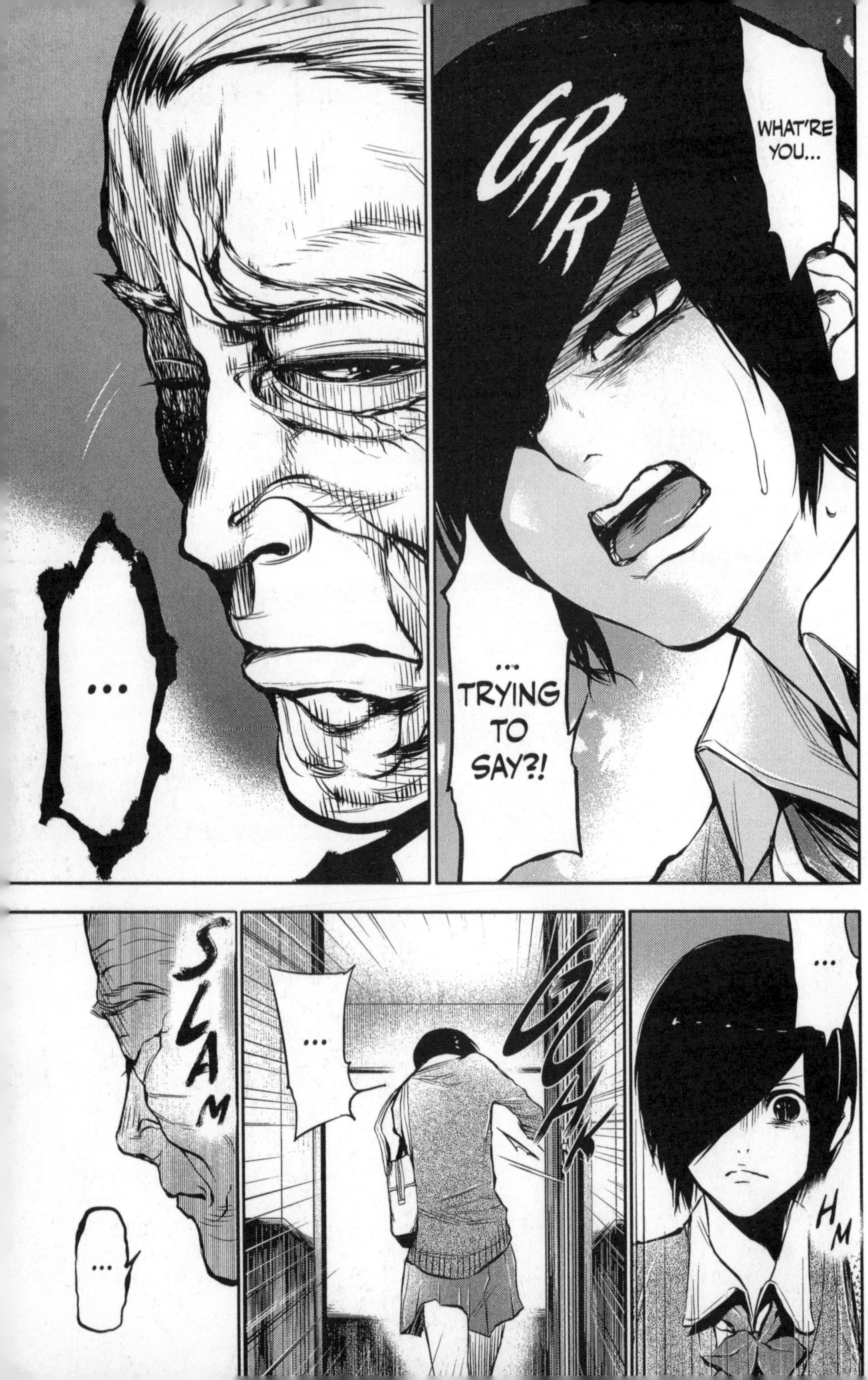
GRR
WHAT'RE YOU...
...TRYING TO SAY?!
...
...
HM
...
SLAM
...

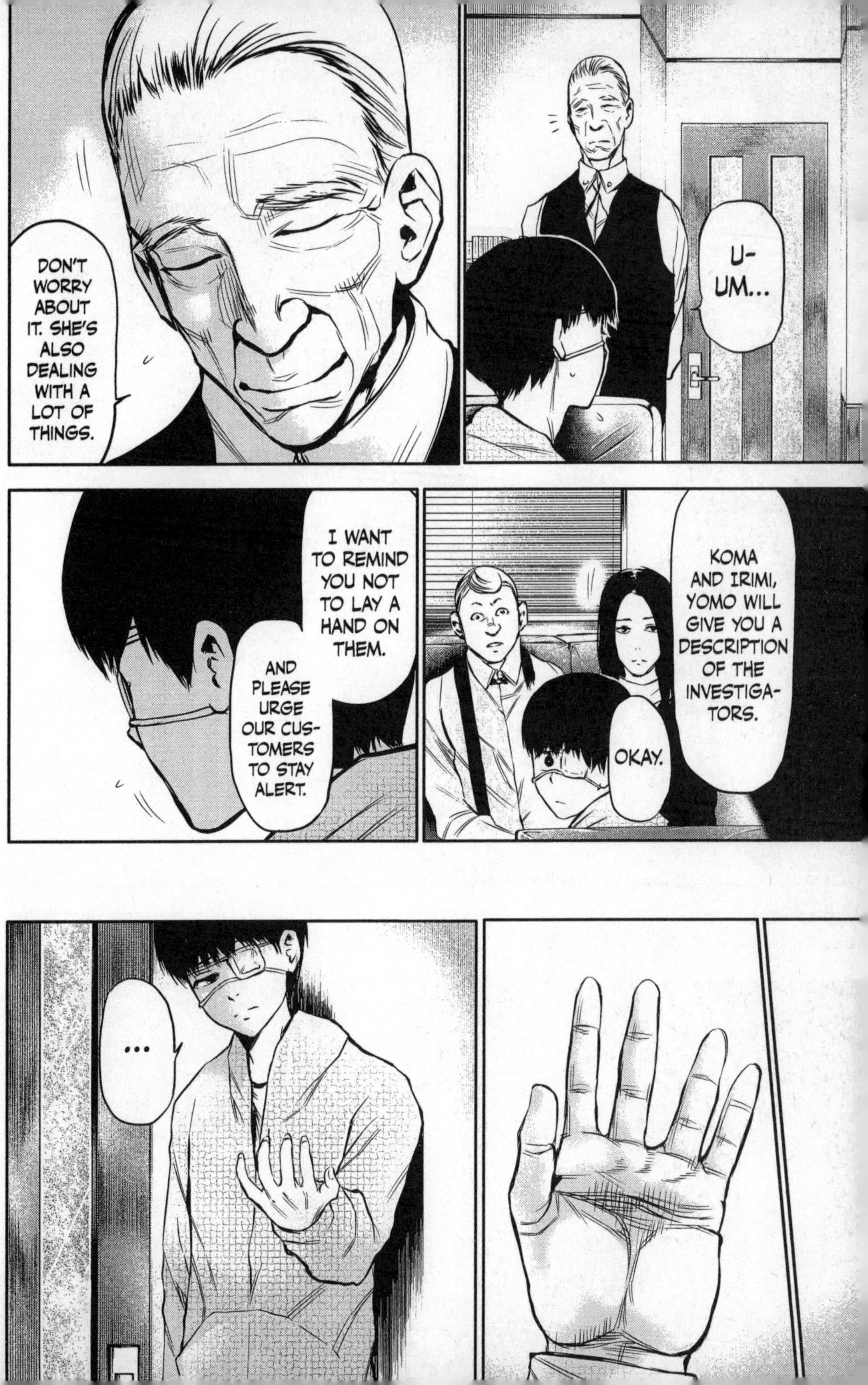
U-UM...
DON'T WORRY ABOUT IT. SHE'S ALSO DEALING WITH A LOT OF THINGS.
KOMA AND IRIMI, YOMO WILL GIVE YOU A DESCRIPTION OF THE INVESTIGATORS.
OKAY.
I WANT TO REMIND YOU NOT TO LAY A HAND ON THEM.
AND PLEASE URGE OUR CUSTOMERS TO STAY ALERT.
...

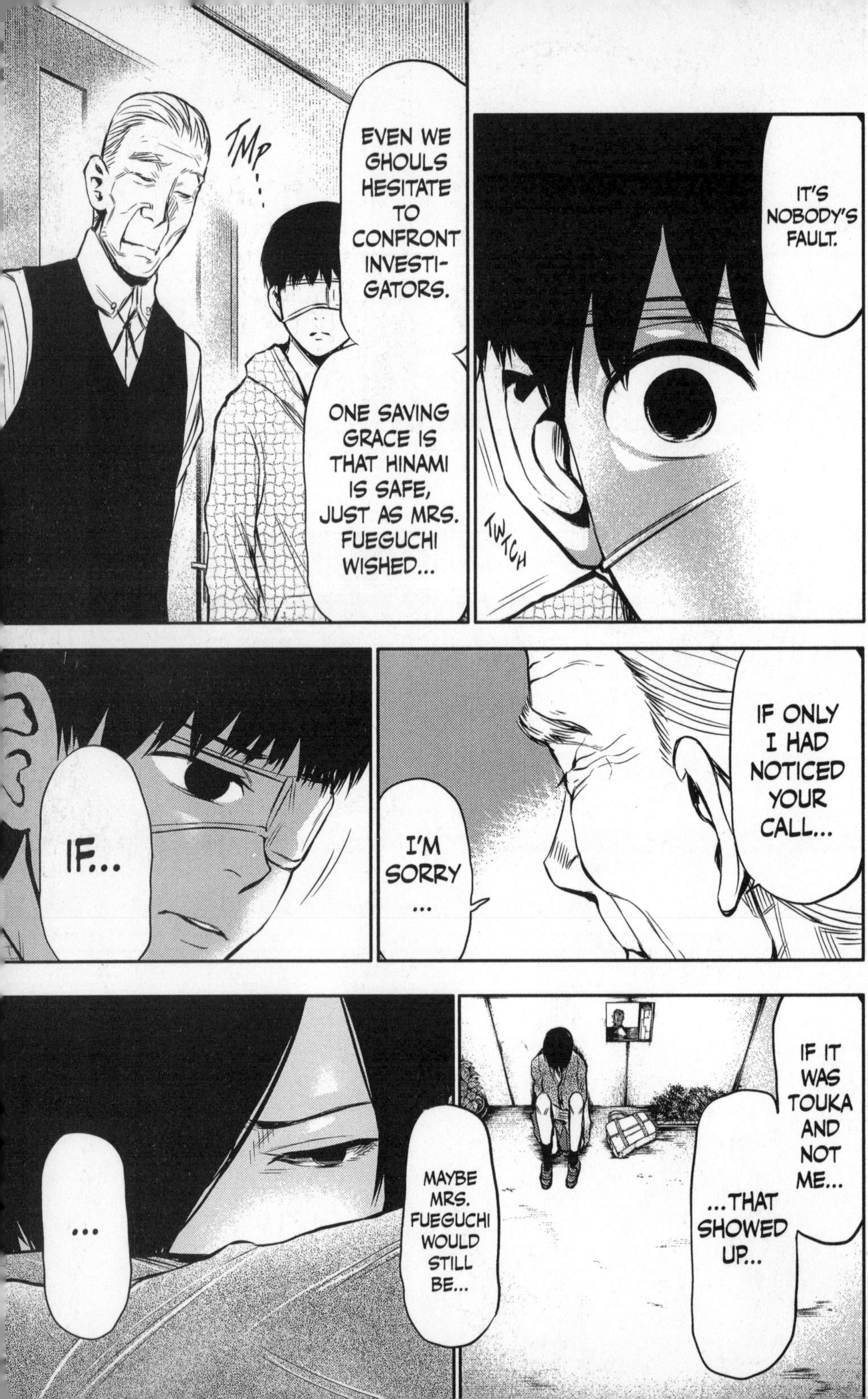
IT'S NOBODY'S FAULT.
TWITCH
TMP...
EVEN WE GHOULS HESITATE TO CONFRONT INVESTIGATORS.
ONE SAVING GRACE IS THAT HINAMI IS SAFE, JUST AS MRS. FUEGUCHI WISHED...
IF ONLY I HAD NOTICED YOUR CALL...
I'M SORRY ...
IF...
IF IT WAS TOUKA AND NOT ME...
...THAT SHOWED UP...
MAYBE MRS. FUEGUCHI WOULD STILL BE...
...

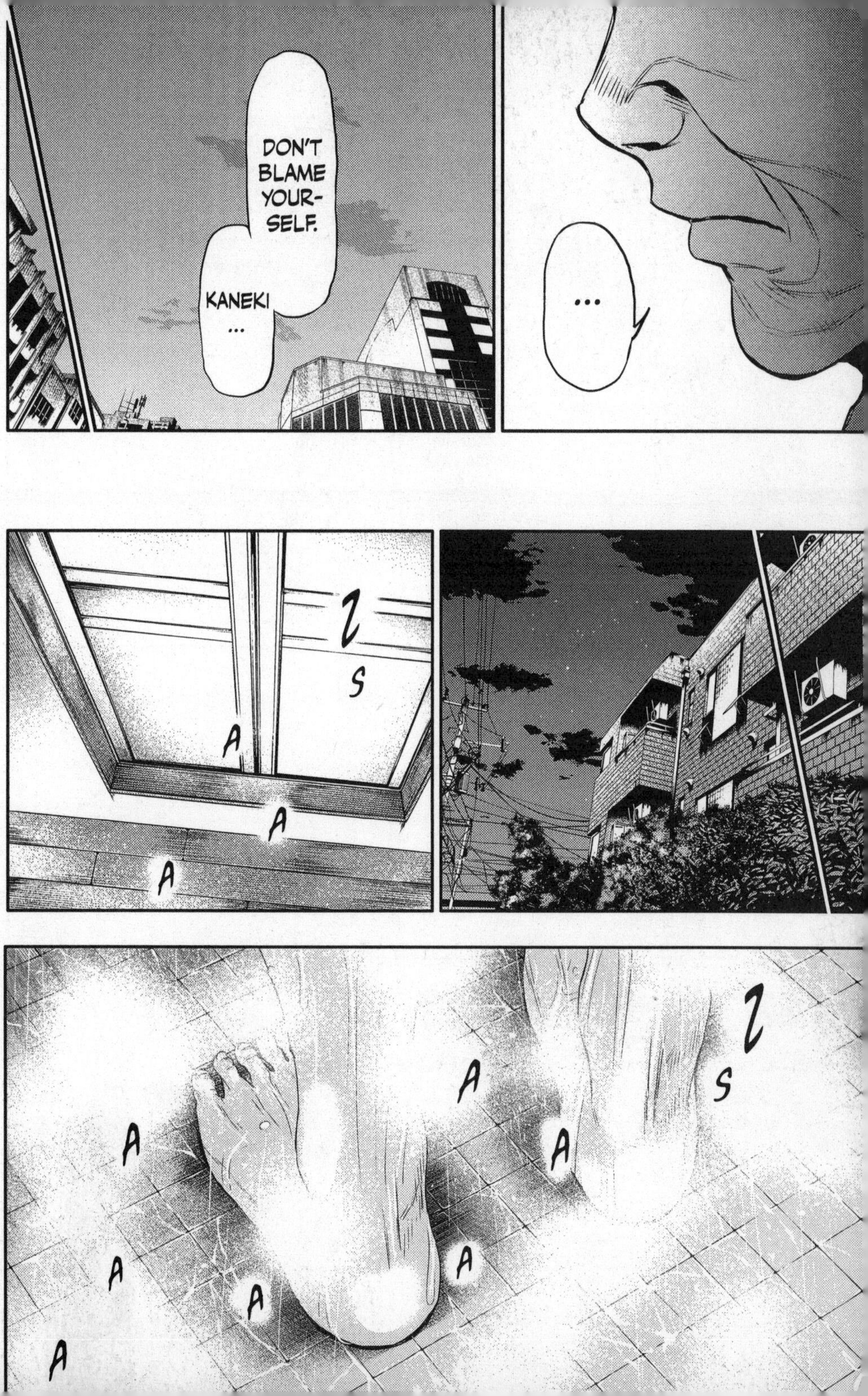
...
DON'T BLAME YOUR-SELF.
KANEKI ...
ZSAAA
ZSAAAAAAA

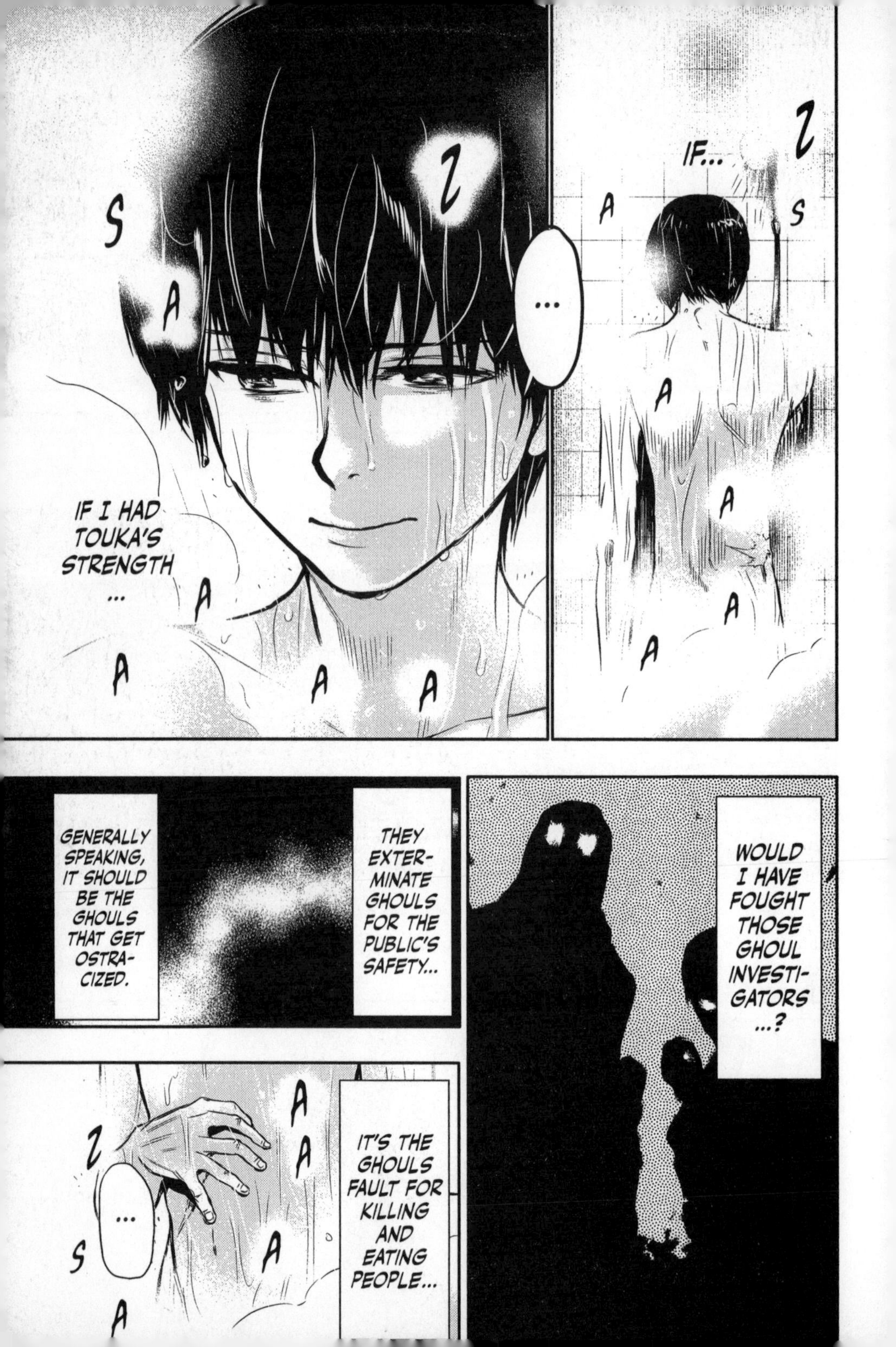
IF...
ZSAAAAA
...
SAZAAAAA
IF I HAD TOUKA'S STRENGTH...
WOULD I HAVE FOUGHT THOSE GHOUL INVESTIGATORS...?
THEY EXTERMINATE GHOULS FOR THE PUBLIC'S SAFETY...
GENERALLY SPEAKING, IT SHOULD BE THE GHOULS THAT GET OSTRACIZED.
IT'S THE GHOULS FAULT FOR KILLING AND EATING PEOPLE...
AAA
...
ZSA

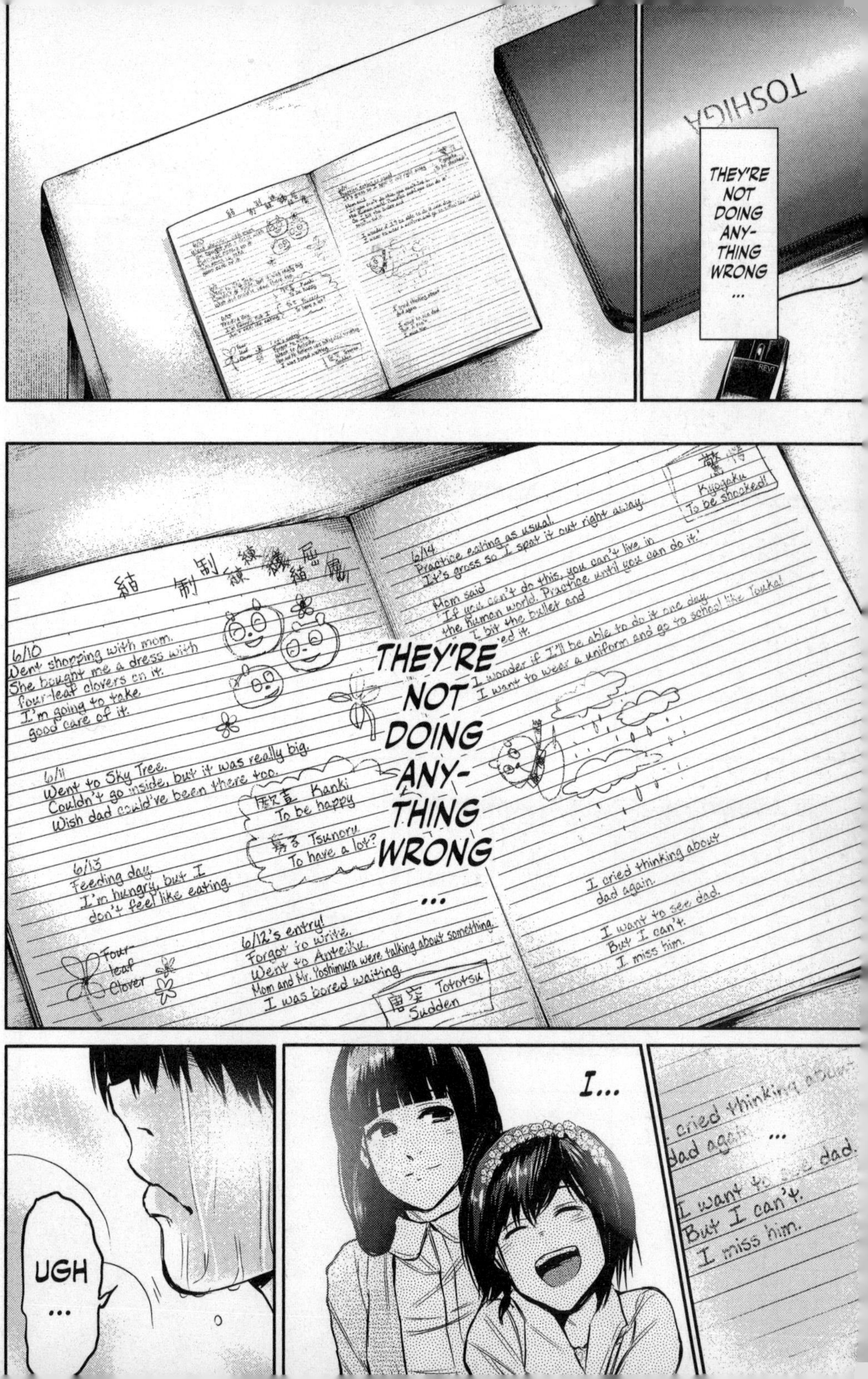
THEY'RE NOT DOING ANYTHING WRONG...
驚愕 Kyogaku To be shocked!
6/14 Practice eating as usual. It's gross so I spat it out right away.
Mom said "If you can't do this, you can't live in the human world. Practice until you can do it." I bit the bullet and
I wonder if I'll be able to do it one day. I want to wear a uniform and go to school like Touka!
I cried thinking about dad again.
I want to see dad. But I can't. I miss him.
6/10 Went shopping with mom. She bought me a dress with four-leaf clovers on it. I'm going to take good care of it.
6/11 Went to Sky Tree. Couldn't go inside, but it was really big. Wish dad could've been there too.
歓喜 Kanki To be happy
募る Tsunoru To have a lot?
6/13 Feeding day. I'm hungry, but I don't feel like eating.
Four leaf Clover
6/12's entry! Forgot to write. Went to Anteiku. Mom and Mr. Yoshimura were talking about something. I was bored waiting.
唐突 Tototsu Sudden
THEY'RE NOT DOING ANYTHING WRONG...
I cried thinking about dad again ...
I want to see dad.
I want to see dad.
But I can't.
I miss him.
I...
UGH...

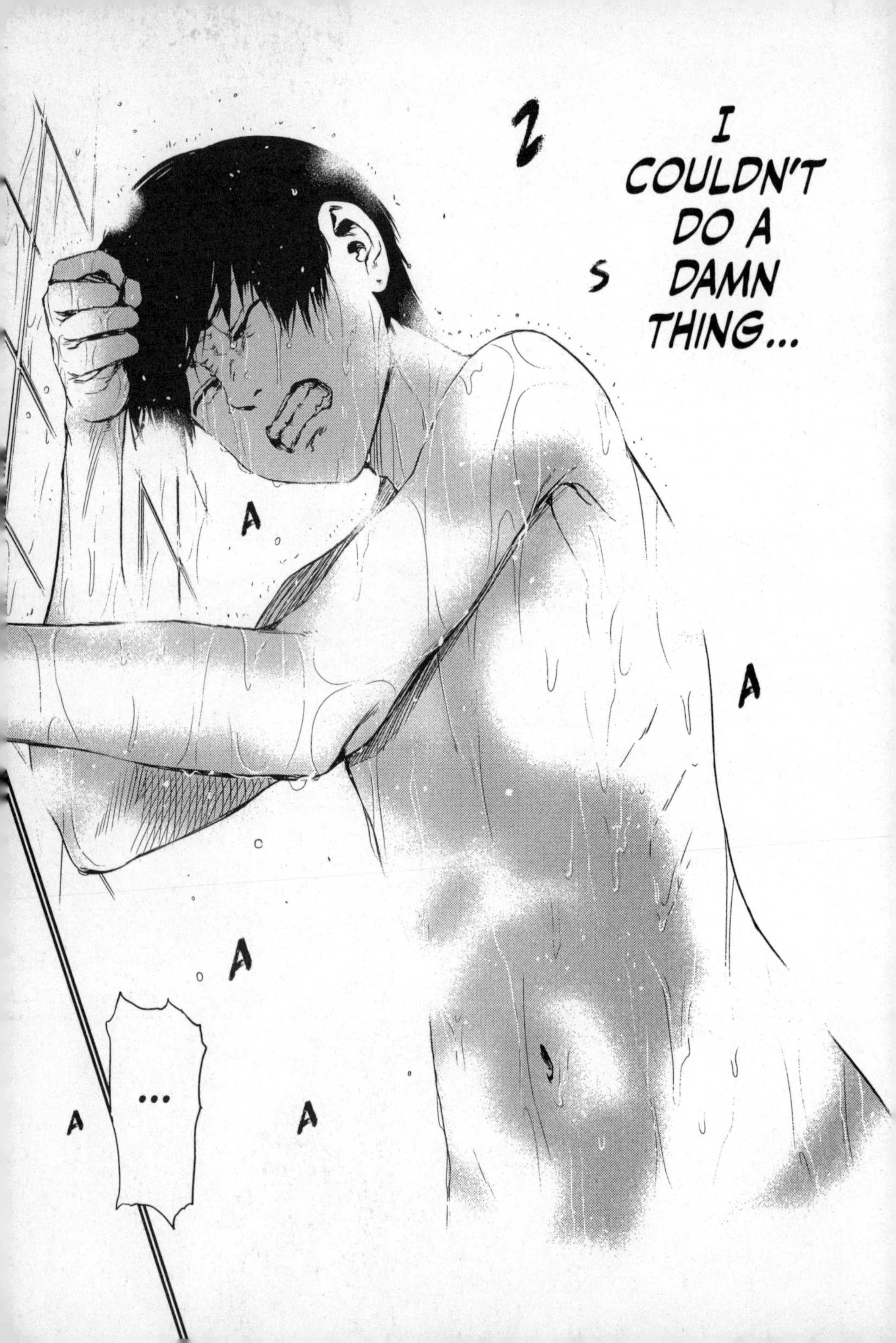
I COULDN'T DO A DAMN THING...
ZSAAAAA
...

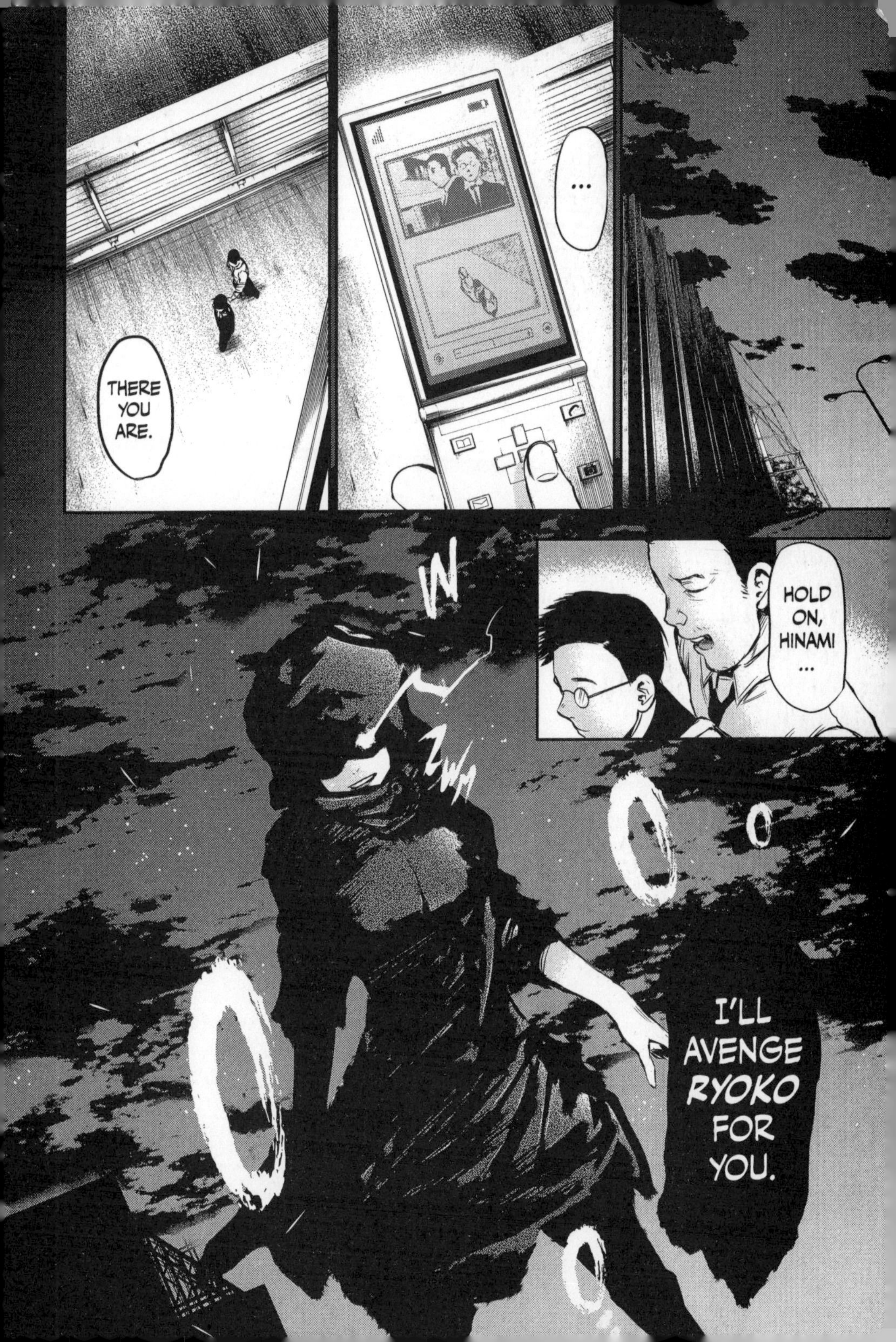
...
THERE YOU ARE.
HOLD ON, HINAMI ...
WZWM
I'LL AVENGE RYOKO FOR YOU.

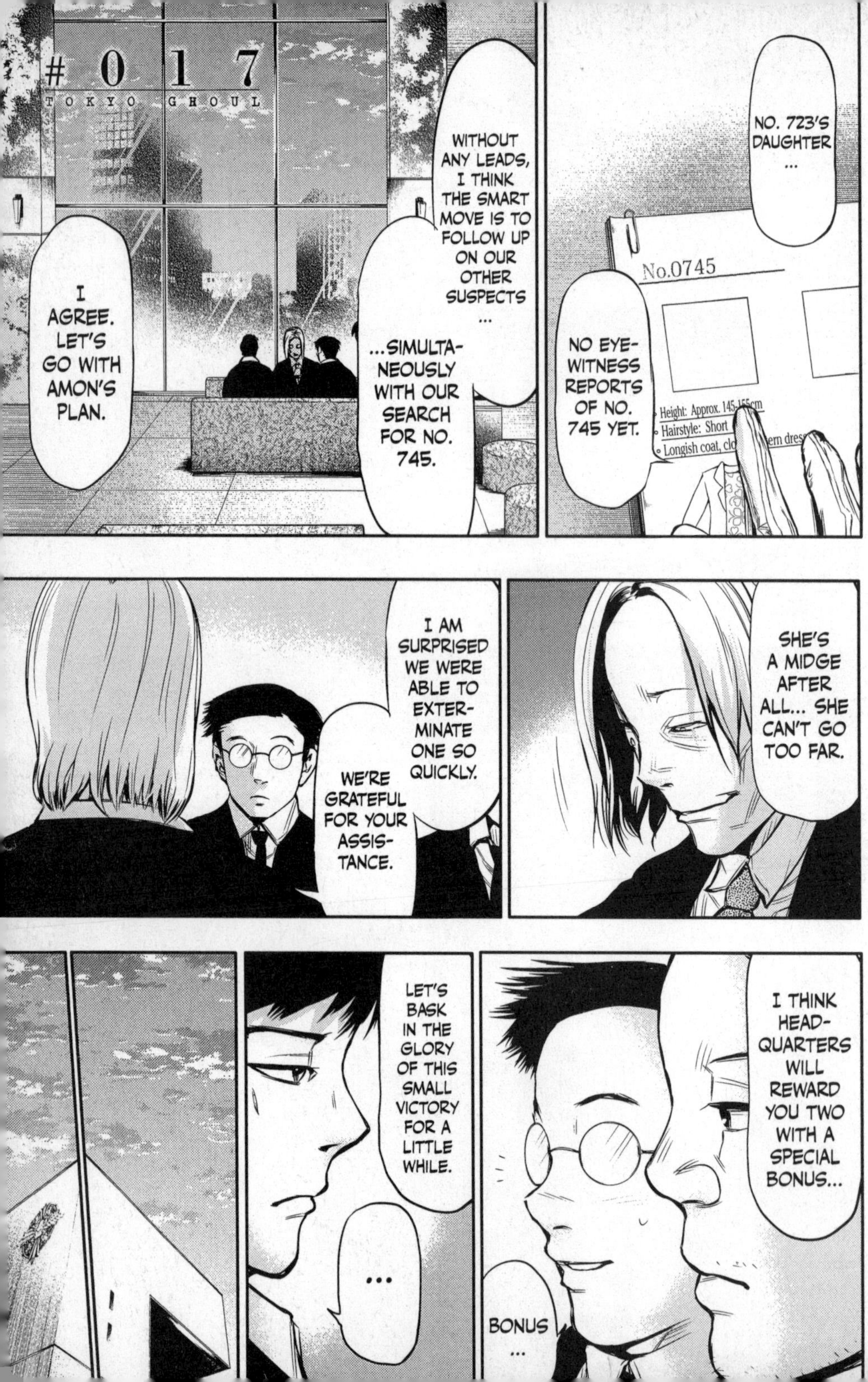
#017
TOKYO GHOUL
NO. 723'S DAUGHTER ...
No.0745
Height: Approx. 145-155cm
Hairstyle: Short
NO EYE-WITNESS REPORTS OF NO. 745 YET.
WITHOUT ANY LEADS, I THINK THE SMART MOVE IS TO FOLLOW UP ON OUR OTHER SUSPECTS ...
...SIMULTANEOUSLY WITH OUR SEARCH FOR NO. 745.
I AGREE. LET'S GO WITH AMON'S PLAN.
SHE'S A MIDGE AFTER ALL... SHE CAN'T GO TOO FAR.
I AM SURPRISED WE WERE ABLE TO EXTERMINATE ONE SO QUICKLY.
WE'RE GRATEFUL FOR YOUR ASSISTANCE.
I THINK HEADQUARTERS WILL REWARD YOU TWO WITH A SPECIAL BONUS...
BONUS ...
LET'S BASK IN THE GLORY OF THIS SMALL VICTORY FOR A LITTLE WHILE.
...

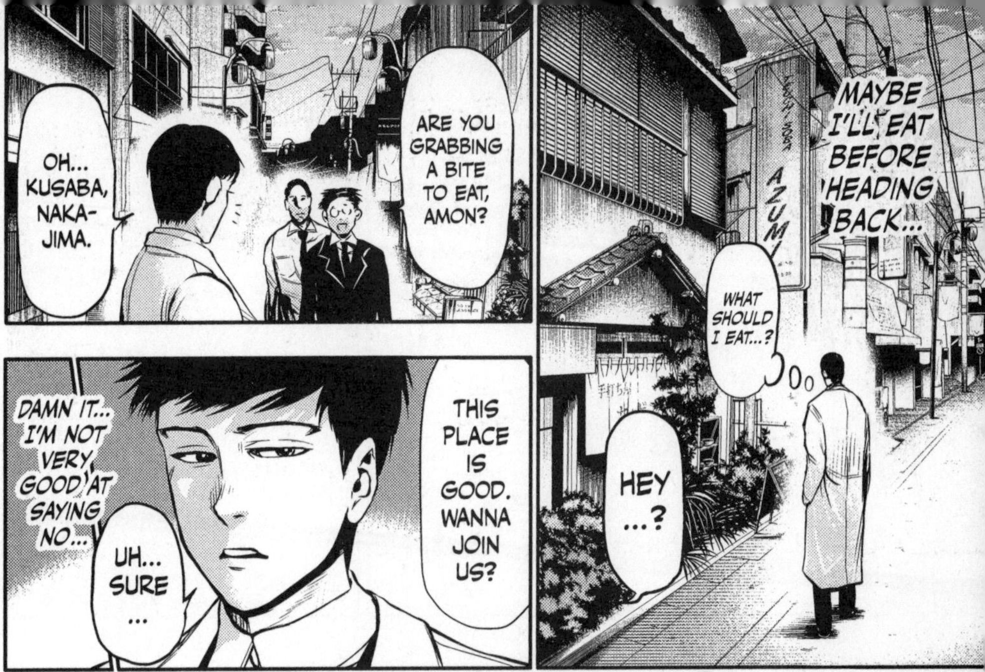
MAYBE I'LL EAT BEFORE HEADING BACK...
AZUMI
WHAT SHOULD I EAT...?
HEY ...?
ARE YOU GRABBING A BITE TO EAT, AMON?
OH... KUSABA, NAKAJIMA.
THIS PLACE IS GOOD. WANNA JOIN US?
DAMN IT... I'M NOT VERY GOOD AT SAYING NO...
UH... SURE ...

017 TOKYO GHOUL [RABBIT MASK]

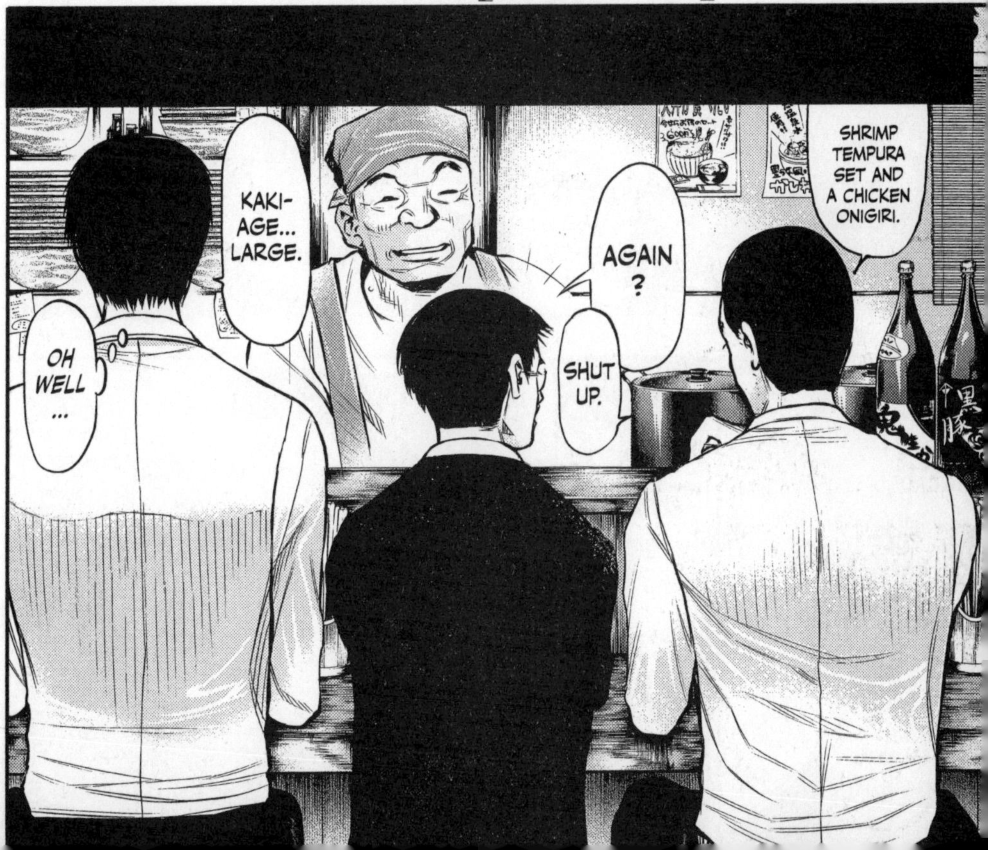
SHRIMP TEMPURA SET AND A CHICKEN ONIGIRI.
AGAIN ?
SHUT UP.
KAKI-AGE... LARGE.
OH WELL ...

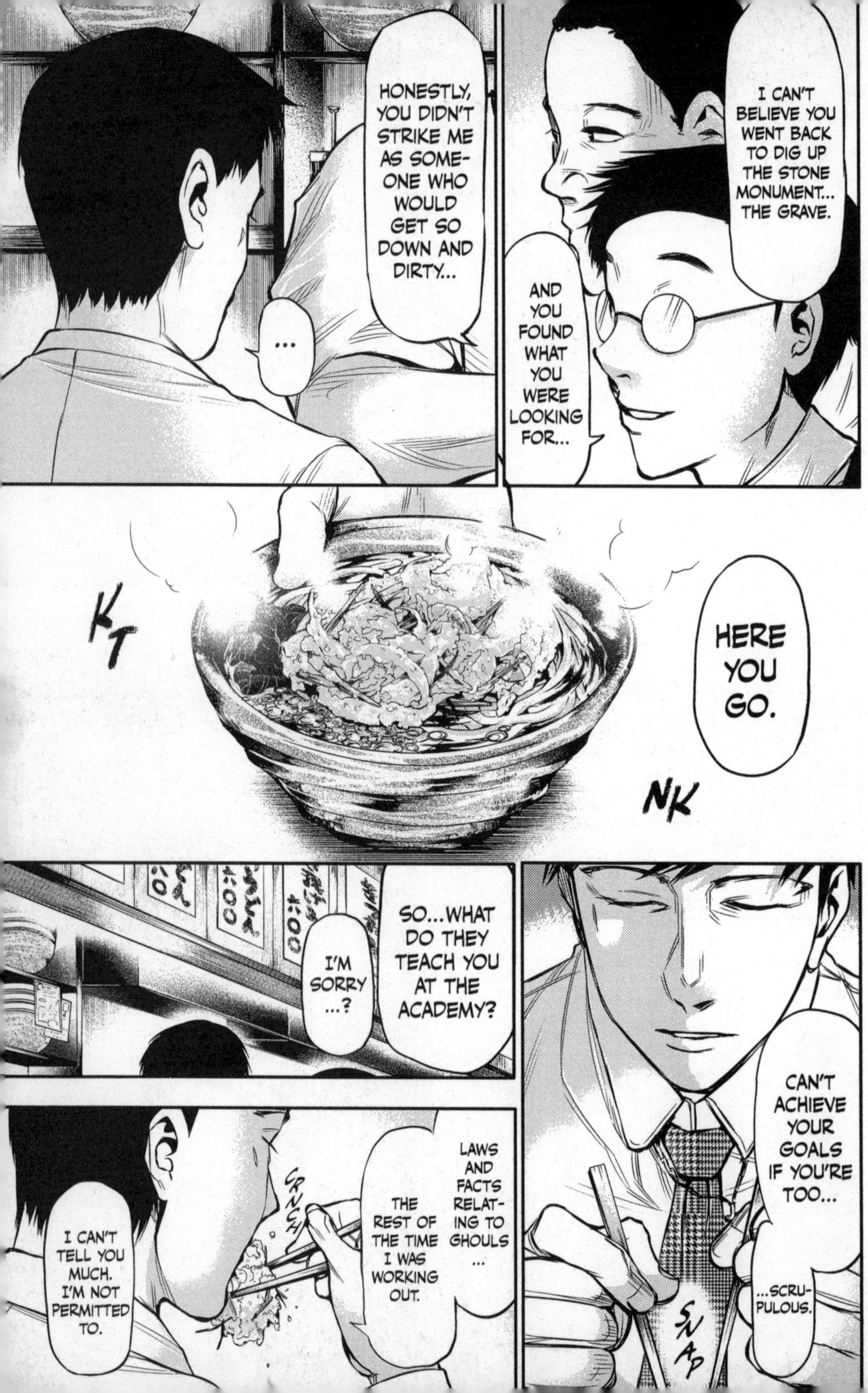
I CAN'T BELIEVE YOU WENT BACK TO DIG UP THE STONE MONUMENT... THE GRAVE.
AND YOU FOUND WHAT YOU WERE LOOKING FOR...
HONESTLY, YOU DIDN'T STRIKE ME AS SOME-ONE WHO WOULD GET SO DOWN AND DIRTY...
...
HERE YOU GO.
NK
KT
SO...WHAT DO THEY TEACH YOU AT THE ACADEMY?
I'M SORRY ...?
LAWS AND FACTS RELAT-ING TO GHOULS ...
THE REST OF THE TIME I WAS WORKING OUT.
CRNCH
I CAN'T TELL YOU MUCH. I'M NOT PERMITTED TO.
CAN'T ACHIEVE YOUR GOALS IF YOU'RE TOO...
...SCRU-PULOUS.
SNAP

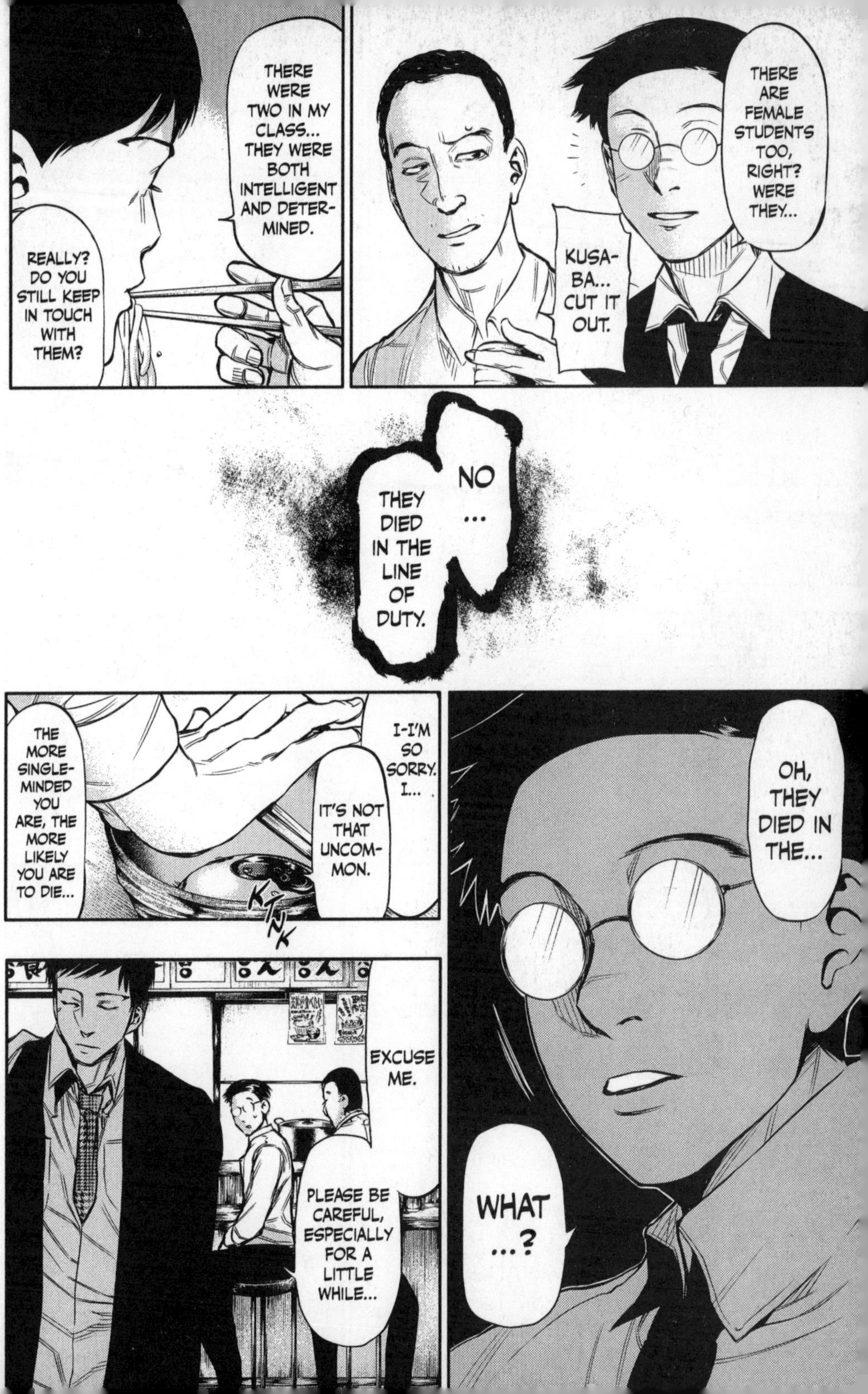
THERE ARE FEMALE STUDENTS TOO, RIGHT? WERE THEY...
KUSABA... CUT IT OUT.
THERE WERE TWO IN MY CLASS... THEY WERE BOTH INTELLIGENT AND DETERMINED.
REALLY? DO YOU STILL KEEP IN TOUCH WITH THEM?
NO...
THEY DIED IN THE LINE OF DUTY.
OH, THEY DIED IN THE...
WHAT...?
I-I'M SO SORRY. I...
IT'S NOT THAT UNCOMMON.
THE MORE SINGLE-MINDED YOU ARE, THE MORE LIKELY YOU ARE TO DIE...
KLINK
EXCUSE ME.
PLEASE BE CAREFUL, ESPECIALLY FOR A LITTLE WHILE...

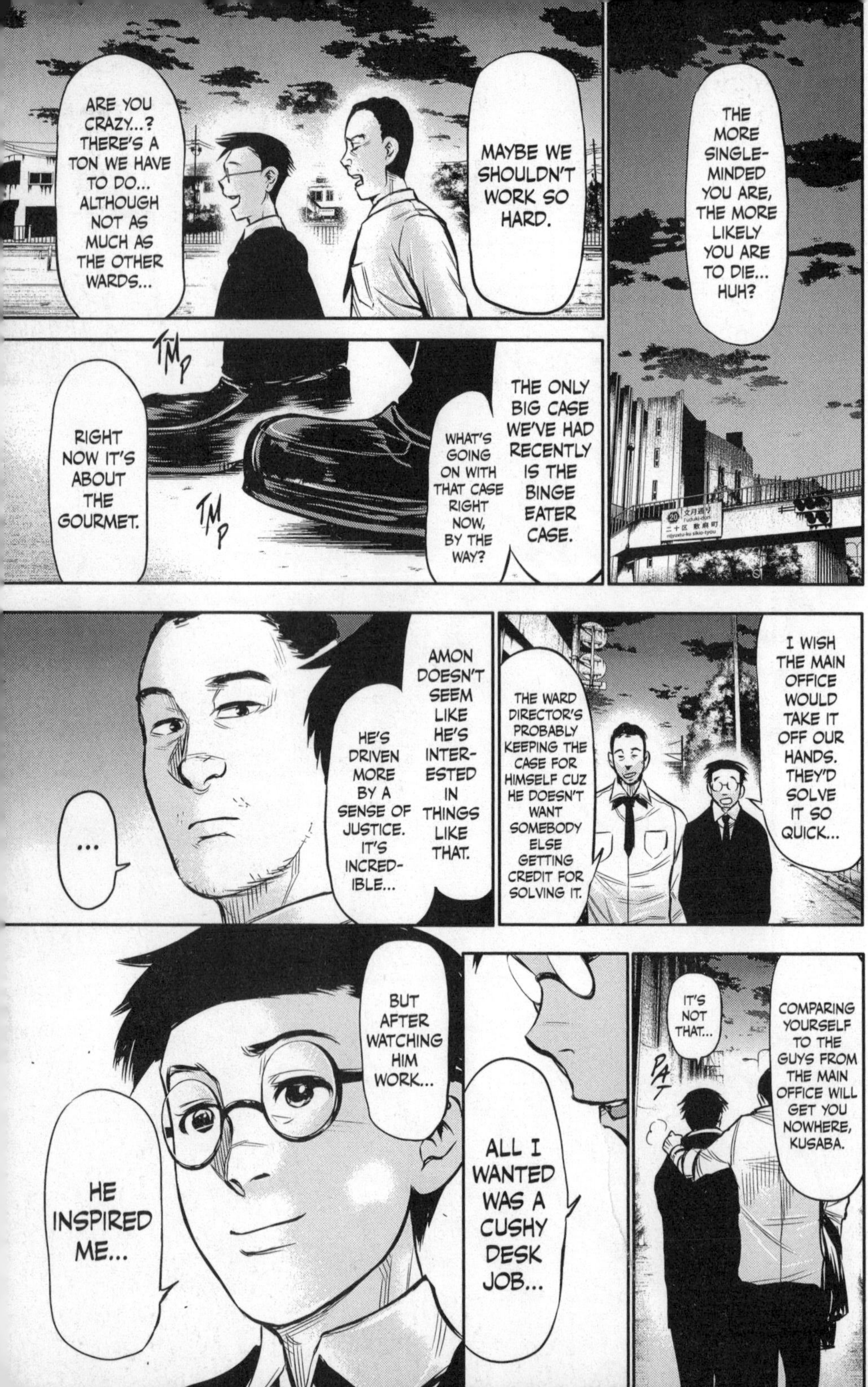
THE MORE SINGLE-MINDED YOU ARE, THE MORE LIKELY YOU ARE TO DIE... HUH?
MAYBE WE SHOULDN'T WORK SO HARD.
ARE YOU CRAZY...? THERE'S A TON WE HAVE TO DO... ALTHOUGH NOT AS MUCH AS THE OTHER WARDS...
THE ONLY BIG CASE WE'VE HAD RECENTLY IS THE BINGE EATER CASE.
WHAT'S GOING ON WITH THAT CASE RIGHT NOW, BY THE WAY?
TMP
RIGHT NOW IT'S ABOUT THE GOURMET.
TMP
I WISH THE MAIN OFFICE WOULD TAKE IT OFF OUR HANDS. THEY'D SOLVE IT SO QUICK...
THE WARD DIRECTOR'S PROBABLY KEEPING THE CASE FOR HIMSELF CUZ HE DOESN'T WANT SOMEBODY ELSE GETTING CREDIT FOR SOLVING IT.
AMON DOESN'T SEEM LIKE HE'S INTERESTED IN THINGS LIKE THAT.
HE'S DRIVEN MORE BY A SENSE OF JUSTICE. IT'S INCREDIBLE...
...
COMPARING YOURSELF TO THE GUYS FROM THE MAIN OFFICE WILL GET YOU NOWHERE, KUSABA.
IT'S NOT THAT...
PAT
ALL I WANTED WAS A CUSHY DESK JOB...
BUT AFTER WATCHING HIM WORK...
HE INSPIRED ME...

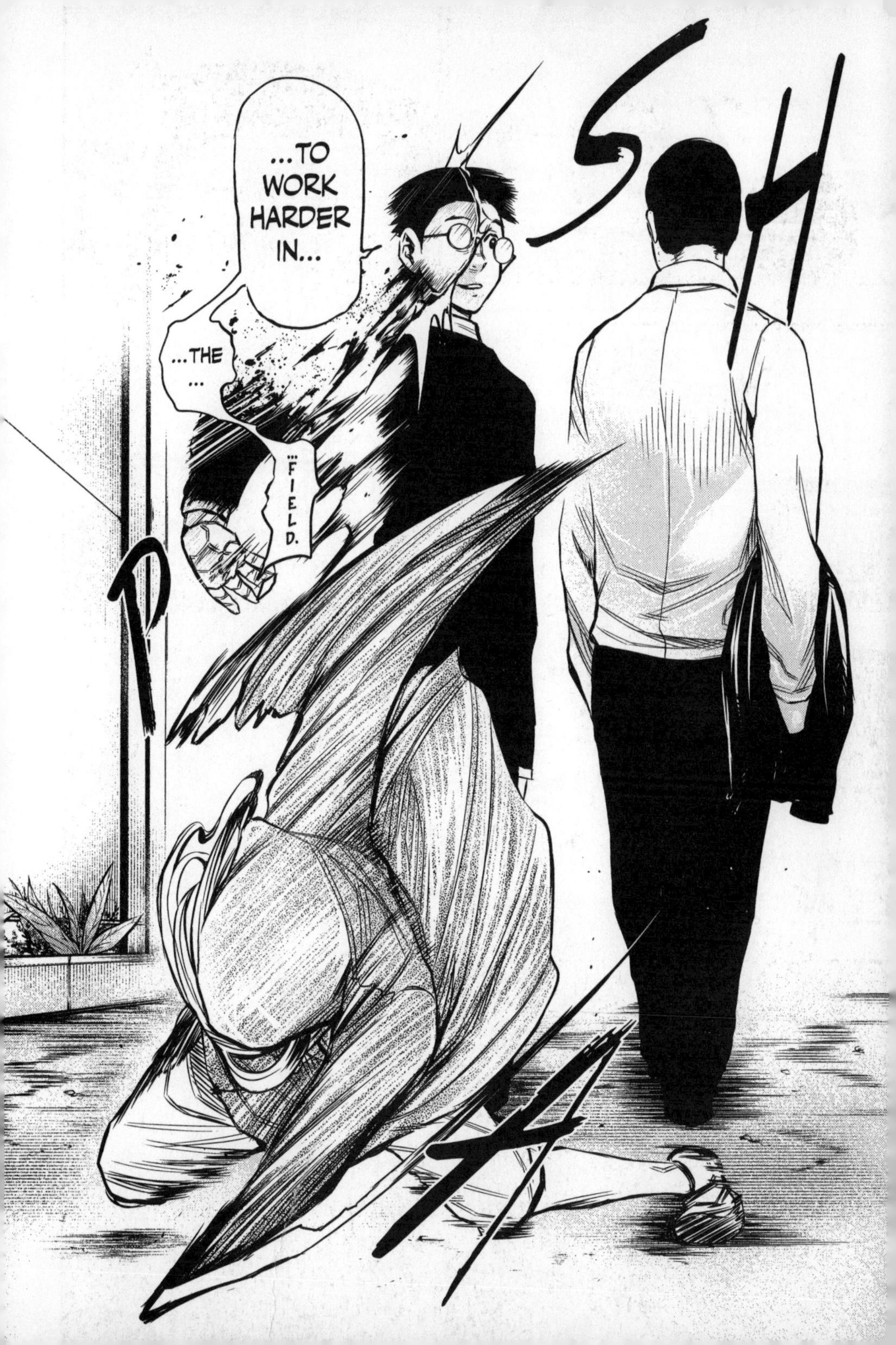

SH
...TO WORK HARDER IN...
...THE ...
...FIELD.
P
SH

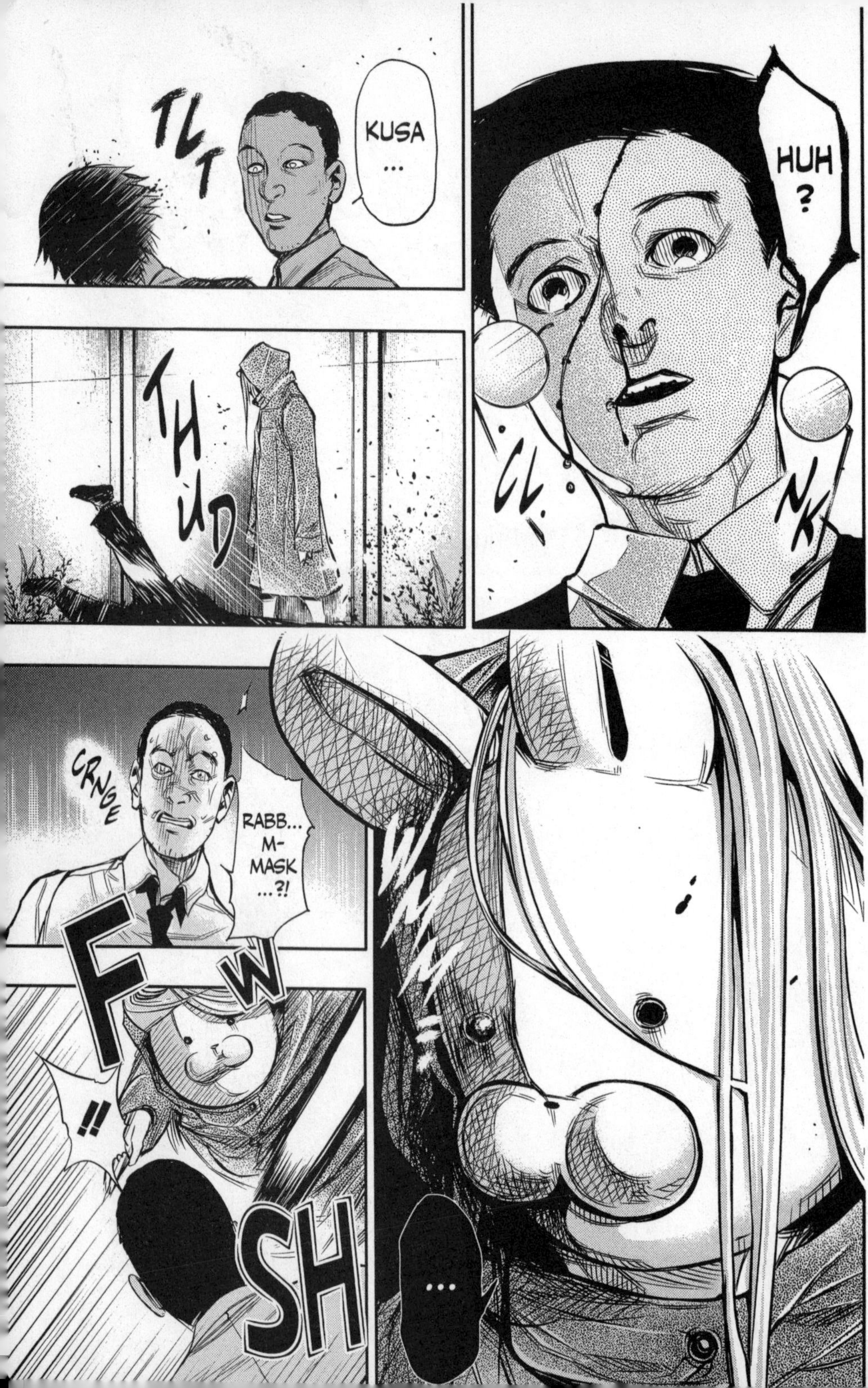
HUH ?
CL
NK
KUSA ...
TLT
THUD
...
CRNGE
RABB... M-MASK ...?!
!!
FW
SH

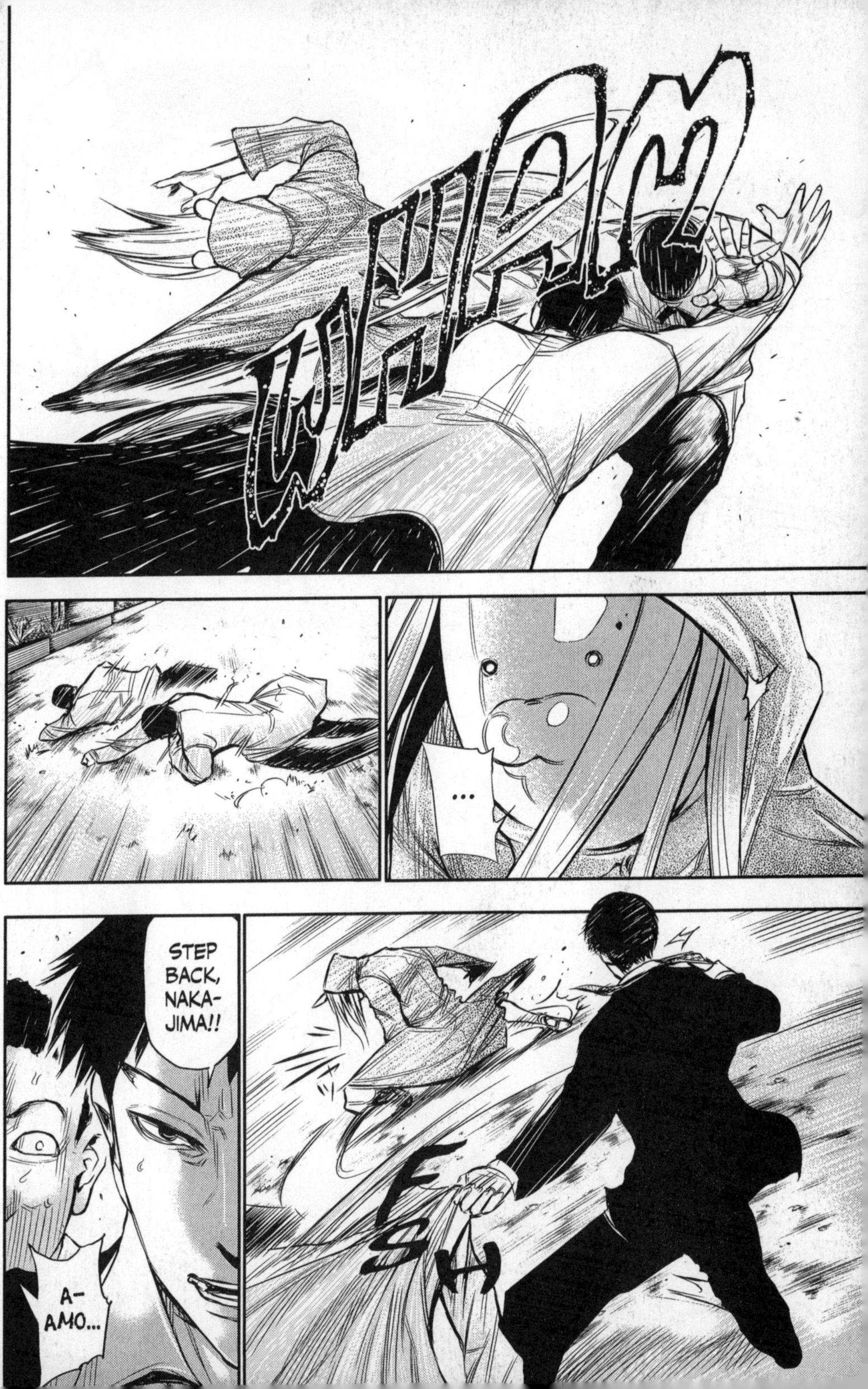
WHAM
...
STEP BACK, NAKA-JIMA!!
A- AMO...

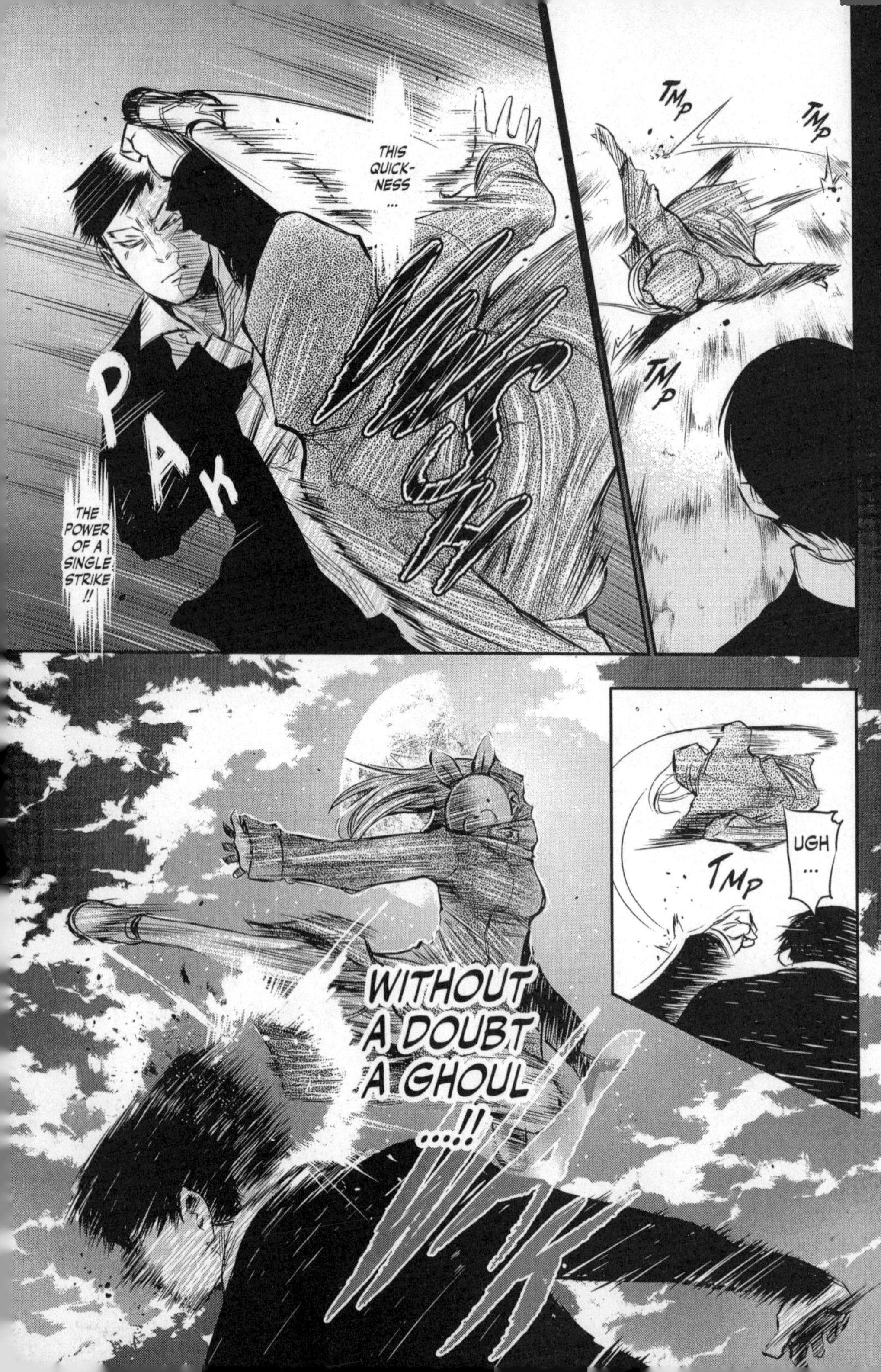
TMP
TMP
TMP
THIS QUICK-NESS ...
PAK
THE POWER OF A SINGLE STRIKE !!
UGH ...
TMP
WITHOUT A DOUBT A GHOUL ...!!

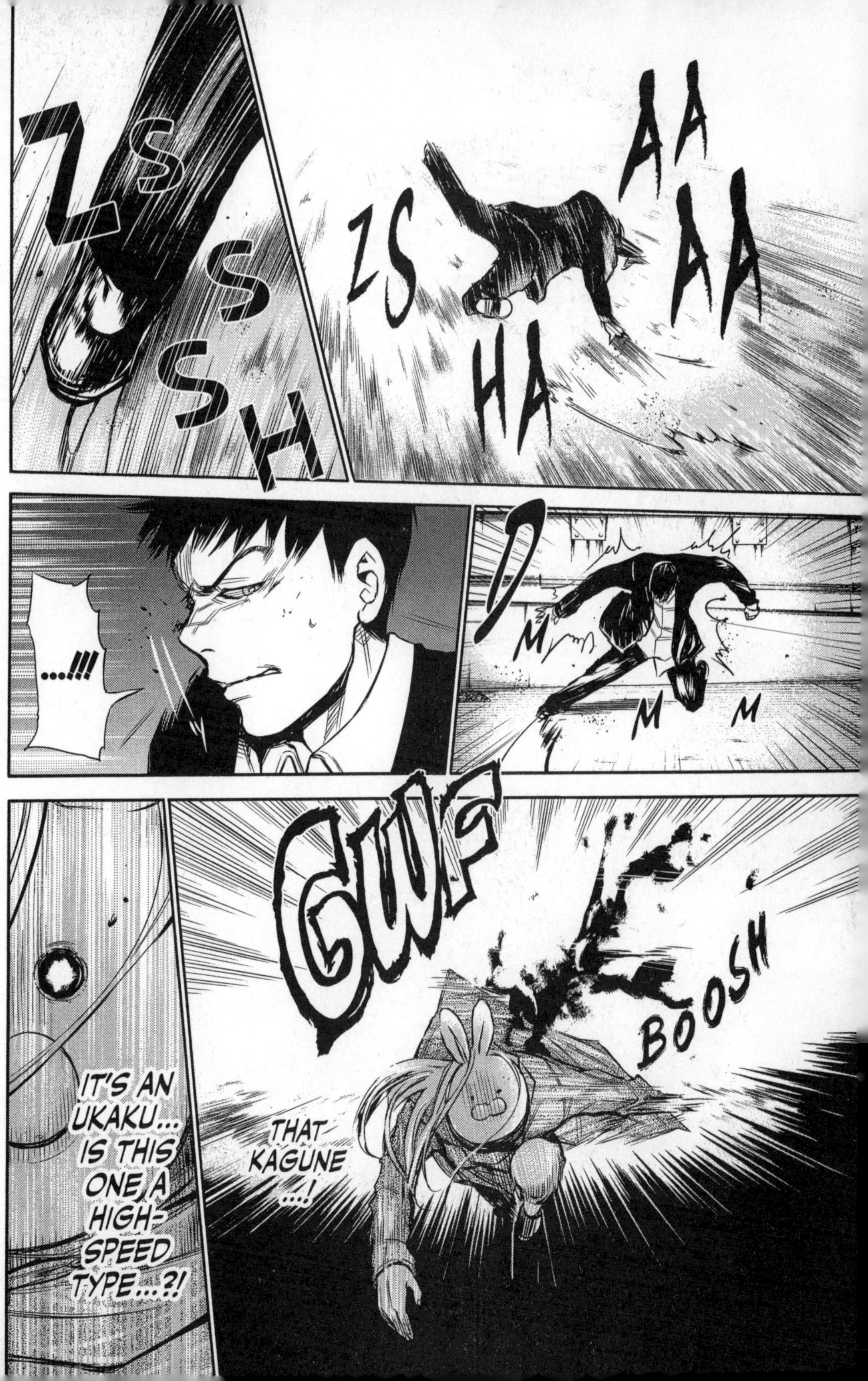
HA AA AA AA
ZS
ZSSSH
DMMM
...!!!
GUUF
BOOSH
THAT KAGUNE ...!
IT'S AN UKAKU... IS THIS ONE A HIGH-SPEED TYPE...?!

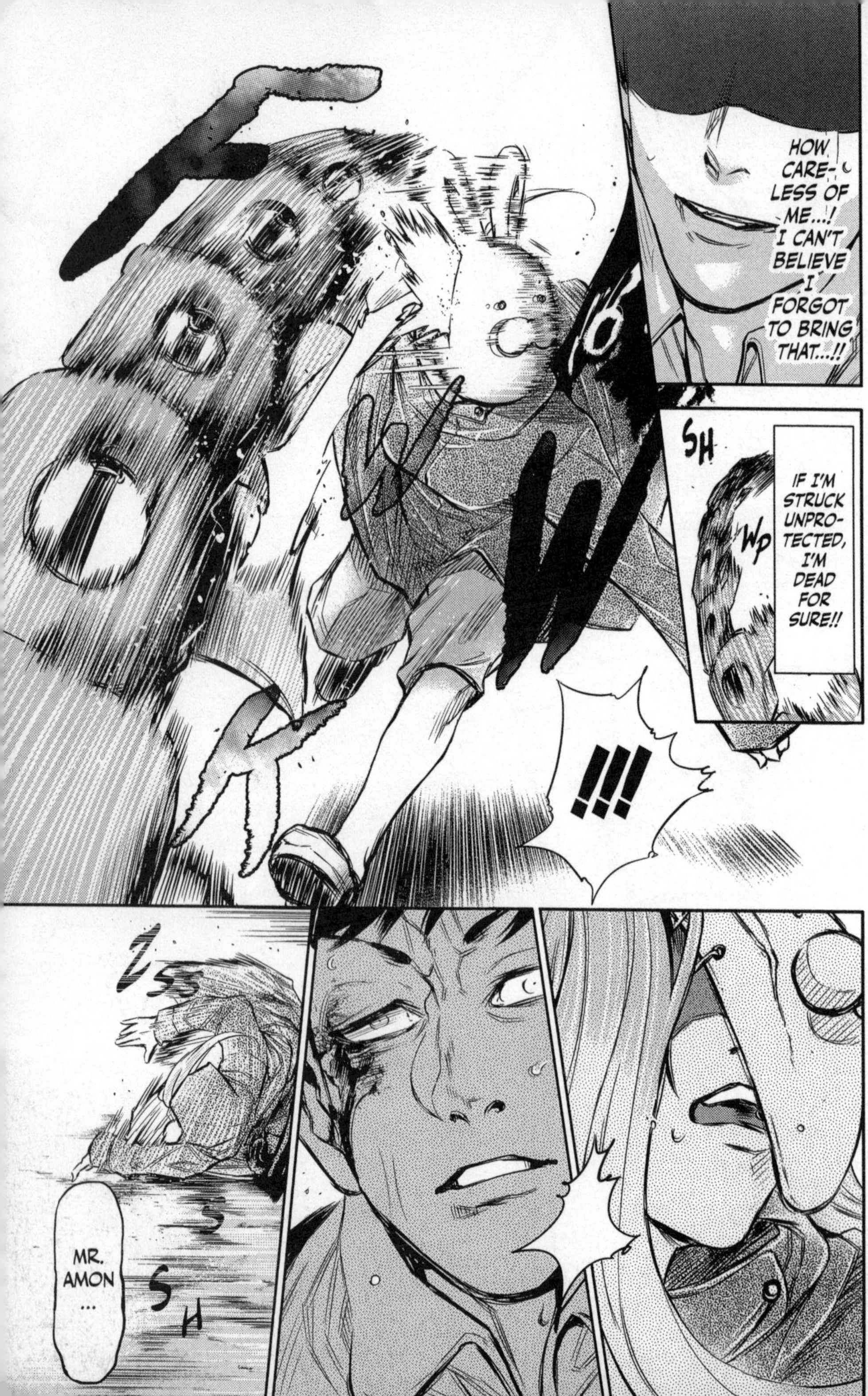
HOW CARE-LESS OF ME...! I CAN'T BELIEVE I FORGOT TO BRING THAT...!!
SH
IF I'M STRUCK UNPRO-TECTED, I'M DEAD FOR SURE!!
WP
!!!
ZSS
MR. AMON ...
SH

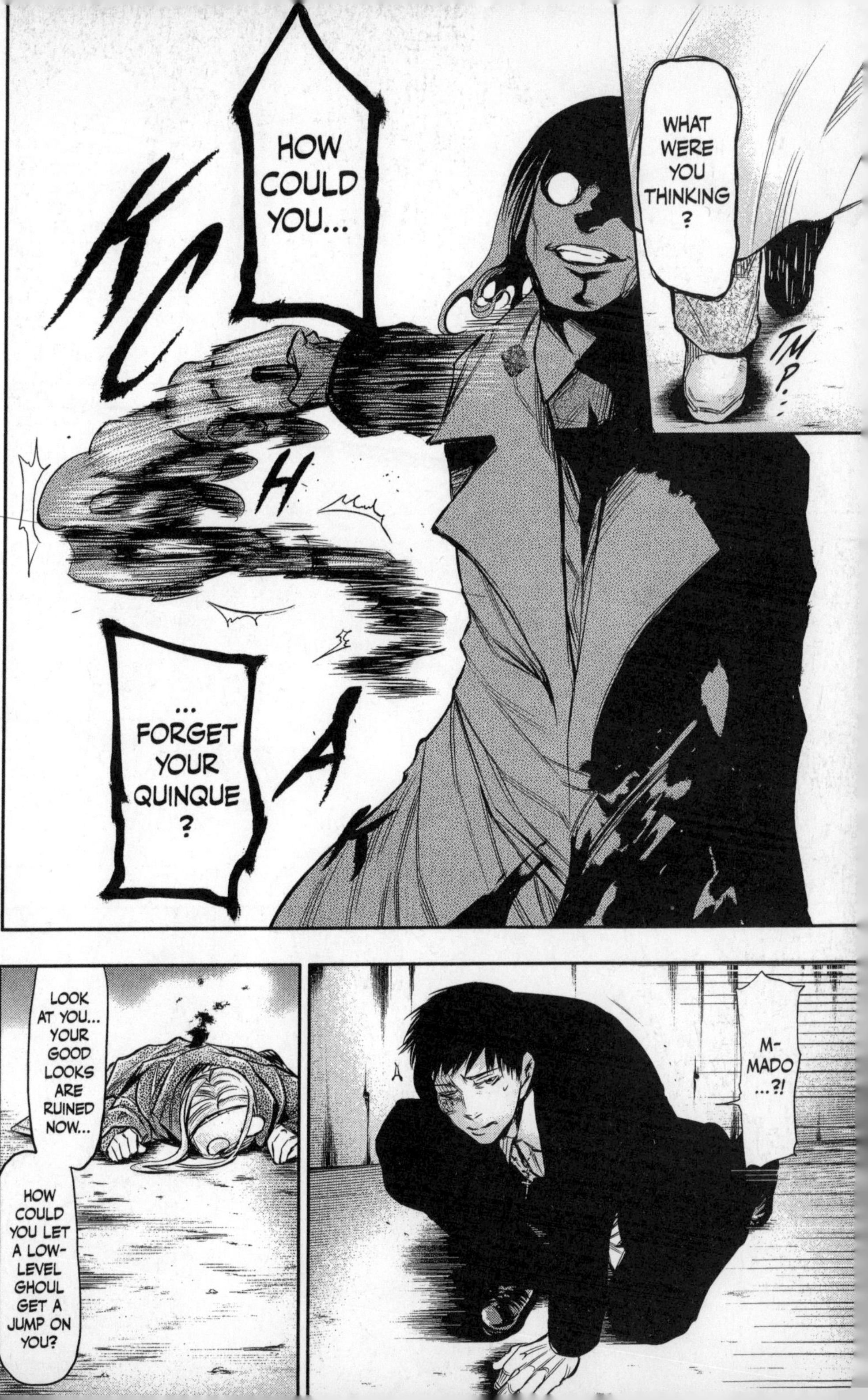
WHAT WERE YOU THINKING?
TMP
HOW COULD YOU...
KCHAK
...FORGET YOUR QUINQUE?
M-MADO...?!
LOOK AT YOU... YOUR GOOD LOOKS ARE RUINED NOW...
HOW COULD YOU LET A LOW-LEVEL GHOUL GET A JUMP ON YOU?

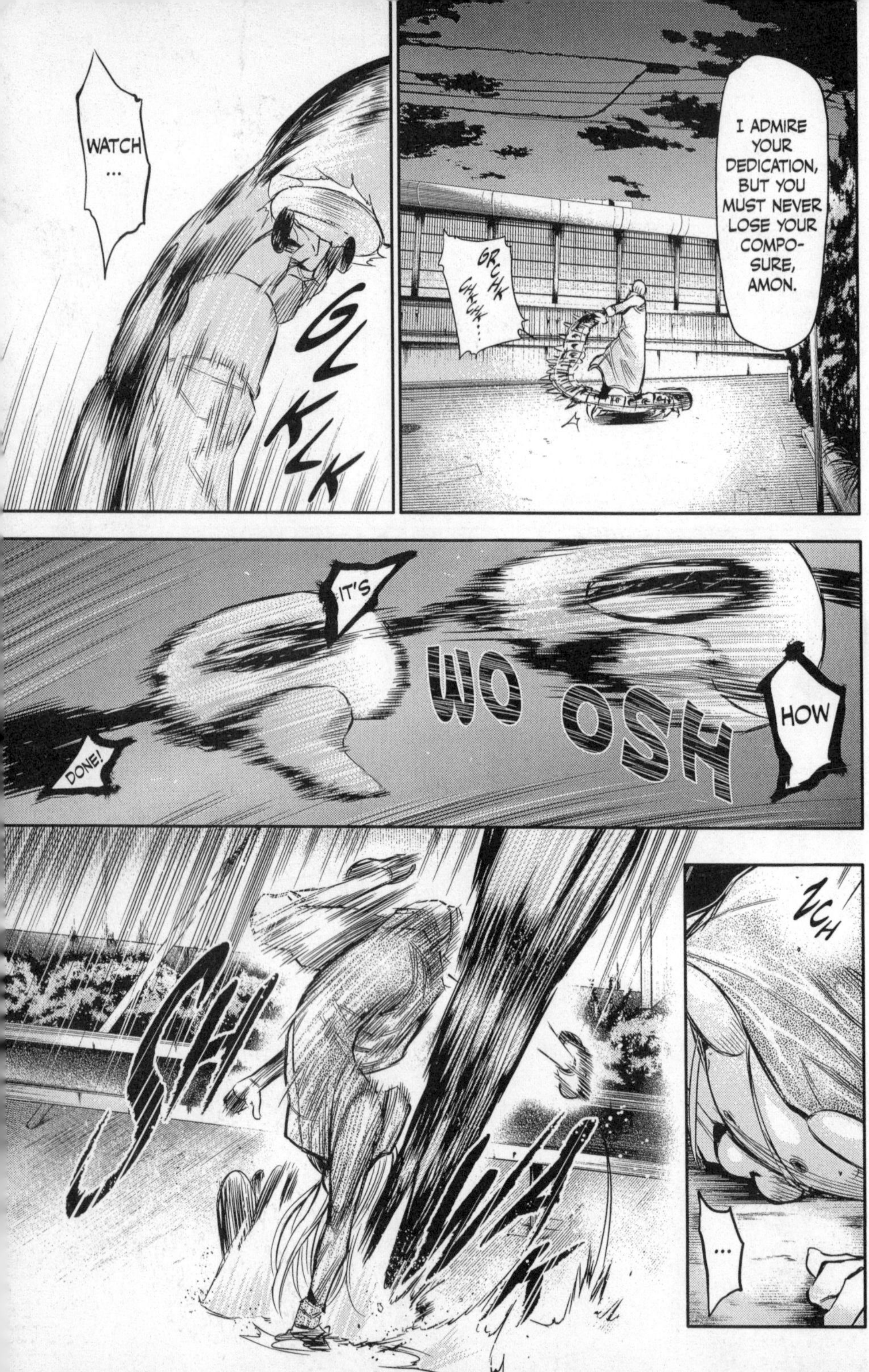
I ADMIRE YOUR DEDICATION, BUT YOU MUST NEVER LOSE YOUR COMPOSURE, AMON.
GRCHK CHCHK...
WATCH...
GLKLK
HOW
WOOSH
IT'S
DONE!
...

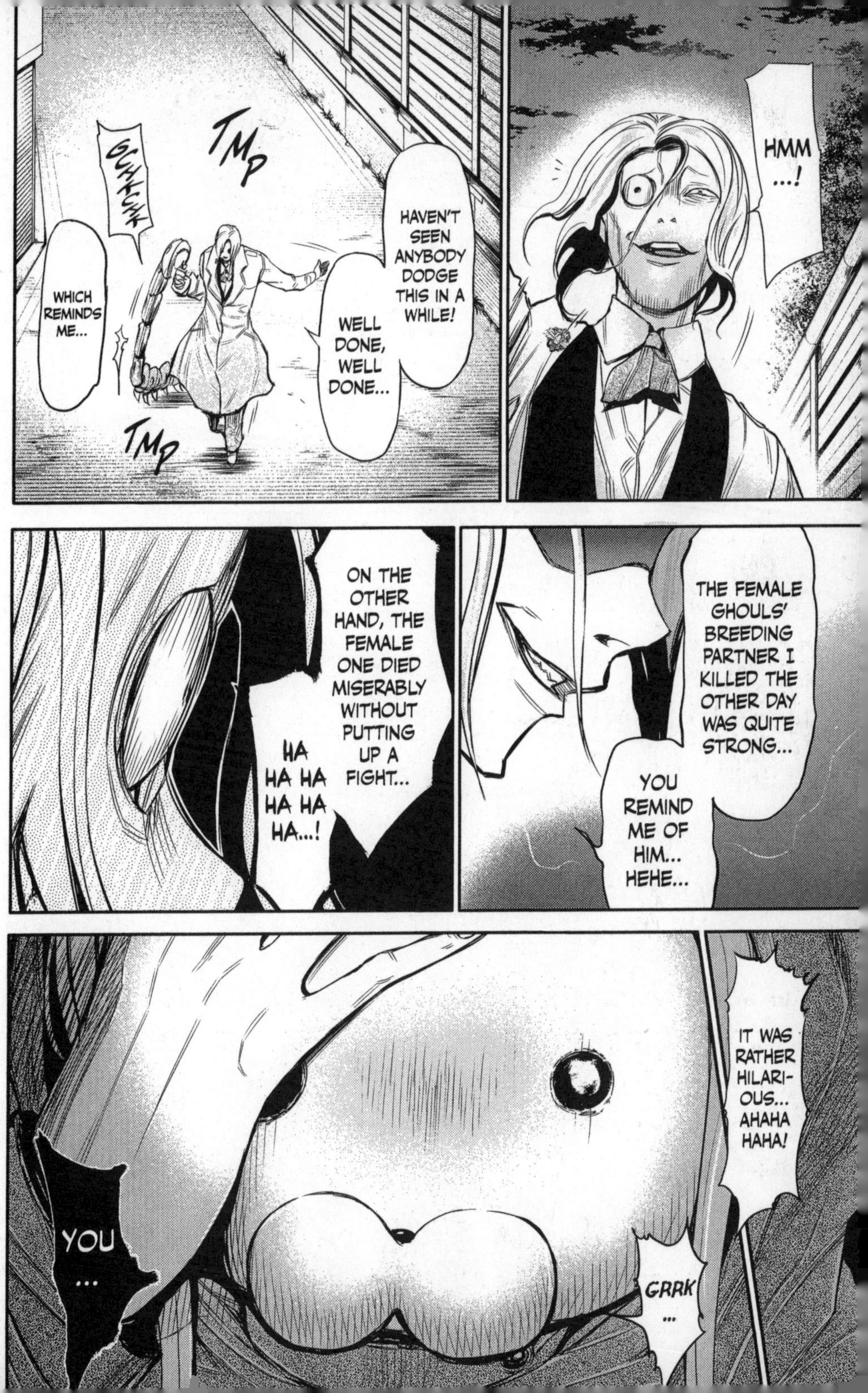
HMM ...!
HAVEN'T SEEN ANYBODY DODGE THIS IN A WHILE!
TMP
WELL DONE, WELL DONE...
GCHKCHK
WHICH REMINDS ME...
TMP
THE FEMALE GHOULS' BREEDING PARTNER I KILLED THE OTHER DAY WAS QUITE STRONG...
YOU REMIND ME OF HIM... HEHE...
ON THE OTHER HAND, THE FEMALE ONE DIED MISERABLY WITHOUT PUTTING UP A FIGHT...
HA HA HA HA HA HA...!
IT WAS RATHER HILARI-OUS... AHAHA HAHA!
GRRK ...
YOU ...

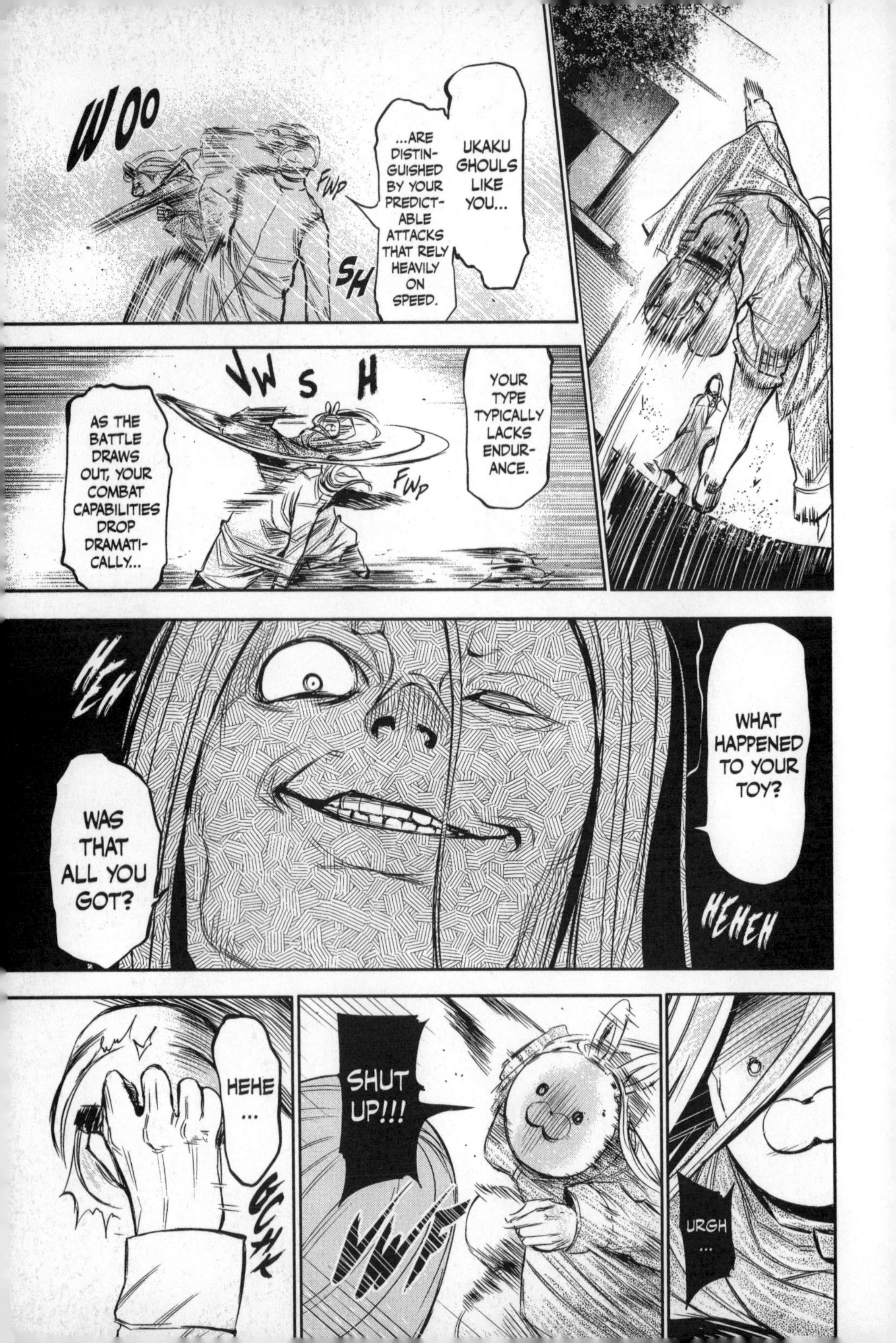
UKAKU GHOULS LIKE YOU...
...ARE DISTIN-GUISHED BY YOUR PREDICT-ABLE ATTACKS THAT RELY HEAVILY ON SPEED.
WOO
FWP
SH
YOUR TYPE TYPICALLY LACKS ENDUR-ANCE.
VWSH
FWP
AS THE BATTLE DRAWS OUT, YOUR COMBAT CAPABILITIES DROP DRAMATI-CALLY...
WHAT HAPPENED TO YOUR TOY?
HEHEH
WAS THAT ALL YOU GOT?
HEH
URGH ...
SHUT UP!!!
HEHE ...

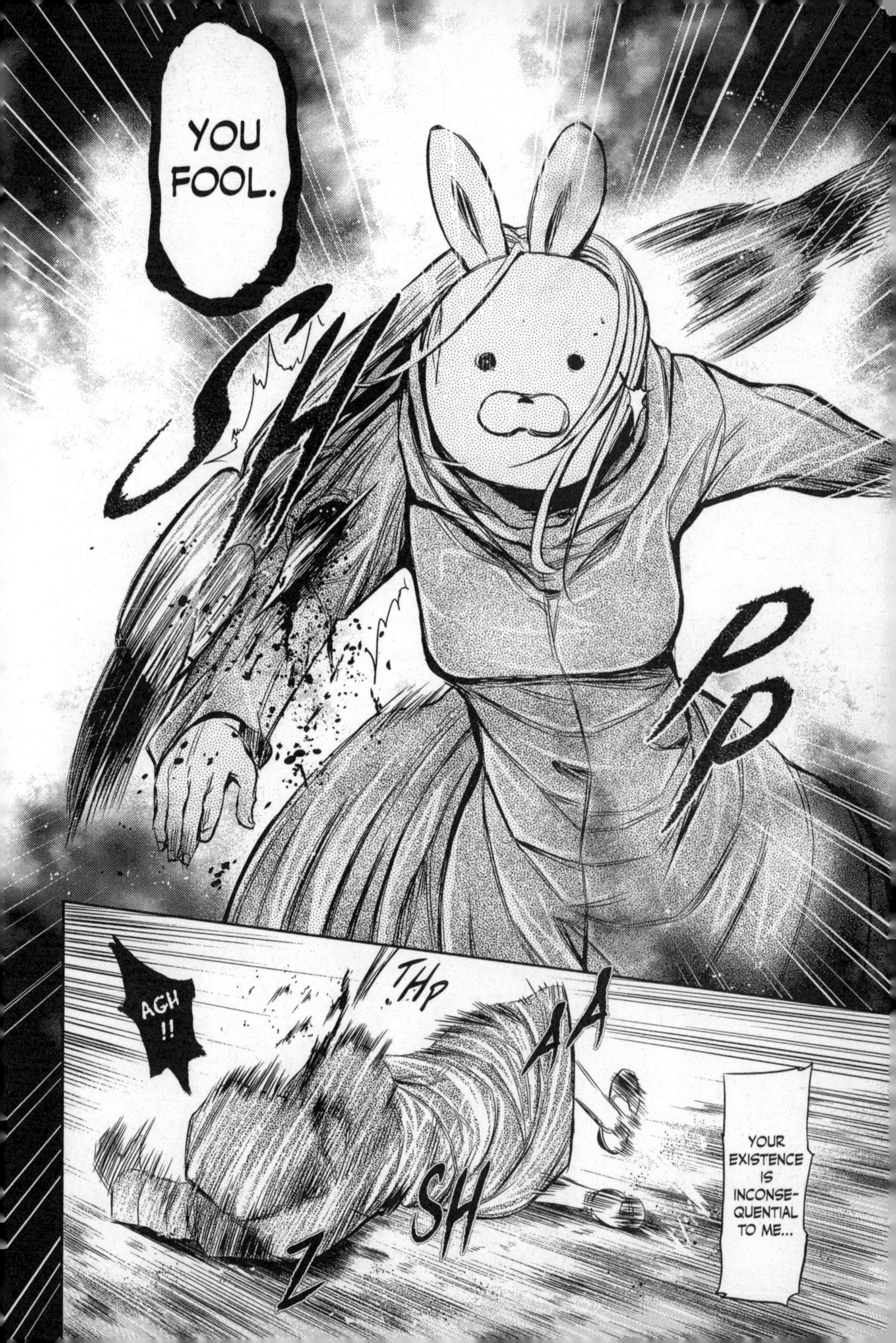
YOU FOOL.
YOUR EXISTENCE IS INCONSE- QUENTIAL TO ME...
THP
AGH !!
ZSH

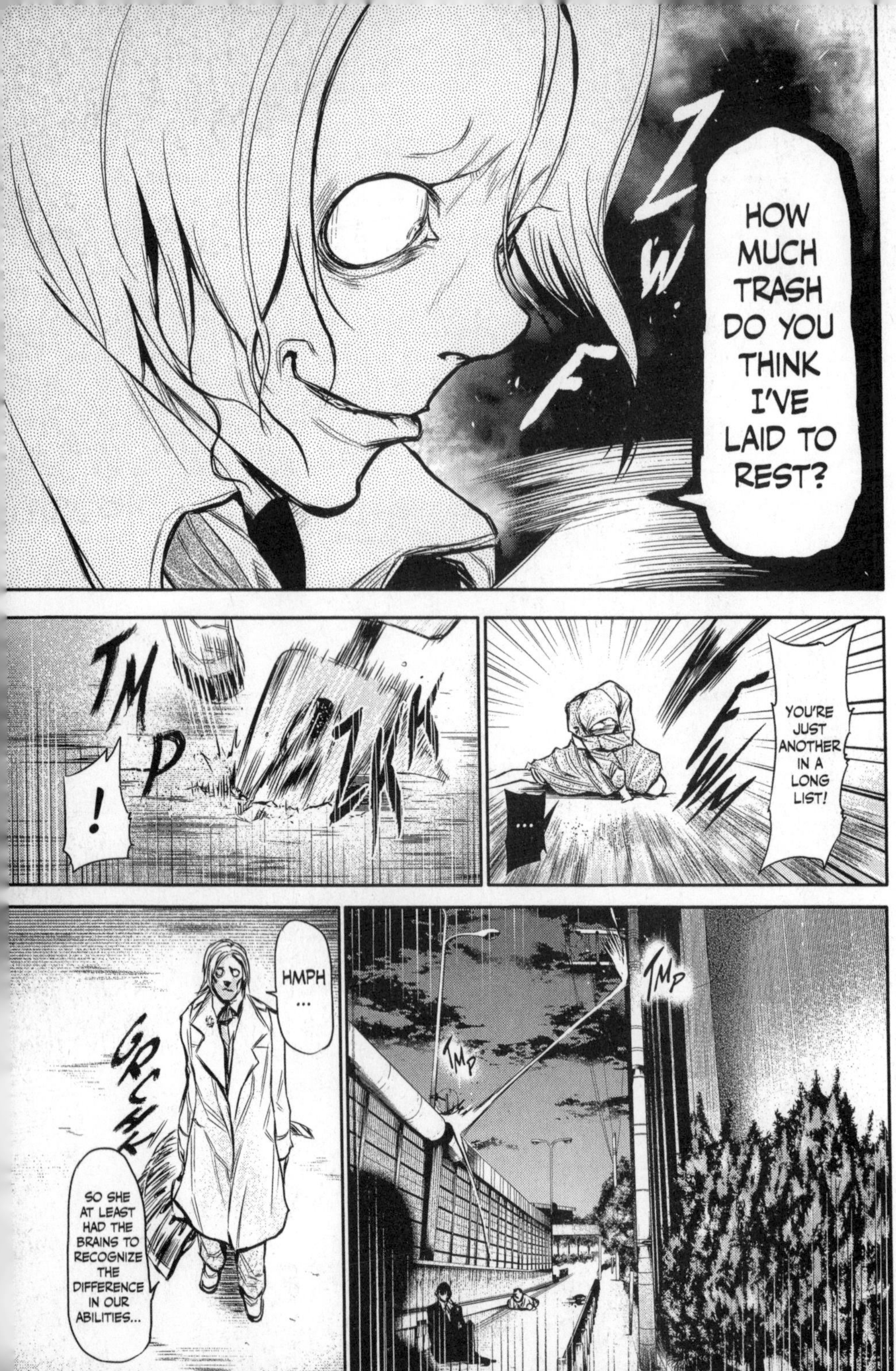
ZWF
HOW MUCH TRASH DO YOU THINK I'VE LAID TO REST?
YOU'RE JUST ANOTHER IN A LONG LIST!
...
TMP
!
TMP
TMP
HMPH ...
SO SHE AT LEAST HAD THE BRAINS TO RECOGNIZE THE DIFFERENCE IN OUR ABILITIES...

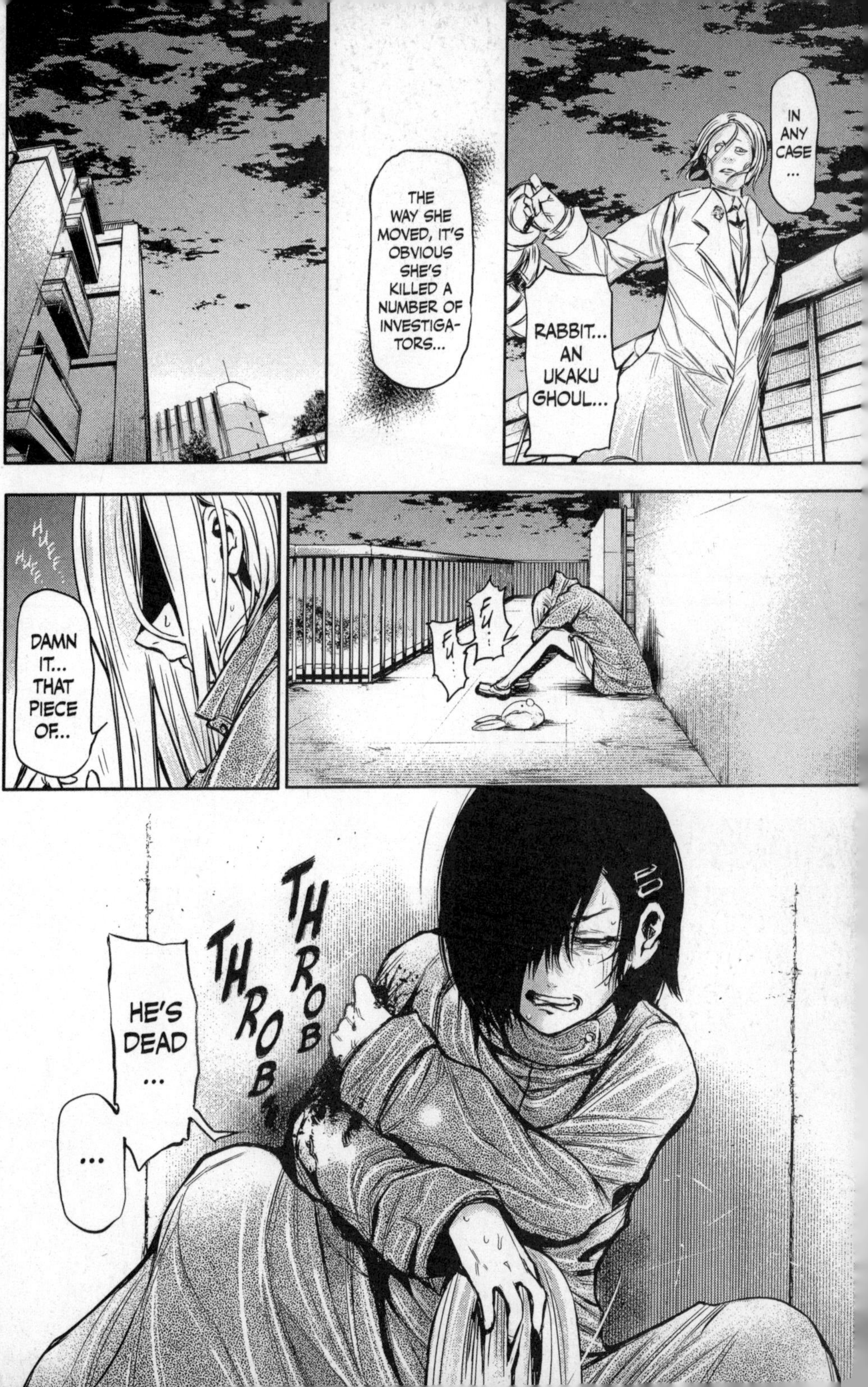
IN ANY CASE...
RABBIT... AN UKAKU GHOUL...
THE WAY SHE MOVED, IT'S OBVIOUS SHE'S KILLED A NUMBER OF INVESTIGA-TORS...
FU...
FU...
HUFF... HUFF...
DAMN IT... THAT PIECE OF...
THROB THROB
HE'S DEAD...
...

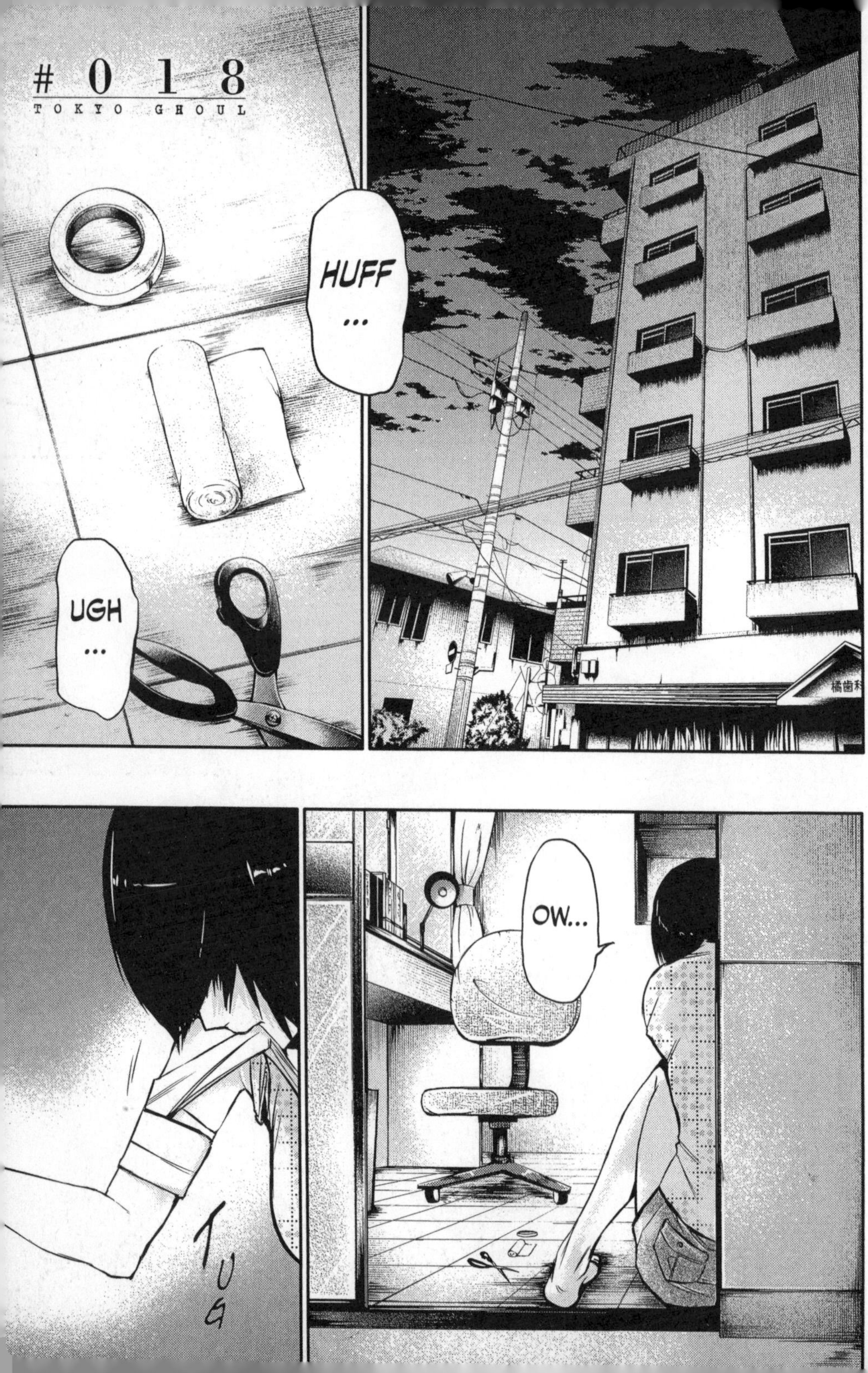
HUFF ...
#018
TOKYO GHOUL
UGH ...
OW...
TUG

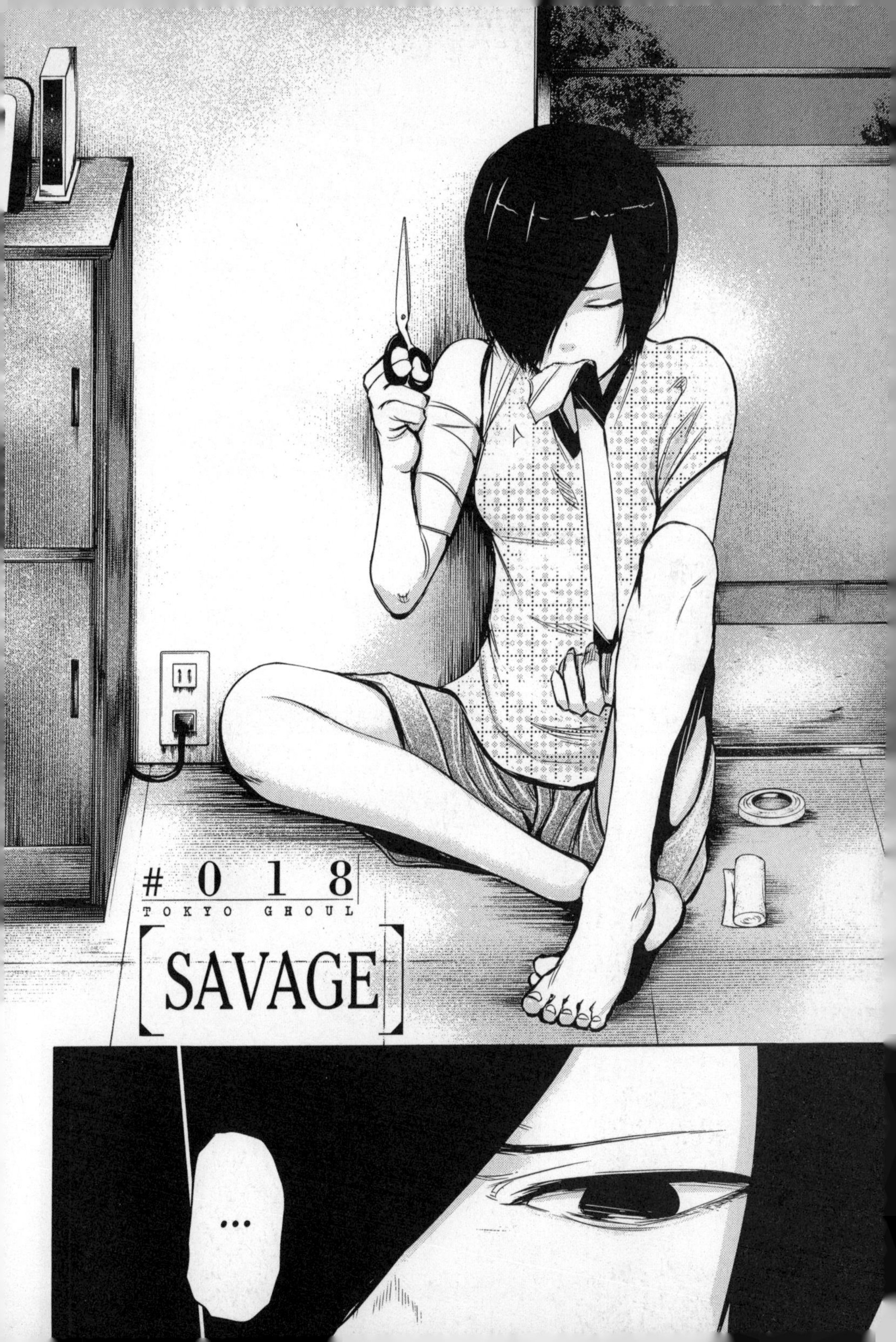
#018
TOKYO GHOUL
SAVAGE
...

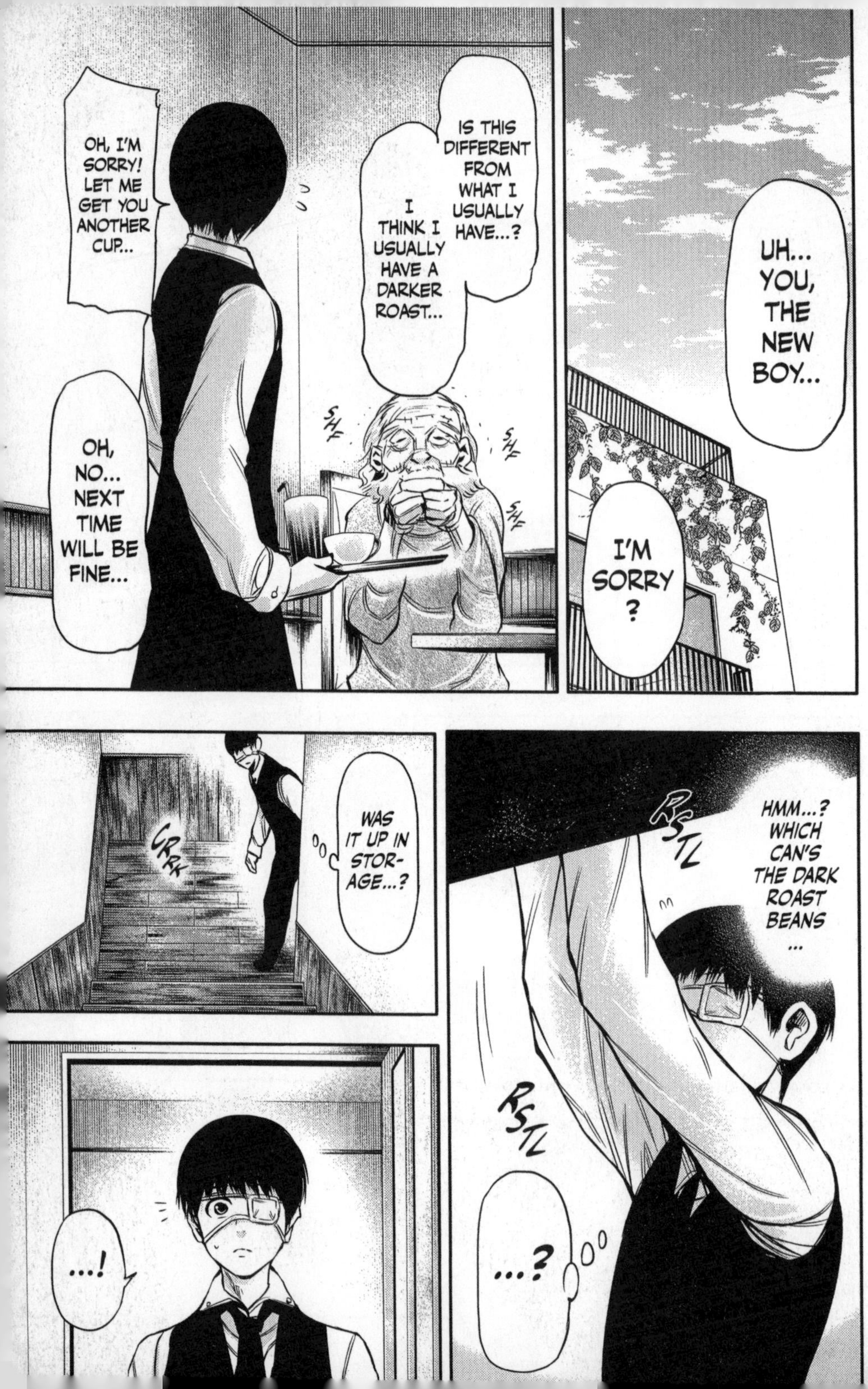
UH... YOU, THE NEW BOY...
I'M SORRY?
IS THIS DIFFERENT FROM WHAT I USUALLY HAVE...?
I THINK I USUALLY HAVE A DARKER ROAST...
SHF SHF SHF
OH, I'M SORRY! LET ME GET YOU ANOTHER CUP...
OH, NO... NEXT TIME WILL BE FINE...
HMM...? WHICH CAN'S THE DARK ROAST BEANS...
RSTL
RSTL
...?
WAS IT UP IN STORAGE...?
CRRK
...!

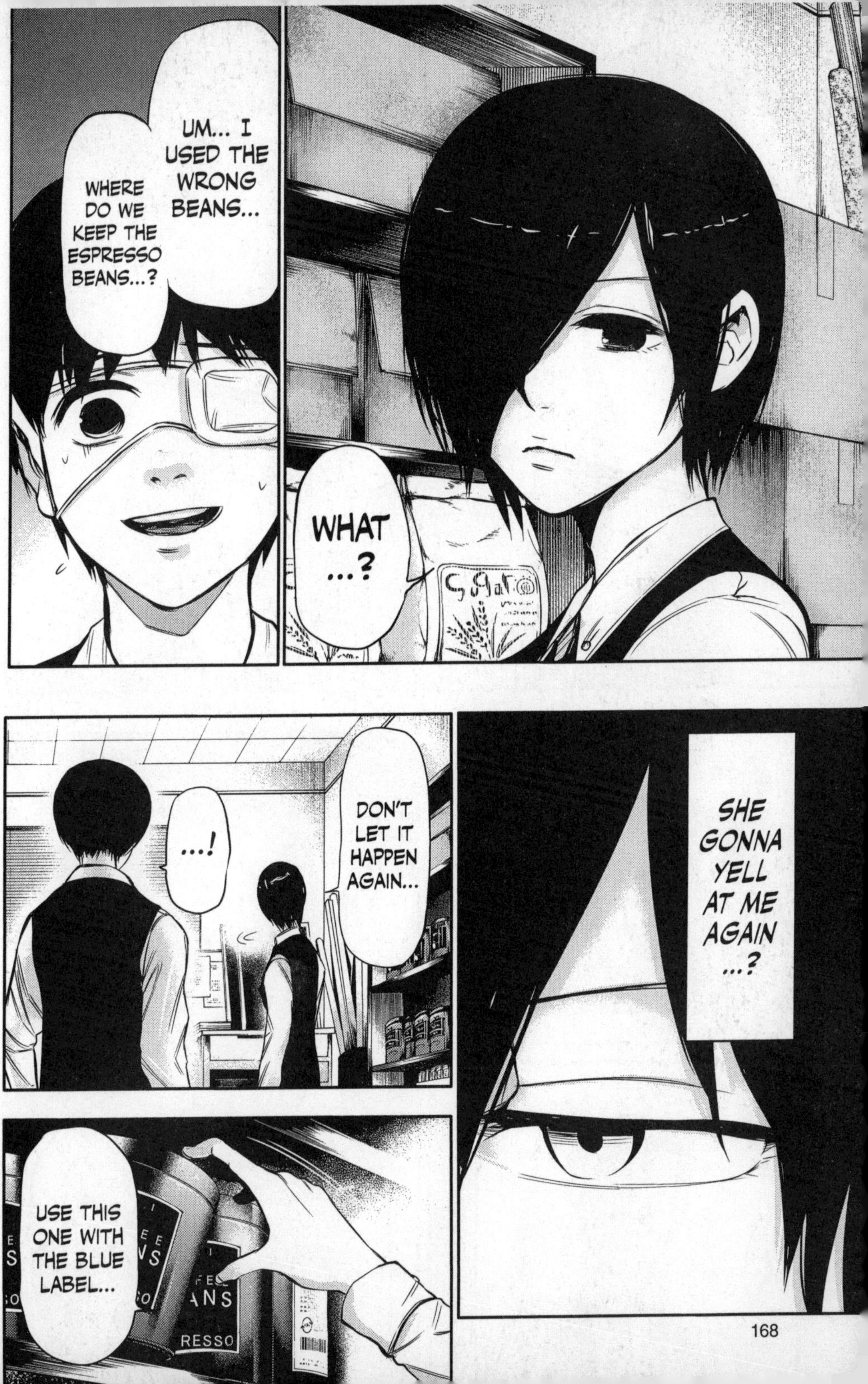
WHAT ...?
UM... I USED THE WRONG BEANS...
WHERE DO WE KEEP THE ESPRESSO BEANS...?
SHE GONNA YELL AT ME AGAIN ...?
DON'T LET IT HAPPEN AGAIN...
...!
USE THIS ONE WITH THE BLUE LABEL...

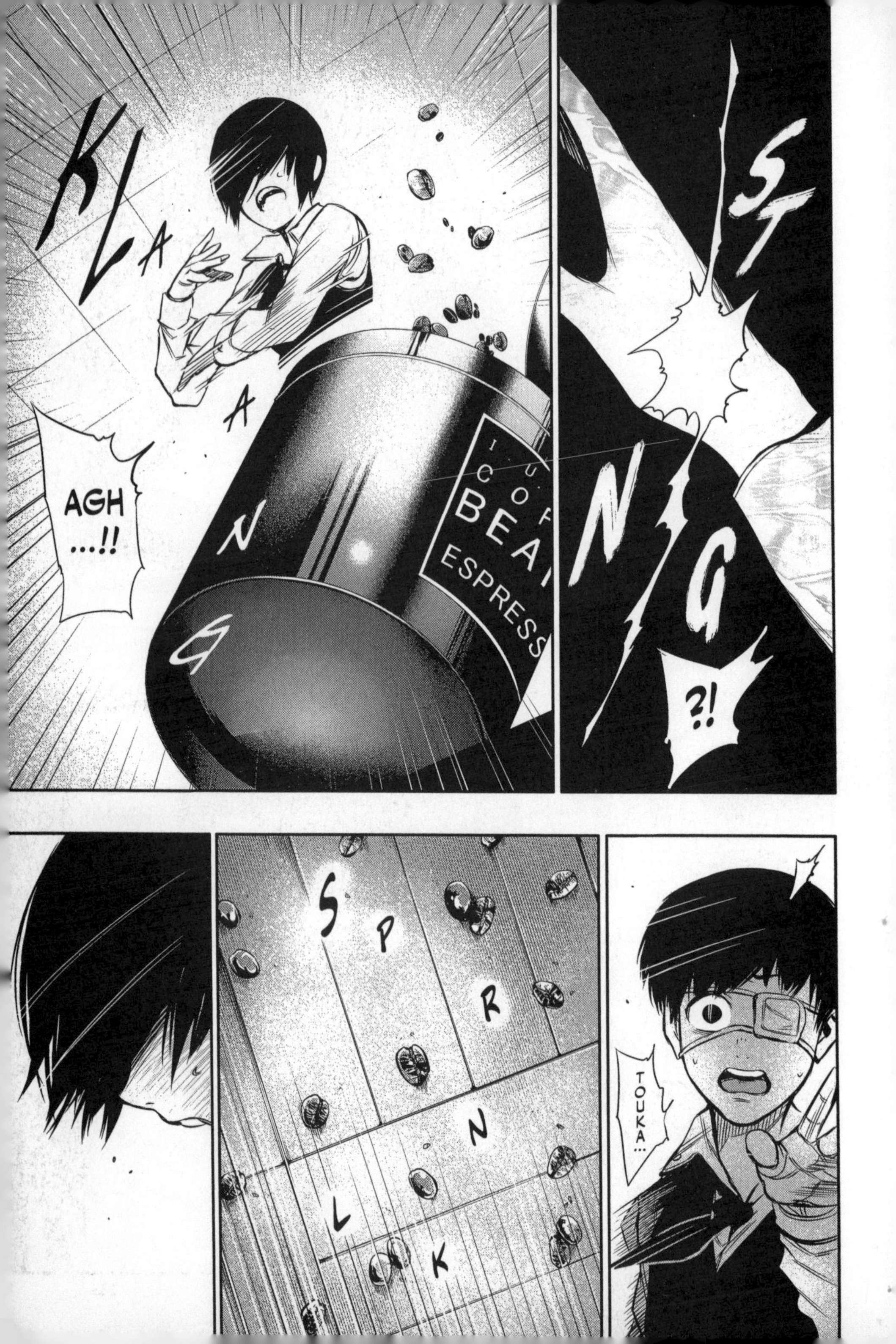

STING
?!
KLAANG
AGH ...!!
COF
BEA
ESPRESS
TOUKA...
SPRNLK

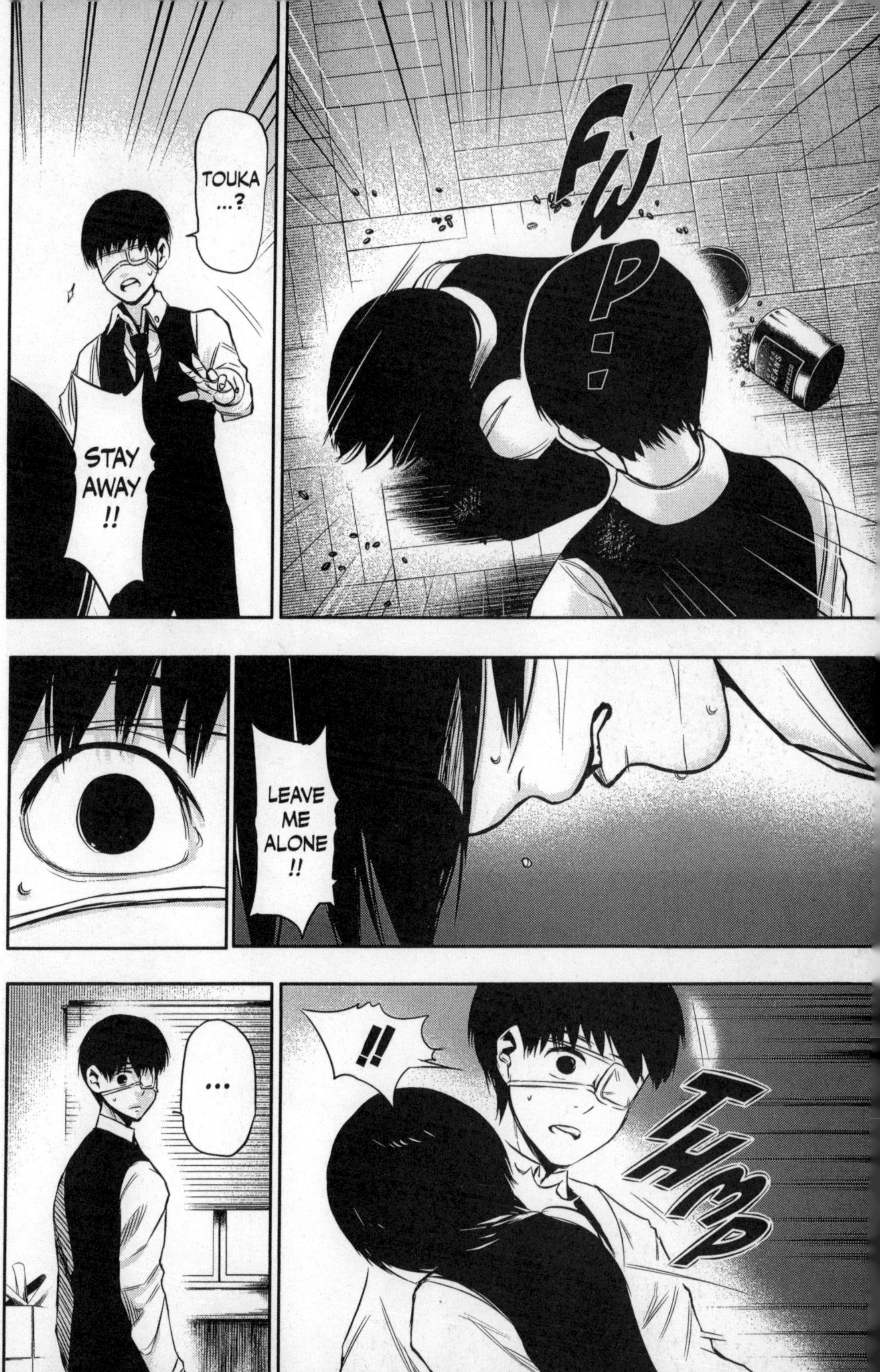
FWP..
TOUKA ...?
STAY AWAY !!
LEAVE ME ALONE !!
!!
THMP
...

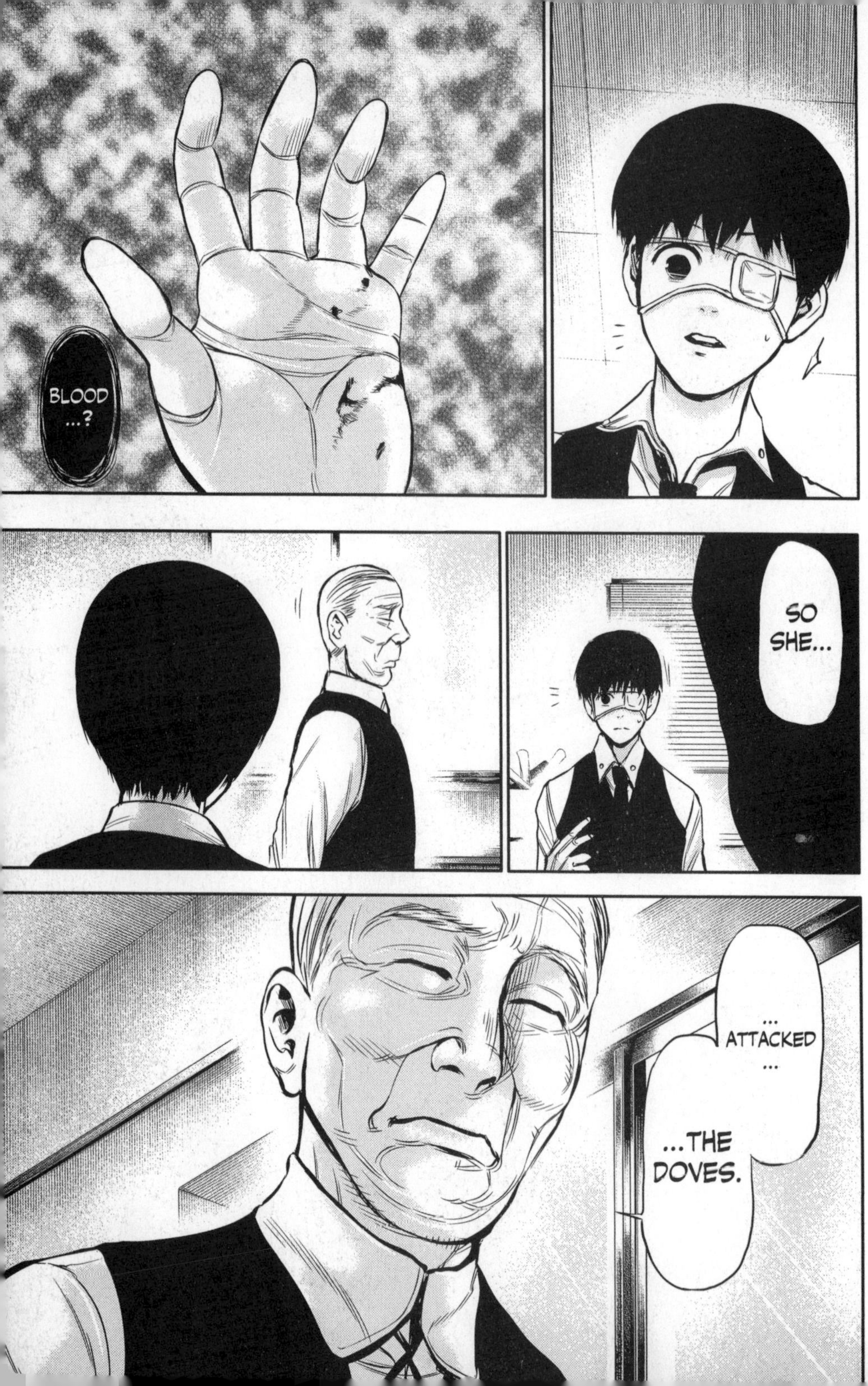
BLOOD ...?
SO SHE...
... ATTACKED ...
...THE DOVES.

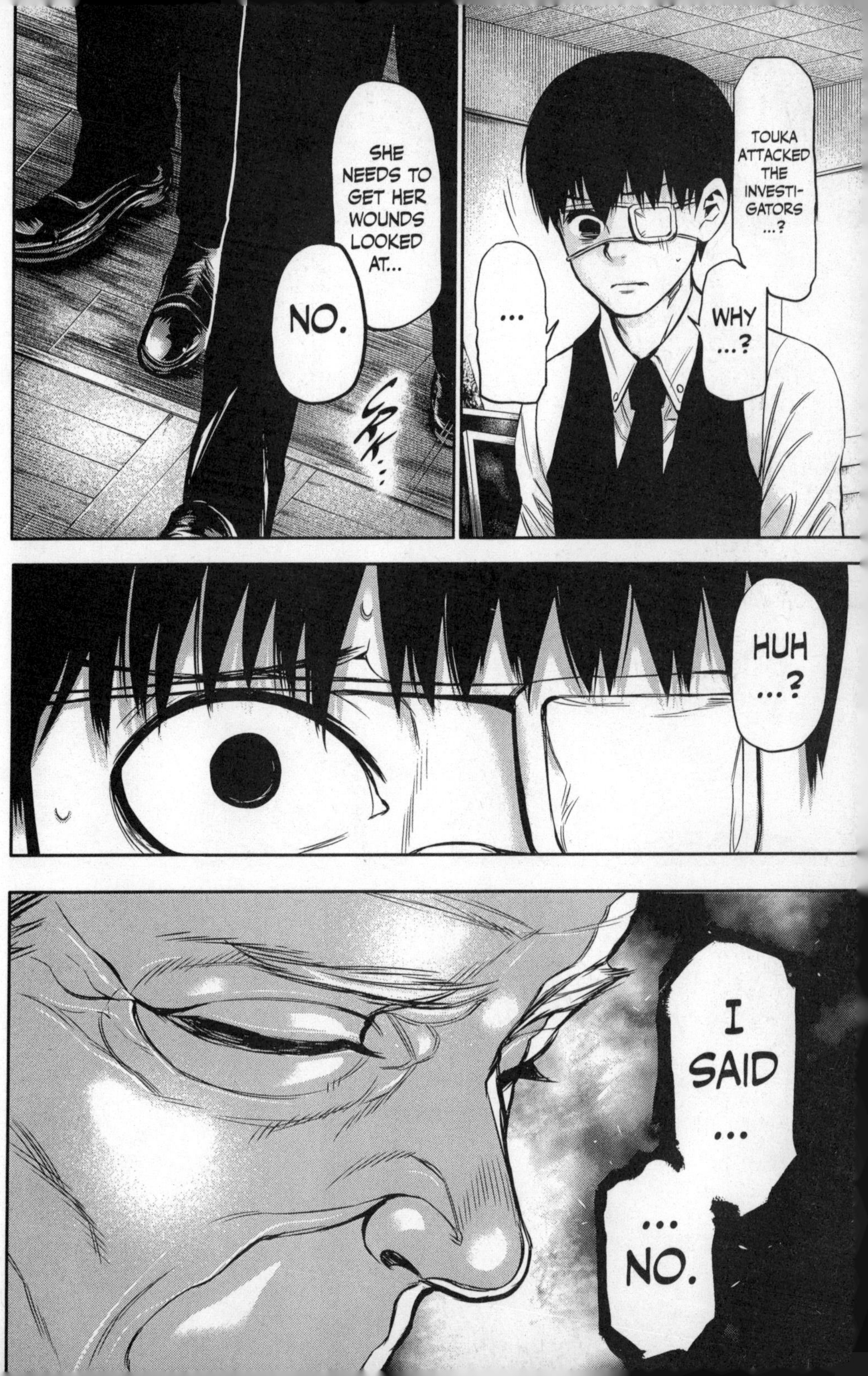
TOUKA ATTACKED THE INVESTI-GATORS ...?
WHY ...?
...
SHE NEEDS TO GET HER WOUNDS LOOKED AT...
NO.
CRK..
HUH ...?
I SAID ...
... NO.

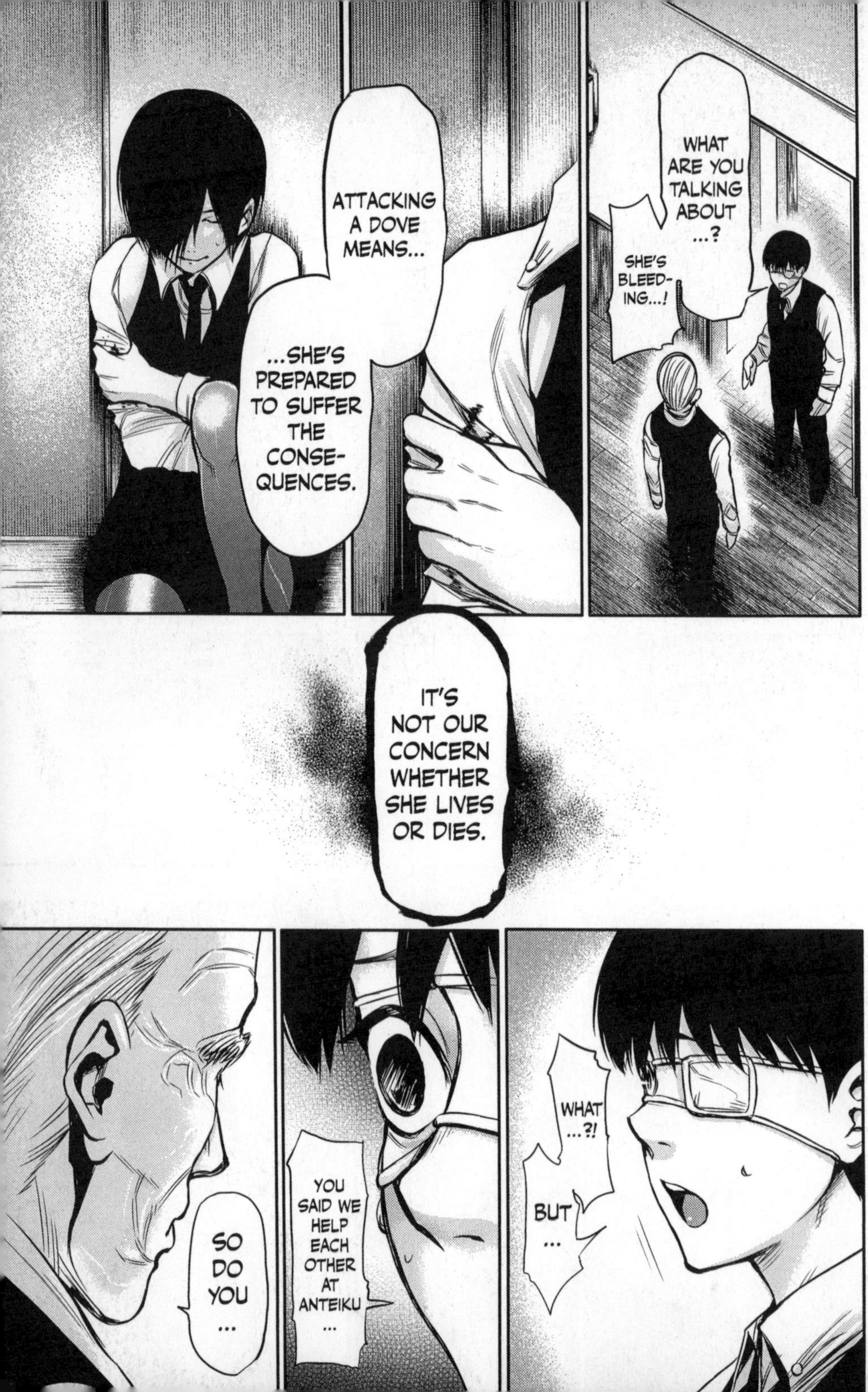
WHAT ARE YOU TALKING ABOUT ...?
SHE'S BLEEDING...!
ATTACKING A DOVE MEANS...
...SHE'S PREPARED TO SUFFER THE CONSEQUENCES.
IT'S NOT OUR CONCERN WHETHER SHE LIVES OR DIES.
WHAT ...?!
BUT ...
YOU SAID WE HELP EACH OTHER AT ANTEIKU ...
SO DO YOU ...

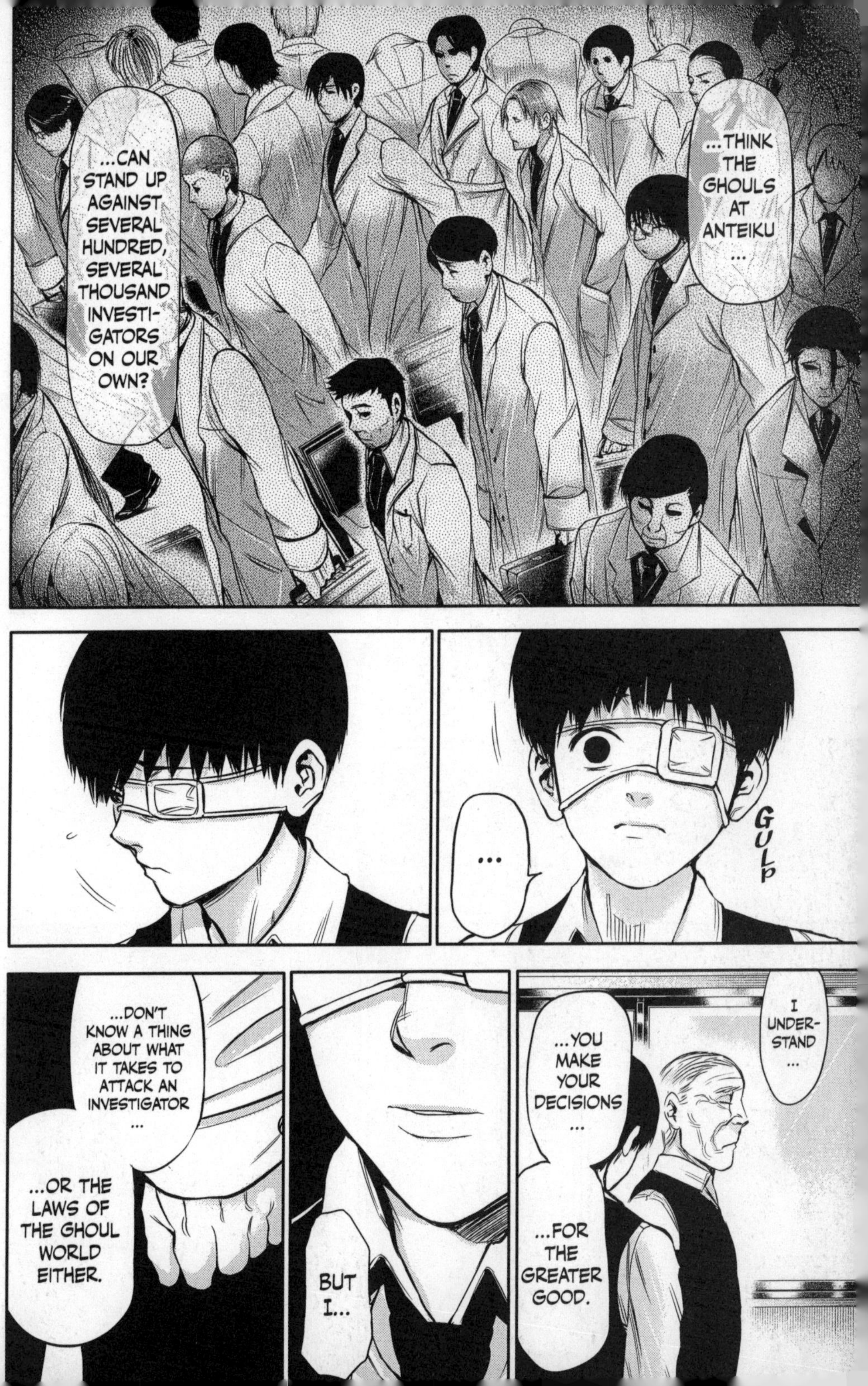
...THINK THE GHOULS AT ANTEIKU ...
...CAN STAND UP AGAINST SEVERAL HUNDRED, SEVERAL THOUSAND INVESTI- GATORS ON OUR OWN?
...
GULP
I UNDER- STAND ...
...YOU MAKE YOUR DECISIONS ...
...FOR THE GREATER GOOD.
BUT I...
...DON'T KNOW A THING ABOUT WHAT IT TAKES TO ATTACK AN INVESTIGATOR ...
...OR THE LAWS OF THE GHOUL WORLD EITHER.

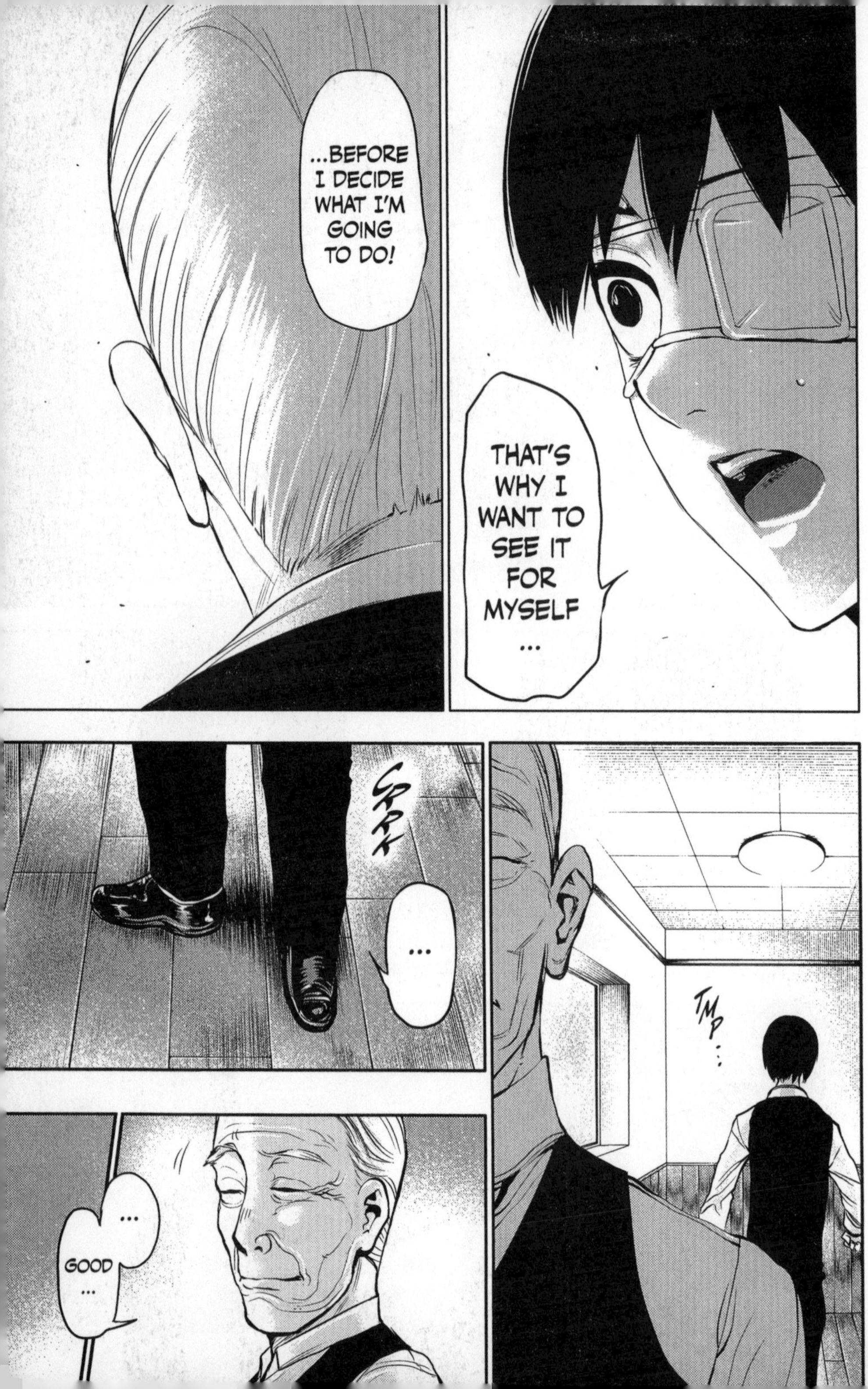
THAT'S WHY I WANT TO SEE IT FOR MYSELF ...
...BEFORE I DECIDE WHAT I'M GOING TO DO!
TMP...
CRRK
...
... GOOD ...

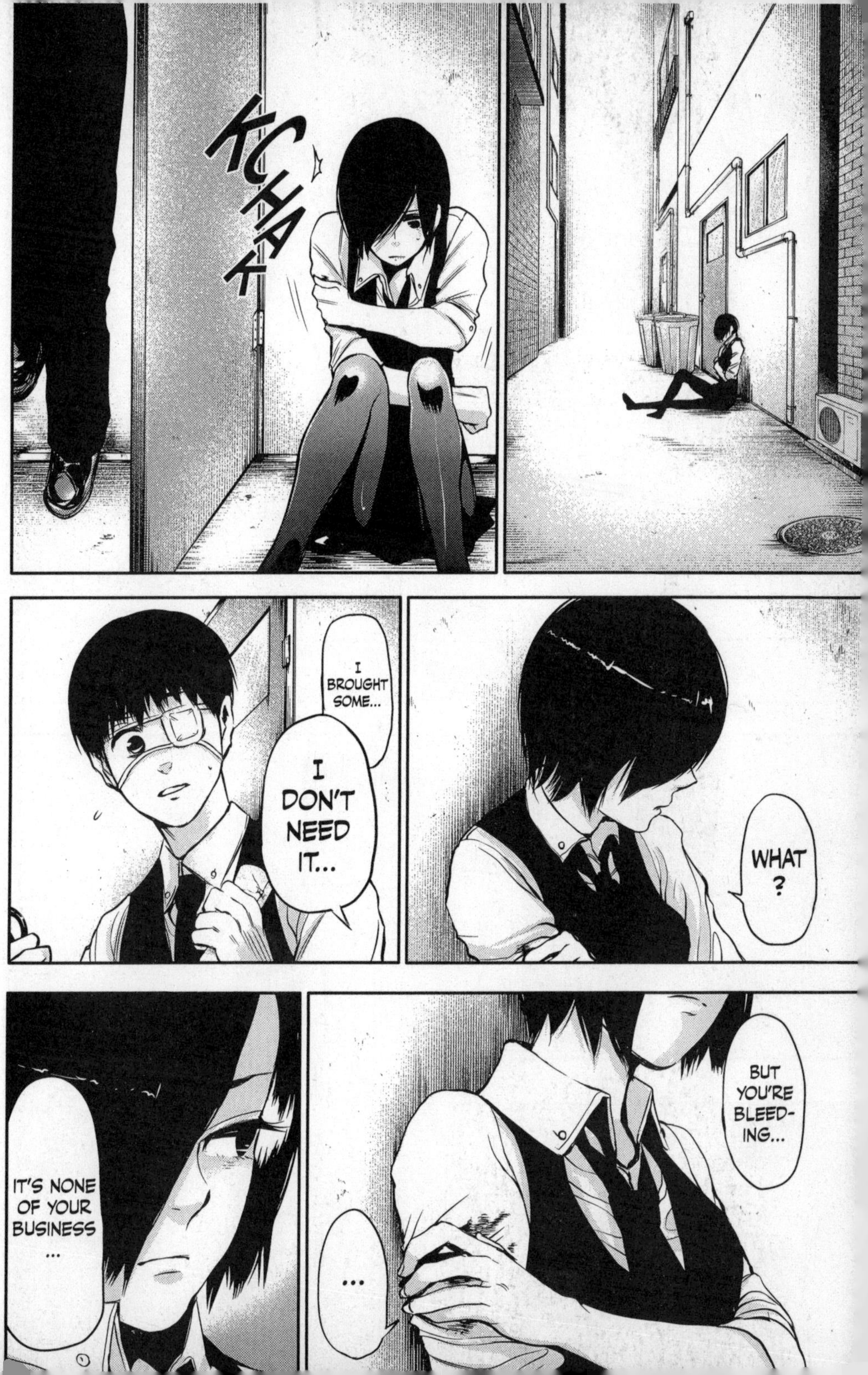
KCHAK
WHAT?
I BROUGHT SOME...
I DON'T NEED IT...
BUT YOU'RE BLEEDING...
...
IT'S NONE OF YOUR BUSINESS ...

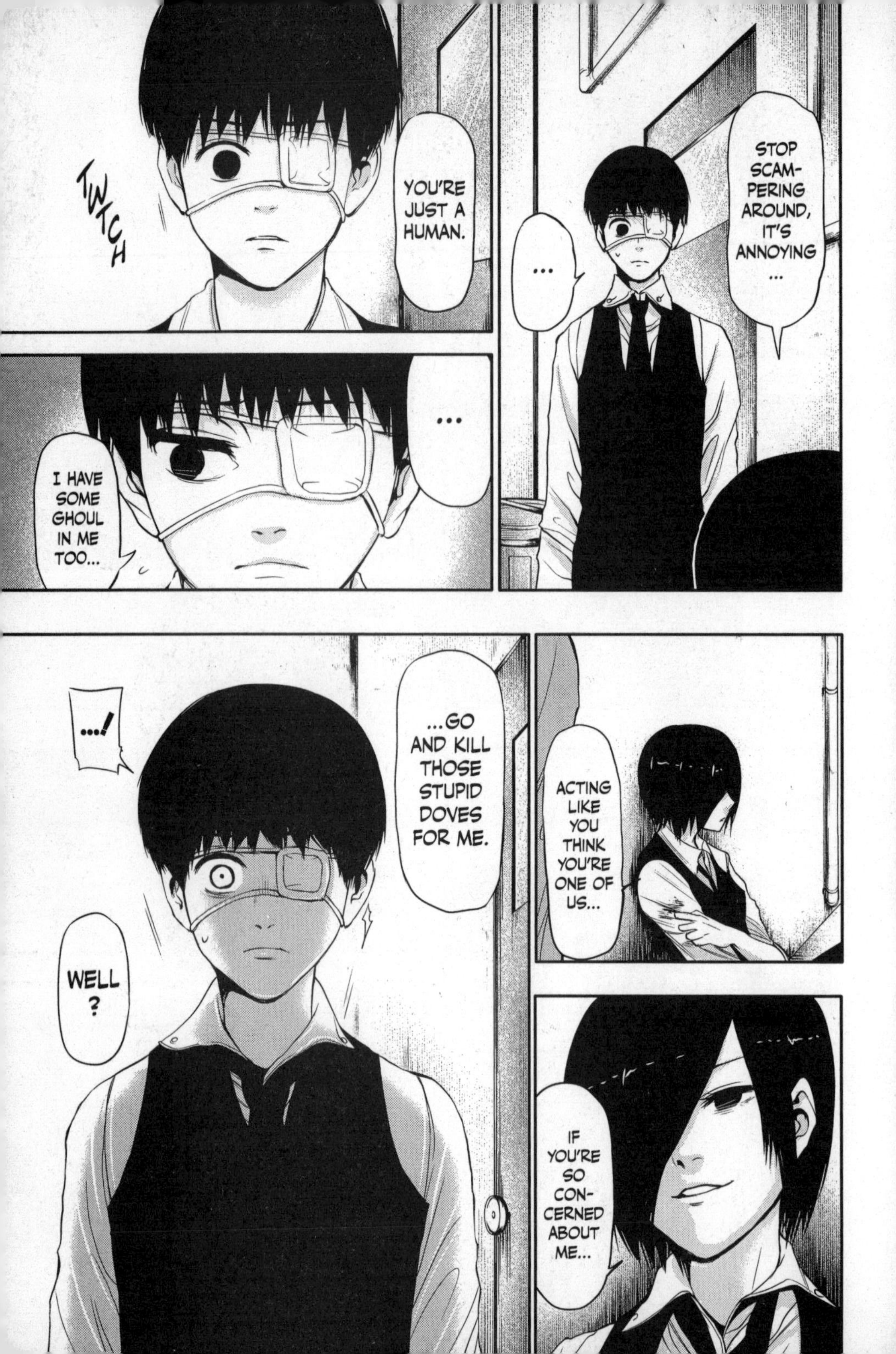
STOP SCAM-PERING AROUND, IT'S ANNOYING ...
...
YOU'RE JUST A HUMAN.
TWITCH
...
I HAVE SOME GHOUL IN ME TOO...
ACTING LIKE YOU THINK YOU'RE ONE OF US...
IF YOU'RE SO CON-CERNED ABOUT ME...
...GO AND KILL THOSE STUPID DOVES FOR ME.
...!
WELL ?

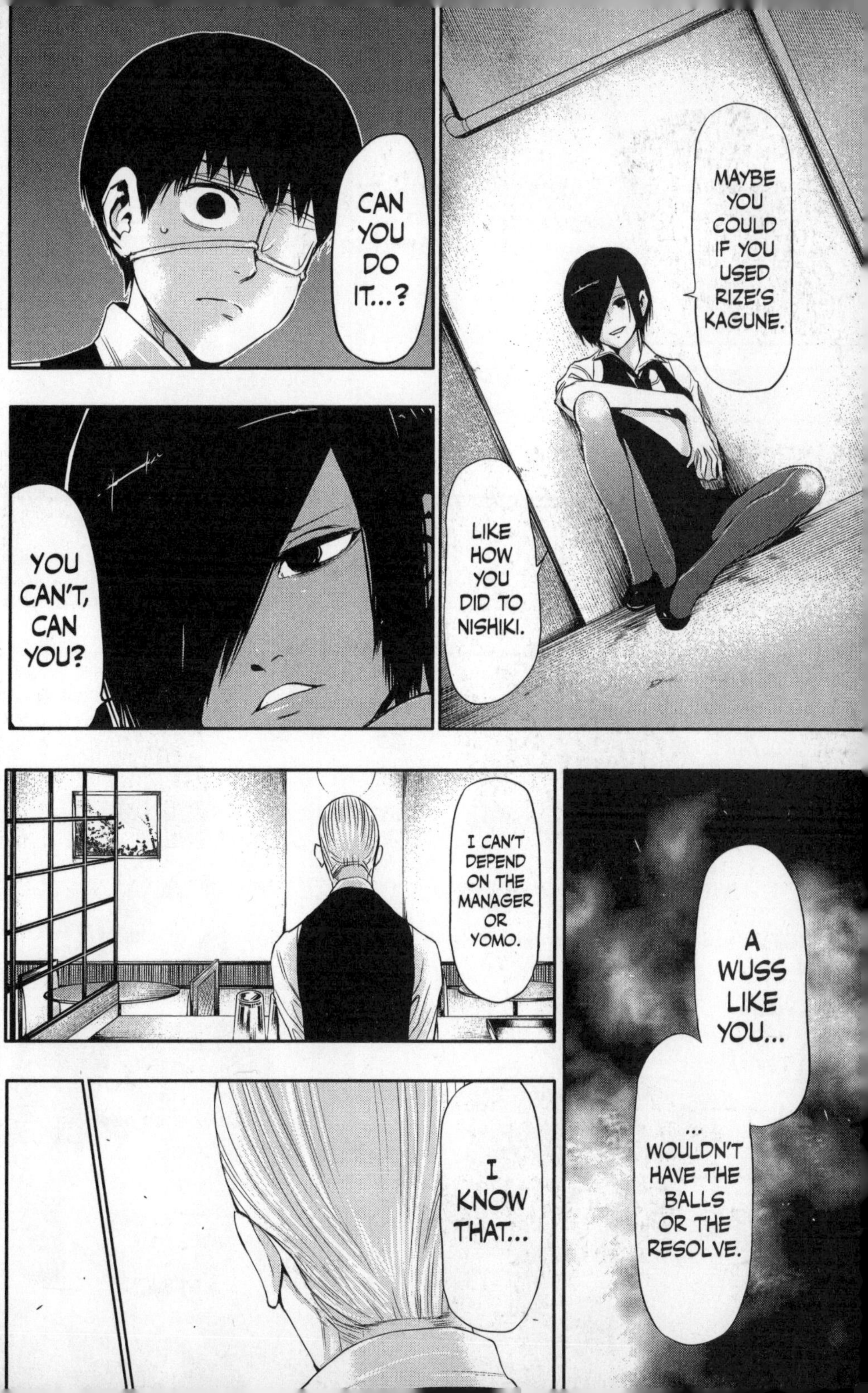
MAYBE YOU COULD IF YOU USED RIZE'S KAGUNE.
LIKE HOW YOU DID TO NISHIKI.
CAN YOU DO IT...?
YOU CAN'T, CAN YOU?
A WUSS LIKE YOU...
... WOULDN'T HAVE THE BALLS OR THE RESOLVE.
I CAN'T DEPEND ON THE MANAGER OR YOMO.
I KNOW THAT...

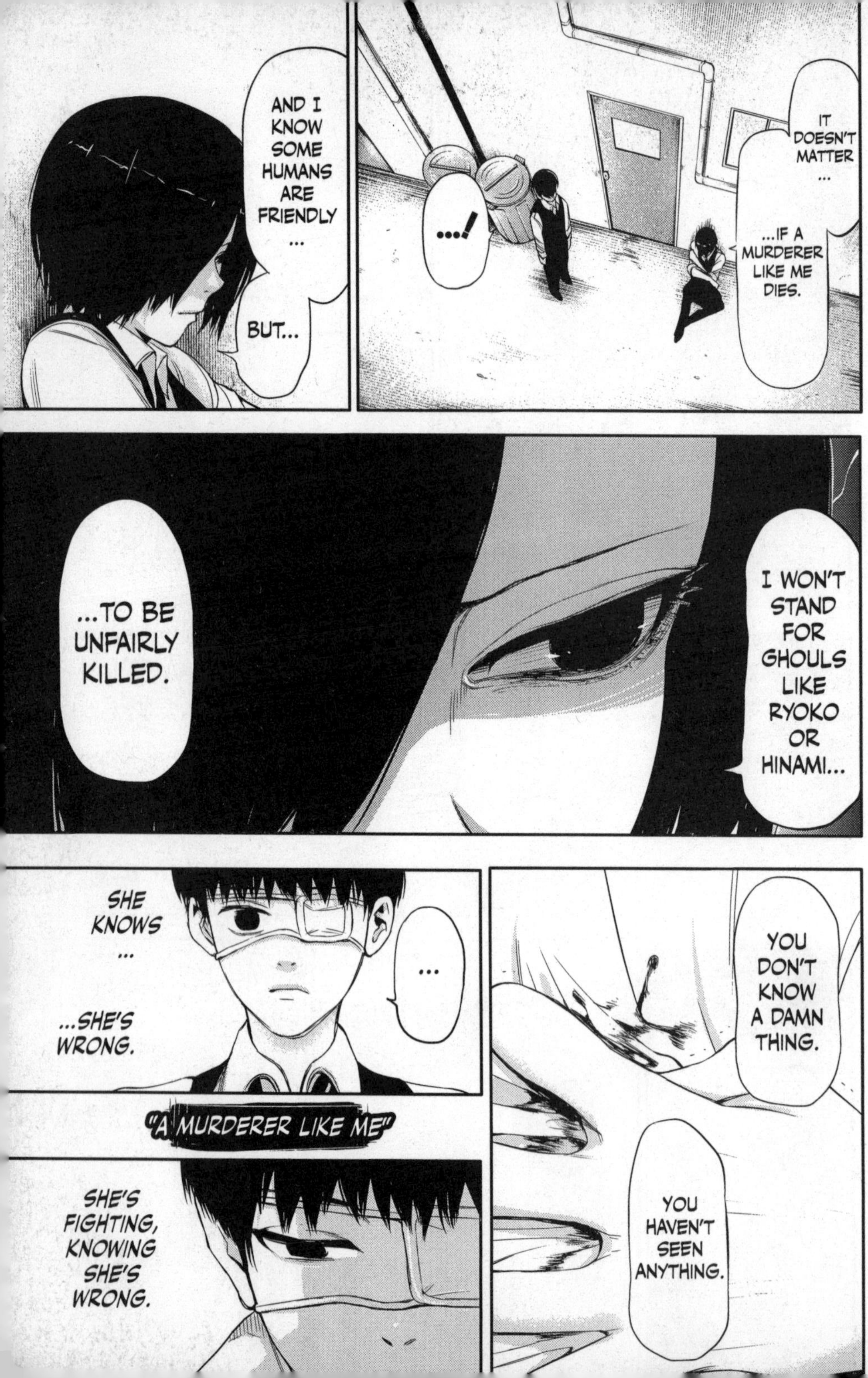
IT DOESN'T MATTER ...
...IF A MURDERER LIKE ME DIES.
...!
AND I KNOW SOME HUMANS ARE FRIENDLY ...
BUT...
I WON'T STAND FOR GHOULS LIKE RYOKO OR HINAMI...
...TO BE UNFAIRLY KILLED.
YOU DON'T KNOW A DAMN THING.
YOU HAVEN'T SEEN ANYTHING.
...
SHE KNOWS ...
...SHE'S WRONG.
"A MURDERER LIKE ME"
SHE'S FIGHTING, KNOWING SHE'S WRONG.

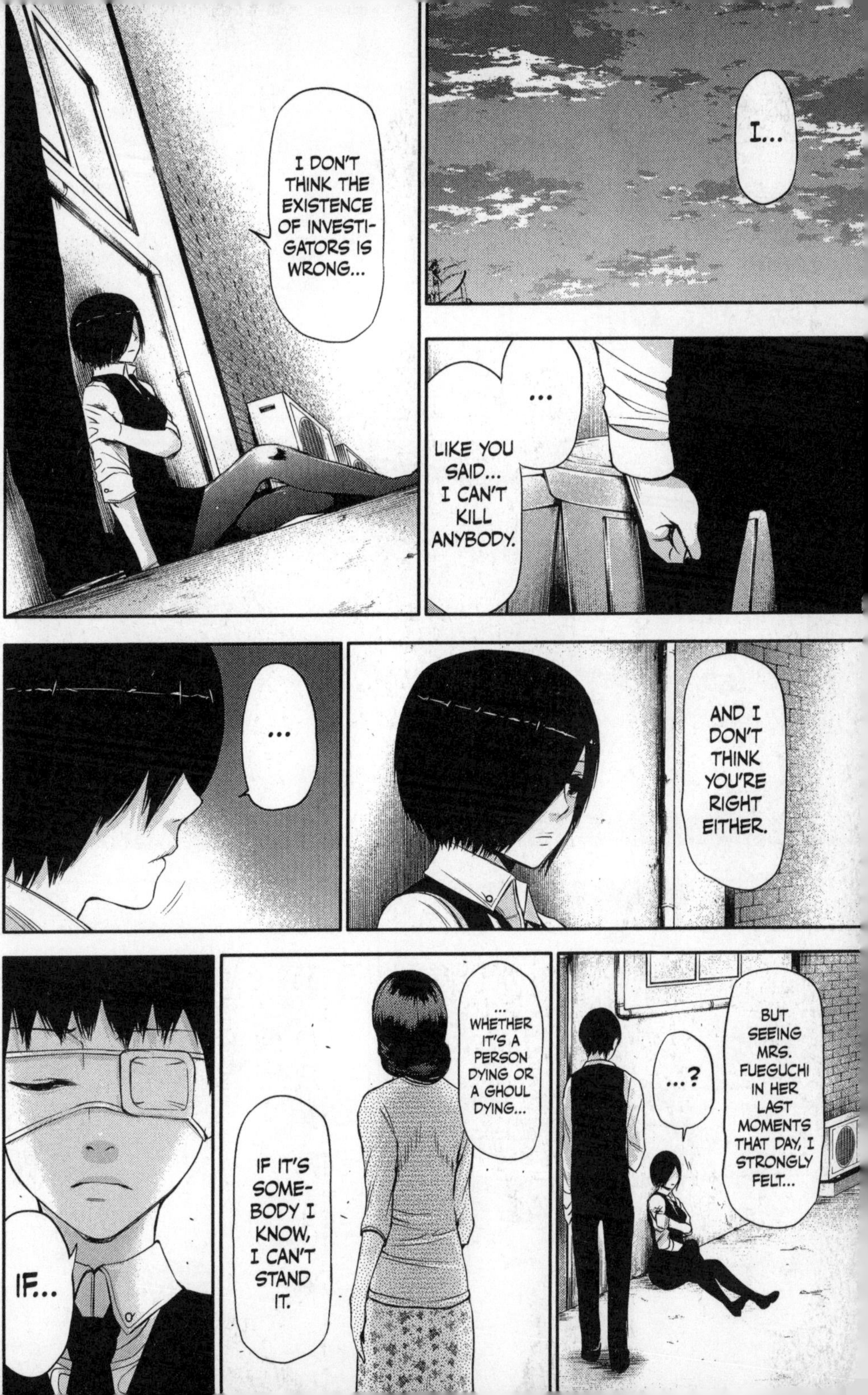
I...
...
LIKE YOU SAID... I CAN'T KILL ANYBODY.
I DON'T THINK THE EXISTENCE OF INVESTI-GATORS IS WRONG...
AND I DON'T THINK YOU'RE RIGHT EITHER.
...
BUT SEEING MRS. FUEGUCHI IN HER LAST MOMENTS THAT DAY, I STRONGLY FELT...
...?
... WHETHER IT'S A PERSON DYING OR A GHOUL DYING...
IF IT'S SOME-BODY I KNOW, I CAN'T STAND IT.
IF...

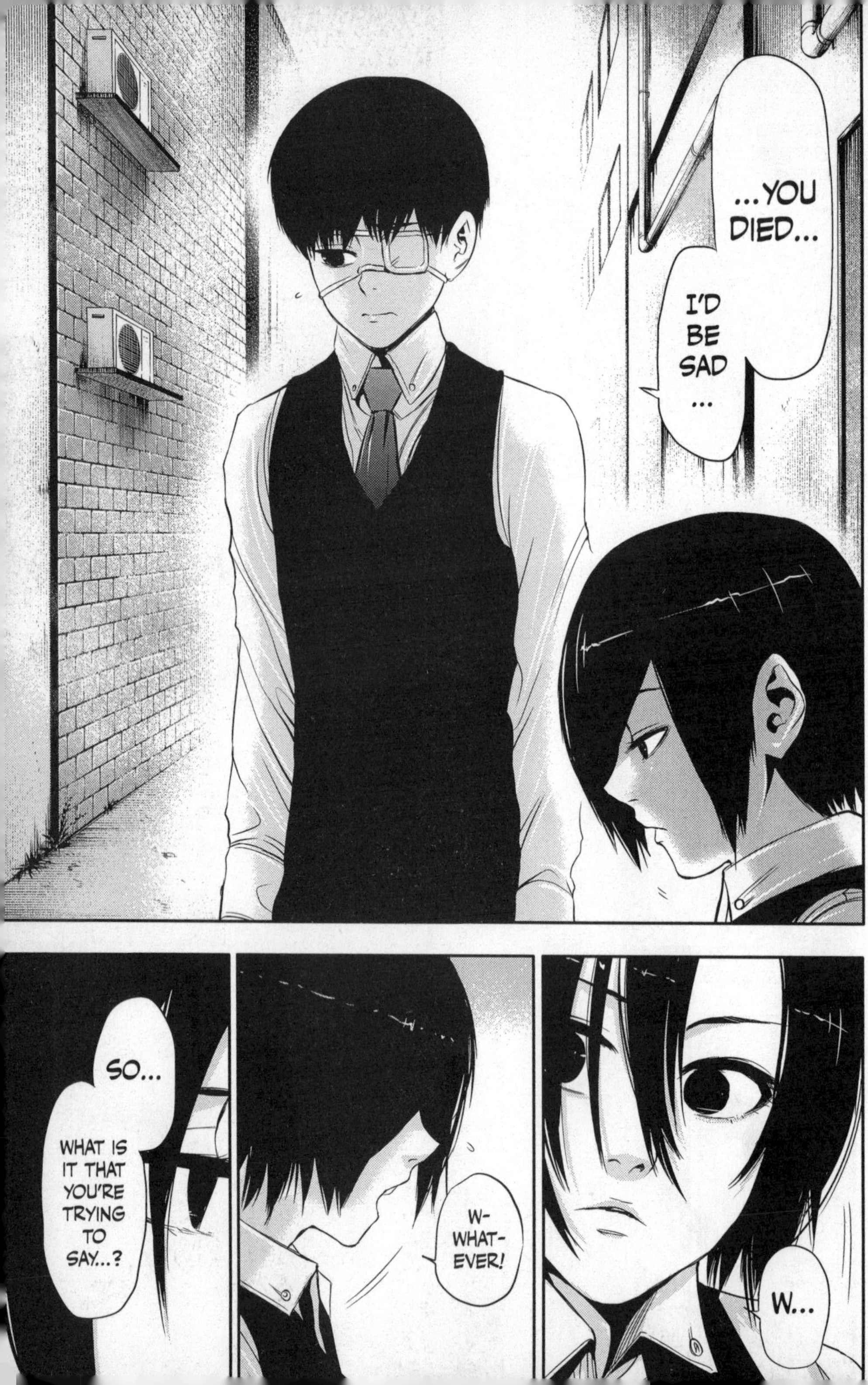
...YOU DIED...
I'D BE SAD ...
W...
W-WHAT-EVER!
SO...
WHAT IS IT THAT YOU'RE TRYING TO SAY...?

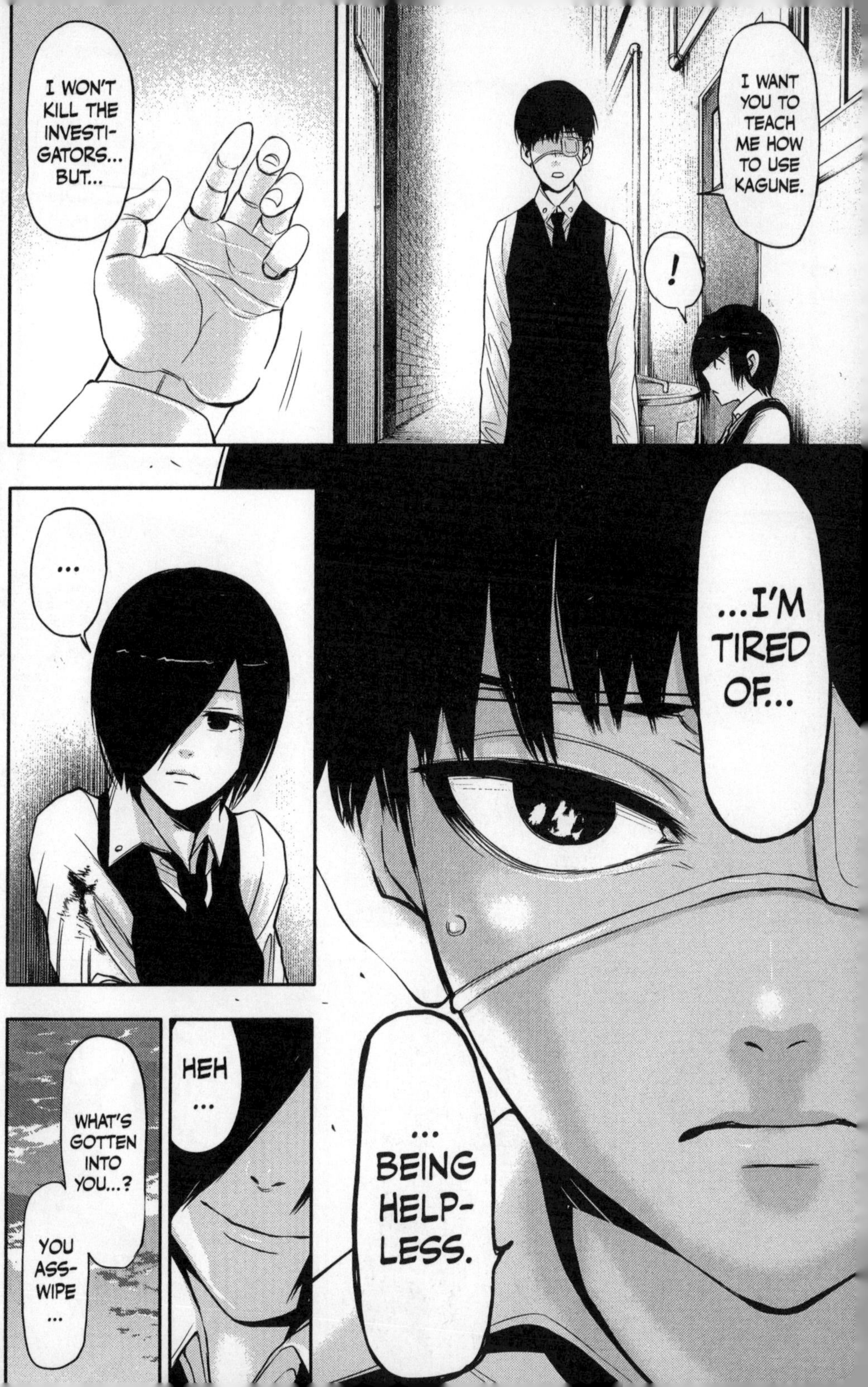
I WANT YOU TO TEACH ME HOW TO USE KAGUNE.
!
I WON'T KILL THE INVESTIGATORS... BUT...
...I'M TIRED OF...
... BEING HELPLESS.
...
HEH ...
WHAT'S GOTTEN INTO YOU...?
YOU ASSWIPE ...

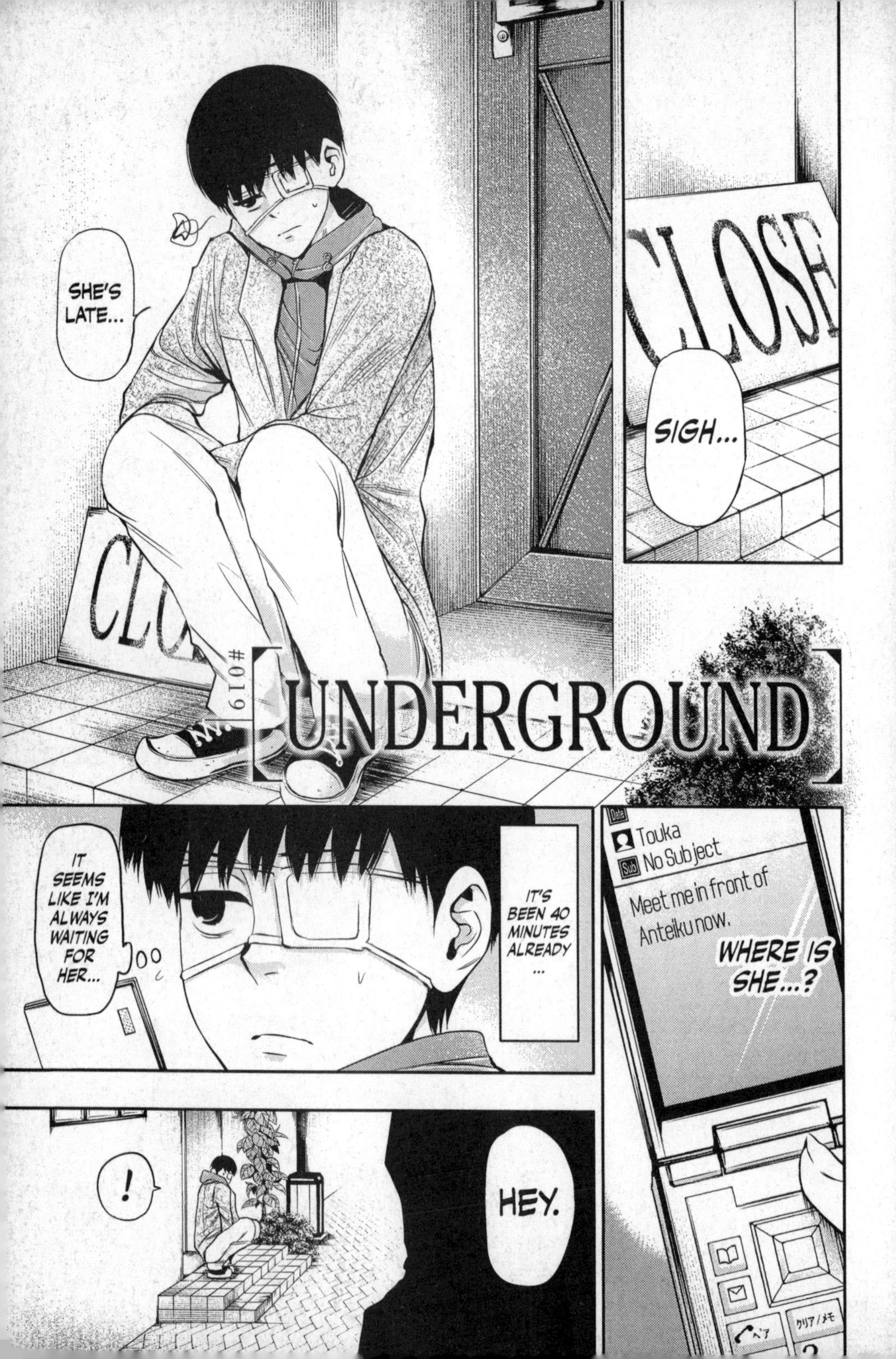
CLOSE
SIGH...
SHE'S LATE...
CLOSE
#019 UNDERGROUND
Date
Touka
Sub No Subject
Meet me in front of Anteiku now.
WHERE IS SHE...?
クリア/メモ
ペア
IT'S BEEN 40 MINUTES ALREADY...
IT SEEMS LIKE I'M ALWAYS WAITING FOR HER...
HEY.
!

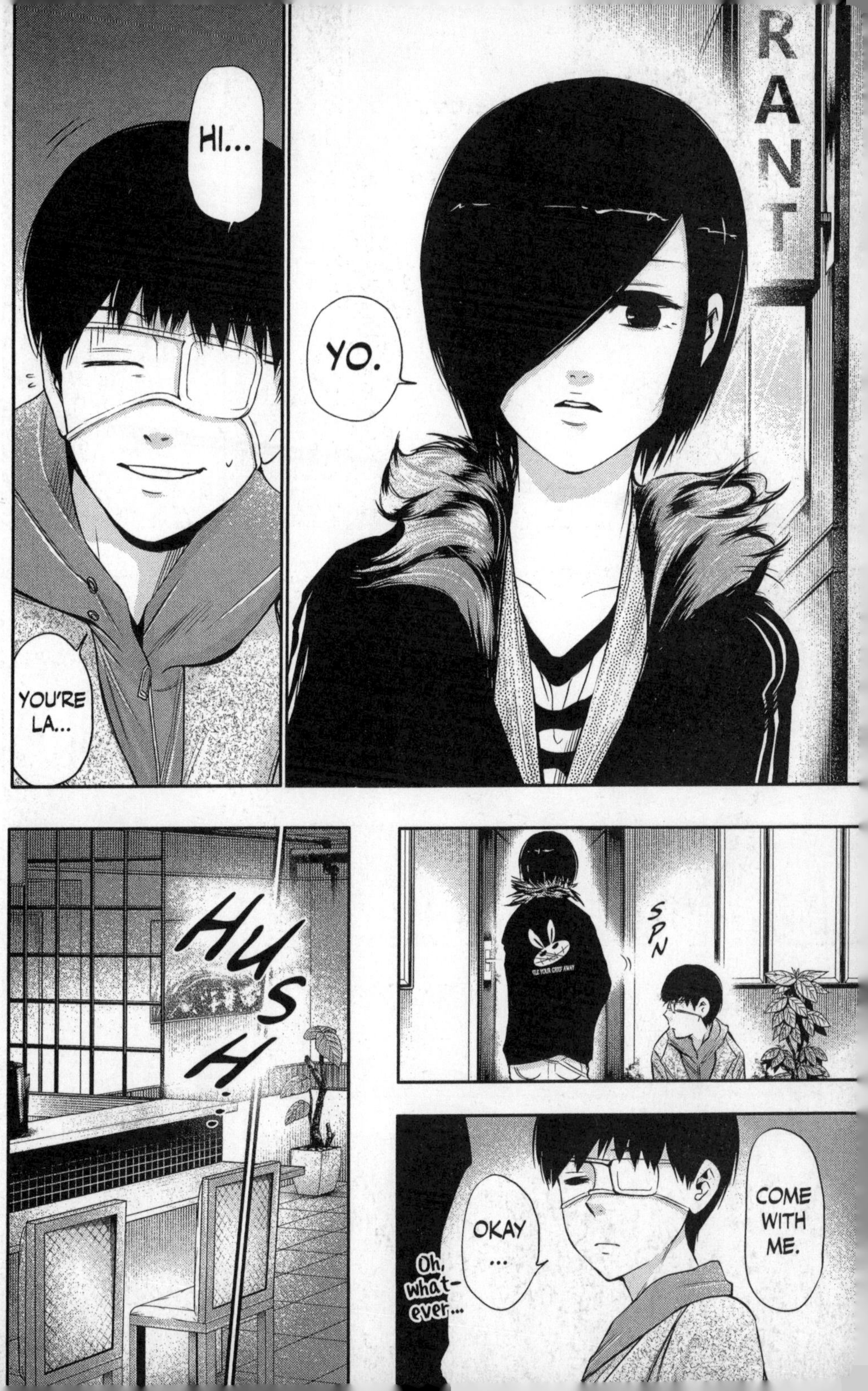
RANT
YO.
HI...
YOU'RE LA...
SPN
COME WITH ME.
OKAY ...
Oh, whatever...
HUSH.

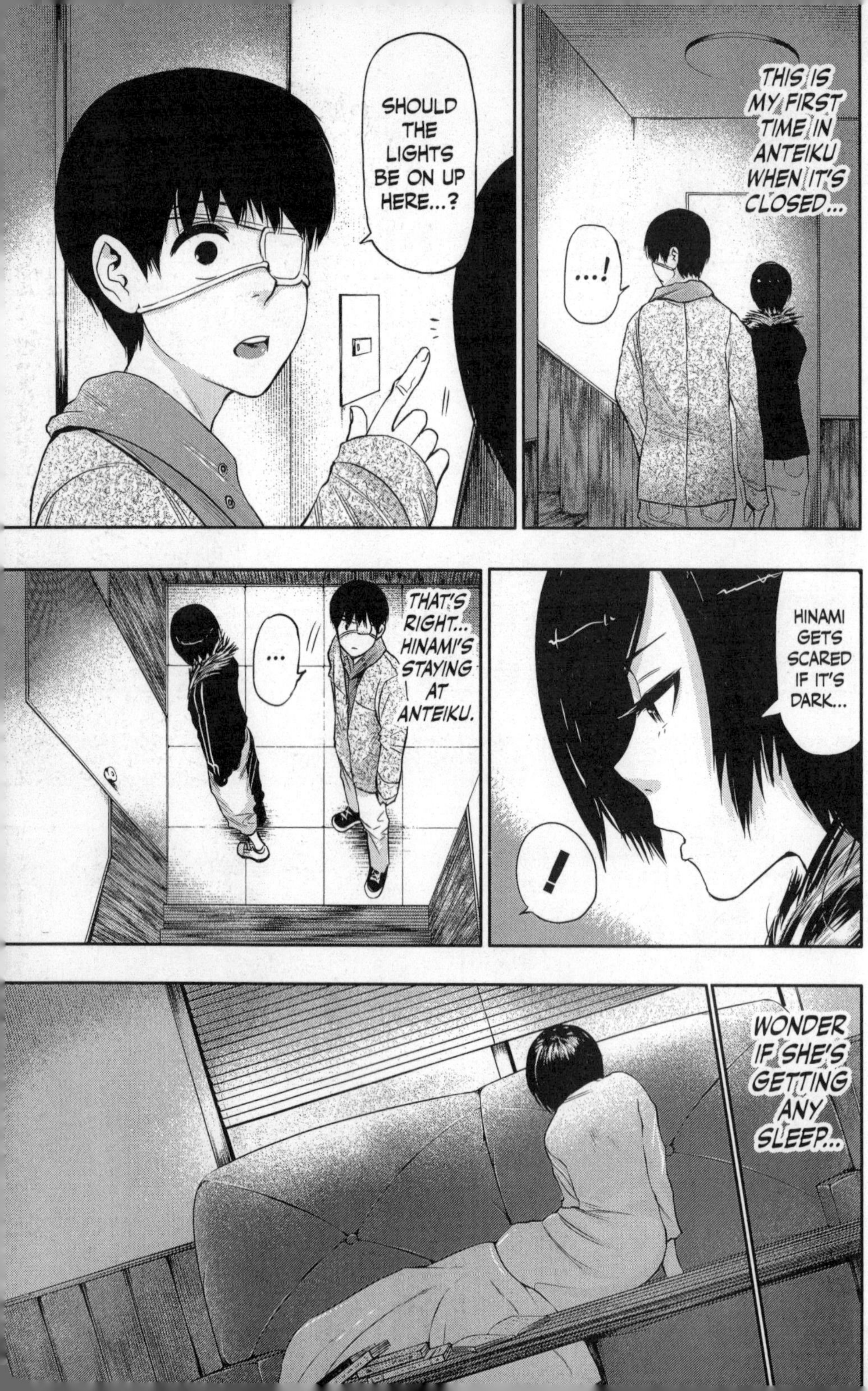
THIS IS MY FIRST TIME IN ANTEIKU WHEN IT'S CLOSED...
...!
SHOULD THE LIGHTS BE ON UP HERE...?
HINAMI GETS SCARED IF IT'S DARK...
!
THAT'S RIGHT... HINAMI'S STAYING AT ANTEIKU.
...
WONDER IF SHE'S GETTING ANY SLEEP...

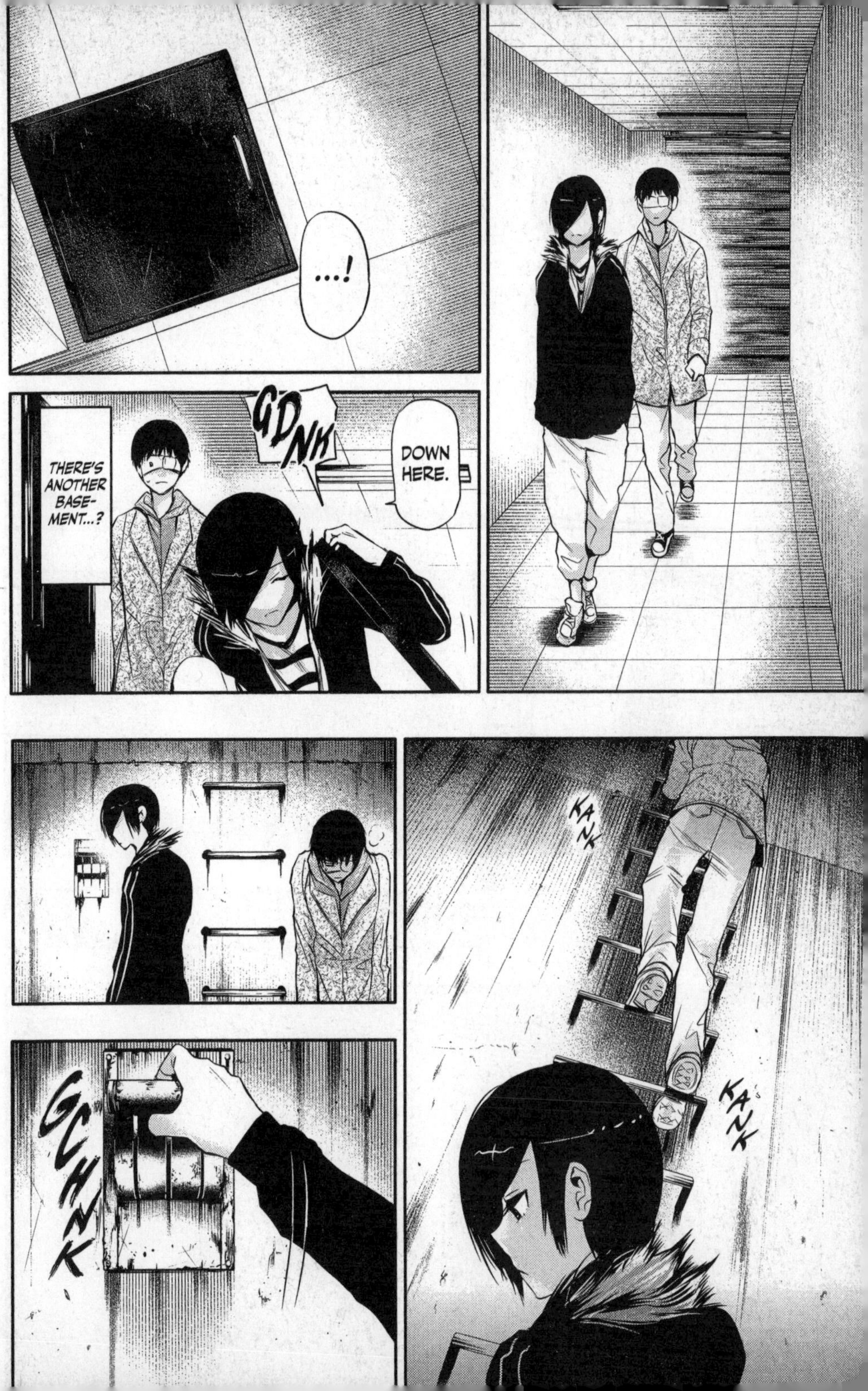
...!
GDNK
DOWN HERE.
THERE'S ANOTHER BASEMENT...?
KANK
KANK
GCHNK

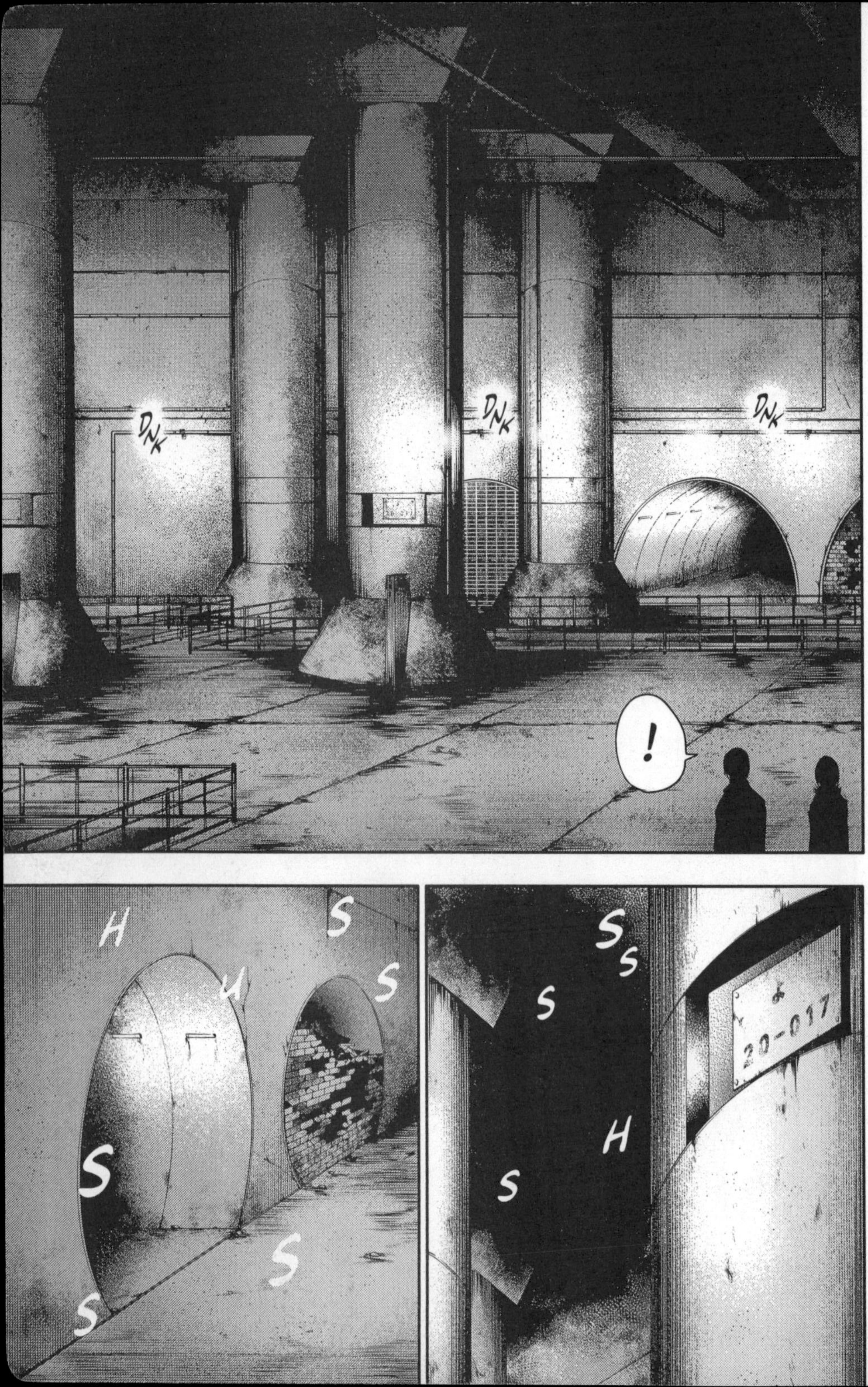
DNK
DNK
DNK
!
20-017
SSSHS
HuSSSSS

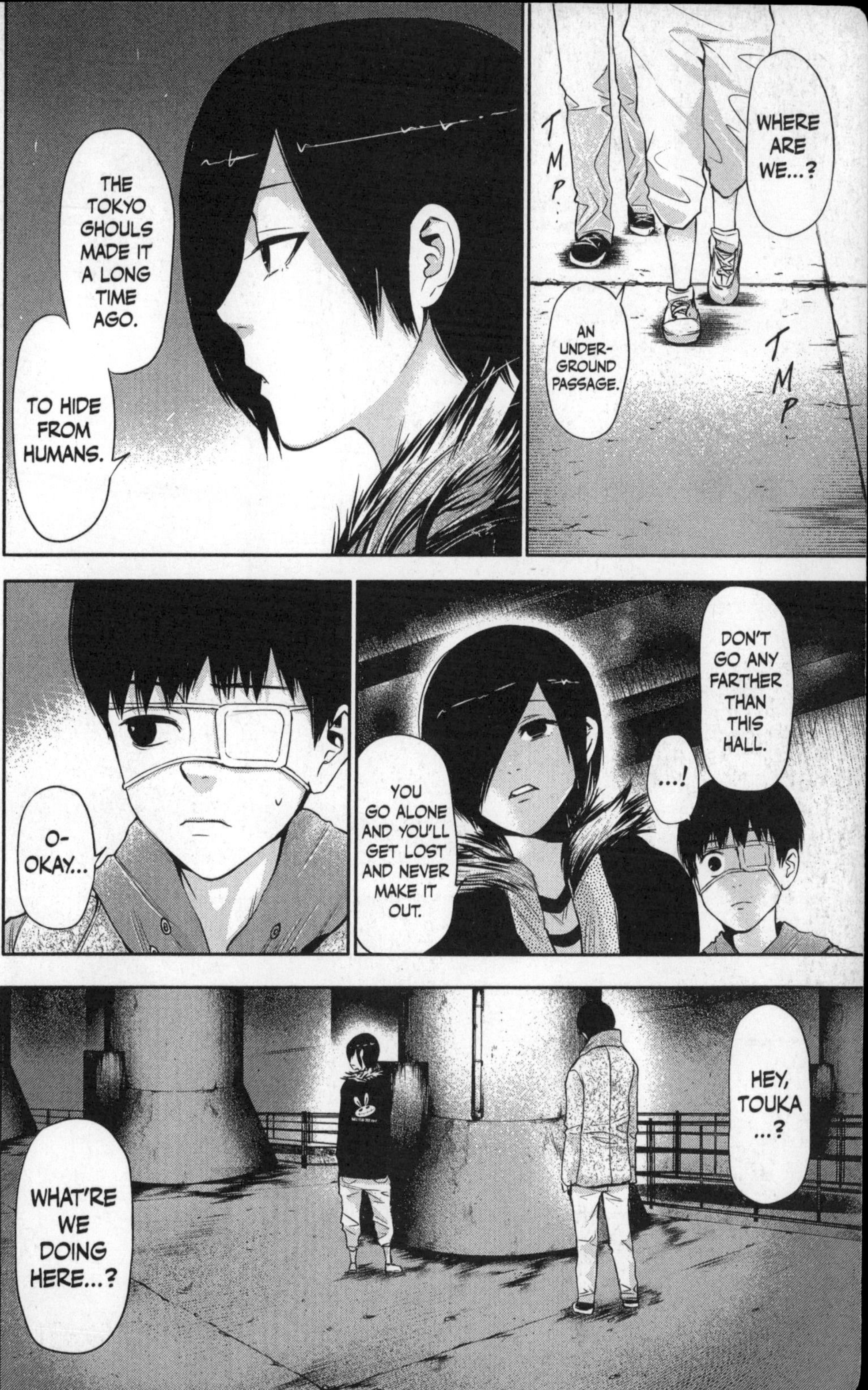
WHERE ARE WE...?
TMP
TMP
AN UNDER-GROUND PASSAGE.
THE TOKYO GHOULS MADE IT A LONG TIME AGO.
TO HIDE FROM HUMANS.
DON'T GO ANY FARTHER THAN THIS HALL.
...!
YOU GO ALONE AND YOU'LL GET LOST AND NEVER MAKE IT OUT.
O-OKAY...
HEY, TOUKA...?
WHAT'RE WE DOING HERE...?

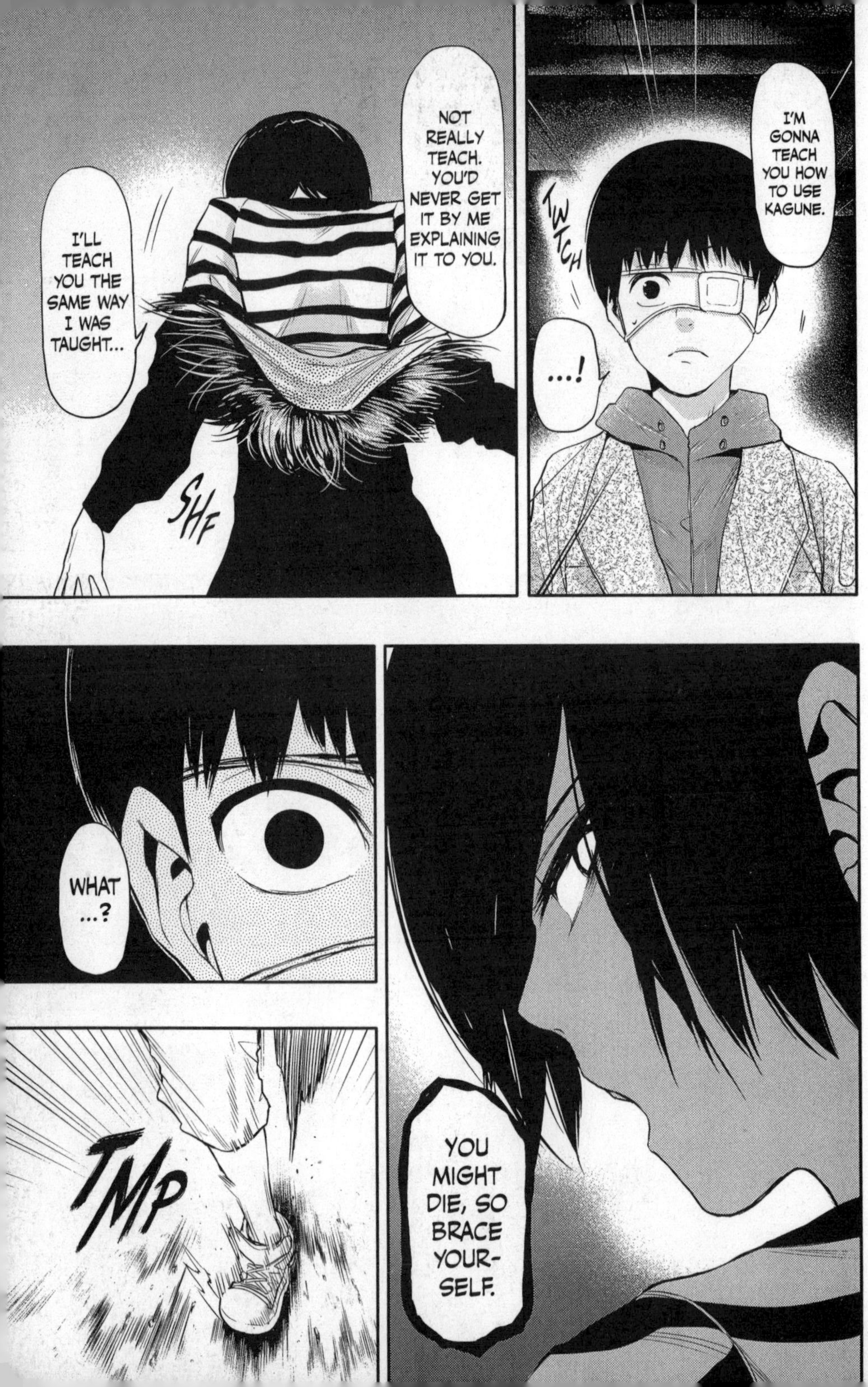
I'M GONNA TEACH YOU HOW TO USE KAGUNE.
TWITCH
...!
NOT REALLY TEACH. YOU'D NEVER GET IT BY ME EXPLAINING IT TO YOU.
I'LL TEACH YOU THE SAME WAY I WAS TAUGHT...
SHF
YOU MIGHT DIE, SO BRACE YOUR-SELF.
WHAT ...?
TMP

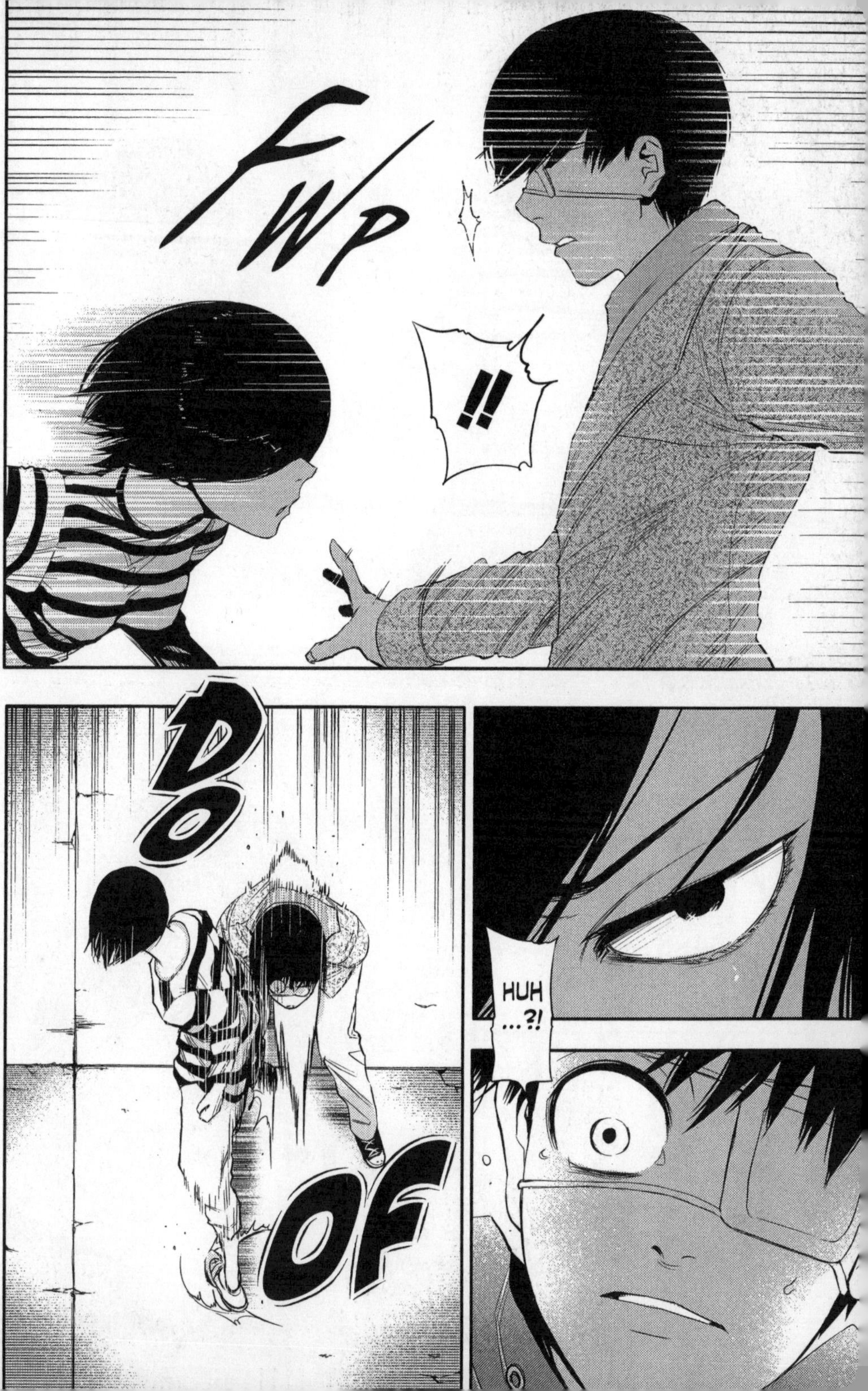
FWP
!!
HUH ...?!
DOOF

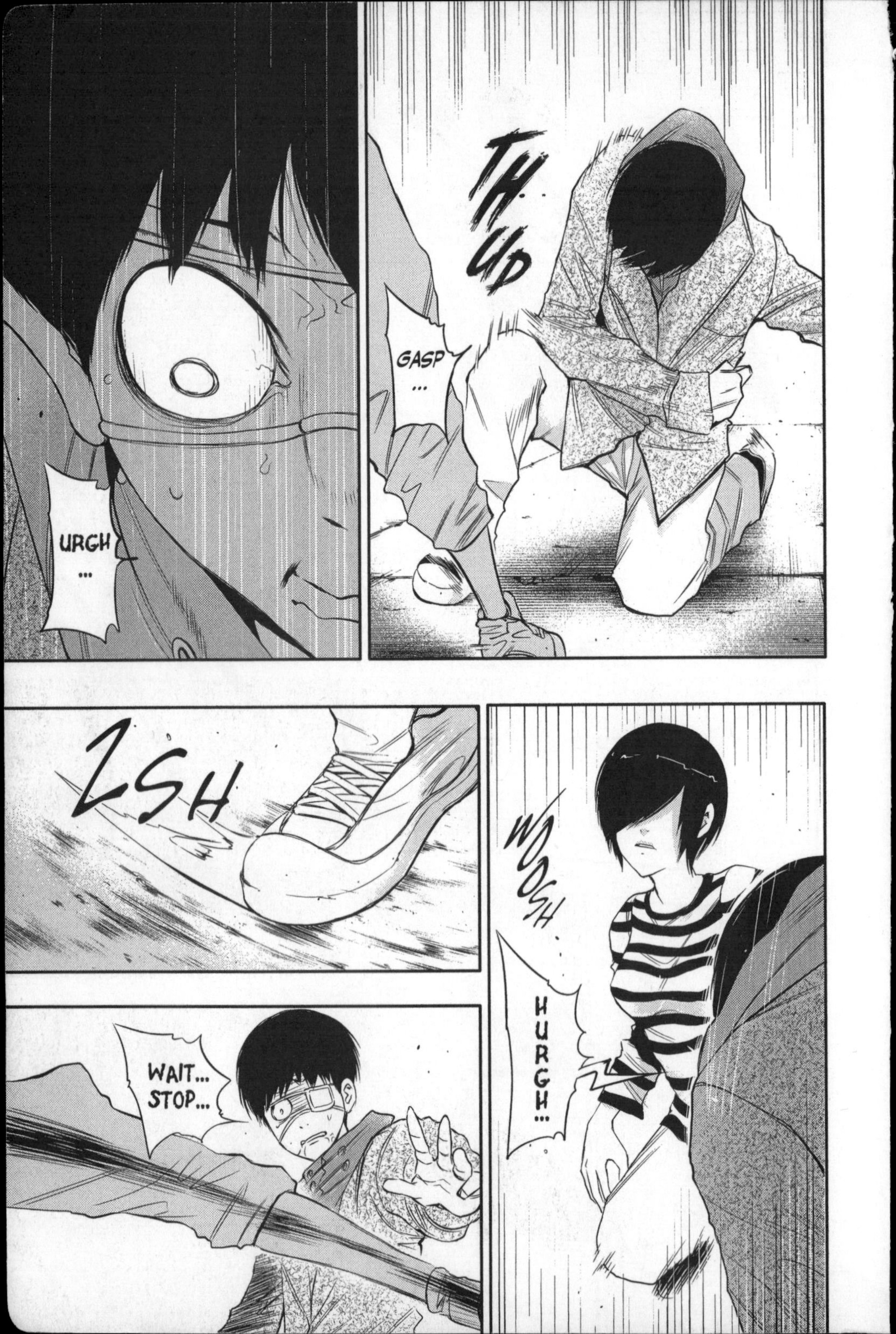
THUD
GASP...
URGH...
WOOSH
HURGH...
ZSH
WAIT... STOP...

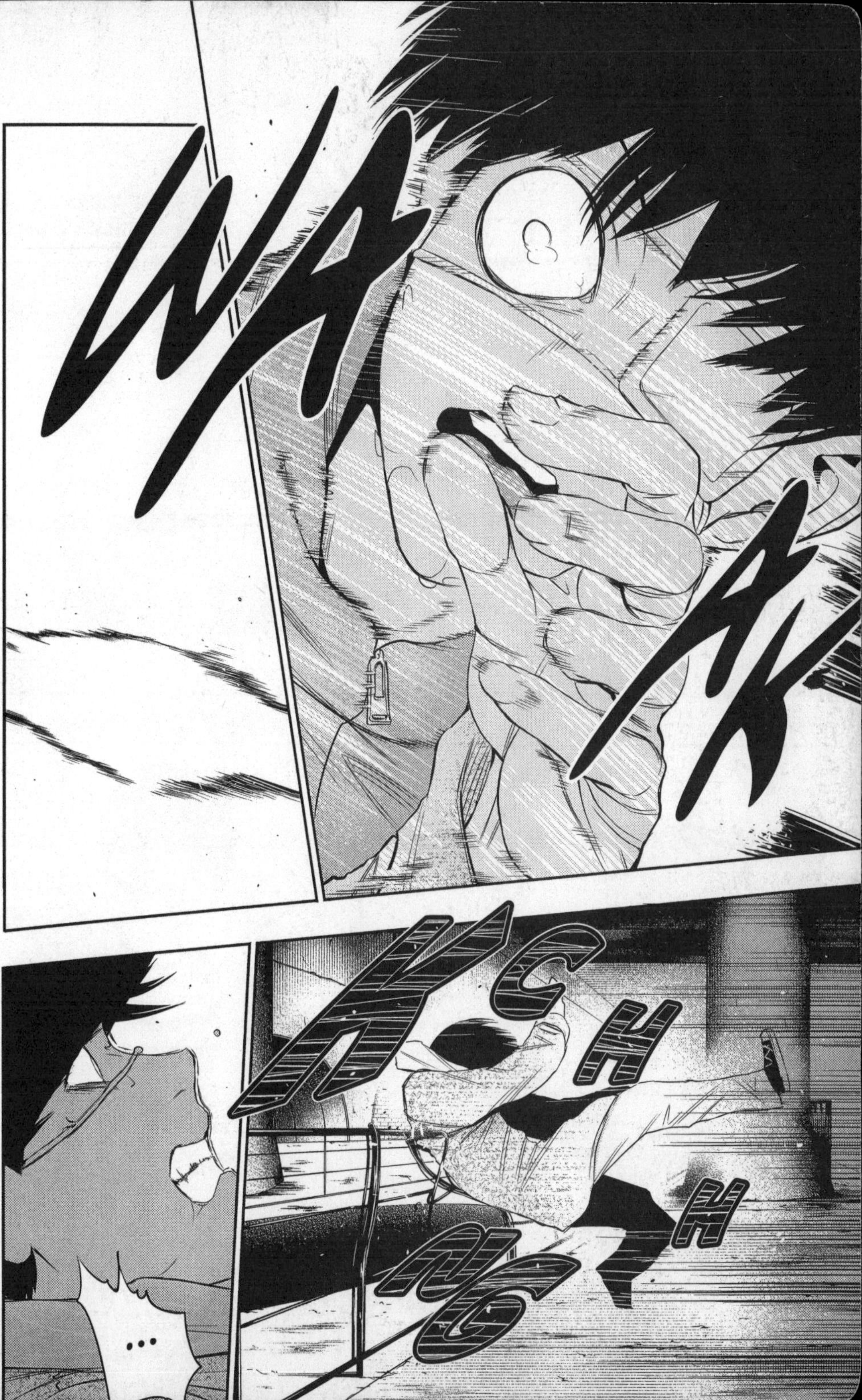
WA
AH
KCHH
NNGH
...

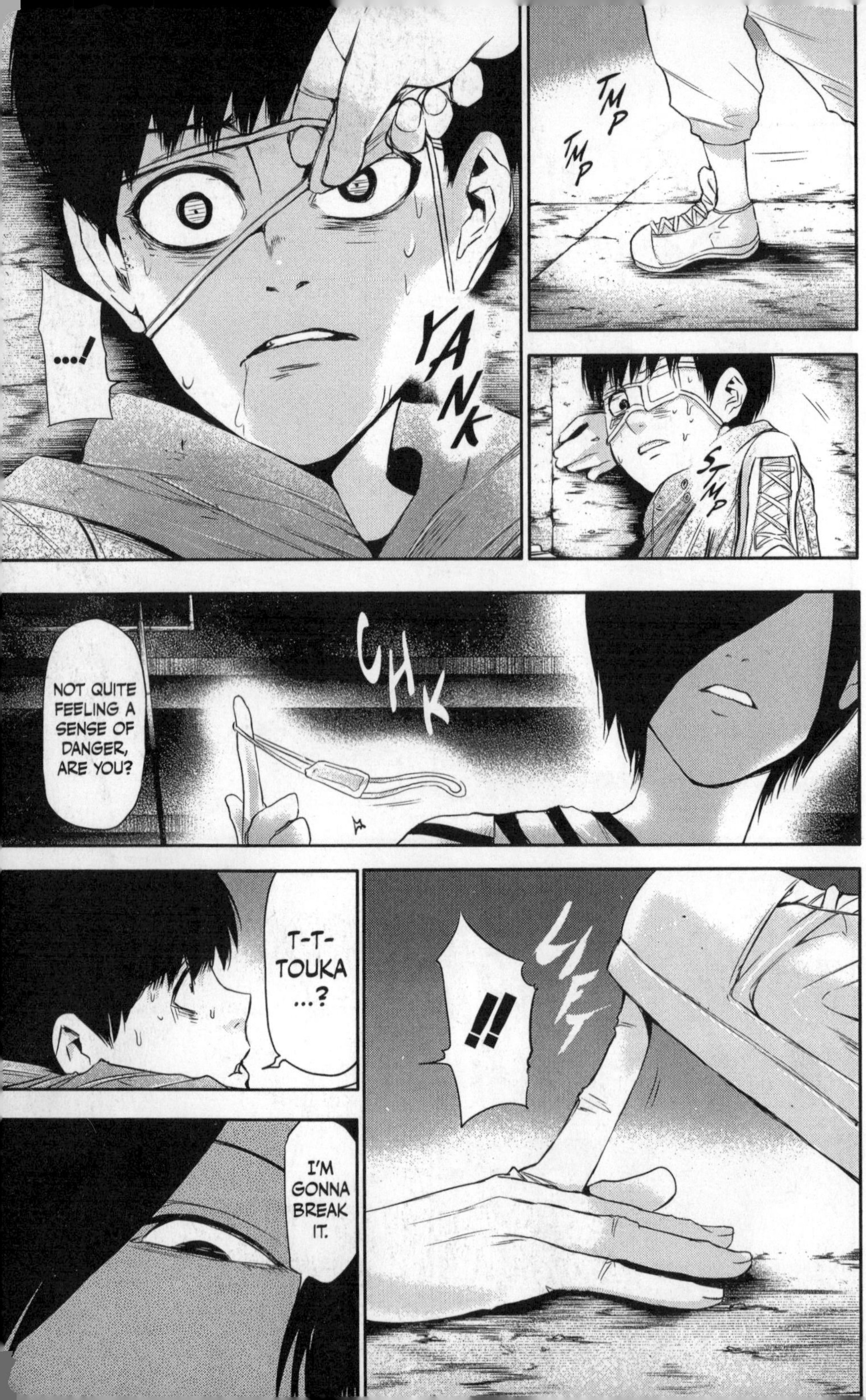
TMP
TMP
STMP
YANK
...!
CHK
NOT QUITE FEELING A SENSE OF DANGER, ARE YOU?
LIFT
!!
T-T-TOUKA ...?
I'M GONNA BREAK IT.

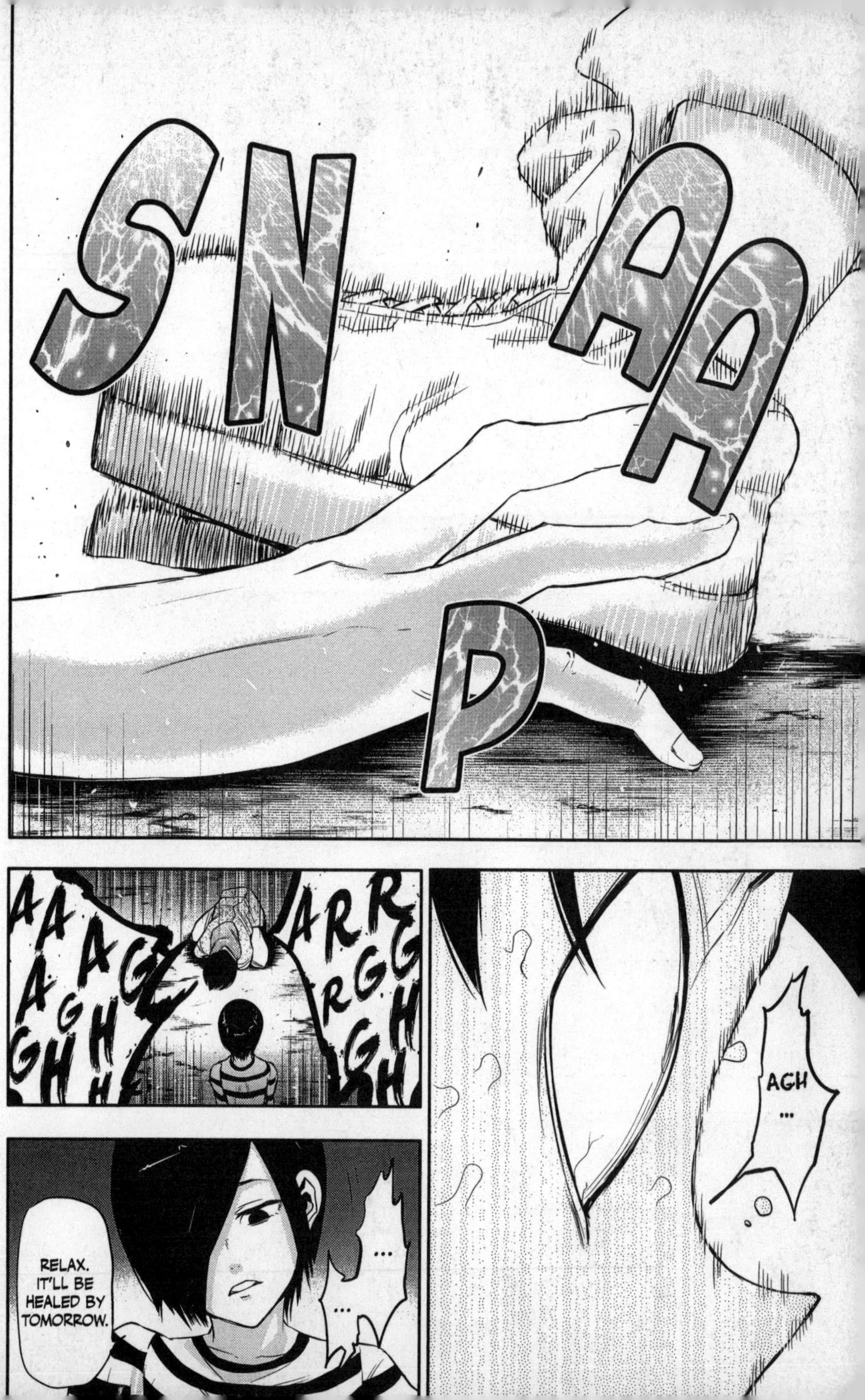
SNAAP
AGH ...
AAAAGGHHH
ARRRGGHHH
RELAX. IT'LL BE HEALED BY TOMORROW.
...
...

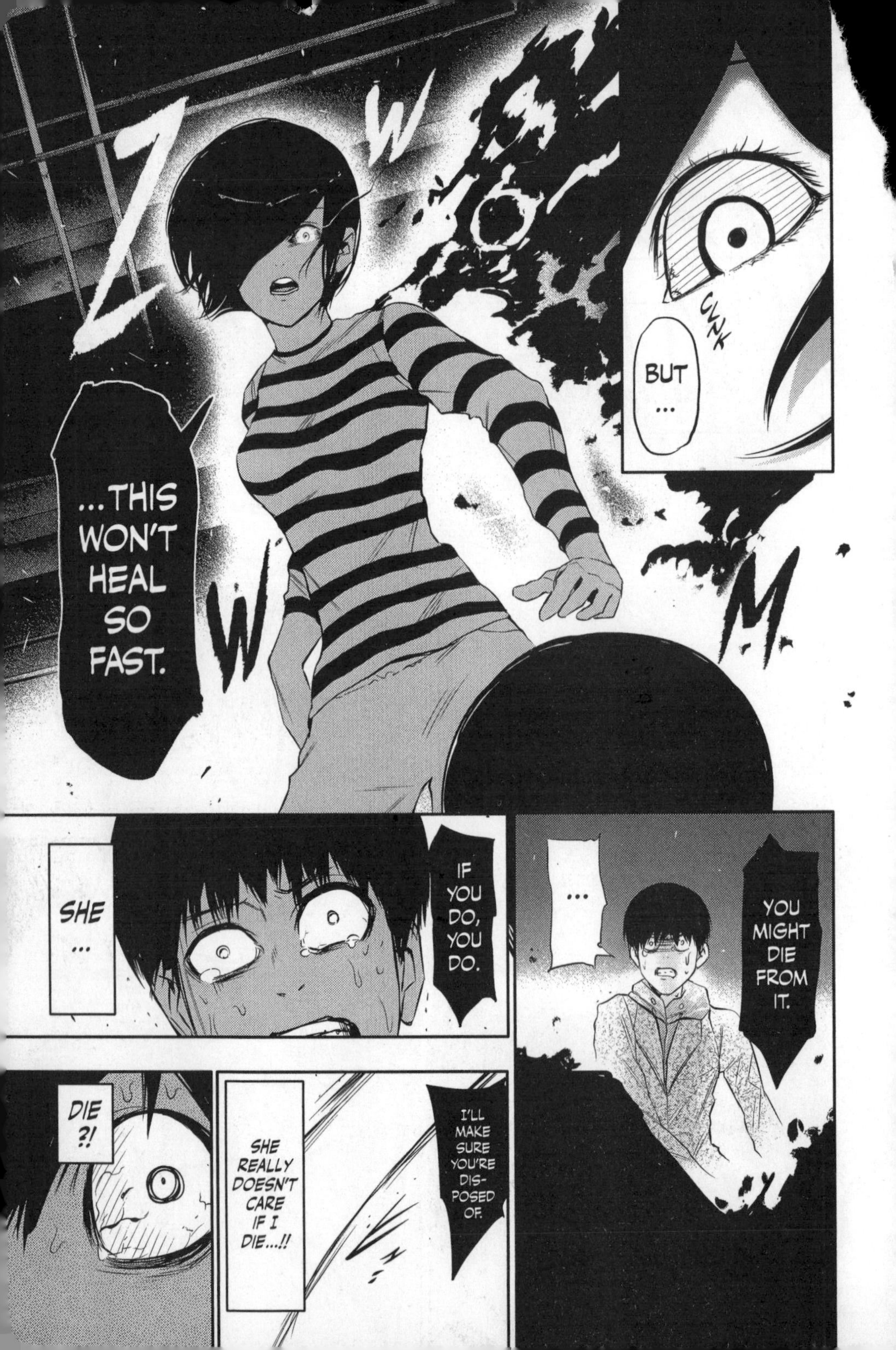
CLNK
BUT ...
...THIS WON'T HEAL SO FAST.
YOU MIGHT DIE FROM IT.
...
IF YOU DO, YOU DO.
SHE ...
I'LL MAKE SURE YOU'RE DIS-POSED OF.
SHE REALLY DOESN'T CARE IF I DIE...!!
DIE ?!

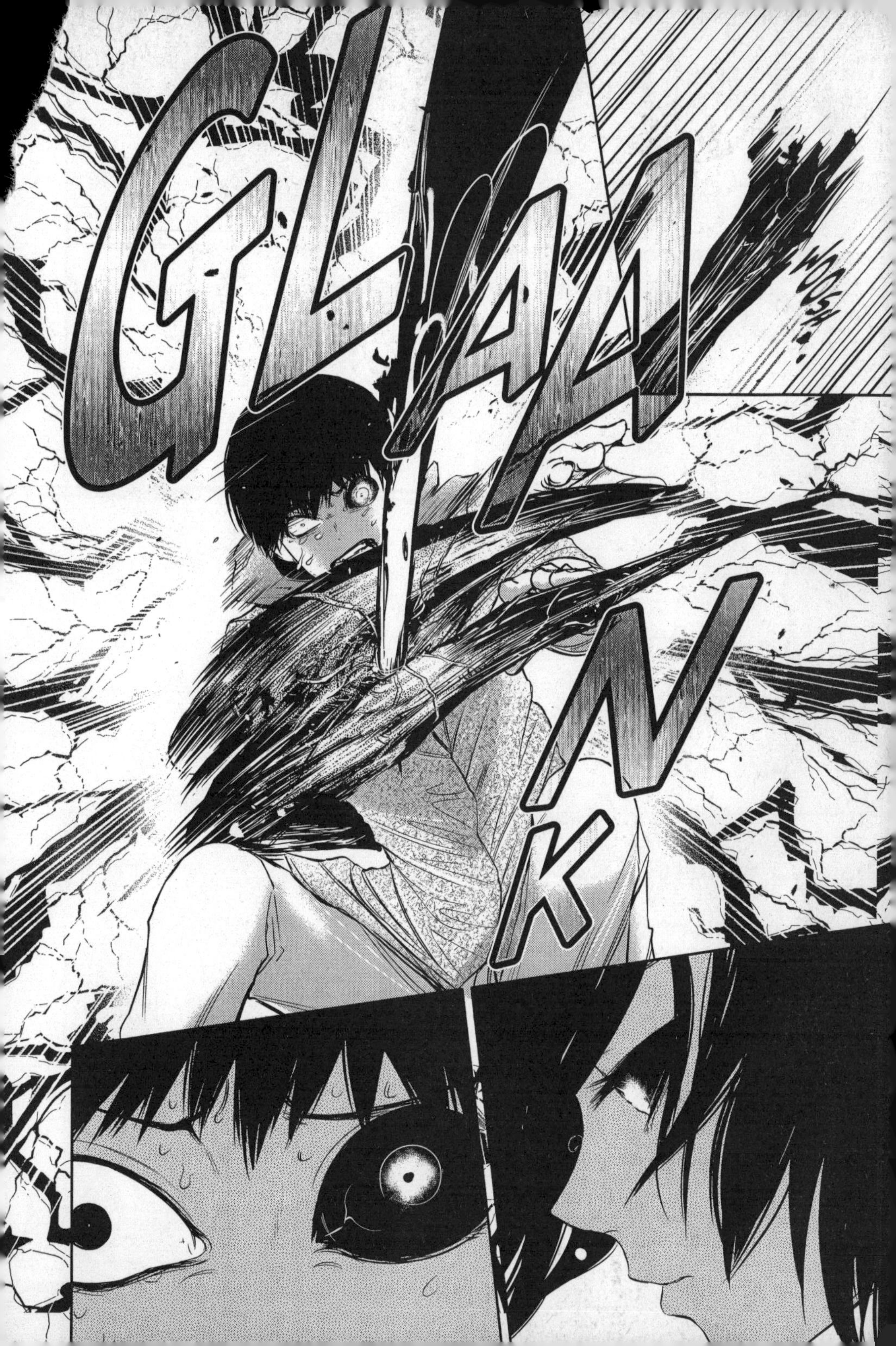
WOOSH..
GLAAANK

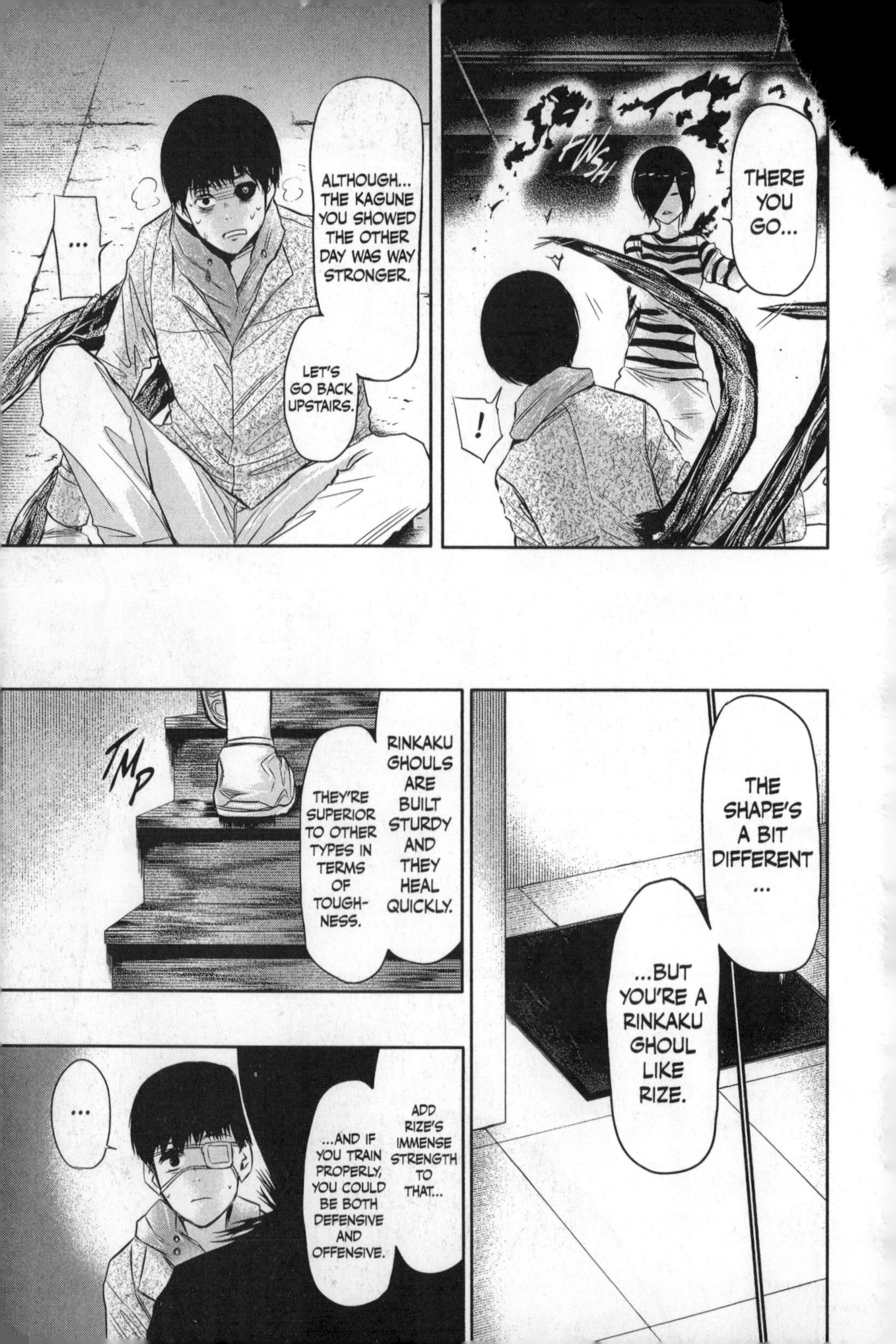
FWSH
THERE YOU GO...
!
ALTHOUGH... THE KAGUNE YOU SHOWED THE OTHER DAY WAS WAY STRONGER.
LET'S GO BACK UPSTAIRS.
...
THE SHAPE'S A BIT DIFFERENT ...
...BUT YOU'RE A RINKAKU GHOUL LIKE RIZE.
RINKAKU GHOULS ARE BUILT STURDY AND THEY HEAL QUICKLY.
THEY'RE SUPERIOR TO OTHER TYPES IN TERMS OF TOUGH-NESS.
TMP
ADD RIZE'S IMMENSE STRENGTH TO THAT...
...AND IF YOU TRAIN PROPERLY, YOU COULD BE BOTH DEFENSIVE AND OFFENSIVE.
...

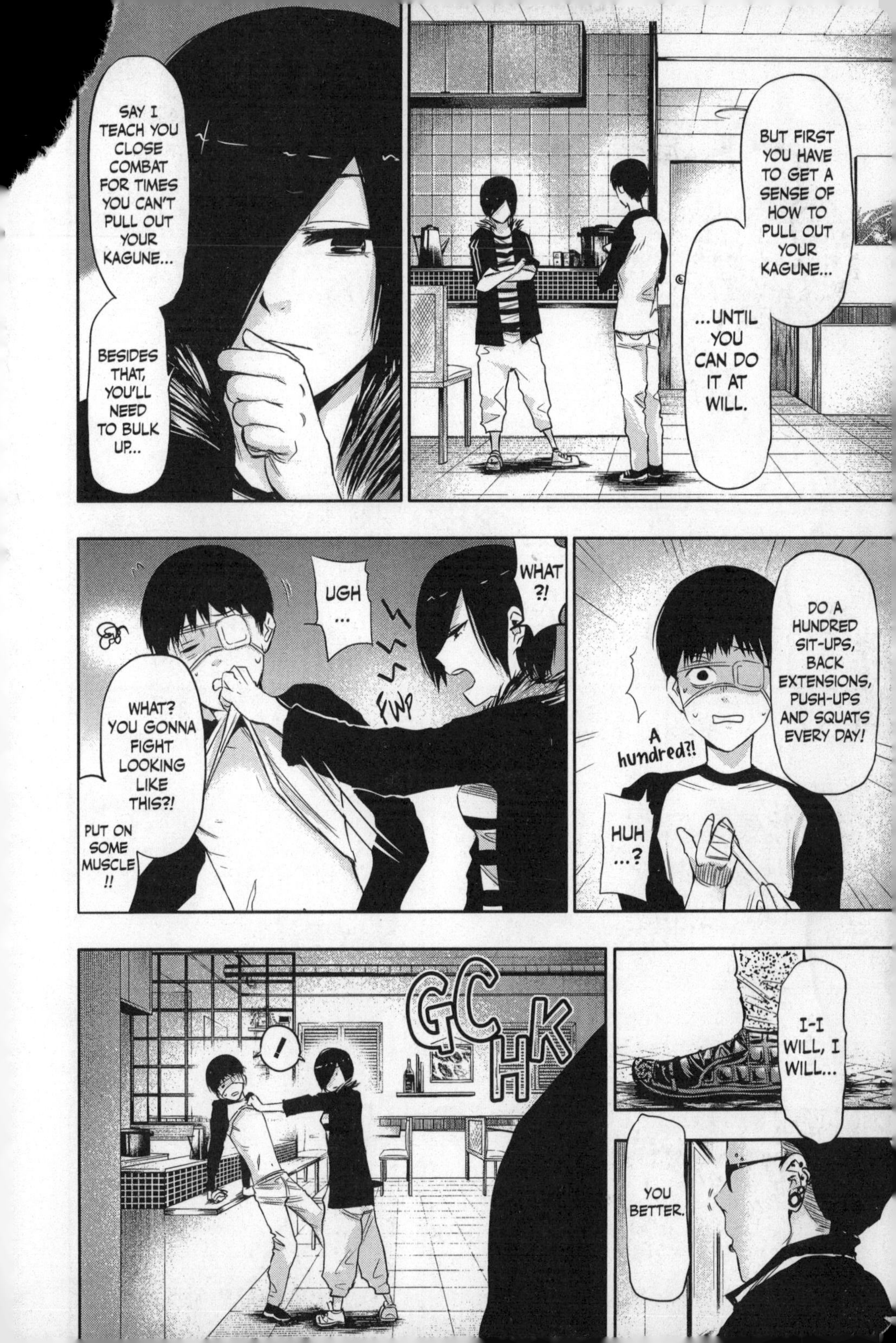
BUT FIRST YOU HAVE TO GET A SENSE OF HOW TO PULL OUT YOUR KAGUNE...
...UNTIL YOU CAN DO IT AT WILL.
SAY I TEACH YOU CLOSE COMBAT FOR TIMES YOU CAN'T PULL OUT YOUR KAGUNE...
BESIDES THAT, YOU'LL NEED TO BULK UP...
DO A HUNDRED SIT-UPS, BACK EXTENSIONS, PUSH-UPS AND SQUATS EVERY DAY!
A hundred?!
HUH ...?
WHAT ?!
UGH ...
WHAT? YOU GONNA FIGHT LOOKING LIKE THIS?!
PUT ON SOME MUSCLE !!
I-I WILL, I WILL...
YOU BETTER.
GCHK
!

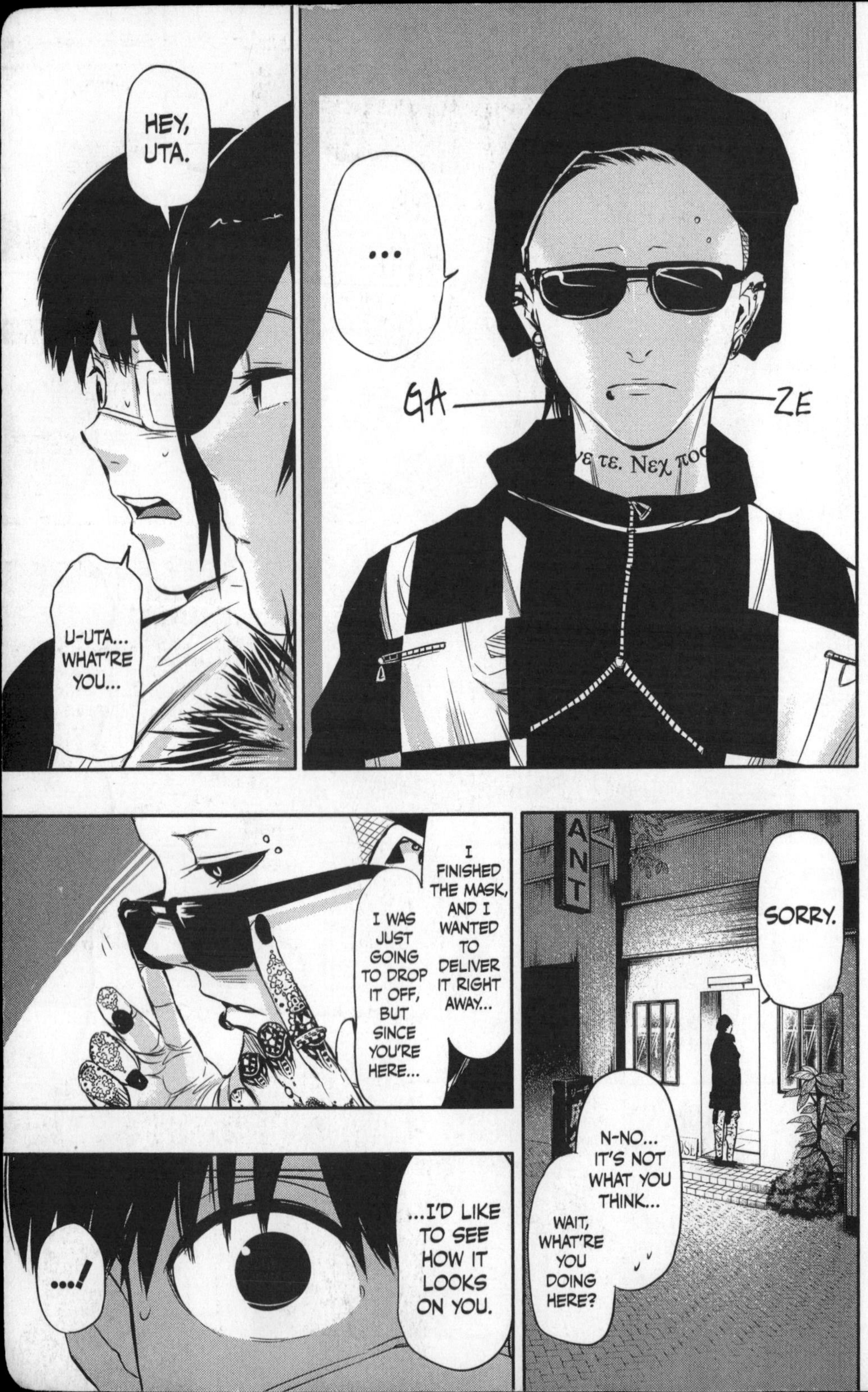
...
GA—ZE
HEY, UTA.
U-UTA... WHAT'RE YOU...
ANT
SORRY.
N-NO... IT'S NOT WHAT YOU THINK...
WAIT, WHAT'RE YOU DOING HERE?
I FINISHED THE MASK, AND I WANTED TO DELIVER IT RIGHT AWAY...
I WAS JUST GOING TO DROP IT OFF, BUT SINCE YOU'RE HERE...
...I'D LIKE TO SEE HOW IT LOOKS ON YOU.
...!

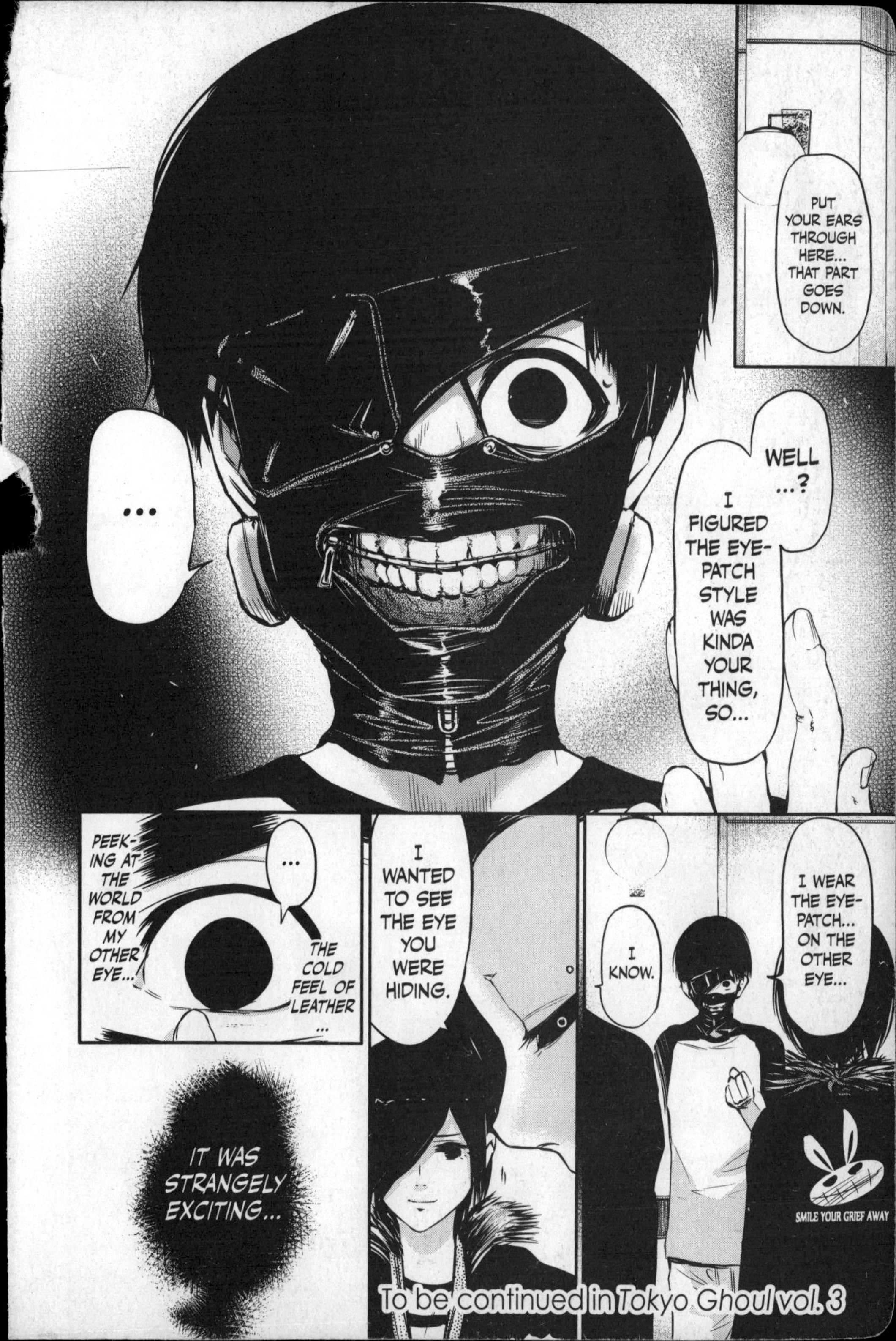
PUT YOUR EARS THROUGH HERE... THAT PART GOES DOWN.
WELL ...?
I FIGURED THE EYE-PATCH STYLE WAS KINDA YOUR THING, SO...
...
I WEAR THE EYE-PATCH... ON THE OTHER EYE...
I KNOW.
I WANTED TO SEE THE EYE YOU WERE HIDING.
...
PEEKING AT THE WORLD FROM MY OTHER EYE...
THE COLD FEEL OF LEATHER ...
IT WAS STRANGELY EXCITING...
SMILE YOUR GRIEF AWAY
To be continued in Tokyo Ghoul vol. 3

Tokyo Ghoul
Sui Ishida

Assistants
eda
Ryuji Miyamoto

Help
Mizuki Ide

Editor
Jumpei Matsuo

Design
Mr. Hideaki Shimada

Four-Cell Ghoul

*It probably has nothing to do with the main story

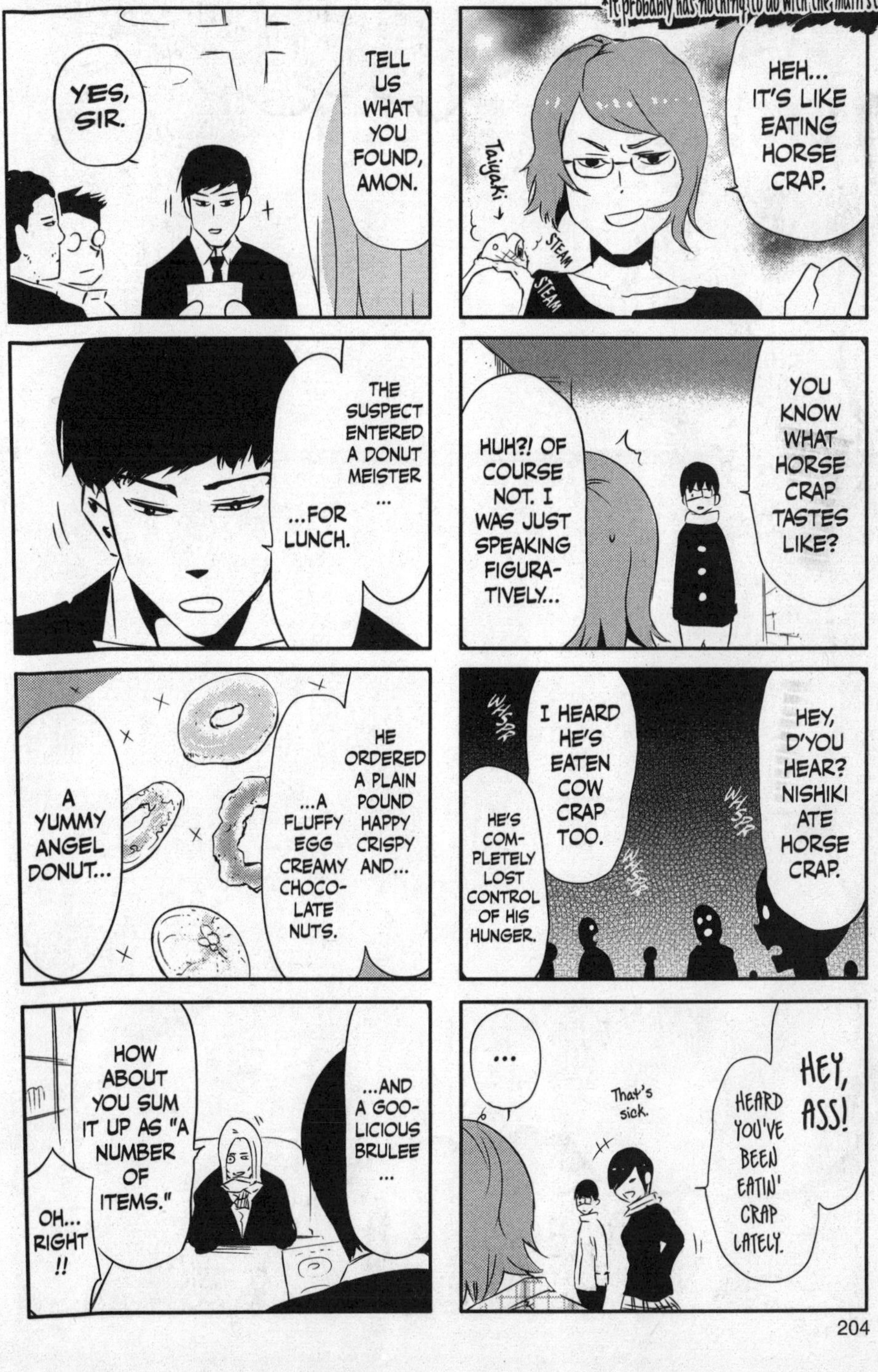
HEH... IT'S LIKE EATING HORSE CRAP.
Taiyaki →
STEAM
STEAM
YOU KNOW WHAT HORSE CRAP TASTES LIKE?
HUH?! OF COURSE NOT. I WAS JUST SPEAKING FIGURATIVELY...
HEY, D'YOU HEAR? NISHIKI ATE HORSE CRAP.
WHSPR
WHSPR
I HEARD HE'S EATEN COW CRAP TOO.
HE'S COMPLETELY LOST CONTROL OF HIS HUNGER.
HEY, ASS!
HEARD YOU'VE BEEN EATIN' CRAP LATELY.
That's sick.
...
TELL US WHAT YOU FOUND, AMON.
YES, SIR.
THE SUSPECT ENTERED A DONUT MEISTER ...
...FOR LUNCH.
HE ORDERED A PLAIN POUND HAPPY CRISPY AND...
...A FLUFFY EGG CREAMY CHOCOLATE NUTS.
A YUMMY ANGEL DONUT...
...AND A GOO-LICIOUS BRULEE ...
HOW ABOUT YOU SUM IT UP AS "A NUMBER OF ITEMS."
OH... RIGHT !!

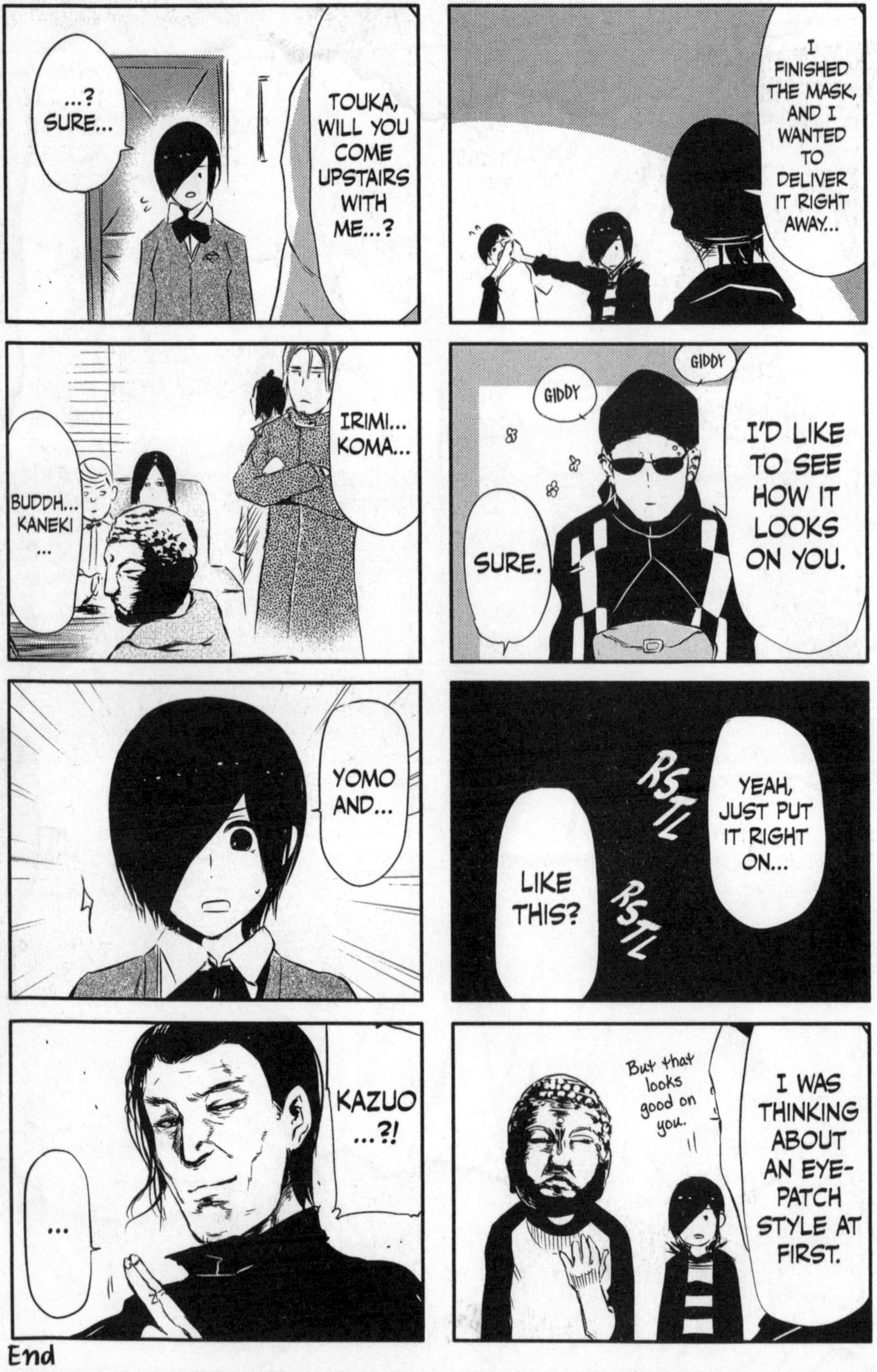

I FINISHED THE MASK, AND I WANTED TO DELIVER IT RIGHT AWAY...
GIDDY
GIDDY
I'D LIKE TO SEE HOW IT LOOKS ON YOU.
SURE.
RSTL
YEAH, JUST PUT IT RIGHT ON...
RSTL
LIKE THIS?
I WAS THINKING ABOUT AN EYE-PATCH STYLE AT FIRST.
But that looks good on you.
TOUKA, WILL YOU COME UPSTAIRS WITH ME...?
...? SURE...
IRIMI... KOMA...
BUDDH... KANEKI ...
YOMO AND...
KAZUO ...?!
...

End

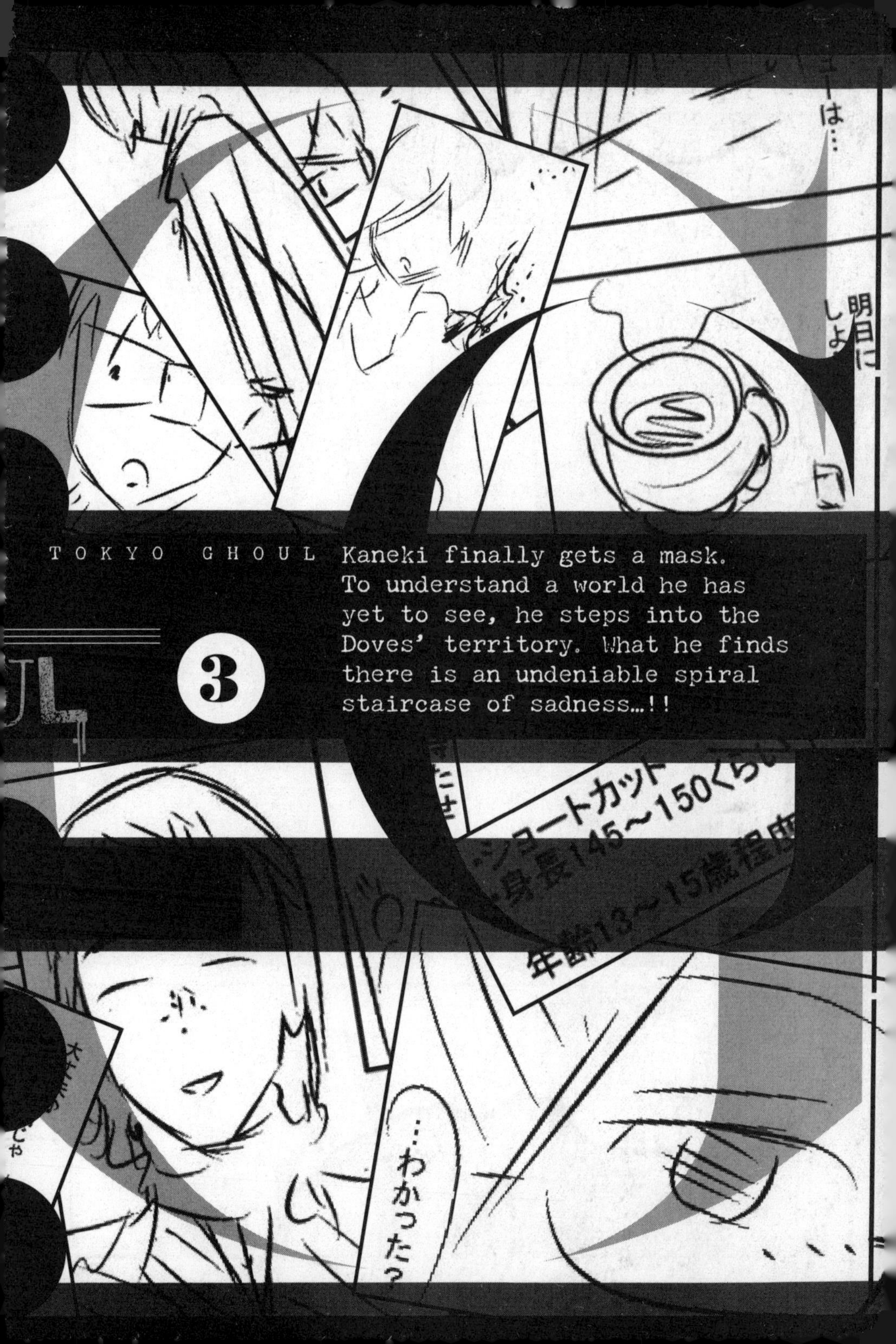
は…
ショートカット
身長145～150くらい
年齢13～15歳程度
…わかった?

TOKYO GHOUL

3

Kaneki finally gets a mask. To understand a world he has yet to see, he steps into the Doves' territory. What he finds there is an undeniable spiral staircase of sadness…!!

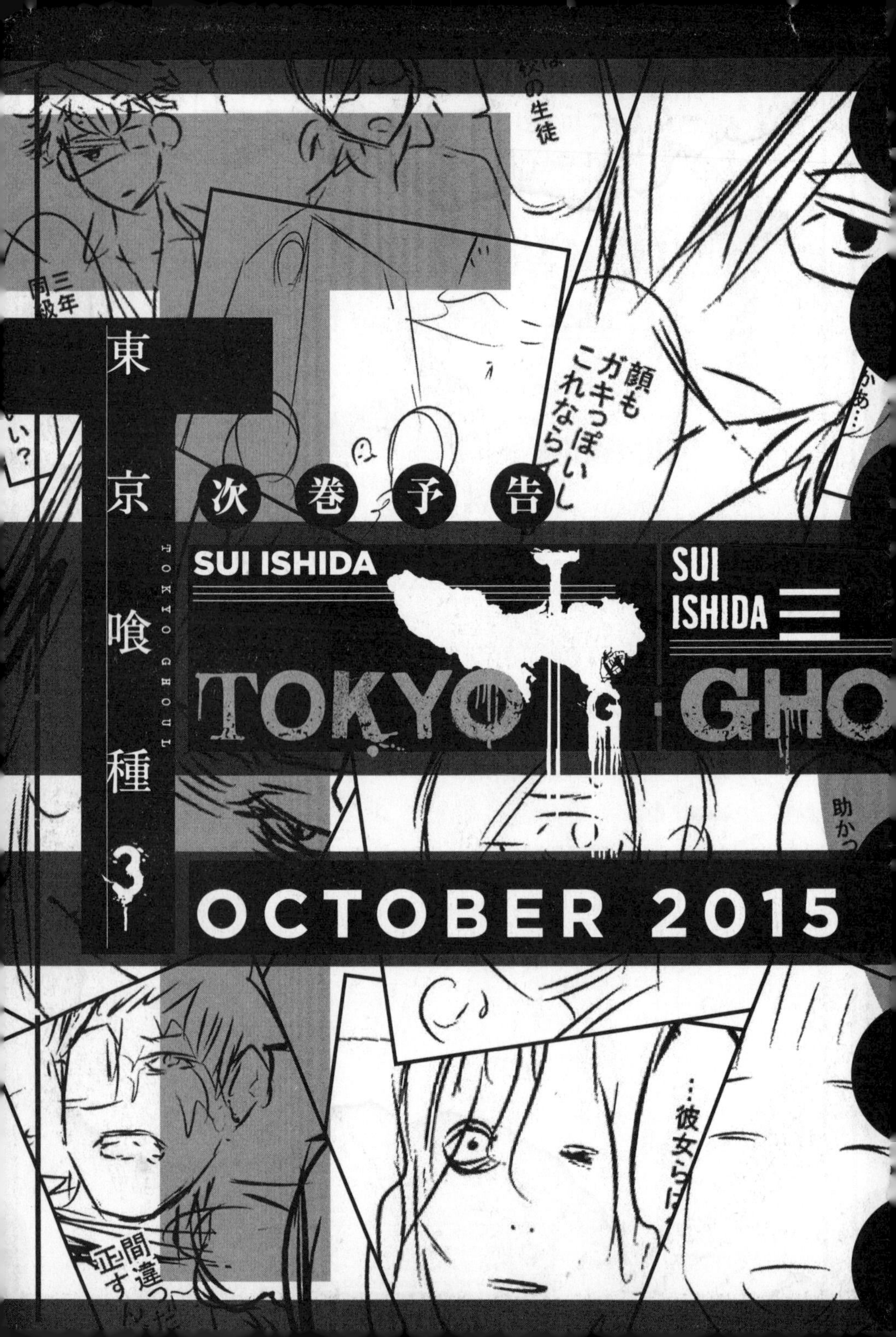
東京喰種 3
TOKYO GHOUL
次巻予告
SUI ISHIDA
TOKYO GHO
SUI ISHIDA 三
OCTOBER 2015
の生徒
三年 同級
顔も ガキっぽいし これなら
かあ…
助かっ
…彼女らは
間違っ

TOKYO GHOUL

P9-DDN-319

[THIS IS THE LAST PAGE]

TOKYO GHOUL
READS
RIGHT TO LEFT

TOKYO GHOUL
東 京 喰 種

VOLUME 2
VIZ Signature Edition

Story and art by
SUI ISHIDA

TOKYO GHOUL © 2011 by Sui Ishida
All rights reserved.
First published in Japan in 2011 by
SHUEISHA Inc., Tokyo.
English translation rights arranged by
SHUEISHA Inc.

TRANSLATION. Joe Yamazaki

TOUCH-UP ART AND LETTERING. Vanessa Satone

DESIGN. Fawn Lau

EDITOR. Joel Enos

Printed in the U.S.A.

Published by VIZ Media, LLC
P.O. Box 77010
San Francisco, CA 94107

10 9 8 7 6 5 4 3
First printing, August 2015
Third printing, August 2015

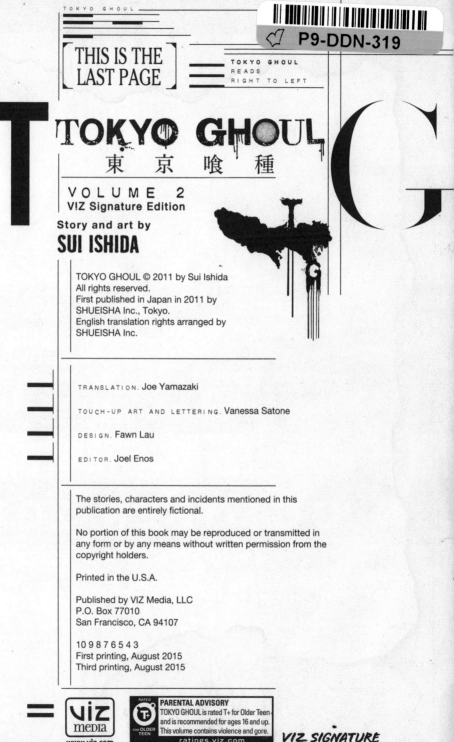

VIZ
MEDIA
www.viz.com

RATED
T+
FOR OLDER
TEEN

PARENTAL ADVISORY
TOKYO GHOUL is rated T+ for Older Teen
and is recommended for ages 16 and up.
This volume contains violence and gore.
ratings.viz.com

VIZ SIGNATURE